THE WEREWOLF BOOK

THE WEREWOLF BOOK

THE ENCYCLOPEDIA OF SHAPE-SHIFTING BEINGS

BRAD STEIGER

foreward by DR. FRANKLIN RUEHL

VISIBLE INK PRESS

DETROIT • LONDON

THE WEREWOLF BOOK
THE ENCYCLOPEDIA OF SHAPESHIFTING BEINGS

Published by Visible Ink Press®, a division of Gale Group, Inc.
27500 Drake Rd.
Farmington Hills, MI 48331-3535

Visible Ink Press is a registered trademark of Gale Group, Inc.

Most Visible Ink Press books are available at special quantity discounts when purchased in bulk by corporations, organizations, or groups. Customized printings, special imprints, messages, and excerpts can be produced to meet your needs. For more information, contact Special Markets Manager, Gale Group, Inc., 27500 Drake Rd., Farmington Hills, MI 48331-3535.

Cover Designer: Michelle DiMercurio
Page Designer: Michelle DiMercurio
Typesetting: LM Design
Cover and back cover photo © The Kobol Collection.

Library of Congress Cataloging-in-Publication Data

The Werewolf Book: the encyclopedia of shapeshifting beings / Brad Steiger; foreword by Franklin Ruehl.
    p. cm.
    Includes bibliographical references and index.
    ISBN 1-57859-078-7 (softcover)
    1. Werewolves Encyclopedias. 2. Metamorphosis—Folklore Encyclopedias. I. Title.
GR830.W4S68 1999
398.24'54'03—dc21
99-32800
CIP

TABLE OF CONTENTS

FOREWORD

Dr. Franklin Ruehl, Ph.D.

Did prehistoric man encounter the werewolf? Was the Babylonian ruler Nebuchadnezzar afflicted with lycanthropy? Could the Greek legend of King Lycaon be true?

First, it should be stressed that the idea of a man morphing into a wolf is actually well within the realm of feasibility. Few among us have not lost their tempers on at least a few occasions. During such outbursts, eruptions of uncontrolled emotions spew forth, making us feel as though we have become transformed into some type of fierce beast.

While feeling as though one is an animal is admittedly a long country mile from actually manifesting the physical characteristics of one, it must be remembered that the brain is a powerful organ. For instance, numerous well-documented cases exist of the stigmata, where individuals display the bleeding wounds of Christ on the Cross, demonstrating the power of mind over matter. And, there are many instances of patients diagnosed with terminal cancer suddenly undergoing spontaneous remissions that medical science cannot in any way explain except as an act of sheer force of will.

Such examples dramatically demonstrate the powerful link between mind and body. So, it is not such a stretch to argue that, in a few rare instances, a human being could periodically express the physical characteristics of some type of a ferocious animal. It may well be that such emotional experiences originally gave birth to the idea that a man could become, at least temporarily, a wild creature of some sort, such as a wolf. The wolf was actually an ideal candidate for that beast, being a canny predator with a wide geographical distribution. This may account for why peoples of many and diverse cultures have independently described the werewolf—the man who becomes a wolf.

Intriguingly, the first depiction of a man-wolf was apparently inscribed on a cave wall, suggesting that even prehistoric *Homo sapiens* may have been cognizant of this incredible duality. The first written account of a werewolf appears in the Scriptures in the Book of Daniel (4:15-33), where King Nebuchadnezzar exhibited symptoms of werewolfism for nearly four harrowing years. And the Greek legend of King Lycaon of Arcadia being transformed into a wolf by Zeus after offending the god by serving him a meal of human flesh gave birth to the scientific term for werewolf, "lycanthrope."

Later, in the fifth century B.C., the celebrated Greek historian Herodotus reported on the Neuri, a strange people who became wolves for a brief time once a year. In the first century A.D., noted Roman poet Virgil described a sorcerer who transmogrified himself into a wolf by use of secret herbs. Also in that century, renowned Roman author Gaius Petronius Arbiter wrote of such shapeshifters in his compilation of short stories, "Satyricon."

Moreover, early physicians, such as Paulos Agina of Alexandria (seventh century A.D.) and Avicenna (ninth century A.D.) and Ali ibn al Abbas (tenth century A.D.), both of Persia, were well aware of the condition. They not only delineated it in detail, but also recommended therapies for it.

Fast forwarding to the Middle Ages, accounts of lycanthropy mushroomed, with an astounding 30,000 individuals charged with werewolfism in France alone between 1520 and 1630. Without a doubt, the most notorious case centered around Gilles Garnier. Garnier was a peasant whose four-month rampage resulted in the deaths of four youngsters in the French village of Dole, youngsters whose flesh he devoured after which he bayed at the moon. His unholy crimes were witnessed by more than 50 locals who swore that they saw him roaming about in the guise of a halfling—half-man, half-beast. And, incredibly, Garnier himself admitted that he was indeed a werewolf. As punishment, he was burned alive on January 18, 1573.

In an intriguing modern case, Dr. Harvey Rosenstock, former clinical associate professor of psychiatry at the University of Texas Medical School, published a paper in the *American Journal of Psychiatry* documenting the case of a 49-year-old woman stricken with lycanthropy. One evening, when the moon was full, she suddenly jumped to the floor and started to crawl about on all fours as she growled and salivated. Worse, she even began chewing and ripping up the furniture. When she gazed into the mirror, she saw not a female's head, but a wolf's.

Ultimately, she was confined to a psychiatric ward where antipsychotic medications appeared to cure her. But, upon release, she once again reprised her lupine behavior at the rising of the next full moon.

Legend tells us that an individual may become a werewolf through several diverse means. Foremost among these is being bitten by a werewolf, which is ably depicted on the silver screen in such films as *The Werewolf of London* (1935) starring Henry Hull and *The Wolf Man* (1941) featuring Lon Chaney Jr. as the infamous Lawrence Talbot. Curses can also lead to the transformation, an idea that was intriguingly presented on the gothic TV soap opera, *Dark Shadows*, with David Selby as the unwilling changeling Quentin Collins. Heredity can also lead to the condition, as suggested in *The Undying Monster* (1941), with John Howard as the lycanthropic heir, and in *Cry of the Werewolf* (1944), with Nina Foch as a rare female descendant of a gypsy werewolf.

In an unusual motif, a vampire (appropriately portrayed by Bela Lugosi) used his occult mastery to reconfigure an underling into a fur-faced man (Matt Willis) in *The Return of the Vampire* (1944). In a fascinating 1992 episode of the TV series, *Beyond Reality* (entitled "Killer Instinct") a laboratory subject (Lawrence Bayne) inhaled lupine pheromones in order to establish a psychic link with a wolf, which he then directed to attack humans as he shared the "thrill" of the kill. And, in 1965's *Dr. Terror's House of Horrors*, in the vignette entitled "Werewolf," a woman became a vicious lycanthrope to free her similarly afflicted entombed husband.

However, cinematic titles can sometimes be misleading. For instance, 1946's *The She-Wolf of London* starred June Lockhart (of *Lost in Space* fame) as a female unfairly being framed as a lycanthrope, with none appearing in the flick. But, the 1992 British TV series of the same name starring Kate Hodge was true to its name. And, on the small screen, the 1953 entry "Ghost Wolf" on *The Adventures of Superman* involved a woman (Jane Adams) being mistaken for a *loup-garou*.

Of course, other circumstances are traditionally believed to lead to lycanthropy, such as being conceived at the time of the full moon, sleeping outdoors on a Friday beneath a full moon, wearing a wolfskin belt or garment, being subjected to demonic possession, and consuming the raw flesh of a rabid wolf, to enumerate just a few.

And Hollywood has conjured up the novel concept of "mad" scientists turning innocents into lycanthropes in their labs, such as in 1942's *The Mad Monster* (with Glenn Strange, the actor who went on to portray the Frankenstein monster three times, as the creature), *The Werewolf* (1956, with Steven Ritch as the hapless victim), and *I Was a Teenage Werewolf* (1957, with Michael Landon in the title role).

Wearing a pentagram (a five-pointed star) affords one protection against a werewolf. Shooting such a beast with silver bullets (as in *The Werewolf of London*) is the best-known means of dispatching the creature. But battering it with a sharp silver implement, such as a silver-handled cane (as used in *The Wolf Man*), is also effective.

Curing a werewolf is also possible, according to popular lore. One way is supposedly by merely calling him by his human name while he is in his animal state. Another method requires the highly dangerous trick of extracting three drops of the entity's blood while in beastly form. Yet a third technique demands that the lycanthrope restrain himself from attacking humans for a full nine years.

Again, Hollywood introduced some inventive means of tackling the problem. In *The Werewolf of London*, devouring a special flower that blooms only during moonlight prevented the dreaded transformation for one night only. In *Dark Shadows*, consumption of a moon poppy while in the werewolf state would end the affliction forever (but when lycanthrope Chris Jennings [portrayed by Donald Briscoe] tried it, his lupine half crushed the flower to bits instead of consuming it). Another *Dark Shadows* lycanthrope, the malevolent Count Petofi (Thayer David), was cured by a gypsy spell, but only upon payment of his right hand, which he then spent the next 100 years in quest of.

And werewolf Lawrence Talbot sought a solution from science. He was twice betrayed by doctors more interested in reanimating the Frankenstein monster than in aiding him (*Frankenstein Meets the Wolf Man*, 1943, and *The House of Frankenstein*, 1944), but finally achieved the desired release from his malady through a brain operation (*The House of Dracula*, 1945). Unfortunately, the Universal Pictures soon returned him to his lycanthropic state in 1948's comedic entry, *Abbott and Costello Meet Frankenstein*.

Conservative physicians, of course, reject all such supernatural notions, preferring to consign lycanthropy's causes to the realm of the mundane. For instance, one theory argues that an injury to the brain's temporal (i.e., side) lobes can set off manifestations of lupine behavior. Another ascribes were-wolfism to a condition known as "hypertrichosis," or excessive hairiness, where a thick, soft growth of hair covers the entire face (even the eyelids) of the sufferer, as well as other body sites.

Perhaps the most imaginative hypothesis yet advanced comes from historian Dr. Mary Matossian of the University of Maryland, who theorized that contaminated rye bread was the causative factor. Specifically, during the Middle Ages, Matossian believed that ergot, a fungal parasite that induces LSD-type hallucinations, became ground into the bread. This caused some individuals to imagine that they were werewolves, and others to believe that they were seeing such entities. Once modern processing techniques were instituted, lycanthropic outbreaks simultaneously decreased.

Of course, other halflings have been depicted in both legend and fiction, such as werelions, werefoxes, wereleopards, and weresnakes. First and foremost is perhaps the classic tale *Beauty and the Beast*, well-rendered on the screen in 1946 (with Jean Marais as the handsome man condemned to live as a lionlike humanoid) as well as on the tube (the 1987–90 series starring Ron Perlman).

One of the most intriguing conceptualizations has been that of werefelids, such as depicted in the 1933 horror flick, *Island of Lost Souls*, where Kathleen Burke portrayed a panther partially transformed into a female by Charles Laughton's evil Dr. Moreau (in a story based on H.G.Wells's 1896 novel). A well-stocked menagerie of other fascinating creatures was also portrayed, including a dog-man and a lion-man. An interesting remake, *The Island of Dr.Moreau*, was released in 1977 featuring Burt Lancaster in the title role. And, in 1942's *Dr. Renault's Secret*, horrormeister George Zucco transformed a panther into a man (J. Carrol Naish), as did Francis Lederer in 1965's *Terror Is a Man*.

Another intriguing rendition was delivered by Simone Simon in 1942's *Cat People*, in which she periodically metamorphosed into a panther due to an inherited legacy from her home village in Serbia. However, the sequel, *Curse of the Cat People*, which Simon also starred in, included not a single such transmogrification. However, 1946's *The Catman of Paris* did capably depict the transformation of a man (Douglas Dumbrille) into a catlike beast. And 1957's *The Cat Girl* starring Barbara Shelley involved another woman periodically turning into a panther.

Man-apes have also been treated several times on the silver screen, such as in 1943's *Captive Wild Woman*, where geneticist John Carradine injected a female ape with human glandular secretions to create a female-ape hybrid (played by Acquanetta). This gave rise to a pair of less-than-spectacular sequels, 1944's *Jungle Woman*, with Naish as a sympathetic scientist trying to study Acquanetta, and 1945's *Jungle Captive*, with vengeful Otto Kruger using the hybrid (now played by Vicky Lane) to dispatch his enemies. Bela Lugosi made himself the subject of experimentation in 1943's *The Ape Man*. Zucco was also at work in 1941's *The Monster and the Girl*, where he introduced a human brain from a wrongfully executed victim of a frame-up (Phillip Terry) into a gorilla to create a justice-seeking ape-man. And Raymond Burr (of *Perry Mason* fame) was reconfigured into an ape as the result of a curse put upon him by the mother of a native girl he had wronged.

A weresnake was intelligently delineated in 1955's *Cult of the Cobra*, where Faith Domergue periodically morphed into a cobra to exact vengeance on a group of GIs who had witnessed a secret ceremony in India. In 1960's *The Snake Woman*, Susan Travers was born a weresnake because her chemist father had injected her mother repeatedly with snake venom. In one eerie scene, she actually shed her entire human skin in the manner of a snake sloughing off its skin. Jacqueline Pearce was turned into such a snake creature in 1966's *The Reptile* as punishment for her father's forbidden studies. And, in 1973's *Sssssss*, Strother Martin gradually converted Dirk Benedict (of *Battlestar Galactica* fame) into a slitherer as part of a cruel experiment.

In an excellent sci-fi entry from 1959, *The Alligator People*, George Macready inadvertently transmuted Richard Crane (best remembered as Rocky Jones, Space Ranger) into an alligator-man by injecting him with reptilian secretions to cure life-threatening war wounds.

In 1944's *The Return of the Ape Man*, Lugosi added part of Carradine's brain to a resurrected Neanderthal, resulting in a homicidal cave man. And scientists have even transformed themselves into cavemen, such as Robert Shayne in 1953's *The Neanderthal Man* and Arthur Franz in 1958's *Monster on the Campus*.

Even plants and animals have been commingled, such as in 1973's *The Mutations*, starring Donald Pleasence as a botanist tampering with nature.

And, in one of the oddest reconfigurations, in the 1945 serial *Manhunt of Mystery Island*, anyone sitting in a special chair was physically transformed into the notorious pirate, Captain Mephisto.

Surprisingly, this overview actually represents but a mere fraction of the totality of accounts, theories, and collateral information that has been accumulated over the centuries concerning werewolves and related shapeshifters. A truly comprehensive record of such entities has been long overdue, so it is with great pleasure that I introduce the book you are holding in your hands, Brad Steiger's monumental *Werewolf Book: The Encyclopedia of Shape-Shifting Beings*. With more than 150 books published on every conceivable aspect of the paranormal, Brad is singularly qualified to tackle such a challenging project. In particular, his 1982 opus, *Monsters Among Us*, stands as a landmark work in the field of cryptozoology. Brad's meticulous scholarship and unrelenting thoroughness guarantee that this text will capably fill the void that has long existed in the study of lycanthropy, and will definitely set the standard in the field for all future such works.

Dr. Franklin Ruehl is an expert writer and speaker on paranormal topics and was the host and producer of Mysteries from Beyond the Other Dominion, *one of the original shows to appear on television's Sci-Fi Channel. He also holds a Ph.D. in nuclear physics.*

ACKNOWLEDGMENTS

I wish to thank my agent, Agnes Birnbaum of Bleecker Street Associates, for her guidance and encouragement; my editor, Brad Morgan, for his helpfulness and unfailing cheerfulness; Dr. Franklin Ruehl for his willingness to help whenever called upon; Twylah, who taught me the wisdom of the Wolf Clan; my mother, who first warned me about the cornwolves and the outlaws in our fields; my children, who always loved sitting on my lap and being safely frightened during Friday night's "creature feature" on television; and my wife, Sherry, who has good-naturedly endured my Lawrence Talbot wolf man impressions during each full moon for the past 13 years.

At Visible Ink and the Gale Group, I'd also like to thank the following people for their help in making this book possible: Julia Furtaw, Martin Connors, Carol Schwartz, Christa Brelin, Justin Karr, Kim Marich, Lauri Taylor, Michelle DiMercurio, Cindy Baldwin, P. J. Butland, Evi Seoud, Rita Wimberley, Mary Grimes, Pam Reed, and Randy Baldwin. Outside editor Gina Misiroglu and typesetter Linda Mahoney deserve special thanks for their hard work.

INTRODUCTION: WE HAVE MET THE WEREWOLVES AND THEY ARE US!

Brad Steiger

One can read a frightening book about vampires or a host of other scary monsters and feel secure in the knowledge that they are merely creatures born of the dark side of human imagination seeking to define the shadow world beyond death and the awful things that go bump in the night. Werewolves, however, constitute a very different, and much more frightening, reality. Werewolves are real!

Not only do werewolves really exist, but everyone who will ever read this book has the seed of the wolf within his or her psyche. Since prehistoric times the bloodline of the wolf has blended with that of our own species, and each one of us bears the personal responsibility of honoring the noble aspects of our lupine heritage and, at the same time, keeping the savage bloodlust under control. It is to be hoped that the vast majority of those who read this book have mastered the challenge of sublimating and channeling their lycanthropic impulses into positive and constructive outlets.

In December 1998, biologist John Allman of the California Institute of Technology stated in his new book, *Evolving Brains*, that canines and humans formed a common bond more than 140,000 years ago and evolved together in one of the most successful partnerships ever fashioned. The wolf's strength, stamina, keen sense of hearing, and extraordinary sense of smell helped humans to hunt prey and to overcome predators. Because humans *(Homo sapiens)* teamed up with wolves, they became better hunters and thus supplanted the rival species of *Homo erectus* and *Neanderthal.*

Humans and wolves even share a similar social structure. Both species employ a cooperative rearing strategy for their offspring, with both parents participating in the feeding and rearing process. In most mammals, the care of the young is left almost exclusively to the mother. Wolves practice fidelity and mate for life, thus setting an early model for the family structure that humans violate more than their canine partners. Wolf packs also have dominant members, like any tribe or community, and humans probably began the domestication process by assuming the role of the dominant wolf and achieving acquiescence from the lupine leader. In turn, wolves may have perceived humans sharing food with their pups as the act of responsible members who helped support the pack.

If, as Allman and other researchers have suggested, the human species may have greatly depended upon wolves for its continued existence, then it may be clearly understood why early humans may have modeled so much of their behavior, especially in the area of survival skills, upon the wolf. As these pre-historic "wolf men" learned over time to hunt in packs and, with the assistance of their wolf allies, to subdue much larger predators, then certain elements of lupine savagery may well have been "inherited" along with the more noble aspects of a sense of community and mutual support.

While most of us have become "domesticated" and hearken to the inner voice of conscience that has been strengthened by moral and spiritual values cultivated over centuries of civilized behavior, those individuals who have suc-cumbed to the more vicious seed of the wolf within them walk among us today as those sadistic sex criminals who slash, tear, rip, rape, mutilate, and cannibal-ize their victims. When one compares the details of the offenses charged to alleged werewolves during the witchcraft mania of the Middle Ages with the offenses attributed to such sex criminals as the Chicago Rippers, Harry Gordon, Richard Ramirez, Henry Lee Lucas, and Jeffrey Dahmer, it becomes clear that there exists a true werewolf psychosis that can cause people to believe that they are transformed into wolves or can cause them to commit cruel and vicious crimes as if they were wolves scratching, biting, and killing their prey.

While the werewolf as sex criminal constitutes a very grim reality and a seri-ous physical threat to unsuspecting members of society who are its potential vic-tims, the werewolf as a creature of superstition poses a psychic threat to those who may trespass beyond the boundaries of logic and reason into the dangerous and uncharted regions of the supernatural. The werewolf of tradition is the deliberate creation of a human who, motivated by a desire for power or revenge, has sought to release the beast within and accomplish the transformation of human into wolf. Therefore, one becomes a werewolf through a self-willed and carefully structured magical quest to achieve a metamorphosis into wolf. In those instances wherein one has become a werewolf against his or her will, it is because a powerful and evil sorcerer has created the terrible transformation through the malignant energy of a curse.

As werewolves became popular characters in folklore and fireside tales, the monster was made all the more frightening by stating that the slightest scratch from a werewolf's claw could transmit the curse to its victim. Motion picture portrayals of werewolves perpetuated this addition to the lycanthropic legend and created many new ones. For millions of contemporary men and women, the very word "werewolf" conjures up images of the actor Lon Chaney Jr. in *The Wolf Man* (1941), creeping through the nocturnal mists, a good man tortured by the knowledge that the bite of a werewolf has caused him to endure a monthly metamorphosis into a monster. Although a wolf, we still recognize Chaney as a man, fully clothed, walking upright in a peculiar loping movement. In later motion pictures, such as *The Howling* (1981), *An American Werewolf in London* (1981), and *An American Werewolf in Paris* (1997), vastly improved visual effects allow us to witness the complete transformation of man into wolf.

In *The Werewolf Book: The Encyclopedia of Shape-shifting Beings*, you will encounter a great deal of material linking the werewolf with witchcraft as it was defined in the Middle Ages by the learned church fathers and the sadistic Inquisitors. In the European tradition, the history of the werewolf as legend and superstition cannot be separated from the witchcraft mania and the vast ecclesiastical machinery of the Inquisition that sought to stamp out all traces of those who worshiped the goddess Diana and all those who endeavored to become such shapeshifters as cats, bats, and werewolves.

In the spiritual traditions of other cultures, shamans are expected to seek the assistance of their spirit helpers, who appear most often in the form of their totem animals. In certain instances, to explore more effectively the spiritual dimensions, shamans may even assume the persona of their totemic animal and become for a time a wolf, a raven, an owl, or whatever creature has granted its power to their quest. In Europe of the Middle Ages, those who employed any kind of shamanic practices were in danger of being tortured and dragged to the stake to be burned to death.

Because of this centuries-old association of witchcraft with the forces of evil and the belief that its practitioners are all agents of Satan, many creatures of forest and farmyard seen in the company of alleged witches and sorcerers were also judged to be masquerading demons. Millions of cats were identified as the companions of witches and were given summary trials (just like their human counterparts) and burned. Wolves, the great teachers and early allies of humankind, were condemned as satanic beasts, along with large black dogs, owls, bats, and all reptiles. At the same time, it was decreed that Satan had granted the most heinous of evildoers the ability to shapeshift into these same animals and transform themselves into werewolves and other monsters of the midnight hour.

As a student of the strange, the unusual, and the unknown, I have always held a particular fascination for the folklore and legends of the werewolf. Throughout all of our known history as an evolving species, I perceive the supernatural fear of the werewolf as our inner awareness of the beast within us, a savage self that must be controlled so that it may not consume ourselves and those around us.

The wild hunts with the wolf packs in prehistoric times provided early humans with the flesh of animals and freed our kind from dependency upon the plant life that could only be gathered in limited areas. The ability to hunt game allowed early humans to migrate and to establish new communities beyond the far horizon. However, once those passive fruit collecting, seed-and-root gathering clans of early humans became meat-eaters, there may well have been times when the only flesh available was found in the bodies of other humans. Human wolf packs may have slain members of other clans in order to be among the fittest to survive.

Since we may all be descended from those carnivorous lycanthropes, we must be ever vigilant to keep the beast within firmly shackled with our civilized sense of morality and a deep sense of ourselves as spiritual beings. Some theorists believe that prehistoric members of the human evolutionary family favored the forested areas where they subsisted on leaves and fruits, very much like the great apes. Certain scholars of the human psyche have gone so far as to suggest that there is a portion of our species' latent genetic memory that abhors the shedding of blood and the eating of flesh and feels a unconscious sense of guilt whenever we eat meat.

This may be the most frightening book that you will ever read. As you explore the encyclopedic entries of werewolfism and shapeshifting down through the centuries, you may begin to feel your own psyche stirring with certain ancient memories. As you examine the accounts of those who have succumbed to the stirrings of the savage beast within, you may find yourself repelled by lives so twisted by evil. Remember to remain balanced and to emphasize within your own concept of self and soul that you are one with the strengths of community and family and that you cherish the moral values that great spiritual masters have bequeathed to us both by their teachings and by their examples.

Once you have your spiritual and moral values firmly in place, there is nothing wrong in savoring a few vicarious chills as you explore the legends, folklore, and facts of the werewolf. However, it might be a good idea to read this book either in the full light of day or with a bright lamp providing plenty of illumination. Quite likely the wild hunt of the werewolves is an inherited fear that can strike even the most sophisticated and civilized of us when night falls and the moon is full.

ABOUT *THE WEREWOLF BOOK*

The Werewolf Book contains nearly 250 descriptive entries arranged in a single alphabetic sequence. Some are brief (100 to 300) words, while others are longer (1000 to 3000 words) and explore major topics associated with werewolves (explanations for lycanthropy, Lon Chaney Jr., and spiritual shapeshifting, for example).

Within the text of each entry, those entities that have their own entry elsewhere in the book appear in boldface. Also, some topics could have been placed under a number of names (such as Bigfoot and Yeti). Where one subject could have easily been treated under a different heading, a cross-reference heading has been added that provides the location of the entry related to that heading.

For example: **BIGFOOT** *see:* ABOMINABLE SNOWMAN OR YETI

There are a number of special features in *The Werewolf Book*. The first, following the introduction, is a chronology of the werewolf, which provides a handy summary of the major events in the development of the werewolf myth from early history to the present. It notes such key events as the torture of suspected shapeshifters and witches during the Inquisition, the werewolf scare caused by The Beast of Gevaudon in eighteenth-century France, and more modern events, such as the horrible crimes of Jeffrey Dahmer and the recent release of the film *An American Werewolf in Paris*.

Another feature is the comprehensive "Werewolf Resources" section. This appendix provides a listing of werewolf-related materials that are available in print, on film, and in other media. Included in the Resources section are: a guide to werewolf sites on the World Wide Web; a list of novels and other works of fiction that feature a werewolf or other shapeshifter; a list of nonfiction books about lycanthropy; and a filmography of werewolf and shapeshifter movies.

The filmography is a concerted effort to include all commercially released movies that feature a werewolf or a shapeshifter as the central character or a key character integral to the plot. The filmography also includes a wide variety of other were-creatures, including those morphing entities that come from outer space.

The films, which date back as far as the early 1900s, are listed in alphabetical order. Each entry contains the name of the film, a brief description of the plot (when available), and other names by which the film was released. Additional information includes (where known) the date of the original release; whether the film is black and white (**B**) or in color (**C**); the country of origin; the production company [in brackets]; principal cast members and the director. If no country is listed, the film was produced in the United States.

WEREWOLVES: A CHRONOLOGY

140,000 BCE According to research published in 1998, humans and wolves establish a common bond more than 140,000 years ago. DNA evidence shows that dogs began to evolve from their wolf ancestors about 135,000 years ago and that humans and their canine companions literally evolved together.

75,000 BCE Discoveries of the earliest human altars reveal evidence of bear, wolf, and other animal cults. The identification of humans or gods with animals is one of the most common elements of myth and religion.

25,000 BCE The Franco-Cantabrian cave artists of over 25,000 years ago leave portraits depicting ghostly creatures and a variety of two-legged beings with the heads of animals and birds. The ethnologist Ivar Lissner suggests {*Man, God and Magic*} that the Stone-Age artists were portraying "intermediary beings who were stronger than common men and able to penetrate more deeply into the mysteries of fate, that unfathomable interrelationship between animals, men, and gods." What the ancient cave painters may have been saying is that the "...road to supernatural powers is easier to follow in animal shape and that spirits can only be reached with an animal's assistance."

6000 BCE Cave drawings in Catal Huyuk depict hunters draped in leopard skins, thus demonstrating how early humans learned to hunt by aping animal predators.

3000 BCE Creation of the Sphinx, the lionheaded beast-woman that has for centuries symbolized the higher spiritual nature triumphing over the world of matter.

2000 BCE Suggested date when the *Epic of Gilgamesh* was written down, giving us, in the character of Enkidu the first literary expression of a werewolflike being.

1000 BCE Stories depicting the power of transformation are immensely popular among the Greeks. Heroes and deities freely change themselves and others into various animals and serpents.

850 BCE Suggested date for Homer's *Odyssey*, a work filled with accounts of werecreatures and shape-shifters, such as Circe, who transformed her lovers into swine.

750 BCE The date given for the legendary founding of Rome by Romulus and Remus, brothers who were suckled by a she-wolf.

***c.* 540 BCE** Nebuchadnezzar, mighty king of Babylon, suffers a mental affliction which causes him to allow his hair and beard to grow long and to roam and to live as if he is an animal for nearly four years.

500 BCE The Scythians, a nomadic Eurasian people, record their beliefs that the Neuri turn themselves into werewolves during an annual religious festival.

400 BCE Damarchus, a werewolf from the Greek city state of Arcadia, is said to have won boxing medals at the Olympics.

100–75 BCE The great Roman poet Virgil speaks of the powers of the werewolf Moeris, from whom he claims to have learned many secrets of magic, including the raising of the dead.

28 Jesus of Nazareth performs a successful exorcism on two werewolf/ghoul-like men who live among the dead in the cemetary outside of Gadarenes on the shore of the sea of Galilee.

55 Simon Magus, a great magician, attempts to ursurp the role of Jesus in the early Christian movement by claiming to be the true Messiah. It is recorded that he has the power to transform himself into a variety of animal and human shapes and to accomplish miracles. He soon runs afoul of Peter and the other disciples.

150 Apuleius' *Golden Ass* records the poet's travels to Thessaly where he beholds a wide assortment of magical practices and the transformation of humans into animals after he, himself, is changed into an ass .

175 Pausanias, a Greek traveler, geographer, and author visits Arcadia and sees the Lycanian werewolves.

***c.* 410** In his *City of God*, the great clergyman St. Augustine relates the account of certain sorceresses in the Alps who give their unsuspecting victims a special kind of cheese that transforms them into beasts of burden.

435 St. Patrick arrives in Ireland and discovers that among his flock are many families of werewolves.

650 Paulus Aegineta describes "melancholic lycantropia," as a black and dismal frame of mind that causes some people to leave their homes and to wander the cemetaries, taking refuge among the tombstones.

As these lycanthropes become increasing melancholy, they see themselves as werewolves.

725 The approximate date for the authorship of *Beowulf*, the earliest extant poem in a modern European language. Although the text is written in Old English it depicts the struggles of a Viking champion, a likely member of a boar cult, against a monster.

731 Venerable Bede's *Ecclesiastical History of England* describes a host of were-animals that haunt the night.

774 *The Chronicles* of Denys of Tell-Mahre describe the wolflike monsters that terrorized the region known today as Iraq.

840 Agobard, the Archbishop of Lyons, writes in his *Liber contra insulam vulgi opinionem* of the evil demons of the mountains that appear as manbeasts.

872 The first reference to the *berserker*, those fierce warriors who enter battle clothed only in wolfskins or bearskins, appears in *Haraldskvaeoi*.

906 The *Canon Episcopi* by Abbot Regino of Prum condemns as heretical any belief in witchcraft and or in the power of sorcerors to change people into animals. If anyone believes they have the ability to fly through the air or to transform a human into a creature of another species, they are being deceived by Satan into maintaining such a delusion. At this time the Christian clergy is more interested in stamping out all allegiance to the goddess Diana and regards as primitive superstition any suggestion that witches possess any kind of magical powers or that men and women can be transformed into werewolves and other beings. Unfortunately, in 1233, the Church smothers all such rational thinking with the thick black smoke of the Inquistion.

930 Pope Leon hears of two sorceresses in Germany who for their own amusement transform certain of their unwitting guests into animals. One victim regains his human form by eating roses.

1000 Deacon Burchard, later archbishop of Worms, publishes *Corrector*, which updates Regino's *Canon Episcopi* and stresses that only God can change one thing into another. Therefore, claims of wild men and women of the woods who transform people into wolves and perform other magical acts are false. In general usage, the term "werewolf" is meant to apply to an outlaw.

1022 The first fully attested burning of a heretic takes place in Orleans.

1101 Prince Vseslav of Polock, an alleged Ukranian werewolf, dies.

1182 Giraldus Camrensis, a Welsh historian, author of *Itineraium Cambraie*, learns of an Irish tribe whose members transform themselves into wolves during their Yuletide feast.

c. 1195   *Guillaume de Palerne*, "William the Werewolf," composed.

1198   Marie de France composes *Bisclavret*, the "Lay of a werewolf."

1205   The *Chronicles* of Abbot Ralph of Essex describe strange demons that appear after a thunderstorm.

1208   The Cathar sect becomes so popular among the people that Pope Innocent III considers it a greater threat to Christianity than the Islamic warriors who pummeled the Crusaders. To satisfy his outrage, he orders the only crusade ever launched against fellow Christians by attacking the Albigensians, as the Cathars of southern France were known.

1214   In his report to the Emperor Otto IV, Gervaise of Tilbury reports cases in Auvergne in which men were seen to take the form of wolves during the full moon.

1220   Caesarius of Heisterbach, author of *Dialogue of Miracles*, describes numerous accounts of shapeshifting, pacts with Satan, and mysterious flights through the air. The Bishop of Tyre records an incident of a sorceress on the island of Cyprus transforming an English solider into an ass to be used as a beast of burden.

1224   Konrad, the first papal Inquisitor in Germany, condemns witches to the stake for worshipping Satan and producing diabolical monsters to do their biding.

1233   Pope Gregory IX urges other bishops to follow Konrad's lead and to become more vigorous in ridding Europe of shapeshifting witches. It is well known that Satan can appear in the form of a black cat, a wolf, a giant toad or any form he wishes. Thus, it follows logically that his disciples possess the same abilities of diabolical transformation. The Inquisition is founded in 1233 to eradicate the practice of witchcraft. The chief components which define witchcraft are the ability to shapeshift, the capability to fly and/or to ride objects through the air, and the use of cannibalism, child murder, salves, animal familiars, and the invocation of demons to achieve power.

1246   Montsegur, the center of Albigensian resistance, falls. Hundreds of Cathars are burned at the stake. The headquarters of the Inquisition is established in Toulouse.

1252   Pope Innocent IV issues a papal bull, *Ad extirpanda*, that places inquisitors above the law. Every ruler and commoner must assist the work of the Inquisition or face excommunication.

1257   The Church officially sanctions torture as a means of forcing witches, werewolves, shapeshifters, and other heretics to confess.

1275   A woman in Tolouse is found guilty of sexual intercourse with an incubus and of giving birth to a child who is half wolf and half snake.

c. 1300   *Volsunga*, the great Viking saga, depicts an outlaw father and son who become werewolves and establish a dynasty.

1305 The wealthy and powerful Knights Templar are accused of heretical acts, such as invoking Satan, having intercourse with succubi, and worshipping demons that appeared as large black cats.

1312 In spite of 573 witnesses for their defense, the Templars are tortured *en masse*, burned at the stake, and their order is disbanded by Pope Clement V.

1313 As he is being burned to death on a scaffold erected for the occasion in front of Notre Dame, the Knights Templar Grand Master, Jacques de Molay, recants the confession produced by torture and proclaims his innocence to the Pope and the King— and he invites them to meet him at Heaven's gate. When both dignitaries die soon after de Molay's execution, it seems to the public at large that the Grand Master had been innocent of the charges of heresy.

1320 In *Practica*, an influential instructional manual written for inquisitors by Bernard Gui, and in *Fasciculus morum*, a work prepared by an English Franciscan, witch hunters are urged to pay particular heed to apprending women who cavort with the goddess Diana and who transform their victims into other shapes for serfdom in elfland.

1324 Ireland's first witchcraft trial occurs when Alice Kyteler is found guilty of consorting with a demon who could appear as a tall man, a black cat, a shaggy dog, or an Ethiopian.

c. 1336 In a version of Wolfram von Eschenbach's *Parzival*, Klaus Wisse and Philipp Colin insert tales of humans being transformed into animals.

1344 Witch hunters announce that they have found a wolf child at Hesse.

c. 1350 First major outbreak of the Black Death, a form of bubonic plague, which becomes pandemic throughout Europe and much of Asia. Boccaccio's *Decameron* includes satirical tales of diabolical beasts and witches' gatherings that are intended to mock the Inquisitors.

1390 Gypsies begin to appear in Europe.

1407 Werewolves are tortured and burned during witchcraft trials at Basel.

1440 Gilles de Rais is tried and burned for child murders and for worshipping Satan in both human and animal form.

1458 *The Book of the Sacred Magic of Abramelin* is translated from the Hebrew. This legendary manuscript deals with the summoning of tutelary spirits and stresses a strong belief in every person developing the higher self that exists within.

1484 Pope Innocent VIII so deplores the spread of witchcraft in Germany that he issues the papal bull *Summis Desiderantes Affectibus* and authorizes two trusted Dominican inquisitors, Heinrich Institoris (Kramer) and Jakob Sprenger, to squelch demonology in the Rhineland.

1486 *Malleus Maleficarum*, the "Hammer of the Witches" by Institoris and Sprenger, is published and quickly becomes the "bible" of the heretic-hunters. *Malleus* earnestly refutes all those who would claim that the works of demons exist only in troubled human minds. Certain angels fell from Heaven and to believe otherwise is to believe contrary to the true faith. And now these fallen angels, these demons, are intent upon destroying the human race. Any persons who consort with demons and become witches and shapeshifters must recant their evil ways or be put to death.

1521 Three werewolves of Poligny, accused of having eaten children and consorted with wild she-wolves, confess to having achieved their transformation from a magic salve. They are burnt at the stake.

1541 A Paduan werewolf dies after torture, and after his inquisitors hack off his arms and legs searching for the wolf hair that he wore on his inside.

1550 Witekind interviews a self-confessed werewolf at Riga. Johann Weyer (Weir), a critic of the Inquisition takes up the post of doctor at Cleve. Weyer believes in the power of Satan, but he believes that the devil has only deluded certain men and women into believing that they have supernatural powers as witches and shapeshifters, thus causing them to worship dark forces rather than God.

1552 Modern French version of *Guillaume* published at Lyon.

1555 Olaus Magnus records [*Historia de gentibu septenrionalibus*] his observation that the werewolves of Livonia put on a girdle of wolf skin, drink a cup of beer, and utter certain magic words to accomplish their transformation from humans to wolves.

1556 In the eleventh book of his *Marvels*, Job Fincel tells of a lycanthrope of Padua who when his wolf-claws were cut later appeared in human form with his hands cut. Fincel also relates an account of an old chateau inhabited by a number of cat people.

1560 The first publication of Giambattista Della Porta's *Magia naturalis*

1563 Against strong opposition, Johann Weyer publishes *De praestigus daemonum*, arguing that while Satan does seek to ensnare and destroy, the charges that witches and other shapeshifters possess supernatural powers exists only in their minds and imaginations.

1573 Gilles Garnier is burned as a werewolf.

1575 Trials begin for the *benandanti*, a fertility cult in the Friuili that worships Diana.

1580 As if to provide an antidote to Weyer's call for a rational approach in dealing with accusations of witchcraft and shapeshifting, the respected intellectual, Jean Bodin, often referred to as the Aristotle of the sixteenth century, writes *De la demonomanie des sorciers*, the book that causes the flames to burn even higher around thousands of heretics' stakes.

1584   Reginald Scot risks accusations of heresy to support the call for reason championed by Weyer and to write *Discoverie of Witchcraft*.

1588   Alleged date of the execution of a female werewolf after a trial presided over by Grand Justice Henri Bouget, a judge especially noted for his cruelty.

1589   Peter Stubbe is executed as a werewolf at Cologne.

1595   *Daemonolatreia* by Nicholas Remy is hailed as the greatest encyclopedia of witchcraft since *Malleus Maleficarum*.

1598   Roulet is tried as werewolf, but his sentence is commuted. The Werewolf of Chalons, a tailor accused of eating children in his shop, is executed in Paris. The Gandillon family is burned as werewolves in the Jura after a wolf is killed while in the act of attacking a village girl and is witnessed by the mob to return to the human form of Perrenette Gandillon

1599   B. de Chavincourt publishes *Discours de la Lycantropic*.

1600   In Spain, Remy's *Daemonolatreia* is replaced as the new Catholic *Malleus* by the massive encyclopedia *Disquisitiones Magicae* , compiled by the Jesuit scholar Martin del Rio.

1602   The Cardinal-Archbishop of Besancon underwrites the publication of *Examen des sorciers [Discours des sorciers]*, a work assigned to the legal scholar Henri Bouget, an accomplished judge, torturer, and burner of heretics. King James of Scotland becomes so incensed by Scot's *Discoverie of Witchcraft* that he writes his own book, *Demonolgie*, and supervises the large-scale burning of Scot's volume.

1603   Jean Grenier is tried as a werewolf and sentenced to life imprisonment.

1610   Two women are condemned to death as werewolves at Liege. Jean Grenier dies.

1612   In *L'inconstance*, Pierre de Lancre, a noted judge of Bordeaux, writes of his visit to the cell of Jean Grenier and declares that the werewolf had sharp, protruding teeth and appeared more comfortable on all fours than in walking upright.

1630   Prince-Bishop Johann Georg II Fuchs von Dornheim, the infamous *Hexenbischof* (Witch Bishop) constructs a special torture chamber which he decorates with appropriate passages from scripture. He burns at least six hundred heretics and shapeshifters, including a fellow bishop he suspects of being too lenient.

1631   Witch trial judge Pierre de Lancre, author of *Tableau*, dies. By his own boast, he tortured and burned over six hundred persons. Jesuit Friedrich Spree has his hair turned prematurely white when he is assigned as a confessor to accused witches. To protest the cruelties he witnessed in the torture chambers, he writes *Cautio Criminalis*.

1635 Benedict Carpzov publishes *Practica Rerum Criminalium*, a work that is often referred to as the *Malleus* of Lutheranism. Carpzov acknowledges that torture of the innocent is deplorable, but necessary to ferret out the disciples of Satan.

1680 Catherine Montvoisin goes to the stake in Paris, claiming she sacrificed over 2500 infants on her satanic altar.

1692 The Livonian werewolf Theiss is interrogated.

1697 Perrault's *Contes* includes "Little Red Riding Hood"

1764 The Beast of Gevaudon starts a widespread werewolf scare in Auvergne.

1812 Brothers Grimm publish their version of "Little Red Riding Hood."

1824 Antoine Leger is tried for werewolf crimes and sentenced to a lunatic asylum.

1848 The Moon turns blood red during an eclipse and sets off an epidemic of werewolf sightings.

1857 G.W.M. Reynolds publishes *Wagner the Wehr-Wolf*.

1886 Robert Louis Stevenson publishes *Dr. Jekyll and Mr. Hyde*.

1887 The Order of the Golden Dawn is founded. The order is largely based on the *Sacred Magic* of Abramalin and restores a fascination with vampires, werewolves, and spirits of darkness and light. Among its members are such luminaries as Nobel Prize winner W.B. Yeats and the notorious Aleister Crowley.

1888 Jack the Ripper terrorizes London with his werewolflike slashings and mutilations of prostitutes.

1897 Vacher the Ripper mutilates and kills as many as twenty victims before he is apprehended in France. Thomas Russell Sullivan adapts *The Strange Case of Dr. Jekyll and Mr. Hyde* for the stage in Boston.

1898 McGregor Matthews, Visible Head of the Order of the Golden Dawn, translates the *grimoire*, *The Sacred Magic of Abramalin the Mage*.

1908 The first film version of *Jekyll and Hyde* is produced by the Selig company in America.

1909 A Danish film company produces their version of *Jekyll and Hyde*.

1912 The Laemmle production company in America releases their take on *Dr. Jekyll and Mr. Hyde*.

1913 The silent film *The Werewolf* uses a real wolf in the transformation scene. Film production companies in the U.S. and Great Britain release the fourth and fifth versions of *Jekyll and Hyde*.

1919 The approximate date of the founding of the Thule Society in German. A young and earnest Adolf Hitler is among their early members.

1920   Kamala and Amala, the wolf children, are discovered in India. Right-wing terror group, "Operation Werewolf," is established in Germany. Four separate versions of *Dr. Jekyll and Mr. Hyde* are released that year. The most famous interpretation of the four is that of John Barrymore, produced by Famous Players-Lasky.

1922   The Fraternity of the Inner Light is founded by Dion Fortune, who has a dramatic and frightening encounter with a werewolf.

1923   The founding of Hitler's Nazi Party.

1924   Fritz Haarmann, the Hanover Butcher, murders and cannibalizes as many as 50 young men. What he cannot himself devour, he sells as steaks and sausages to his unsuspecting customers.

1932   *Dr. Jekyll and Mr. Hyde* with esteemed actor Frederic March becomes the classic film version of the haunting tale.

1933   Montague Summers publishes his study of *The Werewolf*. Adolf Hitler becomes Chancellor and refers to himself as the "Father Wolf" of the German people.

1934   Author Guy Endore publishes *The Werewolf of Paris*.

1935   Henry Hull stars in *The Werewolf of London*. Albert Fish kills and eats as many as fifteen children in Washington, D.C.

1940   Harry Gordon, the Werewolf of San Francisco, is arrested.

1941   *The Wolf Man* with Lon Chaney, Jr. establishes werewolf arcana according to Hollywood.

1942   Gordon Cummins, London's "Wartime Jack the Ripper," is apprehended.

1944   *The House of Frankenstein* includes mention of a silver bullet terminating a werewolf and adds to the lycanthropic mythology.

1945   Goebbels resurrects Operation Werewolf as a terrorist society.

1957   Ed Gein, the Wisconsin Ghoul, is arrested.

1966   Richard Speck brutally slashes eight student nurses to death in Chicago.

1969   The Charles Manson "family" commits a satanic mass murder in Beverly Hills.

1977   Serial killer David Berkowitz ("Son of Sam") is ordered to murder by a large black dog.

1980   Two innovative motion pictures, *The Howling* and *An American Werewolf in London* , set a new high watermark for motion picture special effects and reestablish werewolf films—and the horror genre in general—as viable commodities at the boxoffice.

1982   The notorious "Chicago Rippers," a savage gang of rapist-mutilators, is apprehended.

1985   Richard Ramirez, the "Night Stalker," receives nineteen death sentences in Los Angeles.

1987   Michael Lupo, "the Wolfman of London," is jailed.

1989   In Paris, Francis LeRoy, "the Werewolf of the Dordgone" is imprisoned for life. A satanic/cannibal cult headquartered in Matamoros, Mexico, is disbanded. The high priest, Aldolfo De Jesus Constanzo, is killed on his own orders rather than be taken into custody, and the priestess, Sara Maria Aldrete, imprisoned.

1992   Jeffrey Dahmer is convicted on sixteen charges of murder, mutilation, and cannibalism.

1994   Moscow's neo-Nazi Werewolves disrupt the showing of Steven Spielberg's *Schindler's List*.

1997   Real-life "Werewolves on Wheels," the Cobra and the Butcher, two motorcycle slashers, are apprehended for the brutal deaths of 37 Pakistani Shiite Muslims in Karachi. Nasib Kelewang told authorities in Indonesia that the ghost of his father ordered him to kill and dedicate to Satan the 42 women whose bodies they unearthed from the sugarcane field near the North Sumatran capital of Medan. Police in Paris engage in a desperate search for the "Bastille Slasher," a vicious rapist who slits the throats of his victims.

1998   Hanoi's "Werewolves on Wheels," a crazed pair of motorcycle slashers who prey on children, are sought by police as the toll of the young victims of the monsters' vicious razors rises higher. "The Ripper of Genoa" is finally captured by Italian police after slashing to death at least eight women.

1999   The U.S. Patent and Trademark Office rejects an attempt to patent a technique for creating animal-human hybrids.

Abbot Ralph (1150–?)

Many ancient chronicles contain accounts of monsters and **demons** that leap from dark ambush to kidnap or devour unsuspecting victims. These demons are frequently described in words that bring to mind the appearance of the classic werewolf—"dark and hairy creatures" with eyes that glow in the dark and "the devil's bestial look on their faces."

In his *Chronicles* (c. 1210), Abbot Ralph of Coggeshall Abbey, Essex, England, wrote about a raging thunderstorm that lashed the countryside on the night of St. John the Baptist in June 1205 and of the lightning that struck and killed "a certain strange monster" at Maidstone in Kent: "This monster had the head of a strange being, the belly of a human and other monstrous members and limbs of animals unlike each other. Its black corpse was scorched and a terrible stench came from it and very few were able to go near."

Abbot Ralph recorded another incident that occurred during a storm on the night of July 29, 1205: "Horrible thunder and lightning raged during the night . . . many thought the Judgment Day had arrived. . . . Next day, certain monstrous tracks of [large, pointed] feet were seen at several places. The prints were of a kind never seen before and many claimed they were the tracks of giant demons."

SOURCES:
Hurwood, Bernardt J. *Terror by Night.* New York: Lancer Books, 1963.

Abbott and Costello Meet Frankenstein

In the early 1940s it would have been unthinkable to have teamed the comedy duo of Bud Abbott and Lou Costello with the Big Three of Monsterdom—**Dracula,** the Wolf Man, and the Frankenstein Monster. It would have seemed outrageous blasphemy to die-hard horror fans to inject Abbott and Costello's brand of silly comedy into a scenario of serious terror. Even though masters of motion picture thrillers, such as Alfred Hitchcock, had learned to include a few humorous moments between peak scenes of suspense in order to allow their audiences to release some tension in laughter, an Abbott and Costello vaudeville routine would quite likely completely destroy the creepy mood of a monster movie.

It probably wouldn't have mattered a great deal to the comedy team just when they encountered the cinema's favorite monsters. They had slowly worked their way up the rungs of national popularity since 1931, first paying their dues in vaudeville and burlesque, then appearing on radio and Broadway. They catapulted to success after they were featured in the musical *One Night in the Tropics* (1940), and after their starring roles in *Buck Privates* (1941) they were steady top box office draws until shortly after World War II when their popularity began to wane. Such lackluster films as *Little Giant* (1946) and *The Wistful Widow of Wagon Gap* (1947) could not find the audiences that had once filled the theaters for their comedy antics, and it appeared as though Abbott and Costello had had their time in the spotlight. Then they encountered the Wolf Man, Dracula, and the Frankenstein Monster.

From one perspective, this unique combination involved pairing two formerly successful motion picture teams in a last-ditch effort to achieve some aspect of their former glory. **Universal Pictures** had first paired two of their monsters in **Frankenstein Meets the Wolf Man** in 1943. After the success of that film, a full cast of creatures was featured in *House of Frankenstein* (1944), operating on the tried and true Hollywood formula of giving the audiences what they want. But by the time all the usual suspects were assembled for *House of Dracula* (1945), it was painfully obvious that the monster mythos no longer had the mystique to attract the huge audiences that once flocked to shiver through the original creature features. *Abbott and Costello Meet Frankenstein* (1948) would be the last time the Big Three of Monsterdom would be assembled for a film—and somehow the bizarre combination of comedy and monsters worked, thus reviving both the laugh appeal of Abbott and Costello and the scream appeal of the horror genre for a new generation of audiences.

While many critics name the film as Abbott and Costello's best and most consistently funny cinematic endeavor, a number of the same pundits deplore the fact that the box office bonanza of *Abbott and Costello Meet Frankenstein* resulted in a number of very weak sequels with very repetitious titles as the comedians romped through the entire horror genre: *Abbott and Costello Meet the Killer* (1949), *Abbott and Costello Meet the Invisible Man* (1950), *Abbott and Costello Meet Captain Kidd* (1952), *Abbott and Costello Meet Dr. Jekyll and Mr. Hyde* (1953), and *Abbott and Costello Meet the Mummy* (1955).

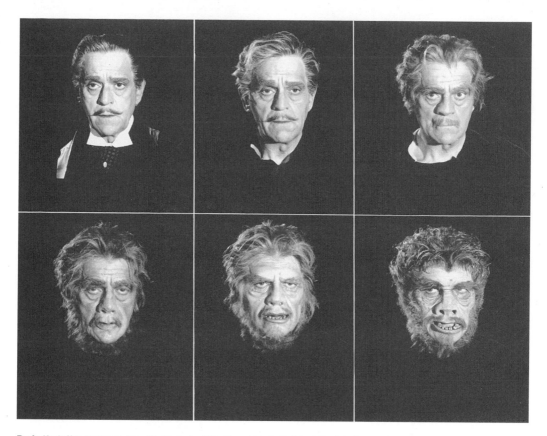

Boris Karloff transforms into Mr. Hyde in *Abbott and Costello Meet Dr. Jekyll and Mr. Hyde*, one of a series of monster flicks from starring the comic duo.

Abbott and Costello Meet Frankenstein deals with the classic plot of finding a suitable brain for the monster—the same problem that first faced Dr. Frankenstein in the 1931 original. Dracula thinks that the simple, easily led brain of Costello would make a perfect fit for the big guy, making him fully subject to his sinister vampiric will.

Lawrence Talbot, the Wolf Man, is once again enacted by **Lon Chaney Jr.** as a sympathetic figure, cursed to be transformed into a werewolf during the **full moon,** and at all other days and nights of the month trying his best to be a nice guy and not hurt anyone. **Bela Lugosi** returned to wear the familiar black cape as Dracula, and Glenn Strange, who would one day play the bartender on the long-running television series *Gunsmoke*, portrayed the hulking Frankenstein Monster with more bulk than either Boris Karloff or Lugosi had to offer when they undertook the heavy makeup of the role. Vincent Price, who would become Hollywood's King of Horror during the 1960s and 1970s, loaned his cultured vocalization to the film as the voice of the Invisible Man.

Abbott and Costello Meet Frankenstein is also known as *Abbott and Costello Meet the Ghosts*, *The Brain of Frankenstein*, and *Meet the Ghosts*.

SOURCES:

Clarens, Carlos. *An Illustrated History of the Horror Film*. New York: Capricorn Books, 1968.

Katz, Ephraim. *The Film Encyclopedia*. New York: Perigee, 1979.

Maltin, Leonard. *Leonard Maltin's 1999 Movie & Video Guide*. New York: Signet, 1998.

Siegel, Scott, and Barbara Siegel. *The Encyclopedia of Hollywood*. New York: Avon Books, 1990.

The Abominable Snowman

For centuries men and women who live or travel in remote areas of the world have told of sighting strange wildmen that appear to be some form of man-beast unknown to conventional science. Folklore has cast these mysterious monsters as werewolves or some kind of apelike creature, and many cynics—especially those who seldom venture to stray from their urban shelters and hike into uncharted areas—believe such accounts are the contents of old campfire spook stories. However, in the last few decades a number of zoologists, biologists, and other field researchers have increasingly begun to place more credence in the stories of unidentified humanlike creatures.

As early as 1913, Moscow scientist Dr. V. A. Khakhlov presented a detailed report on the wild, humanlike creatures that inhabited remote areas of eastern Asia. In 1920, through a mistranslation of the Tibetan word for the mysterious giants of the snow, the term "Abominable Snowman" was coined to describe the creatures.

For the next two decades, reports of the creatures were common, but it was not until the close of World War II and the renewed interest in climbing Mt. Everest that world attention was once again focused on the phenomenon of the unexplained, humanlike footprints that were being found at impossible heights and temperatures. The Himalayan activity reached a climax in 1960 when Sir Edmund Hillary, conqueror of Mt. Everest, led an expedition in search of the elusive snowman, the **yeti.** To the dismay of millions of armchair adventurers around the world, Hillary returned with nothing to show for his efforts but a fur hat that had been fashioned in imitation of the creature's crest.

In the United States, reports of a similar unknown man-beast can be found in frontier journals, in early regional newspapers, and in the legends of many Native American tribes. In the northwestern states and in the Canadian provinces, the mysterious monster is variously known as Sasquatch, Bigfoot, *Wauk-wauk*, or Saskehavis. Most Bigfoot hunters and those scientists seriously interested in the mystery suspect that the creature is a bipedal mammal closely related to *Homo sapiens* and the ape family.

The legendary Bigfoot, as seen in the famous film shot by Roger Patterson.

Eyewitnesses of Sasquatch activity have estimated its height at anywhere from six to nine feet. Estimating its weight from the depths of the depressions made by its footprints puts it well over 400 pounds. The creature's entire body is said to be covered with dark fur from one to four inches in length; but its palms, soles of its feet, nose, and upper facial area are free of hair. The exposed flesh is very ruddy, and its eyes are black. Bigfoot-like beings have been sighted in the more wooded and mountainous regions of the states of California, Oregon, Washington, Idaho, and Alaska; most of the Canadian provinces; the remote areas of South America, Australia, and Africa; the Caucasus Mountains; and the Himalayan mountain range. Although the creature generally avoids contact with humans, it may become violent if attacked, cornered, or surprised.

Little attention was given to Bigfoot sightings in the U.S. until the late 1950s when roadbuilding crews in the unmapped wilderness of the Bluff Creek area north of Eureka, California, began to report close encounters with the forest giants and complained that the monsters were tossing their oil drums and small machinery around at night. Loggers on cleanup were next to discover the tracks and droppings of the Sasquatch. Then, after hunters, hikers, and tourists began to testify to the presence of something big and strange in the California forests, area residents at last came forward with a seemingly endless number of stories about their own encounters with the shrill-squealing, seven-foot giants they had come to regard as a normal part of their existence.

In North America, the greatest number of sightings have come from the following areas: Fraser River Valley; the Strait of Georgia; Vancouver Island, British Columbia; the "Ape Canyon" region near Mt. St. Helens in southwestern Washington; the Three Sisters Wilderness west of Bend, Oregon; and the area around the Hoopa Valley Indian Reservation, especially the Bluff Creek watershed, northeast of Eureka, California.

The most bizarre reports have come from a valley situated at the confluence of the Liard and South Nahanni Rivers at the south end of the Mackenzie Range in the Canadian Northwest Territories. In this strange valley, the grim, unsolved murders of more than a dozen trappers and miners have been blamed on the Sasquatch.

Although the Abominable Snowman remains an enigma, there are a number of wildlife biologists who take the scattered reports of the mysterious creature very seriously and who wish to make the continued search for Bigfoot an earnest scientific undertaking.

SOURCES:

Norman, Eric. *The Abominable Snowmen.* New York: Award Books, 1969.

The Adlet

The Inuit tribespeople have a legend about the Adlet, the dog people, the offspring of a great red dog and an Inuit woman. This beast/human marriage produced five ugly weredogs and five regular dogs, and the disgusted mother set them all adrift on rafts.

The five dogs eventually reached the shores of Europe and begot among them the various white ethnic groups. The weredogs evolved into horrible, bloodthirsty monsters who still haunt the northern icelands in search of human flesh.

SOURCES:

Larousse Dictionary of World Folklore. New York: Larousse, 1995.

Alien Beings

While not every unidentified flying object (UFO) researcher is convinced that the strange aerial objects in our skies originate from some extraterrestrial source, nearly all investigators of the phenomenon believe that the millions of people who report "flying saucers" are seeing something unknown to them. And even if 95 percent of the UFO reports may be explained away as faulty interpretations of natural phenomena, misidentification of conventional aircraft, or sightings of secret government test planes, there remain thousands of reports from serious and sober citizens who have seen something decidedly unidentified and unknown traversing the skies. If the objects are some kind of actual aerial craft, then the question remains, "Who is piloting the darned things?"

From the earliest reports of witnesses sighting alleged alien beings in the late 1940s, the most common descriptions collected by UFO investigators provide a sketchy picture of smallish humanoid beings with gray or grayish-green complexions who stand about five feet tall and are dressed in one-piece jumpsuits. Witnesses who claim to have had very close encounters with these aliens say that they have very large heads with big, lidless eyes. In the majority of accounts of this type, the entities are said to have no noses, only nostrils; no discernible lips, only a straight line indicating a mouth; and no ears. The general appearance of such beings suggests some kind of reptilian or amphibian humanoid.

Other UFO contactees claim an enlightening experience with a far different alien being. They speak of space brothers and sisters who appear to be benevolent, concerned spiritual entities. These extraterrestrials are described as tall, blond, light-complexioned, perfectly proportioned, and completely human in appearance. One might describe them as angelic in their overall countenance.

And then, of course, there are the monsters. Some of them are described as big, hairy, smelly, Bigfoot-like creatures; others are described as rampaging, nightmarish, purple people-eaters; and still others as manic, out-of-control robotlike beings.

Even today, after 50 years of aggressive research on the part of many investigators, few theorists question how many of these entities truly come from outer space and how many may be entities that have been sighted in various guises throughout the course of human history. Few UFO researchers ponder whether or not the alien intelligences might be shapeshifters capable of assuming any size or any life-form that suits their undisclosed purposes or that may be more readily comprehensible to the human percipients.

Hollywood, the chief purveyor of popular culture and folklore, is much quicker to suggest that the beings—extraterrestrial or otherwise—that appear to arrive in spaceships are neither little bug-eyed creatures nor angelic entities, but are shapeshifting creatures assuming whatever form best attains their overall goals, benevolent or hostile. And while the cute, amphibious E.T.-type entities seem benign, more often than not Hollywood screenwriters have decided that the extraterrestrial shapeshifters are intent on doing great harm to the inhabitants of planet earth. In films such as *Invaders from Mars* (1953, 1986), *Invasion of the Body Snatchers* (1956, 1978), *The Thing* (1951, 1982), and *The Faculty* (1998), the spooky scenarios presented to audiences warn of an intelligence that can assume many forms. Most frightening of all, they can assume the image of those nearest and dearest to us. When shapeshifters have the power to appear as our friends and loved ones, then the paranoid admonition to trust no one becomes a deadly truth.

SOURCES:

Stanley, John. *Creature Features*. New York: Boulevard, 1997.

Steiger, Brad, and Sherry Hansen Steiger. *UFO Odyssey*. New York: Ballantine, 1999.

Almasti

In the spring of 1966, Didanov, a man who was highly respected in his Russian village, told Dr. Jeanne-Marie-Therese Koffman, a well-known Russian monster hunter, of his experience with an *almasti*, a wildman of the mountains.

Didanov had traveled to the mountain pastures and had received an invitation to have supper and to spend the night at a shepherds' encampment. Later that night, Didanov watched a strange hairy "animal" stick his head inside the tent where he was sleeping, peer about, then withdraw. Didanov awoke his host and described what he had seen.

The shepherd advised Didanov to pay no attention. It was only an almasti, a wildman who often paid a visit to the camp.

Kevin McCarthy (in suit) and other cast members fighting off *The Invasion of the Body Snatchers.*

The shepherd quickly dozed off again, but Didanov, unnerved by the experience, could not sleep. Then, according to his account in the magazine *Nauka i Religiya* (translated in English for the journal *Sputnik*), the tent flaps opened and the wildman once again entered. Didanov said that he feigned sleep, but, scared stiff, he "screwed up" his eyes and kept watching the bizarre invader: "The thing squatted beside the pots of food, and lifting the lids, it began to eat . . . glancing our way constantly to see if we were asleep. Then it stood up, silently replaced the lids on both pots . . . and slipped out of the tent."

Aubekir Bekanov, a Karbardin villager, told Russian journalists that he had been returning from a late movie in the village when he spied a shadowy figure standing near a fence:

> I turned on my flashlight and found myself face to face with a hairy, manlike creature. I could only stand there rooted to the ground, staring at the monstrous thing. It, in turn, stood there and stared at me. We were both

immobile. When I finally made a move, the almasti jumped the fence in one leap and disappeared into a grove of cherry trees.

The next morning two young girls had their feast of cherries interrupted by the glimpse of a massive, hairy arm shaking the trunk of a tree near them. Later that same day, three other villagers saw the creature among the cherry trees. By the time the almasti chose to quit the village of Kabardin, nine people had witnessed its dark, hairy bulk.

Professor V. K. Leontiev recalled the day in July 1957 when he came across some very strange manlike tracks while he was following the trail of a leopard in the territory known as the Gagan Sanctuary. That night as he was preparing camp, he was startled by a loud, shrill, humanlike cry that he was convinced had been made by no animal.

That day, toward evening, Professor Leontiev caught sight of something very large moving ahead of him on a snowfield. He could see that the creature was walking erect, and he estimated its height as about seven feet tall. Its body was covered with long, dark hair. During the five to seven minutes that he had the almasti in sight, he observed shoulders of unusual width, a massive head, and a man-beast with a generally humanlike appearance.

SOURCES:
Norman, Eric. *The Abominable Snowmen.* New York: Award Books, 1969.
Steiger, Brad. *Monsters Among Us.* New York: Berkley Books, 1989.

An American Werewolf in London

When *An American Werewolf in London* opened in motion picture theaters in 1981, it offered horror buffs and werewolf lovers the proper mix of black, contemporary hip comedy and creepy obeisance missing from the old black-and-white creature feature classics. While **The Howling,** which appeared earlier the same year, has excellent special effects and has been credited for reintroducing werewolves as a viable box office attraction, *An American Werewolf in London* is in a category all its own. The film presents Rick Baker's Academy Award–winning makeup wizardry, which allows the audience to see virtual microscopic close-ups of each agonizing step that the victim of a werewolf's bite must undergo to achieve the process of transmutation. With no detection of stop-action photography and with no awareness of the movie magic involved, the audience witnesses the actor grimacing and screaming in horror as his body sprouts coarse hair, his hands stretch into paws, and his torso twists painfully from bipedal human to four-legged wolf. The effect on the viewers is visceral, forcing them to participate vicariously in the nightmarish process of transmutation. Not since the classic *The Curse of the Werewolf* (1961) has an audience witnessed cinematic transmutation.

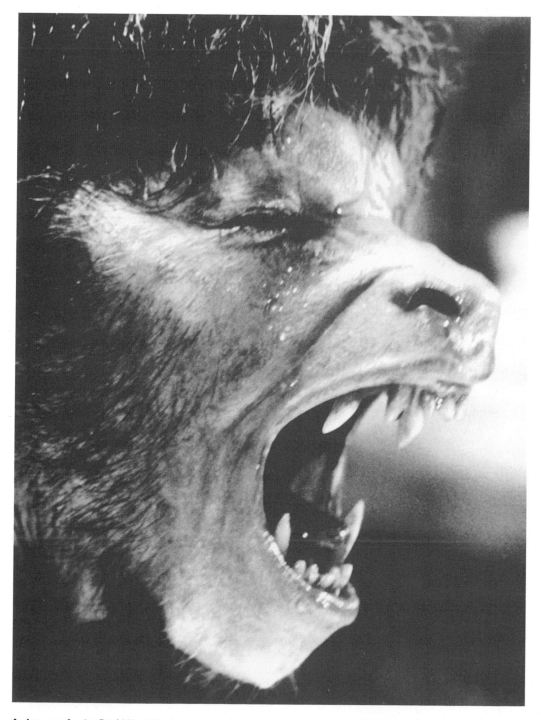

A close-up of actor David Naughton's face as he transforms into a werewolf in *An American Werewolf in London.*

The storyline focuses on two young Americans, David (David Naughton) and Jack (Griffin Dunne), who are hitchhiking around the English countryside. Although they are warned to beware the **full moon** and to stay away from the moors, they find themselves off the main road, near the moors, and alone under a full moon. They are attacked by a large wolf that kills Jack and wounds David before the villagers shoot it. Once struck down, the creature is revealed as a werewolf when it transforms back into its human form.

David is taken to a hospital, where he soon experiences a series of bizarre and frightening visions and dreams in which his friend Jack—who steadily decomposes a bit more in each subsequent ghostly visit—warns him that the bites that he received in the scuffle on the moors will turn him into a werewolf. Jack counsels suicide and a quiet passage to the next life rather than becoming a bloodlusting monster, but by now David has fallen in love with his nurse (Jenny Agutter) and chooses to believe that he is merely suffering from some mental aberration rather than receiving werewolf warnings from a ghost. By the time he realizes he is truly fated to become a werewolf, he is already undergoing the excruciating pain of transmutation. Once the process is complete, he can only fulfill his gory destiny and terrorize London as a werewolf.

Naughton, who achieved earlier fame in a series of television commercials as the congenial, dancing Dr. Pepper enthusiast, underwent a rigorous physical training program to get himself in shape for the nude werewolf transmutation scenes. Although Dunne may steal a few scenes as his decomposing buddy, Naughton portrays his character as likeable and ordinary, thus accentuating the tragedy and the underlying threat that *anyone* could be bitten by a werewolf and suffer a similar fate. Naughton has since appeared in an occasional film in the horror genre (*Amityville: A New Generation*, 1993), and he frequently guests on television programs, from *Seinfeld* and *Melrose Place* to *Diagnosis Murder* and *Touched by an Angel*.

Director John Landis, who previously demonstrated his gift for developing off-beat characterizations in *National Lampoon's Animal House* (1978) and *The Blues Brothers* (1980), employs his sense of the bizarre and darkly humorous to good advantage in *An American Werewolf in London*. Landis joins the fun by giving himself a cameo as a man who is thrown through a London shop window by the rampaging werewolf.

SOURCES:

Skal, David J. *The Monster Show*. New York: W.W. Norton, 1993.
Stanley, John. *Creature Features*. New York: Boulevard, 1997.

An American Werewolf in Paris

The astonishing computer-generated special effects in *An American Werewolf in Paris* (1997) reflect the progress that has been achieved in the technical proficiencies of moviemaking. While the film was not nearly as well received as the cult classic **An American Werewolf in London** (1981), the plot is a great deal more complex. In many ways—in spite of the marvel of beholding the seemingly effortless morphing of humans into wolves—it is more of an old-fashioned horror movie.

Andy (Tom Everett Scott) and his two buddies, Brad (Vince Vieluf) and Chris (Phil Buckman), are on a "Daredevil Tour of Europe," seeing who can outperform others with dangerous stunts. When Andy comes up with the ultimate daredevil feat, bungee-jumping off the Eiffel Tower in Paris, he also manages to save the life of a lovely young woman intent on committing suicide.

Andy decides that Serafine (Julie Delpy) is the woman of his dreams, and he pursues her across greater Paris, not realizing that it is her despair over being a werewolf that drove her to attempt to take her own life.

Things get nasty after Andy and Brad unknowingly visit a underground Paris nightclub that is really a front for a den of werewolves who love to snack on unsuspecting tourists. When Brad is killed and Andy wounded by the werewolves, the film repeats the device used in *An American Werewolf in London* of having the dead and decomposing friend return to warn his bitten buddy of his fate. But in this picture, the hero's love interest is also a werewolf, not a nurse who must stand helplessly by and watch the horrible transmutation occur. Andy must somehow rid himself of the werewolf virus within his own body and find a cure for the curse that has affected Serafine since her birth.

Animal Ancestors

The belief in animal beings goes back to the dawn of humankind's curiosity about its place in the natural scheme of things. In *Algonquin Legends of New England*, C. G. Leland repeats a common Native American myth that states that at the beginning of time humans were as animals and animals were as humans. The mythologies of the aboriginal people of South America echo the same belief: in the beginning, people were animals but also humans. Those myths state that the spiritual aspects of beings that would one day evolve to humanhood first found its first physical expression in the shapes of animals.

Numerous legends from tribes across North America tell of wolfmen, bearmen, cougarmen, and other werecreatures. Stories of women who gave birth to man-beasts are common, as are accounts of tribesmen who took animal brides. Ancient cultures throughout the world formed totem clans and claimed an animal ancestor as the progenitor of their clan.

Although it is always hazardous to make cross-cultural generalities about any subject, there is generally a commonality of belief among

shamans from nearly every known tradition that all creatures on the planet are relatives.

Donna Kay Barthelemy, who spent five years with a cross-cultural shaman studying the ways of many different traditions, agrees. In the shamanistic tradition, she writes: "All creatures are called 'relatives,' and are considered sisters, brothers, grandparents. . . . Nonhuman relatives are considered 'people' and are prayed for . . . the birds (winged ones), the trees (tall standing people), the plants (green-growing people), the four-leggeds, the creepy crawlies, as well as the two-leggeds."

Perhaps because of the association with wolves—which according to recent research began over 140,000 years ago—many tribes in Europe and the Americas believed that their ancestors truly had been **wolves.** Many Native American tribes contain legends that tell how the first tribes that ever existed were wolfpeople. At first, according to these traditions, the wolfpeople walked on all fours. After a time, it seemed a good thing to begin walking upright and—very slowly at first—to become human. So a toe was formed, then a couple of fingers, smaller ears and teeth, and so forth, until they gradually became perfect human beings. Some, however, mourned the loss of a tail, but it was agreed that such an appendage made sitting difficult—and one could always "borrow" one from those spirits who had chosen to remain in wolf, coyote, or fox form.

After a time, clans began to form around the belief that certain animals other than wolves had been ancestors for their families. Some admired the grace of the deer, the strength of the bear, the prowess of the cougar, and so forth, and clan demarcations were established within the tribes.

SOURCES:

Barthelemy, Donna Kay. "Shamanism As Living System." *Quest,* summer 1995.

Steiger, Brad. *Totems: The Transformative Power of Your Personal Animal Totem.* San Francisco: HarperSanFrancisco, 1997.

Ankers, Evelyn (1918–1985)

The lobby posters for the horror film *The Wolf Man* (1941) depict the monster carrying a shapely woman in its arms and warned potential audiences that it would "tear the scream" from their throats. By the time Evelyn Ankers appeared as Gwen Conliffe in the film she was well prepared to lead moviegoers in those screams, for she was already known as the Scream Queen of the movies. An attractive British leading lady who came to Hollywood in 1940, some critics said that she did not so much act as react.

Ankers also appeared in a number of other films in the horror genre, including *Hold That Ghost* (1941), *Ghost of Frankenstein* (1942), *Son of Drac-*

ula (1943), *Captive Wild Woman* (1943), and *Invisible Man's Revenge* (1944). After *The Frozen Ghost* (1945), she was considered by film buffs to be the Queen of the Horror Movies.

Engaged for a time to marry actor Glenn Ford, she broke the engagement when she met actor Richard Denning. They were married on September 6, 1942, and remained so until her death on August 29, 1985. Denning, perhaps best known for his 12-year run as governor Paul Jameson on the television series *Hawaii Five-O*, was no stranger to motion pictures in the horror genre. Among his film credits are *Unknown Island* (1948), *Creature from the Black Lagoon* (1954), *Creature with the Atom Brain* (1955), *The Day the World Ended* (1956), and *The Black Scorpion* (1957).

SOURCES:
Katz, Ephraim. *The Film Encyclopedia*. New York: Perigee, 1979.
Walker, John, ed. *Halliwell's Filmgoer's Companion, 12th Edition*. New York: HarperCollins, 1997.

Anubis

Anubis is the jackal-headed Egyptian god of the underworld, the judge of the dead. Sometimes known as the Great Dog, Anubis was mated to Nepthys, the underworld aspect of the goddess Isis. Dogs were greatly revered in ancient Egypt, and Anubis had a place of great honor in the pantheon of gods.

For Christians in the Middle Ages, images of Anubis reinforced folk legends of werejackals that attacked unwary desert travelers. While some ancient cults saw Anubis as a conduit for healing, others believed the priests with their dog-headed masks were assuming the pagan god's role as judge of the underworld and were stealing the souls of those hapless victims that they only pretended to cure.

SOURCES:
Gaynor, Frank, ed. *Dictionary of Mysticism*. New York: Philosophical Library, 1953.

The Appearance of Werewolves

When werewolves are free of the awful curse that dominates their existence during the nights of the **full moon,** they appear as ordinary men and women—perhaps a bit nervous or restless, perhaps occasionally somewhat melancholy, but essentially normal in every aspect of their physical appearance. They can walk about in full sunlight and need not fear crucifixes or holy water.

Most of the contemporary folklore describing the transformation of human to werewolf is influenced by such Hollywood films as **The Wolf Man** (1941) and **Curse of the Werewolf** (1961), which depict the end result of the process of shapeshifting as a two-legged, hairy, fanged, wolflike entity, lusting

Ferdy Mayne displays an unconventional appearance as a werewolf in *The Howling II*.

for **blood** and flesh. The werewolf continues to walk upright, rather than move on all fours, and is still recognizable as a humanoid creature. During the transmutation, articles of clothing may be ripped or shredded and shoes discarded, but the werewolf remains barefooted and clothed as he seeks for prey under the full moon.

More recent films, such as **An American Werewolf in London** (1981), **An American Werewolf in Paris** (1997), and the series of motion pictures based on **The Howling** (1981), have largely returned to the descriptions of werewolves of ancient legend by portraying a beast that is more wolf than human. In the classic accounts, once the transformation into wolf has occurred, it is difficult to detect any differences between the werewolf and the true wolf without careful examination. The werewolf that has undergone a complete shapeshifting process is somewhat larger than a true wolf, very often has a silvery sheen to its fur, and always has red, glowing eyes.

The werewolf of ancient tradition runs on all fours and has discarded all vestiges of clothing before the process of transmutation begins. If the shapeshifter should be killed while in the form of a wolf, he or she would return to human shape and be found naked.

When those individuals who became werewolves against their will are not under the power of the curse that forces them to become ravenous beasts, they experience all the normal human emotions of shame and disgust for the deeds that they must commit under the blood spell. They may long for death and seek ways to destroy themselves before they take the lives of more innocent victims. However, they soon discover to their dismay that the Grim Reaper can only be summoned to their door by certain means—and self-destruction is not one of them.

On the other hand, those who became werewolves of their own choice and who sought the power of transmutation through incantations, potions, or spells, glory in their strength and in their ability to strike fear into the hearts of all who hear their piercing howling on the nights of the full moon.

SOURCES:

Douglas, Drake. *Horror!* New York: Collier Books, 1966.

Spence, Lewis. *An Encyclopedia of Occultism.* New Hyde Park, NY: University Books, 1960.

B

Badger People

The folk wisdom of Native American tribes sees the badger as a smaller, younger brother to the bear, and the people greatly respect the creature's strength and stout heart. Because its evenly marked black and white stripes suggest a being that somehow stands between night and day, the darkness and the light, some medicine priests believe the badger is a perfect emissary to mediate between the world of spirits and the world of humans. Its powerful, compact body also makes the badger an excellent and secure form to receive the spirit of a shapeshifting **shaman.**

Among certain Native American tribes, the badger's remarkable prowess at burrowing through the earth is regarded as symbolic of the child pushing its way through the womb during the birth process. Badger paw **talisman**s are prized by pregnant women about to come full term and enter labor.

While the Japanese may also respect the badger's strength, they more often perceive the creature as capable of working great violence, and their folklore frequently casts the badger as a favorite form assumed by shapeshifting dark magicians who seek to work evil.

SOURCES:

Hazlitt, W. C. *Dictionary of Faiths & Folklore.* London: Studio Editions, 1995.
Larousse Dictionary of World Folklore. New York: Larousse, 1995.
Steiger, Brad. *Totems: The Transformative Power of Your Personal Animal Totem.* San Francisco: HarperSanFrancisco, 1997.

Basic Ways to Become a Werewolf

There are two basic ways by which one might become a werewolf: voluntary and involuntary.

According to the ancient Greeks, any skilled sorcerer who so chose could become a werewolf. Throughout history, self-professed werewolves have mentioned a "magic girdle" or "magic belt," which they wear about their middles, or a "magic salve" which they apply liberally to their naked bodies. Others tell of inhaling or imbibing certain potions.

Magical texts advise those who wish to become a werewolf to disrobe, rub a magical ointment freely over their flesh, place a girdle made of human or wolf skin around their waist, then cover their entire body with the pelt of a wolf. To accelerate the process, they should drink beer mixed with **blood** and chant a particular magical formula.

Some werewolves claim to have achieved their shapeshifting ability by having drunk water from the paw print of a wolf. Once this had been accomplished, they ate the brains of a wolf and slept in its lair.

One ancient text prescribes a ritual for the magician who is eager to become a shapeshifter. He is told to wait until the night of a **full moon,** then enter the forest at midnight. Then, according to the instructions:

> Draw two concentric circles on the ground, one six feet in diameter, the other 14 feet in diameter. Build a fire in the center of the inner circle and place a tripod over the flames. Suspend from the tripod an iron pot full of water. Bring the water to a full boil and throw into the pot a handful each of aloe, hemlock, poppy seed, and nightshade. As the ingredients are being stirred in the iron pot, call aloud to the spirits of the restless dead, the spirits of the foul darkness, the spirits of the hateful, and the spirits of werewolves and satyrs.

Once the summons for the various spirits of darkness have been shouted into the night, the person who aspires to become a werewolf should strip off all of his clothing and smear his body with the fat of a freshly killed animal that has been mixed with anise, camphor, and opium. The next step is to take the wolfskin that he has brought with him, wrap it around his middle like a loincloth, then kneel down at the boundaries of the large circle and remain in that position until the fire dies out. When this happens, the power that the disciple of darkness has summoned should make its presence known to him.

If the magician has done everything correctly, the dark force will announce its presence by loud shrieks and groans. Later, if the would-be werewolf has not been terrified and frightened away by the dark one's awful screams and groans, it will materialize in any one of a number of forms, most likely that of a horrible half-human, half-beast monster. Once it has manifested in whatever form it desires, the dark force will conduct its transaction with the magician and allow him henceforth to assume the shape of a wolf whenever he wears his wolfskin loincloth.

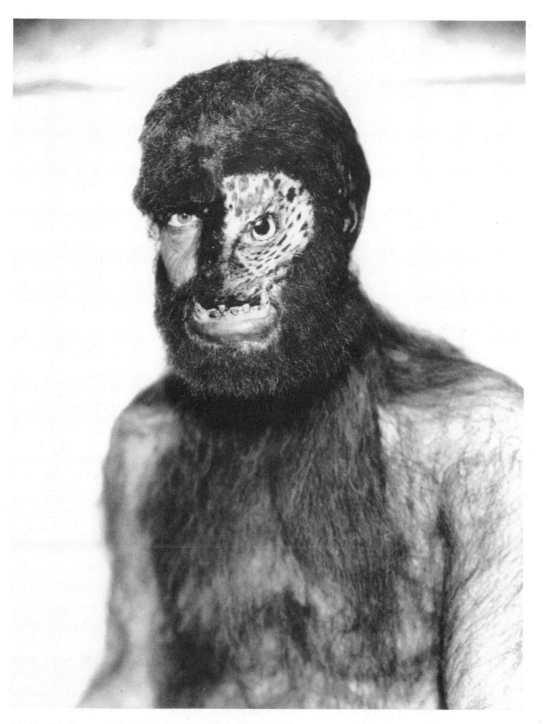

A half-owl, half-man creature from the film *Island of Lost Souls.*

By far the most familiar involuntary manner in which one becomes a werewolf is to be bitten or scratched by such a creature. In the same category would be those men and women who are transformed into werewolves by being cursed for their sins or by being the victim of a sorcerer's incantations.

Another involuntary means of becoming a werewolf, according to some old traditions, is to be born on Christmas Eve. The very process of one's birth on that sacred night, according to certain ecclesiastical scholars, is an act of blasphemy since it detracts from the full attention that should be given to the nativity of Jesus. Thus, those born on that night are condemned to be werewolves unless they prove themselves to be pious beyond reproach in all thoughts, words, and deeds throughout their lifetime.

SOURCES:

Eisler, Robert. *Man into Wolf*. London: Spring Books, n.d.

Spence, Lewis. *An Encyclopedia of Occultism*. New Hyde Park, NY: University Books, 1960.

Bathory, Elisabeth (1560–1614)

Grisly surprises awaited the raiding party as they slipped unnoticed through the massive doors of the Castle Csejthe in Hungary on New Year's Eve, 1610.

In the great hall lay the pale, lifeless form of a young woman, the **blood** completely drained from her naked body. A few steps away lay a girl sprawled grotesquely and pitiably on the floor. Her breasts had been slashed repeatedly, and she was unconscious from loss of blood. Chained to a pillar was another young woman who had been burned and savagely whipped to death.

Hurrying to the dungeons below, the raiders found several dozen girls and young women, many of whom had been bled. Others had not yet been touched and were fattened and in good health—like domesticated animals awaiting slaughter.

It was on the second floor of the castle that the raiders surprised Countess Elisabeth Bathory, her guests, and members of the household in the midst of a drunken and depraved orgy. The raiding party, which consisted of the prime minister, the governor, a priest, and several soldiers and police, later said that the details of the loathsome bacchanal were too awful to be repeated.

Later, at her trial, it was charged that the blood of at least 600 girls and young women stained the soul and bathed the blood of Elisabeth Bathory, the Countess of Blood. Although the countess has often been portrayed as the quintessential vampire, many researchers have expressed their opinion that she qualifies equally well as a werewolf slasher and Satanist, for there is little evidence that she ever drank the blood of her victims—but she did bite and slash a number of them to death. In her vile cosmology, blood was the elixir of youth and a crucial element in black magic rituals. In Elisabeth's quest to remain ever young, she had arrived at the belief that by bathing in the vital fluid of other women she would be able to preserve the famous beauty that she had debauched with countless orgies.

Elisabeth married Count Ferencz Nadasdy when she was only 15 years old, but was already famous for her pale, almost translucent flesh, raven black hair, sensual lips, and blazing eyes. She was delighted when she discovered that the count was a devotee of **witchcraft**, **sorcery,** and the worship of Satan.

The newlyweds had come into the world endowed with two of the most powerful names in Hungary. The Nadasdys were known as fierce warriors and harsh taskmasters. To their serfs, the Nadasdys were miserly with rewards and gifts and generous only with the lash and the dungeon. The Bathory bloodline combined psychosis and public service, cleverness and corruption, benevolence and brutality. Gyorgy, the conscientious prime minister of Hungary, was Elisabeth's cousin—but so was Sigismund Bathory, the savage, unstable prince of Transylvania. It is little wonder that Ferencz and Elisabeth soon devoted themselves to sophisticated sadism and princely perversions.

Perhaps Elisabeth would have remained simply a jaded aristocrat of her times, dabbling in black magic for amusement, if her well-matched mate had stayed at home. But the count became increasingly preoccupied with becoming Hungary's black hero of the battlefield, and he left the bed of his lady for months at a time.

It was during one of these periods of loneliness, boredom, and aching frustration that the beautiful countess turned to an even more intense study of witchcraft. She ordered her faithful Ilona Joo, who had been her nurse since childhood, to summon the most famous alchemists, witches, and sorcerers to Castle Csejthe. And they came—strange creatures from the depths of the forest, werewolves, **vampires,** defrocked priests, demented alchemists, and those who practiced torture for pleasure.

Although Elisabeth entered into a variety of diabolical studies with wild frenzy and abandon, the sexuality that had been aroused by the masterful Count Nadasdy grew even more frustrated, and she ran away for a time with a young nobleman who was reputed to be a vampire. Her cadaverous lover could not compare with the virile count, however, and Elisabeth returned to Castle Csejthe to throw herself at Nadasdy's feet in supplication. The count understood the passions that inflamed his beautiful wife, and he eagerly forgave Elisabeth for her unfaithfulness.

Vowing everlasting fidelity to her husband, the countess swore to give herself completely only to the study of **satanism** during her husband's absences, and shortly after her 26th birthday she presented Nadasdy with the male heir for which he had so long been striving. She gave birth to three other children in as rapid succession as nature would allow, and until the count's death, she set aside her study of the dark arts and completely occupied herself with the demands of motherhood.

It was after the death of Ferencz Nadasdy that Elisabeth began to notice with an ever-growing horror that the face famous throughout all Hungary for its beauty was beginning to display a few lines of aging. Desperately, she turned once again to witchcraft to seek a potion that would restore her youth and loveliness.

Elisabeth discovered the magic elixir quite by accident. One day a serving maid so angered her that she struck her violently and drew blood. Amazingly, her frenzied senses told her, where drops of blood from the wench had speckled her own flesh, the skin appeared to be softer, whiter, than it was before. She had stumbled upon the true formula for eternal youth: complete and regular submersion in the blood of a young maid.

For the next 11 years, the terrified peasants and villagers locked themselves in their houses after dark and listened in horror to the screams of anguish and tortured pain that drifted down to them from Castle Csejthe. From behind their curtained windows they watched with dread as the black carriage drawn by black horses descended from the castle to search for fresh victims. Not one of the girls and young women who were abducted ever managed to escape the castle alive.

The Countess of Blood kept her dungeons filled with girls who were fed like animals being fattened for the butcher. Elisabeth liked her victims to be plump, reasoning that stouter women would have healthier blood in their veins, thereby providing better properties of rejuvenation for her beauty baths.

The countess believed that the rubbing of towels on her delicate skin had a corrosive effect. Hence, she required captive girls to lick the blood off her flesh after she emerged from the tub. If any girl displayed displeasure while engaged in the gruesome chore, she would be hideously tortured to death.

Elisabeth Bathory's regular in-castle assembly of witches, vampires, werewolves, and alchemists easily convinced her of the advisability of ritual **human sacrifice** to ensure Satan's blessing of their magic spells and her rejuvenating blood baths. Dark-side witches also gained Elisabeth's permission to conduct sadistic magical experiments on the girls. The countess herself grew to crave demonstrations of torture as a daily activity. Her cruelly inventive mind devised countless devices by which to flay, burn, freeze, and bleed the captive girls.

Rumors of such tortures and emphatic reports of large-scale abductions of young women reached the ears of the authorities years before any action was taken. After all, Countess Elisabeth belonged to two wealthy and powerful

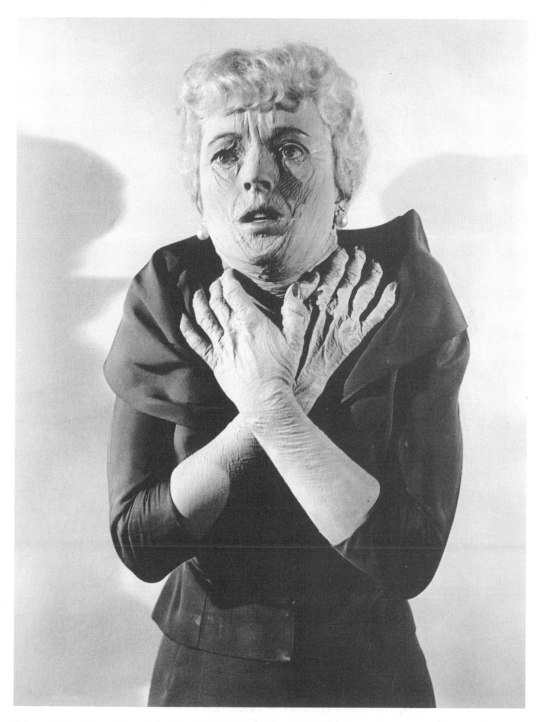

Actress Coleen Gray portrayed the title character in the film *The Leech Woman*.

families—Bathory and Nadasdy—and no one in Hungary dared to investigate the truthfulness of such terrible charges and accusations. Eventually, the prime minister, the countess's own cousin, led the raiding party of Castle Csejthe on New Year's Eve, 1610. Even the most loathsome and disgusting rumors had not prepared them for the hellish scenes they discovered.

All of the countess's assemblage of witches and sorcerers were put to torture and then either beheaded or burned alive. Elisabeth herself was walled up in her apartment in Castle Csejthe with only tiny slits for ventilation and the passing of food.

Still strikingly beautiful and youthful at 50, the Countess lived for four years without uttering a single word to her captors. Perhaps she could only listen to the ghostly echoes of the screams of pain and the pleadings for mercy of her 600 victims.

SOURCES:

Eisler, Robert. *Man into Wolf.* London: Spring Books, n.d.

Hurwood, Bernardt J. *Vampires, Werewolves, and Ghouls.* New York: Ace Books, 1968.

Steiger, Brad. *Demon Lovers: Cases of Possession, Vampires, and Werewolves.* Inner Light, NJ: 1987.

Bear People

It requires little imagination to understand why the bear became a favorite totem animal wherever they coexisted in the same environment as primitive humans and why so many clans claim direct descent from an ancestor who was originally a bear. Among all ancient people who encountered the bear and who left some kind of record of those meetings, the powerful, lumbering giant was held in the greatest respect as the one who knew all things, the one who could speak directly with the gods.

When the bear walks upright on its two hind feet, it appears very much like a stout, powerfully built man with short, bandy legs. When it moves through the forest on the hunt, it seems to saunter in a leisurely manner, confidently assured that no one will challenge its majesty.

Many tribal **shamans** address the bear reverently as "Grandfather," and there is a widespread belief that the spirit of the bear never dies. It is common for traditional Native American medicine priests to adopt "bear" as a part of their name, and shapeshifting shamans frequently take the form of a bear because of its supernatural powers.

Among the old tribes of northern Europe, the warriors known as the **Berserker** wore bearskin shirts into battle in dedication to the goddess Ursel, the she-bear. To the Vikings, the bear symbolized the lone champion, prepared to fight to the death in single combat against all odds. To wear the bearskin in battle was to become one with the bear's indomitable spirit.

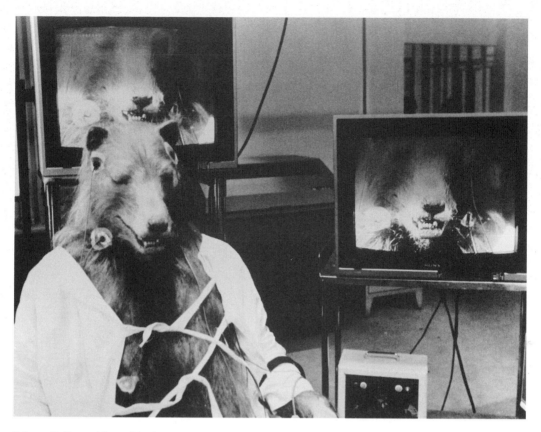

Science fiction and horror blend as a werewolf is tortured in *The Howling III.*

In the opinion of a number of scholars, the eighth-century saga of *Beowulf*, the Swedish hero who defeats the monster Grendal and its hideous underwater troll mother, is an example of the "bear's son cycle," found among the folklore of European, Asian, and Native North American people. In these sagas, the child has a bear for one or the other of his parents and acquires the strength of a bear to fight supernatural beings for the good of his people.

SOURCES:

Davidson, Ellis H. R. *Gods and Myths of the Viking Age.* New York: Barnes & Noble, 1996.

Gaskell, G. A. *Dictionary of All Scriptures and Myths.* Avenel, NJ: Gramercy Books, 1981.

Simek, Rudolf. *Dictionary of Northern Mythology.* Translated by Angela Hall. Rochester, NY: Boydell & Brewer, 1993.

Steiger, Brad. *American Indian Medicine Dream Book.* Atglen, PA: Whitford Press, 1993.

The Beast of Le Gevaudan

What or who was the Beast of Le Gevaudan has puzzled students of unexplained mysteries for more than two centuries. Le Gevaudan is a barren, 75-mile stretch of hills and valleys in the rugged mountain range that runs along the edge of the Auvergne plateau in southern France. Although Lyons and Toulouse are populous cities, the outlying area is sparsely settled.

In the 1760s, rural residents of the area were terrorized by a werewolf that allegedly killed hundreds of people during a bloody three-year reign of bestial butchery. "***Loup-garou***! Werewolf!" became a cry that terrorized the whole of Le Gevaudan. Outlying farms were abandoned as the monster preyed upon the peasants. Entire villages were deserted as the beast moved boldly into these communities in search of new victims.

The creature was described as a hairy beast that walked upright on two legs. Its face was sworn to be like that of Satan, and its entire body was said to be covered with dark, bristly hair. Those who were fortunate enough to escape the beast's clutches always mentioned an "evil smell" that emanated from its foul hide. Deep claw marks on the bodies of its victims indicated that the monster sucked **blood** from the corpses.

On the night of January 15, 1765, a blizzard raged in the mountains. When his 15-year-old son did not return from tending sheep, Pierre Chateauneuf lit a torch and went in search of the boy. The horrified father discovered the mutilated body of his son near the bawling flock.

The grieving Chateauneuf carried the body down the slopes to their small farm home in the valley. He lay the pitiful corpse on the plankwood floor of his home, covered the form with a quilt, and slumped sorrowfully into a chair. It was then, Chateauneuf later told the authorities, that he saw the beast staring at him through a window. The werewolf's eyes were glassy, like those of a wild animal, and its dark face was covered with hair.

The angry farmer dashed to a wall, pulled down a musket, and fired point-blank at the creature. The black, hairy monster had apparently anticipated the man's attack, for it dropped down before the musket was discharged. Chateauneuf testified later that as he reloaded the musket and ran outside, he saw the beast running across the snow toward his orchard. It looked like a man running in an animal's skin. The frightened, grieving farmer heard the howl of the wind, saw the giant footprints being erased in the drifting snow, and, reluctantly, returned to his home. He knew that it would have been death to follow the creature into the mountains.

Shortly after the death of the Chateauneuf youth, local farmer Jean-Pierre Pourcher told authorities that he had been out hunting rabbits when the beast rose up before him out of a nearby thicket. Pourcher said that he fired at the monster, but he was trembling too much from fear to be an accurate marksman. The Beast of Le Gevaudan, he stated to investigators, could run on all four legs or upright, in a loping, humanlike movement.

Five days later, several children were playing in a field outside the village of Chamaleilles. Little Jean Panafieux dashed into some brush for concealment during a game of hide and seek and found himself confronted by the beast. Although two giant hands clamped around his throat, Jean's feeble cries managed to alert his playmates and they ran into the village for help. Andre Portefaix, a young farmer, grabbed a pitchfork and stabbed viciously at the werewolf. Other men from the village soon joined Portefaix, and, with clubs and stones, they drove the beast back into the surrounding hills.

Dragoon captain Jacques Duhamel scoffed that such creatures, identified as werewolves, were nothing but superstition and old wives' tales, but Portefaix carried a petition from the villagers directly to Louis IX at Versailles, and the king ordered a detachment of dragoons to search the mountains of Le Gevaudan. After the soldiers had left the region, the murderous rampage of the beast increased with savage fury. The years of 1765, 1766, and 1767 are spoken of as the "time of the death" in the mountains. Parish records reveal daily attacks by the monster, who seemed to choose housewives and children as its principal victims.

The Marquis d'Apcher organized a posse of several hundred armed men, and after tracking the beast for many days they succeeded in surrounding the creature in a grove of trees near the village of Le Serge d'Auvert. As dusk deepened into darkness, the monster charged its pursuers and was shot down. Jean Chastel was given credit for the kill.

According to Chastel's testimony, he had retired a short distance from his companions to read his prayer book. He happened to glance up from his devotions and saw the beast coming directly toward him, walking erect. Chastel said that he had prepared himself according to certain ancient traditions. His double-barreled musket was loaded with bullets made from a silver chalice that had been blessed by a priest.

The bullet from the first barrel of Chastel's musket struck the monster in the chest. It let out a fierce howl and charged its attacker. Chastel aimed the next shot directly for the monster's heart. The werewolf dropped dead at his feet, the silver bullet in its heart.

Since that dramatic final encounter with the Beast of Le Gevaudan there has been constant debate concerning the type of creature slain by the Marquis's posse. Some researchers have argued that the beast was some type of rare leopard, others a wild boar with deadly tusks and tough, dark bristles. Chastel himself described his trophy as possessing peculiar feet, pointed ears, and a body completed covered with coarse, dark hair. The general consensus among the members of the hunting party claimed that the beast was a true werewolf, half-human and half-wolf.

It is known for certain that the carcass of a large wolf was paraded through the streets of several villages in the area as proof that the terrible beast had truly been killed.

Abbe Pourcher of St. Martin de Bourchauz parish in the mountains recorded statements from those people who had encountered the beast and survived its attack. He also interviewed members of the posse that had slain the creature. In his final report, he wrote that he remained mystified by the true identity of the Beast of Le Gevaudan. He also noted that certain rumors started that a large wolf carcass had been paraded through the village streets because the actual beast had been too terrible to display.

Tourists may still see Abbe Pourcher's records and view the double-barreled musket that finally downed the awful Beast of Le Gevaudan. And cemetery and municipal records attest to the hundreds of people who were killed by the murderous monster—whether werewolf, wolf, or other being.

SOURCES:
Hurwood, Bernhardt J. *Terror by Night*. New York: Lancer Books, 1963.
Norman, Eric. *The Abominable Snowmen*. New York: Award Books, 1969.
Steiger, Brad. *Monsters Among Us*. New York: Berkley Books, 1989.

"Beauty and the Beast"

The most famous survival of the ancient beast marriage tales is "Beauty and the Beast." Stories of a human married to an animal are popular in folklore throughout the world, and in many cultures it is the union between animal and human that produces the tribe or the clan that perpetuates the legend.

The version most familiar to contemporary audiences is that recorded by Mme. Leprince de Beaumont in her *Magasin des Enfans* (1756). Beauty is the youngest of three daughters of a merchant who is traveling away from home in a desperate effort to reestablish his failing business. While on his journey, he is caught in a terrible storm and seeks refuge in a castle. During his stay, he is provided with all the blessings of hospitality, but he sees no one.

The next morning as he is leaving, he admires his unseen host's magnificent garden, and his thoughts turn to Beauty. Before he left home, the two oldest daughters begged for elegant gowns and expensive gifts, but all Beauty wished from her father was a rose. Surely, he imagines, no one could object to his taking just one rose from the garden.

The enraged Beast suddenly appears, prepared to slay the merchant for such a breach of etiquette. When he hears the frightened man's explanation, he agrees to let him go on the condition that one of his daughters return to his castle. If this demand is not met, Beast will hunt him down and kill him.

Jean Marais as "The Beast" in director Jean Cocteau's famous version of *Beauty and the Beast.*

Beauty volunteers, and her purity of heart allows her to overlook Beast's monstrous appearance. She is treated with the greatest of courtesy and respect by the Beast, and she stays with him until she looks in Beast's magic mirror and sees that her father is very ill. She is granted her wish of returning to visit her father for only one week. The weeks go by, and Beauty stays with her father until she has a vision in which she sees that Beast is dying. Beauty rushes back to the castle and promises to become Beast's wife. Her love dissolves a curse that had transformed a handsome young man into an ugly monster.

Many scholars have stated that in the original version of the tale, the beast was a werewolf. While there is no folklore that suggests a werewolf can be redeemed by the love of a virtuous maiden, the tale could represent love and compassion as antidotes for the bestial impulses within all humans. Variations of "Beauty and the Beast" abound throughout the world. In certain regions of the Middle East, Beast is a boar, complete with large, curved tusks. Among some African tribes, he is a crocodile.

"Beauty and the Beast" has become such an integral archetypal element within the psyche that it has been filmed at least seven times, most notably by the Walt Disney Studios in their award-winning animated version. A contemporary updating of the story, transforming the Beast's castle to a subterranean world beneath New York City, became a successful television series (*Beauty and the Beast*, 1987–1990), starring Linda Hamilton and Ron Perlman.

SOURCES:

Gaskell, G. A. *Dictionary of All Scriptures and Myths.* Avenel, NJ: Gramercy Books, 1981.

Hazlitt, W. C. *Dictionary of Faiths & Folklore.* London: Studio Editions, 1995.

Larousse Dictionary of World Folklore. New York: Larousse, 1995.

Beaver People

The Osage tribe has a legend that until Wabashas, the first human, was created, the Great Spirit had appointed the beaver to be chief over the birds, beasts, and fish of the forest. Chief Beaver considered disputing the Great Spirit's decision that he should leave the coveted position of the leadership of all the animals until he saw the sharp points on the heads of the arrows in Wabashas's quiver—then he decided humans and beavers should be brothers. In fact, Chief Beaver would offer Wabashas the hand of his lovely daughter in marriage to cement their friendship.

In the eyes of the Osage, and perhaps all the tribes of the northeast, the beavers in their streams were called the little wise people. The industrious creatures built their communities of lodges and kept to themselves and provided great healing powers whenever the tribes had need of their medicine.

For the **shamans** of many tribes, the beaver serves as a familiar spirit being that accompanies them on journeys out of the body. To shapeshift and become one of the beaver people during one's apprenticeship period is to enable the medicine practitioners to learn well the ways of healing and spirit wisdom.

SOURCES:

Emerson, Ellen Russell. *Indian Myths*. Minneapolis, MN: Ross & Haines, 1965.

Gaskell, G. A. *Dictionary of All Scriptures and Myths.* Avenel, NJ: Gramercy Books, 1981.

Hazlitt, W. C. *Dictionary of Faiths & Folklore*. London: Studio Editions, 1995.

Berserkers

Since earliest times, more levelheaded persons have observed that when a man becomes absolutely filled with rage, he is no longer quite human. One may say that he has given the control of his reason back to the beast within— or one might even say that the enraged man is "beside himself," that he has become something more than himself. Either the beast within or some other supernatural power has now endowed the angered, raging man with more strength and more deadly determination to work harm against his enemy than he had before he became so angry, so *berserk*.

Among the old tribes of northern Europe, the warriors known as the berserkers (in Old Norse, *Berserkir*) were so filled with the savage joy of battle that they tossed aside their armor and wore only bearskin shirts into battle in dedication to the goddess Ursel, the she-bear. To the Germanic tribes, the bear was a masterful martial artist, and the angered she-bear protecting her cubs was the most formidable challenge a warrior could ever face. The bearskin shirts were worn with the hope that its wearers could absorb the great beast's fighting prowess and its enormous endurance and strength.

Those Viking Berserkers who considered the wolf to be their totem donned wolf coats and charged into battle howling like **wolves,** giving warning to the enemy that they were a cross between man and beast and that they would soon change their shapes and become even more vicious in their attack.

The oldest reference to the Berserkers is in a poem composed to honor the Norwegian king Harald Fairhair after his victory at Hafrsfjord in about 872. In the thirteenth century, the skald Snorri gives a detailed account of Berserkers in action at the beginning of his *Ynglinga Saga* 6: "Odin's men went [into battle] without armor and were as wild as dogs or wolves. They bit their shields and were stronger than bears or bulls. They killed many men but they themselves were unharmed either by fire or by iron; this is what is called *berserksgangr* [berserk-fury]."

Snorri indicates the connection between Odin, the Berserkers, and the *ulfheonar* (wolfskins), stating that they are "his warriors." It should be noted that in addition to being the father of the gods and the god of war, Odin/Wodan is also the god of cult ecstasy. His very name confirms this, Rudolf Simek points out, since in Old Norse it means "fury." And, Simek continues, "The Berserk fury bears all the traits of ecstatic states of consciousness: insensitivity to fire and pain (as well as not bleeding) are phenomena known from shamanic trances." Therefore, in his opinion, the concept of Berserks and the wolfskins originate "in special forms of old masked cults in Scandinavia, which manifest themselves in the existence of masked bands of warriors dedicated to Odin."

SOURCES:

Davidson, Ellis H. R. *Gods and Myths of the Viking Age.* New York: Barnes & Noble, 1996.

Simek, Rudolf. *Dictionary of Northern Mythology.* Translated by Angela Hall. Rochester, NY: Boydell & Brewer, 1993.

Sgt. Bertrand, Francois (1824–1849)

Although Guy Endore is said to have based the central character in his classic novel **The Werewolf of Paris** (1933) on the actual person of Sgt. Francois Bertrand, it is clear that from the very beginning the man was a ghoul, rather than a werewolf. When Bertrand was arrested for the heinous crimes that shocked Paris in 1847, his fellow soldiers were stunned. It seemed incomprehensible to them that their 25-year-old comrade could be the monster that had profaned the sanctity of Parisian graveyards.

In the eyes of his friends, Bertrand was intelligent, lucid, handsome, and sensitive. If anything, he was rather delicate and unusually quiet for a professional soldier. Nevertheless, it was established beyond all doubt that Francois was the tormented ghoul that had unearthed cadavers from their coffins to give vent to his perverse craving for human flesh.

Bertrand himself was of little help in analyzing the gruesome nature of his crimes. He could only say that he had been driven by forces beyond his control. He was powerless to disobey the awful compulsion that bid him to dig up the newly dead and tear at their flesh with his sword, his bare hands, and his teeth. According to the young soldier, when the madness seized him, he was beset by a rapid beating of his heart, a terrible trembling of his body, and a violent headache. As soon as he could slip out of the military barracks, he would make his way to a cemetery where he would dig at the unsettled soil of a fresh grave. Once he had exhumed the corpse, he would strike at it with his sword until he had slashed the body to shreds. This terrible deed of desecration and mutilation accomplished, he would experience a release that would immediately free him of his throbbing headache and other physical symptoms.

On one occasion, while walking with a comrade, Bertrand sighted a freshly dug grave in a cemetery and immediately began to suffer the agony of

Paul Clemens portrays a humanoid creature in the film *The Beast Within*.

his private torment. Nervously he tried to make carefree conversation with his companion, but his thoughts kept returning to the newly dug plot in the little cemetery. He knew that he must return to it that night.

Even though it was on a bitterly cold evening in the dead of winter, Bertrand's morbid compulsion would not allow him to rest. In order to leave the military camp without been seen, he had to swim a wide ditch in which huge chunks of ice bobbed. In order to enter the cemetery, he was forced to scale a high wall. But to Bertrand, in the trancelike obsession of his private curse, the bitter cold and the physical obstacles did not affect him.

When the parents of the recently buried teenaged girl came to bring a wreath to her grave the next morning, they were shocked to discover the unspeakable violation that had been wrought upon their daughter's corpse.

Sgt. Bertrand satisfied his grisly perversion on dozens of Parisian graves before an outraged populace demanded doubled efforts on the part of the police to apprehend the ghoul and to put a stop to the desecration of their loved ones' final resting places.

When he was finally captured after a night of indulging his ghoulish passions, Bertrand told his captors that he was completely unable to explain his actions. As difficult as it might have been for his jailers to hear, he proclaimed that he had always been a very religious person, offended by indecent talk and actions. The Ghoul of Paris spent his final days in a madman's cell where he, in turn, could no longer offend the sanctity of the grave by his indecent and perverse actions.

SOURCES:

Hurwood, Bernardt J. *Vampires, Werewolves, and Ghouls.* New York: Ace Books, 1968.
Masters, R. E. L., and Eduard Lea. *Perverse Crimes in History.* New York: The Julian Press, 1963.
Steiger, Brad. *Demon Lovers: Cases of Possession, Vampires, and Werewolves.* Inner Light, NJ: 1987.

BIGFOOT *see:* ABOMINABLE SNOWMAN AND YETI

Bisclaveret

French romances frequently include werewolves among their cast of characters. One of the earliest (c. 1165) and most remarkable examples is the Lay (from the French *Lais*, a story of about 1,000 lines, usually meant to be sung) by Marie de France entitled *Bisclaveret*, the Lay of a Werewolf.

In Brittany, *bisclaveret* is the name given to the werewolf, which, in that region, is a human who has been transformed by magic into a vicious beast.

SOURCES:

Spence, Lewis. *An Encyclopedia of Occultism.* New Hyde Park, NY: University Books, 1960.

Still photo from a 1977 film shot by Ivan Marx that supposedly shows Bigfoot on the loose in Northern Califorina.

Black Dog

While the Somerset region in England has a tradition of a large, benevolent black dog that accompanies lone travelers as a kind of protector and guide, the vast majority of black dog folklore depicts the dark canine as an ominous creature that forebodes death to those who behold it.

Great Britain, especially, seems to have more than its share of demonic hounds. The very glance from the devilish eyes of the black hound of Okehampton Castle on Dartmoor means death within the year. The Black Dow Woods in Wiltshire are haunted by a black dog whose appearance signals a death before Christmas. Knaith, Lincolnshire, is the site where many frightened travelers have seen a large black dog with a woman's face.

For over 400 years, Newgate Prison has been haunted by the black dog, which appears shortly before executions. According to legend, in 1596, a man named Scholler was brought into prison to face accusations of witchcraft. Before the man could even come to trial, starving prisoners had killed and eaten him. Not long thereafter, the black dog appeared, its huge canine jaws eager for revenge. Whether the phantom hound was the spirit of Scholler returned in another form or whether the beast was his familiar come to avenge its master, the cannibalistic prisoners were so terrified of the apparition that they murdered their jailers and escaped. According to the legend, however, the black dog hunted down each one of the men who had dined on Scholler. Then, its mission of revenge completed, it returned to Newgate to haunt the prison walls.

In August 1977, before serial killer David Berkowitz was sentenced to 365 years in prison, he stated that he had been ordered to kill his victims by **demons** speaking through his neighbor's black Labrador retriever.

SOURCES:

Gaskell, G. A. *Dictionary of All Scriptures and Myths.* Avenel, NJ: Gramercy Books, 1981.

Wright, Bruce Lanier. "Hell Hounds and Ghost Dogs." *Strange,* spring 1998.

Blood

The emotional impact that blood has retained upon even our sophisticated, space-age generation is demonstrated in the number of people who faint at the very sight of it. Surely it did not take long for the most primitive ancestors of our species to learn that when the sticky red fluid was draining from the body as a result of a tiger's claw or a sharp rock, the victim's life oozed out along with the blood. For early humans, blood was life itself, and it is not at all surprising to discover the vast number of magical and religious rituals that center around the vital fluid. And since blood contains the very essence of an individual person or animal, it becomes apparent why it was often deemed extremely expedient to drink the blood of a lion, a bear, a wolf, or a great vanquished warrior foe if one wished to absorb the inherent elements of strength and courage possessed by the fallen beast or enemy champion. At the same time, when early hunters crouched around their fires at night, they knew with awful foreboding that there were fierce animals, **demons,** and monsters prowling the darkness, hungering for human blood.

In the Bible, Leviticus 17:14 says of blood that "it is the life of all flesh, the blood of it is the life thereof; therefore I said unto the children of Israel, Ye shall not eat of the blood of no manner of flesh; for the life of all flesh is the blood thereof: whosoever eateth it shall be cut off."

The blood of lambs was sprinkled on the doorposts of the children of Israel at the first Passover to prevent the Angel of Death from entering their homes during the terrible plagues that ravaged Egypt. The cup of wine shared by celebrants of the Lord's Supper represents the blood shed by Jesus on the cross as he offered himself as sacrificial lamb to take away the sins of the world.

With such powerful religious representations of blood and such awesome scriptural admonitions against the ingesting of blood, what monsters could be more hideous than the werewolf or the **vampire** that lust after human blood?

Some theorists believe that since fossil evidence indicates that ancient members of the human evolutionary family favored forested areas where they subsisted on leaves and fruits, our species's latent genetic memory abhors the shedding of blood and the eating of flesh and feels a certain unconscious guilt whenever we eat meat. On some deep level of consciousness, the knowledge that humans are not basically carnivorous arouses an unconscious sense of immorality and sin whenever we partake of nourishment that we know involved the shedding of blood. And the ancestral memory of those primitive, savage, nocturnal lupine hunters who clothed themselves in wolfskins and slaughtered animals for food for their human pack fills us with dread when night falls. The wild hunt of the werewolves becomes an inherited fear that strikes even the most sophisticated of civilized men and women when the moon is full.

When the traditional Native American must take the life of an animal in order to survive, the practitioner of the medicine ways kills only after uttering a prayer, as if he or she were performing a sacrament. The entity (the soul of the animal) and its group spirit must be told that such an act is necessary in the turning of the great Wheel of Life. It may well be that the traditional asking of a blessing before meals is our unconscious method of duplicating the ancient propitiatory prayer after the shedding of blood.

SOURCES:
Eisler, Robert. *Man into Wolf*. London: Spring Books, n.d.

Bodin, Jean (1530–1596)

Before Jean Bodin died of the plague in 1596, he had been hailed as the Aristotle of the sixteenth century. His *Republique*, published when he was but a youth, was praised as containing the very spirit of the law. A celebrated jurisconsult, a leading member of the Parliament of Paris, and a highly respected intellectual, Bodin was known throughout Europe as a formidable scholar of history, political theory, and the philosophy of law. By writing *Demonomanie des Sorciers*, however, Bodin became one of the men most responsible for keeping the fires of the Inquisition burning brightly.

The *Demonomanie* was first published in Paris in 1581 and again under the title of *Fleau des demons et des sorciers* in 1616. In the first and second books of this monumental work, Bodin offers his proofs that spirits communicate with humankind, and he itemizes the characteristics by which one might distinguish good spirits from their evil counterparts. Those who seek to enter pacts with Satan in order to achieve diabolical prophecy, the ability to fly through the air, and the power to shapeshift are dealing with evil spirits. Bodin acknowledges that he is well aware of spells by which one might change into a werewolf or to summon incubi or succubi for carnal ecstasies.

The third book details methods by which the work of sorcerers and shapeshifters might be prevented and destroyed, and the fourth book lists ways by which witches, werewolves, and other servants of Satan may be identified. The massive work concludes with a refutation of the arguments of **Johann Weyer** who, Bodin concludes, is in grave danger of committing heresy by stating that witches and shapeshifters are merely people with unsound minds.

SOURCES:

Masters, R. E. L. *Eros and Evil*. New York: The Julian Press, 1962.
Russell, Jeffrey Burton. *Witchcraft in the Middle Ages*. Ithaca, NY: Cornell University Press, 1972.
Spence, Lewis. *An Encyclopedia of Occultism*. New Hyde Park, NY: University Books, 1960.
Trevor-Roper, H. R. *The European Witch-Craze*. New York: Harper & Row, 1967.

Bogey

For countless generations children in the English-speaking world have been threatened into obedience by the Bogeyman who inhabits the darkness and can quickly materialize to snatch away naughty boys and girls if they aren't careful. Perhaps parents would be a bit more cautious in their summoning of such an entity if they knew that the Bogey is traditionally a shapeshifting demon that may have begun its nefarious career by haunting bogs, but since delights in carrying off the souls of unsuspecting, especially errant children.

DE ANIMAL. SYLVES.

De ferocia Hominum in Lupos conuerforum.

CAP. XLV.

An engraving from the "Historia Gentibus Septentrionalibus" by Olaus Magnus showing flying demons and shapeshifting creatures.

Interestingly, the Bogey is also a common figure in Native American mythology, and during some dances special masks are worn to turn the tables on the spirit and to frighten him away from the children of the village.

SOURCES:

Gill, Sam D., and Irene F. Sullivan. *Dictionary of Native American Mythology.* New York: Oxford University Press, 1992.

Larousse Dictionary of World Folklore. New York: Larousse, 1995.

Boguet, Henri (1550–1619)

In 1584, a werewolf was seen attacking a small girl in a village located in the Jura Mountains of France. When the child's 16-year-old brother came to her rescue, the werewolf turned on the boy and killed him. Enraged villagers, hearing the cries and sounds of struggle, cornered the werewolf and clubbed it to death. Amazed, they beheld the grotesque beast in its death throes turn into the nude body of a young woman they recognized as Perrenette Gandillon.

A giant vulture, which is similar to the bird-creature known as the *bruxsa*, attacks a woman in the film *The Vulture*.

In his *Discours des Sorciers* (1610), Henri Boguet, eminent judge of Saint-Claude in the Jura Mountains, writes that an official investigation of the matter led to the arrest of the entire Gandillon family, and he states that he personally examined and observed them while they were in prison. According to his testimony, the Gandillons walked on all fours and howled like beasts. Their eyes turned red and gleaming; their hair sprouted; their teeth became long and sharp; their fingernails turned horny and clawlike.

As a judge, Boguet was known for his cruelty, especially toward children. He had no doubt that Satan gifted witches with the ability to change shape into a variety of animal forms, especially the wolf, so that they might devour humans, and the cat, so they might better prowl by night. In another case recounted in *Discours des Sorciers*, he tells of eight-year-old Louise Maillat, who in the summer of 1598 was possessed by five **demons**: wolf, cat, dog, jolly, and griffon. In addition the little girl was accused of shapeshifting into the form of a wolf.

SOURCES:

Masters, R. E. L. *Eros and Evil.* New York: The Julian Press, 1962.
Russell, Jeffrey Burton. *Witchcraft in the Middle Ages.* Ithaca, NY: Cornell University Press, 1972.
Spence, Lewis. *An Encyclopedia of Occultism.* New Hyde Park, NY: University Books, 1960.
Trevor-Roper, H. R. *The European Witch-Craze.* New York: Harper & Row, 1967.

Boxenwolf

In the Schaumburg region of Germany, werewolves are called *boxenwolves* because it is believed that they have made a pact with Satan that allows them to achieve transformation into **wolves** by the act of buckling a diabolical strap about their waists.

Boxenwolves are noted for their cunning and the great delight they receive from tormenting people. If one suspects an individual of being in league with Satan and a secret boxenwolf, his or her true identity can be revealed by holding a piece of steel over the person.

SOURCES:

Lyncker, Karl. *Deutsche Sagen und Sitten in Hessischen Gauen.* Translated by D. L. Ashliman. Cassel: Verlag von Oswald Bertram, 1854.

Bruxsa

The *bruxsa* is a Portuguese shapeshifter that combines elements of both the werewolf and the **vampire.** Usually a woman who has magically invoked a demon, the bruxsa leaves her home at night and transforms herself into a hideous, gigantic bird-creature.

After an evening of cavorting with others of her diabolical kind and terrifying lonely travelers on dark roads, the bruxsa returns home to suck the **blood** of her own children.

SOURCES:

Larousse Dictionary of World Folklore. New York: Larousse, 1995.

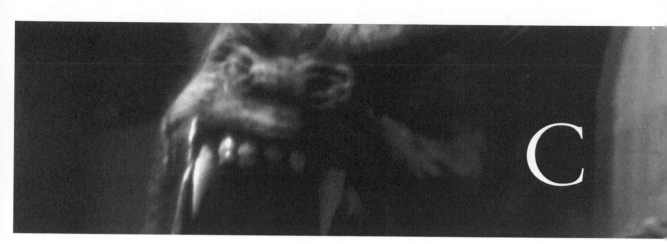

C

Cambrensis, Giraldus (c. 1146–1220)

Until the end of the eighteenth century, Ireland was known in England as "the Wolfland," a country that abounded with accounts of werewolves. As early as the twelfth century, Giraldus Cambrensis (*Topographia Hibernica*) spoke of a priest who was met by a wolf in Meath who beseeched the cleric to accompany him to be with his dying wife.

The wolf explained that they had been natives of Ossory, whose people had been cursed for their wickedness by St. Natalis to change their shapes into that of **wolves** for a period of seven years. The priest was at last persuaded to give the she-wolf the sacrament when she was able to turn her skin down a little and reveal that she was an old woman.

SOURCES:
Eisler, Robert. *Man into Wolf.* London: Spring Books, n.d.

Cannibalism

There are a number of serious scholars who believe that human beings descended from carnivorous lycanthropes. Although humankind may have begun as peaceful tribes of fruit-collecting, seed-and-root planting agriculturalists, climatic changes at the end of the Pluvial period forced human ancestors to become meat-eaters—and sometimes meat could only be found in the flesh of other humans. While the childbearing women and children huddled in cave or hut, human wolf packs attired in wolfskins hunted down whatever meat fell into their hands—animals or slain members of other tribes. Thus, according to these scholars, human beings bear within the genes of the werewolf, the man-beast who will eat even his fellows in order to be among the fittest to survive.

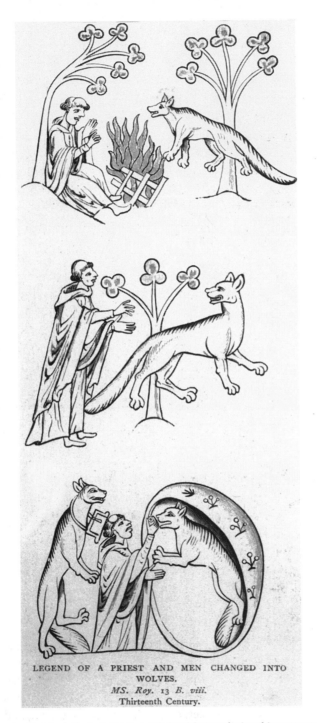

LEGEND OF A PRIEST AND MEN CHANGED INTO
WOLVES.
MS. Roy. 13 *B. viii.*
Thirteenth Century.

A thirteenth-century drawing depicting a legendary tale involving a priest and two werewolves.

At the same time, some scholars argue, there exists an atavistic sense of guilt within the collective human psyche that our species so freely partakes of the flesh of other beings to increase the bulk of our own flesh. Thus while the eating of all flesh is at best a necessary evil, to taste human flesh would be the most abhorrent of taboos.

Of course the strict vegetarian may consider the consumption of any creature's flesh to be as bad as cannibalism, but for some unbalanced minds the ancient taboo of dining on the meat of one's own kind may also represent the greatest single act of rebellion against all rules and laws of established decency, proper social behavior, and ecclesiastical doctrines. And, in a sense that is extremely sickening to the sensitive mind and the weak of stomach, there may also be a great empowerment in eating the flesh of one's enemies. How better to gain the strength of a mighty foe than to eat his flesh and absorb his prowess? And how better for a werewolf to achieve the strength of a dozen men than to eat a dozen men? And as frightening as it may seem to the sensibilities of twentieth-century idealists, evidence supports the existence of cannibals among us:

In July 1970, tall, bearded Stanley Dean Baker contacted Monterey County, California, detective Dempsey Biley and the resident FBI agent at the substation and convinced the astonished officers that he had a rather unique problem. "I am a cannibal," Baker confessed.

Baker explained that he had killed and dismembered a young social worker, James Schlosser, who had made the fatal mistake of giving him a ride outside of Yellowstone Park. He admitted murdering Schlosser while he slept, then cutting out his heart and eating it.

Investigating officers discovered a blood-stained survival knife near a river bank and noticed a patch of ground saturated with **blood.** To their disgust, the officers found what appeared to be human bone fragments, pieces of flesh, teeth, and what appeared to be the remains of a human ear. Informants came forward to relate ghastly accounts of Baker's demonic activities around his home base of Sheridan, Wyoming. A teenage boy told of devil worshipping rites that had occurred in the Big Horn Mountains. He testified that small wild animals had been eaten alive and human blood had been drunk.

In 1993, Omaima Nelson testified before a court in Orange County, California, that after she and her husband Bill quarreled, she struck him in the head 24 times with an iron, then stabbed him with a knife. Next, the 24-year-old woman hacked his body into pieces with a meat cleaver, cut all the flesh from his bones, and ground the leftovers in the garbage disposal. Twelve hours later, she fried her husband's hands and feet, baked his head in the oven, and stored it in the refrigerator.

When these tasks were completed, she told court-appointed psychiatrist David Sheffner that she barbecued her husband's ribs. She sat at the table and commented that the ribs were sweet and delicious—and nice and tender.

In January 1998, South African police in Johannesburg found the mutilated remains of three children with their heads and feet hacked off and feared that 12 other missing children had met a similar fate. Certain of South Africa's tribal **shamans** seek human flesh to add special potency to their mystical potions. The flesh of children is thought to be the most powerful.

SOURCES:
Eisler, Robert. *Man into Wolf.* London: Spring Books, n.d.
Steiger, Brad. *Bizarre Crime.* New York: Signet, 1992.

Capture of the Chicago Rippers

The trademark of the notorious Chicago Rippers was the kidnapping and gang rape of a female victim, followed by stabbing her to death and mutilating her by removing her left breast. The years of 1981 and 1982 were filled with ghastly accounts of at least six victims who fell prey to the depraved slashers.

In September 1982, an 18-year-old prostitute miraculously survived the brutal attack of the Chicago Rippers and was left for dead beside the North Western railroad tracks. From her bed in an emergency room, she told police of being picked up by a client in a red van.

A few nights later, a police patrol stopped a van answering the description given by the young woman and the driver, 21-year-old Edward Spreitzer, and his 19-year-old passenger, Andrew Kokoraleis, were taken in for questioning—and the lives of countless future victims were saved.

Spreitzer told police that the van belonged to his employer, Robin Gecht. A quick check of the files turned up numerous convictions for sexual assault and violence on Gecht's rap sheet. Later, he was identified by the teenage prostitute as the man who had first attacked her.

Under steady questioning, Spreitzer and Kokoraleis admitted their participation in the gory series of mutilation murders and also implicated Andrew's younger brother Thomas Kokoraleis. Later, all except Gecht confessed to the disgusting two-year reign of terror and ripper deaths that they had visited upon Chicago. To add to the revulsion of their atrocities, they also admitted that the severed breasts from their victims had been used in ritual cannibalism.

Spreitzer was indicted on six murder charges and sentenced to die by lethal injection. Andrew Kokoraleis was sentenced to death for the murder of Lorraine Borowski, with a 30-year term for imprisonment for her kidnapping, and life for the murder of Rose Davis, with 60- and 30-year terms for rape and kidnapping. Thomas Kokoraleis won a reversal from the court of appeals on a technicality regarding his conviction for the Borowski murder. Plea-bargaining reduced his sentence after his second trial to 70 years' imprisonment. Robin Gecht's insistence that he had not participated in the murders and the lack of evidence to the contrary managed to win him 120 years in prison for attempted murder and rape.

SOURCES:

Lane, Brian, and Wilfred Gregg. *The Encyclopedia of Serial Killers.* New York: Berkley Publishing, 1994.

Steiger, Brad, and Sherry Hansen Steiger. *Demon Deaths.* New York: Berkley Publishing, 1991.

Cat People

There is perhaps no other animal on earth that inspires such lengths of devotion and dedication—and such animosity and abhorrence—as the cat. In European tradition, the black cat is the favorite familiar of the witch; and during the course of the Inquisition, almost as many cats as witches were condemned to be burned at the stake.

An old black-letter book titled *Beware the Cat!* (1540) warns that black cats may be shapeshifting witches. A person might kill a black cat, believing that one has also killed the witch, but the act does not necessarily guarantee the elimination of the servant of the devil—for a witch has the power to assume the body of a cat nine times.

During the terrible witchcraft trials of the Inquisition, men and women under torture confessed to kissing cats' buttocks and toads' mouths and cavorting with them in blasphemous ceremonies. Some women confessed that Satan first appeared to them in the form of a cat, for it was commonly held that cats were allied with the Prince of Darkness in the great rebellion against God.

A Navajo named Manuel once told the story of his grandfather Esteban's experience with two witches who could transform their bodies into cats. It happened in 1909, when Esteban was a 15-year-old shepherd, herding his father's flock of sheep not far from the Arizona–New Mexico border. One day he stopped at a small hut a few miles from his family's hogan in which two sisters, Isabel and Carmelita, lived alone.

The sisters were very courteous to him, and they gave him some cool water and some fry bread. Isabel seemed to be about his own age, and Carmelita appeared only a few years older. Since they were very pretty girls and there was little to do in the evenings in the small village, Esteban began to slip out at night to visit them. The sisters were exciting company, and they

Barbara Shelley played the title character in the movie *The Cat Girl.*

sang songs that he had never heard anywhere else. As Carmelita played the guitar, the two sisters sang of people with great powers, of witches and **serpent people** and shapeshifters.

Although Esteban cherished the secret nocturnal hours he spent with the beautiful sisters, he always left their hut before midnight so he could silently return to his parents' home and be there asleep in his bedroll for his father's morning call to work. Such diligence became increasingly difficult when the girls began to tempt him with promises of what fun he could have if he stayed with them until after midnight.

One day, as he daydreamed about the enchanting sisters, Esteban allowed a number of sheep to stray from the herd. By the time he was able to round them up and return them to his furious father, it was late at night. Still, his desires forced him to set out for the hut of Isabel and Carmelita in spite of the lateness of the hour.

Carl Esmond, who starred in *The Catman of Paris,* terrorizes Marie Audet after transforming into his feline state.

As he knocked on their door, his common sense told him that he was doing a foolish, perhaps even discourteous thing. Isabel and Carmelita might be sleeping. On the other hand, the girls had so often suggested that they stayed up most of the night, playing the guitar and singing.

After knocking unsuccessfully on their door, Esteban cautiously opened the latch and stepped inside. He was disappointed to discover that the girls were not at home—and he was startled to find their hut empty except for a half-dozen very large cats that began to yowl fiercely at him the moment he entered the hogan. He knew that Isabel and Carmelita kept no cats. These creatures had to be homeless strays that had invaded their kitchen in search of food. In frustration and disgust, he kicked the cat nearest him and left the hogan.

He had not walked far when he felt a sharp pain in his ankle. The cat that he had kicked had bitten him. And he was startled to see that all six of the stray animals were attacking him.

Esteban received several bites and scratches, but he gave much worse than he received. He dealt several of the cats powerful kicks in their ribs, and he picked up one of their number and dashed its brains out against a large rock.

The next evening when he called upon Isabel and Carmelita to inquire where they had been the night before, an angry old woman met him at the door and told him that he was no longer welcome there. Although she wore a shawl, Esteban could see that her head was bandaged. Directly behind her were the shadowy figures of four old hags who glared at him with hatred such as he had never before perceived.

When he protested that he wished to speak with Carmelita or Isabel, he was told that Carmelita did not want to see him ever again and that Isabel had been killed the night before when she fell and struck her head on a rock.

Esteban's senses began to whirl. His ankle began to throb anew with pain as he recalled the large cat that had sunk its fangs into his flesh before he dashed its brains out against a rock. Frightened out of his wits when he realized that the vicious cats from the evening before were the same witches he now saw before him, Esteban ran all the way home and confessed everything to his father, who immediately ordered a sing, ritual of purification to cleanse him and to drive away any evil that might have lingered near him in spirit form. Esteban lived forever with the memory of the wrinkled old crones who had used their **sorcery** to create the illusion that they were beautiful young women instead of shapeshifting witches.

Ceasg

A type of mermaid that haunts the Scottish highlands, the *ceasg's* upper body and facial features are those of a beautiful and well-endowed woman—but her lower half is that of a very large salmon.

The *ceasg*, like her distant relative the selkie, may become kindly disposed to a handsome young man who captures her attention—or her heart—and she may also grant him three wishes. In the tradition of the beast marriage, the *ceasg* may assume complete human shape and marry her lover. Her children will be born with a passion for the sea and soon give evidence of preternatural knowledge of navigational skills.

Like most supernatural beings, the *ceasg* can also express a threatening nature if she is wronged. If she feels that humans have treated her disrespectfully, she may choose to use her beauty to lure sailors into treacherous waters and their certain deaths.

SOURCES:
Larousse Dictionary of World Folklore. New York: Larousse, 1995.

Chaney, Lon Jr. (1906–1973)

For millions of people around the world, the first image of a werewolf that comes to mind whenever they hear or read the word is that of Lon Chaney Jr. in *The Wolf Man* (1941). Although some critics have suggested the Jack Pierce makeup made Chaney look more like a wild boar than a wolf, those theatergoers who were children when they first slunk down in their seats during the vivid stop-action photography that made the big, rugged actor appear to change from congenial fellow to fearsome werewolf will never forget the experience.

Chaney was born in Oklahoma City on February 10, 1906, as Creighton Chaney, the son of the famous silent screen actor Lon Chaney who was known as the "Man of a Thousand Faces." Chaney Jr. made his screen debut in a western serial in 1932, and then in 1935 changed his name to Lon Chaney Jr., perhaps with the hopes that his father's prestige as a legendary film star would add some good fortune to a show business career that seemed stalled at first base. Chaney played thugs and assorted villains in such films as *Scarlet River* (1933), *Captain Hurricane* (1935), *Slave Ship* (1937), *Mr. Moto's Gamble* (1938), and *Union Pacific* (1939) until he received his career breakthrough as the slow-witted, hulking Lennie in *Of Mice and Men* (1939).

The next year Chaney played a crippled, scarred prehistoric warrior fighting dinosaurs in *One Million B.C.*, and **Universal Pictures** bosses, who were always on the lookout for another Boris Karloff or another Lon Chaney Sr., first took notice of the 34-year-old actor as potential monster material. His horror film debut as the electrically supercharged murderer in *Man-Made Monster* (1941) did not achieve great box office success, but later that same year Chaney became the definitive motion picture werewolf in **The Wolf Man,** a position that would remain virtually unchallenged until British actor **Oliver Reed** undertook the process of cinematic transmutation in *The Curse of the Werewolf* (1961).

Although Chaney's unbitten **Lawrence Talbot** was a charming, upbeat, intelligent character, once Talbot had been attacked and bitten by a werewolf, the actor brought about the same kind of audience sympathy for a big man beset by forces beyond his control that he had instilled in his characterization of the mentally challenged Lennie. The screenwriter, Curt Siodmak, had originally written Talbot as an American technician who travels to Wales to install an observatory telescope at Talbot Castle. Studio bosses insisted that the werewolf be a member of the Talbot family, so Siodmak threw in a couple of lines of dialogue that explained Lawrence's American accent as the result of a stateside education and time spent away from the family castle. With small matters such as misplaced accents and a Welsh landscape that seemed a

Lon Chaney Jr. in full werewolf makeup in his most famous role as *The Wolf Man.*

Lon Chaney Jr. reprised his role as the Wolf Man in the 1944 film *House of Frankenstein.*

peculiar amalgam of several European countries, the werewolf as portrayed by Chaney became the favorite movie monster of World War II.

Siodmak had first envisioned the film as a vehicle for Boris Karloff, Universal's favorite monster man, but it was the screenwriter himself who once observed that he believed Lon Jr. to have endured rather sadistic treatment from his famous father and had emerged from his father's shadow as something of a tortured person. Perhaps Siodmak believed that Lon Jr. would be able to dredge those anguished depths to portray a man twisted and tortured by supernatural forces far beyond any mortal's ability to comprehend or resist.

Chaney went on to play all the famous monster roles that had been created by Karloff and Lugosi. He was the Frankenstein Monster in *The Ghost of Frankenstein* (1942) and **Dracula** in *Son of Dracula* (1943). He also assumed the rotting bandages originally worn by Karloff's Im-Ho-Tep as the Mummy Kharis in *The Mummy's Tomb* (1942), *The Mummy's Ghost*, and *The Mummy's Curse* (both 1944). He was Lawrence Talbot still fighting the curse of the werewolf in **Frankenstein Meets the Wolf Man** (1943), *House of Frankenstein* (1944), *House of Dracula* (1945), and **Abbott and Costello Meet Frankenstein** (1948). He put on the Wolf Man makeup for the last time in 1960 for an episode of the television series *Route 66*, "Lizard's Leg and Owlet's Wing."

In addition to donning the cape of Dracula, sprouting the bristled hair of the Wolf Man, enduring the sparking electrodes of the Frankenstein Monster, and supporting the rotting bandages of the Mummy, Chaney also acted in numerous other horror films, such as *Cobra Woman* (1944), *Weird Woman* (1944), *Calling Dr. Death* (1943), *Frozen Ghost* (1945), and *Pillow of Death* (1946).

Lon Chaney Jr. appeared in 150 motion pictures during the course of his career and had guest starring roles in dozens of television series, including *Rawhide*, *The Lawman*, *The Rifleman*, *Wagon Train*, *Zane Grey Theater*, *Have Gun Will Travel*, *General Electric Theater*, and *Wanted: Dead or Alive*.

SOURCES:

Clarens, Carlos. *An Illustrated History of the Horror Film*. New York: Capicorn Books, 1968.

Katz, Epharaim. *The Film Encyclopedia*. New York: Perigee, 1979.

Stanley, John. *Creature Features*. New York: Boulevard, 1997.

Walker, John, ed. *Halliwell's Filmgoer's Companion, 12th Edition*. New York: HarperCollins, 1997.

Children Raised by Wolves

Many people have become familiar with Rudyard Kipling's tale of the boy **Mowgli,** who was raised by wolves in the jungles of India, through the three cinematic treatments of the story. In 1942, *The Jungle Book* was made into a captivating live-action feature starring the actor Sabu as Mowgli. In 1967,

Walt Disney translated the adventures of the wolf boy into an animated musical version, then, in 1994, filmed the Kipling story once again, this time with live actors and Jason Scott Lee as Mowgli.

In his *Man into Wolf* (c. 1950), **Robert Eisler** makes the point that Kipling's *The Jungle Book* achieved worldwide success because of the appeal that it makes to archetypal ideas of the human race. He also states that the "wolf cubs" among the Boy Scouts was suggested by the romanticized wolf-boy Mowgli and characterizes such expression as "a curious and harmless revival of activistic lycanthropic ideas."

While the vast majority of people may be skeptical about claims that human infants could be reared by wolves, there are some well-documented accounts of wolves and other animals becoming surrogate parents to human children.

In 1920, the Reverend J. A. L. Singh, an Anglican missionary who supervised an orphanage at Midnapore, India, was beseeched by villagers from Godamuri who sought his help in ridding them of **ghosts.** More intrigued than alarmed by the superstitious villagers, Reverend Singh journeyed to Godamuri and ordered a tiger-shooting platform constructed in the area where the evil spirits had been seen.

After some time, three full-grown wolves emerged from their lair. The adults were followed by two pups and a ghost—a hideous-looking being with hands, feet, and torso like a human, but with a large grotesque head that was more like a giant fur ball than a face. Close at its heels came another awful creature, exactly like the first, although smaller in size.

Reverend Singh suddenly found himself all alone on the tiger-shooting platform. And when he returned to the village, he found no amount of persuasion could convince anyone from Godamuri to return to the lair to capture the terrible ghosts.

Six days later, he returned with help recruited from nearby villages and flushed the wolves out of their den. In a corner of the wolf den, they were forced to kill a female that had stayed to defend the two ghosts, who now faced Reverend Singh with bared teeth. To his astonishment, he could at last see the two evil jungle spirits for what they really were: two young girls who had been raised by wolves.

The missionary took the two wolf-girls back with him to the orphanage at Midnapore where he first cut the huge, matted mass of hair from their heads, and then undertook the arduous task of rearing them as human children. Reverend Singh estimated their ages to be about nine and two. Neither of them was able to utter a single human sound. They walked about on all fours and could not be forced to stand erect. He christened the older girl Kamala, the younger, Amala.

The wolf-girls ate and drank canine-fashion by lowering their faces into their bowls. If not attended at mealtimes, they would scamper out to the courtyard and eat with the dogs, fighting with them for the choicest bits of raw meat. From their wolf environment, Kamala and Amala had developed a keen sense of smell, so they could detect the bones and stores of meat that their canine comrades had buried. They not only relished the caches of rotting flesh that the dogs had hidden, but they would chase off any vultures they might spot beaking a choice bit of carrion.

The wolf-girls slept most of the day, then prowled around at night while the rest of the orphanage slept. Whenever the opportunity presented itself, Kamala and Amala escaped for a nocturnal hunt for small game in the surrounding jungle.

It was only after several months that the girls tolerated loincloths. Personal hygiene had been a major problem from the very beginning of their stay at the orphanage, for toilet training is not required among jungle creatures who follow the instincts of the pack.

Little Amala died 11 months after her capture, and Kamala gave evidence of her first human emotion when she shed a few tears upon the death of her sister. It was about the same time that Kamala began to respond to Reverend Singh's patient ministrations, relinquishing some of her ferocious, wolflike ways. With daily massage and measured exercise, she was eventually able to stand erect and to walk in a conventional human manner.

Kamala's table etiquette advanced to the point where she could eat at the table with guests who might be visiting the orphanage. By 1927, her vocabulary included 30 words, she was helping Reverend Singh by watching the younger children, and she had begun to attend church services.

Sadly, as Kamala's adjustment to human society improved, her health began steadily to fail. On September 26, 1929, at the approximate age of 17, the last of India's wolf-girls died of uremic poisoning.

In October 1990, welfare workers in Springs, South Africa, discovered a case wherein the family dog had apparently been given almost full responsibility for the care of Danny, a 24-month-old boy. The child's mother admitted that she had left her son in the kennel to be raised by Skaapie, the dog, because she was an alcoholic and usually too drunk to care for him herself.

Child welfare workers said that Danny scampered about on all fours, barked, and whined. It was obvious to welfare worker Les Lancaster that the boy had spent so much time with Skaapie that he had assumed the behavior patterns of a dog. For her part, Danny's mother said that she provided him with a daily bowl of food, and she was happy that Skaapie had assumed all other maternal duties.

David Rintoul undergoes the painful transformation into a werewolf in the film *Legend of the Werewolf*.

When the officials took Danny away from his life in the dog kennel, they also separated him from his devoted, caring surrogate mother. Devastated by the loss of her "puppy," Skaapie died two weeks after their separation.

One of the most astonishing cases of surrogate animal parenting was made public in China's Liaoning Province in September 1991 when authorities at the China Medical Institute in Shenyang revealed that 16-year-old Wang Xian Feng had been raised from the ages of two to six by pigs. The bizarre situation had been discovered by a botanist searching for rare flowers who happened upon a small girl foraging for food among a herd of pigs. The girl was on all fours, squealing, grunting, and shoving her face into the grass just like the members of her family of swine.

According to the Anshan Psychology Research Institute of the China Medical Institute, they sent researchers to investigate the botanist's claims and the members of their team witnessed the child sucking a sow. Later, they observed her grunting, pushing pigs out of the way, and shoving her face into a trough to eat. At night, she would curl up next to the pigs to share body heat against the cold.

The girl was removed from the swine herd and taken to the institute for study and observation. Although at first the child could only grunt and squeal, an expert in children's learning disorders eventually taught Xian Feng to speak and behave like a human. By the time she was 16, she was evaluated as a sweet, simple, lovable girl by all who knew her.

SOURCES:

Eisler, Robert. *Man into Wolf.* London: Spring Books, n.d.

Steiger, Brad, and Sherry Hansen Steiger. *Strange Powers of Pets.* New York: Donald I. Fine, 1992.

The *Chindi*

According to Navajo artist David Little Turtle, the *chindi* is a shapeshifter that acts as a kind of avenging angel to those who show disrespect to any of the Earth Mother's creatures. "It can assume any shape," he says, "or, perhaps more accurately, it can inhabit any living thing. Almost any traditional Navajo has at least one chindi story to tell. He or she will tell you about coming home at night and seeing a coyote walking on its hind legs."

According to Navajo tradition, one of the ways of knowing that an animal harbors a chindi is that it will walk upright, like a human. Another sure way of identifying an animal that harbors a chindi is that the fact that its eyes will appear dead. If your headlights hit the animal's eyes and they do not reflect the light, you will know that a *chindi* has possessed the creature.

How the *chindi* responds to an innocent person depends upon that individual's attitude toward the Earth Mother and whether or not he or she has a good heart.

If a *chindi* is set against you for any reason, the only way you can stop the energy is draw a medicine circle around you and sing or say a prayer for protection. "It need not be a Navajo chant," Little Turtle maintains. "Sing or say aloud any prayer you know. The important thing is your attitude. If the *chindi* sees that you have a good heart, the evil energy will boomerang and return to the one who set it upon you."

And what about the worst-case scenario? What if a wolf or coyote or fox appears at your door walking on its hind legs and you don't know how to draw a proper medicine circle or sing the right kind of prayer? Can you stop it with a silver bullet?

Little Turtle believes that there is no kind of bullet that can stop a *chindi*. "If you kill the host animal," he explains, "the *chindi* will simply enter another animal. And another and another . . . until it has worked its vengeance upon you."

The tragic account of the Navajo Long Salt family is the most completely documented story of the *chindi's* persistence in exacting vengeance. Incredibly, the avenging spirit pursued the members of this one clan for over 100 years.

The Long Salt family's ordeal began in 1825 when a man of the family became ill because of nightmares that constantly troubled his sleep. He confided in his brothers that he was being visited by the angry spirit of a man that he had killed.

His older brother protested that the man had been their family's enemy for years and that he had been slain in a fair fight. According to tribal law, the killing had been justified.

The tormented man explained that the spirit was restless because he had been struck down before he could sing his death song. They must find a medicine priest to rid him of the troubled spirit—or he would surely die.

The Long Salts sought assistance from an old, blind medicine priest from the Tsegi country. At their request, he held a three-day *b'jene* (sing)—a purification ritual—over the afflicted brother. After the final day of the ritual, the troubled man sighed his relief and his gratitude that the restless spirit had departed and that he could now sleep peacefully.

For his pay, the blind priest had asked for five butchered sheep from the Long Salt family's herd. The requested recompense was surely fair, and the powerful Long Salt clan, who at that time numbered over 100 members, possessed many sheep. But since the flock was grazing at a considerable distance from the old priest's village, the two Long Salt men assigned the task of slaughtering the sheep decided to substitute five wild antelope in their place. After all, the old man was blind. He wouldn't be able to tell the difference between the animals, and they would preserve five valuable sheep for the family's own use.

The Long Salt elder who awarded the priest the five carcasses was himself unaware that antelope had been substituted for the specified sheep. With the animals' heads cut off and their lower legs removed at the knees, even those at the ceremony rewarding the medicine man were unaware of the deceit that two members of their family had perpetrated.

A few weeks later, an older member of the Long Salt family who had been healthy and without illness died suddenly. Then a very young and robust Long Salt male fell dead for no perceptible reason. As his pregnant wife and other family members sang their mourning songs, a uneasy feeling began to grow that something was not right.

Every few weeks after the young husband's death, a member of the Long Salt family would become ill, begin to waste away, and then die in suffering. To the wiser members of the family, it was becoming increasingly obvious that a *chindi* had been set against them. But why?

When at last the two men confessed substituting the antelope for the sheep, a council of family leaders agreed that selected delegates would meet with the medicine priest and seek to rectify the situation without further delay.

The old priest admitted that he had discovered the deception and had become very angry. He also acknowledged that he had set a *chindi* against them with the instructions that the entire Long Salt family should be eliminated one by one.

The representatives of the Long Salts beseeched him to call off the avenging spirit. They tried to make him understand that they, too, had been duped by two deceitful and lazy members of the clan. They did not intend to cheat him. And already many members of their family had been killed by the *chindi*.

The elderly medicine priest carefully evaluated their words and deemed them sincere. He told them that he was not an evil man, but he had been forced to uphold his dignity and reputation. He would remove the curse, but he must charge them a price somehow commensurate with the laws of the spirit world that had required him to set the chindi upon them.

The Long Salt delegates answered that they would not question his judgment. They would pay whatever price he asked in order to call off the *chindi* and to save the lives of their family members.

The old priest called his son to his side, complaining that he was now very tired—too weary to determine a proper compensation. He bade the Long Salts return in 10 days. At that time, both parties would agree to the terms of payment.

The Long Salts were dismayed, but they knew better than to protest the old man's decision.

On the morning of the tenth day, the delegation from the Long Salts was prompt in keeping the appointment at the hogan of the blind medicine man. But they were greeted by a family in mourning. The elderly priest had passed to the land of the grandfathers three days earlier.

The desperate Long Salts asked the man's son if he had called off the chindi before he died. To their horror, they were unable to determine if the curse had been lifted. The priest's son could only tell him that he knew that his father had thought much about the problem before he died.

By the time the Long Salt delegation returned home, several members of the family lay ill and dying.

In the August–September 1967 issue of *Frontier Times*, John R. Winslowe wrote that he met the last surviving member of the Long Salts in 1925, a slender teenaged girl named Alice:

> Curiously, anyone marrying into the family met the same fate as a **blood** Long Salt. Alice's mother died when the girl reached seven and she was attending the Tuba City boarding school at the Indian agency. Alice's father became skin and bones, dying two years later. . . . The remaining three Long Salts [Alice's two uncles and an aunt] were ill, crippled, and helpless. Friends cared for them, watching them fade into nothing before their eyes.

An aging but determined Navajo named Hosteen Behegade adopted Alice Long Salt and swore that he would protect her from the *chindi's* mission to destroy the sole surviving member of once proud and prosperous family. Behegade was incensed that so many people had to die because of the deceit of two lazy men who had tried to deceive an old priest, and he devised a plan to keep moving, to somehow stay one step ahead of the *chindi*.

In the winter of 1928, the desperate wanderers found themselves seeking refuge from a blizzard in a hogan three miles from the trading post on Red Mesa. The blizzard developed into the worst snowstorm in years. Surely not even the *chindi* could find them amid the deep-piling snow and the fierce howling wind.

The next morning, Alice Long Salt lay dead. The final propitiation had been exacted. At last the *chindi* would return to the unknown realm from which it had come, its 100th mission of revenge completed.

The Chronicon of Denys of Tell-Mahre

For centuries now, scholars have puzzled over *The Chronicon* of Denys of Tell-Mahre, a leader of the Syrian Jacobites. From what can be determined, the ancient scribe was born in Mesopotamia (now Iraq) and recorded a remarkable account of the appearance of frightening and terrifying creatures just before the reign of the Greek-Byzantine ruler Leo IV c. 774:

> They fled from no man, and, indeed, killed many people. . . . They were like **wolves,** but their faces were small and long . . . and they had great ears. The skin on their spine resembled that of a pig. These mysterious animals committed great ravages on the people in the Abdin Rock region, near Hoh. In some village they devoured more than 100 people; and in many others, from 20 to 40 or 50. If a man did pursue them, in no way did the monsters become frightened or flee. Instead, they turned on the man. If men loosed their weapons on a monster, it leaped on the men and tore them to bits.

> These monsters entered houses and yards, and . . . climbed in the night onto terraces, stole children from their beds and went off without opposition. When they appeared, dogs were afraid to bark.

A photo from *Frankenstein Meets the Wolf Man,* in which Lon Chaney Jr. once again portrayed the Wolf Man.

For these reasons, the country suffered a more terrible experience than it had ever known before. . . . When one of these monsters attacked a herd of goats, cattle, or a flock of sheep, they took away several at one time. . . . These monsters finally passed from the land and went into Arzanene [a district in southern Armenia along the borders of Assyria] and ravaged every village there. They also ravaged in the country of Maipherk and along Mt. Cahai and caused great damage. . . .

At this point, several pages are missing from the ancient manuscripts. Many scholars have long maintained that Denys of Tell-Mahre was only writing a fanciful tale. Others debate whether the monsters were packs of aggressive wolves driven by hunger to invade villages or if they were herds of wild pigs who were fiercely unafraid to turn upon those men who sought to hunt them down. There are many such accounts from antiquity that contain descriptions of strange, hairy creatures with glowing eyes that leap on their victims from dark ambush.

SOURCES:

Hurwood, Bernhardt J. *Vampires, Werewolves, and Ghouls.* New York: Ace Books, 1968.

Coyote People

The coyote has a very unique place among the Native American tribes of the Southwest. For many, Brother Coyote participated with the Great Mystery in the very act of creation. For others, humans first assumed the form of coyotes before they evolved to their present physical shape.

According to Native American tradition, it is Brother Coyote who gave the tribes the knowledge of how to make fire, how to grind flour, and how to find the herbs that would bring about healings. But Brother Coyote is also a trickster. While it is true that he brought fire and food and healing wisdom to the tribes, he also brought death. The **shamans** soon learned that when you ask such a creature to grant you a wish, you must be very careful that there is not some trick attached to it.

The traditional Navajo generally regard the coyote as the very essence and symbol of dark-side witchcraft. If a Navajo were to set out on a journey and a coyote should cross his path, he would go back home and wait for three days before he set out again. And once the missionaries told the Navajo about Satan, they were certain that he used the coyote as his steed to travel about working nocturnal evil.

David Little Turtle, a Navajo artist, reports of the shepherd near Window Rock, Arizona, who was out hunting one night when he caught a glimpse of a large coyote running behind a clump of mesquite.

As he walked around the bush with his rifle at the ready, a female voice startled him by shouting at him not to shoot or he would kill a member of his own clan. The shepherd was further astonished when the coyote pulled back its skin to reveal a woman he immediately recognized as one of his cousins.

She promised to conduct a powerful purification ceremony called a sing for him and, in return, he would promise to say nothing of the incident to anyone. The shepherd had long suspected his kinswoman of being a shapeshifter, but to see her in the act of transforming herself into a coyote had made him feel as though his brain were spinning. Once the witch had obtained his vow of secrecy, she slipped the coyote skin back over her head and ran off with such speed that she became but a blur of motion.

David Little Turtle says that the Navajo believe in many types of were-animals. In referring to the account of the shepherd encountering his kinswoman as a coyote, he explains that the witch probably kept the skin of the animal hidden somewhere in a cave or in her home. When she wanted to join with other witches or move about at night with great speed, she would put on the magic skin.

"Other witches might keep the hide of a bear, a fox, a wolf, or a mountain lion hidden away for such purposes of night travel," he says. "When they gather together in secret meeting places, the witches plot against their enemies, initiate new members, and sometimes eat human flesh or have sexual intercourse with corpses."

A Native American psychiatrist in Phoenix, Arizona, explains that the werecreatures in which the Navajos believe are not quite the same as the popular werewolf of European traditions. "Interestingly, though," he conveys, "it is the wolfmen or the coyotemen who are most common among the North American tribes as in Europe. The difference is that the creatures of various tribal beliefs are more often supernatural entities who are shapeshifters that can assume the form of humans and—at will—can travel many, many miles in the blink of an eye and appear as **wolves** or as men dressed in wolf's clothing."

An attractive young Navajo woman, a convert to Roman Catholicism, tells of her brother's experience while hitchhiking late one night to their grandmother's home:

> It was in February and it was pretty cold. It was past midnight, and he just couldn't go any farther. There are these little bus stops on the roads where they pick up schoolchildren, so he was sitting there, debating whether or not to spend the night there or to keep walking the second half of the 50 miles to Grandmother's home.
>
> Then he saw this animal that he thought was a big dog. He wanted some company, so he whistled at it. It came running up to him, then it stood up on its hind legs. My brother was so scared! He said the big dog or big coyote had a man's face—and the face was painted with little white dots and other kinds of signs. Then the thing ran off on four legs, and my brother said it dawned on him what he had seen. He had never really believed in such

Not nearly as popular as werewolves and other shapeshifters, alligators and crocodiles did have their moment in the sun in the low-budget 1959 film *Alligator People*.

creatures until then. Now he knew that it was true that some medicine people really have the power to travel long distances in no time at all in the form of a wolf or a coyote.

My brother did not tell our grandmother about his experience until many months later; if he had, Grandmother would have become frightened and insisted that we have a sing to chase away any evil spirits.

Crocodile People

Many African tribes believe that crocodiles house the souls of murder victims who have returned to seek revenge. These tormented spirits may assume a limited human form or may shapeshift between reptile and human.

A more common belief is that the crocodiles are themselves the present incarnations of tribal ancestors. Propitiation may be offered to the large reptiles to insure their benevolent guidance, rather than their disgust or animosity with present generations of their tribe.

To the ancient Egyptians, the fearsome river beast was often identified with Osiris, lord of the fertilizing power of the Nile, god of death and rebirth. The crocodile god, Sebek, was often associated with Ra, the creator sun god.

Beast marriages with crocodiles are common in the folklore of many African tribes, and as a totem animal, the great reptile represents ancient wisdom in the powerful frame of a proud survivor.

The ancient Hebrews saw the crocodile as leviathan, "the great dragon that lies in the midst of rivers" (Ezekiel 29:3). In the old Christian tradition, leviathan evolved from crocodile to a great demon dragon, symbolizing Satan at his most repulsive and powerful.

SOURCES:

Gaskell, G. A. *Dictionary of All Scriptures and Myths*. Avenel, NJ: Gramercy Books, 1981.

Larousse Dictionary of World Folklore. New York: Larousse, 1995.

Cummins, Gordon Frederick (1917–1942)

Gordon Frederick Cummins, a 25-year-old Royal Air Force (RAF) cadet, earned the notorious sobriquet "the Wartime Jack the Ripper," by killing at least four women, and possibly two or more others. Like his infamous namesake, Cummins picked up women on the streets, killed them, and cruelly mutilated their bodies.

Cummins's first victim was found in an air-raid shelter during the early hours of February 9, 1942. A chemist's assistant named Evelyn Hamilton had been strangled with her own scarf. The next night, he struck again, killing a former Windmill showgirl, Evelyn Oatley, and horribly mutilating her body with the cutting edge of a can opener.

A few nights later, the mutilated corpse of a prostitute was found in the small flat where she serviced her clients. Before the police barely had time to declare the crime scene, they were forced to deal with the body of Mrs. Doris Jouannet, the wife of a hotel manager, who had been strangled and slashed in her home. Then, as incredible as it must have seemed to the police, the Wartime Jack the Ripper had struck again within hours of the discovery of the body of Mrs. Jouannet. Fortunately for the victim, this time the Ripper had been frightened away by a passerby who sensed that the activity in a doorway in Piccadilly was something more than amorous between the cadet and the lady. Carelessly, Cummins had dropped his RAF-issue gas mask when he fled the scene.

Later that same evening, he was at it again, attempting to strangle a woman in her flat in Paddington. This woman had decided not to be another victim of the Ripper, and she fought back viciously, throwing every ounce of her determination to survive into her blows of resistance. At the same time, she employed one of the oldest and time-tested of women's weapons—screaming bloody murder. Within a short time, a good share of the neighborhood was chasing the Ripper, who this time hastily discarded his RAF uniform belt in his effort to escape vigilante justice.

With two such bits of evidence in hand, police work became routine. The gas mask even bore Cummins's Air Force number, and the fingerprints on the mask and the belt matched those found at the crime scenes. Gordon Frederick Cummins, the Wartime Jack the Ripper, was hanged at Wandsworth Prison on June 25, 1942.

SOURCES:

Lane, Brian, and Wilfred Gregg. *The Encyclopedia of Serial Killers.* New York: Berkley Publishing, 1994.

The Curse of the Werewolf

There are those devotees of werewolf movies who affirm that this is the very best of the films depicting the evolution of a lupine character. Filmed with the style and high production values that Great Britain's Hammer Films brought to all of its horror pictures, *The Curse of the Werewolf* (1961) is very loosely based on Guy Endore's novel, **The Werewolf of Paris** (1933).

Leon (**Oliver Reed**), the werewolf of the film, is shown to be of the lineage that is certain to produce a lycanthrope. Set in eighteenth-century Spain, the opening scene depicts a beautiful mute servant girl (Yvonne Romain) who is resisting the unwanted advances of her employer, a cruel marquis (Anthony Dawson), who has recently taken a bride. The servant is punished by being thrown into the dungeon cell of a wretched beggar who, after years of imprisonment, has become a disgusting mass of sores and filth. The wild-eyed beggar (Richard Wordsworth) manages to rape the girl and impregnate her before he dies from the exertion of the brutal attack. The servant girl, in turn, manages to escape the dungeon, kill the vicious marquis, and go into hiding with a sympathetic professor (Clifford Evans) and his housekeeper. As fate has it, she delivers the child on Christmas Eve, which according to old tradition predisposes the newborn to become a werewolf. The unfortunate young woman dies in childbirth, but she is spared the future horror of seeing her son fulfill his demonic legacy.

By the time Leon (Justine Walters) is six years of age, it is certain from his predatory attack on flocks of sheep that he is a werewolf. The professor is advised by the village priest that only love can hold the lupine instincts at bay, and through the caring ministrations of his benefactor, Leon (Oliver Reed) matures into manhood unaware of the curse that slumbers within him. When he finds romance with Christine (Catherine Feller), his bestial impulses are even further subdued.

All goes awry when a fun-loving friend cajoles Leon into accompanying him to a cheap dancehall. The sordidness of the surroundings begin to provoke the demon within and the confused Leon becomes ill because of the conflict within him. Now out of control, he kills one of the women and the friend who had taken him there. He flees into the wilds, a ravaging werewolf.

His loving adopted father seeks to keep Leon chained to prevent his rampages. Christine, learning the truth about her sweetheart, believes that her love can quiet the beast within him. But before this idyllic plan can be put into effect, Leon is arrested for the series of murders that he has committed.

No village jail in eighteenth-century Spain was constructed to withstand the rage of a maddened werewolf when the moon is full. Leon escapes and is finally put to rest by a silver bullet forged from a crucifix and fired by his beloved adoptive father.

SOURCES:

Clarens, Carlos. *An Illustrated History of the Horror Film*. New York: Capricorn Books, 1968.
Douglas, Drake. *Horror!* New York: Collier Books, 1966.

D

Dahmer, Jeffrey (1960–1994)

A very well-known example of a contemporary werewolf is Jeffrey L. Dahmer, who killed, dismembered, butchered, and ate portions of the flesh of at least 18 human victims. As a modern serial killer, Dahmer portrays the most common and graphic expression of the lycanthrope in today's culture—an individual (almost always male) who leads a double life, then ventures forth sadistically to slash, rip, murder, mutilate, and very often partake of the flesh of his prey. Although much was made of the theory that Dahmer suffered from a mental disease called paraphilia, a sexual attraction to inanimate objects—in his case, dead bodies—the grisly fact remains that he was the sole person responsible for the death of his victims.

Basically a nightstalker, Dahmer would hang around gay bars or shopping malls until closing time, then approach his victim and ask if he would like to accompany him for sex, for drinks, or to take photographs. If the target was somewhat reluctant, Dahmer would not hesitate to offer money as an added inducement. Once he had managed to lure a young man to his apartment, Dahmer would either drug or strangle him, then gradually dismember him.

Thirty-one-year-old Dahmer was arrested on July 24, 1991, when his most recently selected victim, a teenager, managed to escape from the cannibal's apartment and run out into the street, still wearing the handcuffs that were supposed to hold him until Dahmer carved him with a butcher knife. Investigating police officers who first entered the ghastly flat at 213 Oxford Apartments, Milwaukee, Wisconsin, must have felt as if they had descended into one of the lower rings of hell. They discovered nine severed heads—seven in various stages of being boiled; two kept fresh in the refrigerator—four male torsos stuffed into a barrel, and several assorted sections of male genitalia being stored in a pot. Other scraps of human flesh and portions of limbs and bodies were scattered throughout the apartment. The wretched stench of putrefaction was beyond the experience of the most seasoned police officer.

Although generally regarded as a polite, harmless, and quiet young man, Dahmer had a prior police record of a number of minor sex offenses against children. He had been released from prison on probation in 1989 after serving time for having abused a 13-year-old boy. But even dating back to his high school days, Jeffrey Dahmer had been pronounced "a generally weird dude" by his fellow students. In 1989, Dahmer's father had requested that his son receive psychiatric treatment.

Although Jeffrey Dahmer most certainly expressed extremely aberrant behavior, it was argued that he could still distinguish right from wrong. His defense attorney suggested that Dahmer had no awareness that he was mentally ill, he just thought that he occasionally did bad things. The state prosecutor countered by stating that the sadistic cannibal was not possessed of a diseased mind, but a disordered one.

It did seem as though Jeffrey Dahmer was truly suffering from some kind of **possession** by a terrible beast within his psyche. Throughout the trial, he sat quietly, almost expressionless, as if he had little personal interest in the outcome of the proceedings. On the one hand, he described how he cooked the biceps of one of his victims, seasoned it with salt, pepper, and steak sauce— then, with apparent sincerity, said that he was at a loss to believe that any human being could have done the things that he had done. Before he was sentenced, he rose to make a kind of public apology in which he stated that he had never hoped for his freedom, that he wanted death for himself. Because nearly all of his victims were from minority groups, he wanted it clearly understood that his terrible crimes were not motivated by racial hatreds. Quoting from his statement to the court:

> One of the reasons [that I decided to go through this trial] was to let the world know that these were not hate crimes . . . I wanted to find out just what it was that caused me to be so bad and evil, but most of all . . . I decided that maybe there was a way for us to tell the world that there are people out there with these disorders, maybe they can get help before they end up being hurt or hurting someone. . . . In closing I just want to say that I hope God has forgiven me; I know society will never be able to forgive me for what I have done. . . .

On May 1, 1992, Jeffrey Dahmer was sentenced to life imprisonment on 16 charges of aggravated murder. On November 28, 1994, while he was mopping the bathroom floor in maximum security, Dahmer was killed by Christopher Scarver, a convicted murderer on antipsychotic medication.

Dahmer's mother requested that his brain be preserved in formaldehyde for future study, but his father appealed to the court to honor his son's request for cre-

Infamous serial killer and cannibal Jeffrey Dahmer is a perfect example of the modern lycanthrope who cannot control his animal impulses.

mation. On December 12, 1995, more than a year after Jeffrey Dahmer's death, the county circuit judge found for his father and ordered the brain destroyed.

SOURCES:

Lane, Brian, and Wilfred Gregg. *The Encyclopedia of Serial Killers*. New York: Berkley Publishing, 1994.

Steiger, Brad, and Sherry Hansen Steiger. *Demon Deaths*. New York: Berkley Publishing, 1991.

Dante, Joe (1946–)

Joe Dante is one of many top-notch directors who came up through the ranks at Roger Corman's New World Pictures organization. Under Corman's aegis, Dante directed *Piranha* (1978) and learned how to make a motion picture on time and on budget. Made for $700,000, and featuring such horror flick veterans as Bradford Dillman, Kevin McCarthy, Barbara Steele, Bruce Gordon, Dick Miller, and others, *Piranha* became New World's top grosser.

In an interview with Paul Mandell, Dante says that he made **The Howling** (1981) because he thought it would be fun to make a werewolf picture. Although the project began with a novel written by Gary Brandner, Dante felt the author's original setting was more in a "period" vein, and he wanted to update the werewolf theme to make it more contemporary and more accessible to modern audiences. Dante, together with Terry Winkless and John Sayles, who had written the script for *Piranha* and has since written and directed such cinematic successes as *Return of the Secaucus 7* (1980), *Brother from Another Planet* (1984), and *Lone Star* (1996), "mapped out the new story with the newsgirl, the TV studio, and the ending. That all evolved as we went along."

Dante filmed *The Howling* in 28 days: "We shot one week in Mendocino. It was a beautiful, backwoodsy area. That was only part of the forest in the picture. The rest was Griffith Park. That's as far as our budget allowed. . . . We planned to shoot most of the effects footage after principal photography was finished."

When asked about the incredible effects achieved by special effects artist Rob Bottin for the film, Dante stated that some of the storyline was written around what they felt they could have the werewolf do: "We used some of the Rouben Mamoulian Jekyll and Hyde tricks, using colored filters during stage photography and slowly removing them for transition effects. . . . We may have taken it at a faster or slower speed, and in some cases, even shot things backwards. But it's all happening before your eyes. There are no lap dissolves or opticals for Rob's werewolf transitions. We used every trick in the book to get away with what we did."

Since achieving success with *The Howling* and jumpstarting the werewolf film as a genre, Joe Dante has directed such films as *Gremlins* (1984), *Inner-*

In this scene from a nineteenth-century storybook, French villagers hunt a werewolf that has been terrorizing their village.

space (1987), *The 'Burbs* (1989), and *Small Soliders* (1998). As an actor he has appeared in small roles in a variety of films, including *Cannonball* (1976), *Sleepwalkers* (1992), and *Beverly Hills Cop III* (1994).

SOURCES:

Mandell, Paul. "Dante's Inferno Blazes Again." *Fantastic Films,* August 1981.
Mitchell, Blake, and Jim Ferguson. "The Howling." *Fantastic Films,* August 1981.
Walker, John, ed. *Halliwell's Filmgoer's Companion, 12th Edition.* New York: HarperCollins, 1997.

de Rais, Gilles (1404–1440)

In 1415, as a boy of 11, Gilles de Rais became heir to the greatest fortune in France. At 16, he greatly increased his net worth by marrying the extremely wealthy Catherine de Thouars. When he had barely turned 20, he rode by the side of Joan of Arc and fought with such fierce merit that King Charles awarded Gilles the title of Marshal of France. Gilles de Rais was a man so noted for his devotion to duty and his personal piety that he came to be regarded as a latter-day Lancelot. But, like Lancelot before him, Gilles entered into an ill-fated love affair that destroyed him.

Although it was undoubtedly an affair that was conducted entirely on a spiritual level, Gilles fell in love with Joan of Arc, the strange young mystic whose "voices" dictated that she save France. He became her guardian and protector, but when she was captured, tortured, and burned at the stake, Gilles de Rais was transformed into a fiend of such infamy, such hellish and unholy proportions, that his depraved acts are virtually unequaled in the annals of perverse crimes against society. The life of this pietist-turned-monster has been examined in depth by many scholars, and most of them seem to agree that de Rais's crimes and acts of sacrilege were quite likely inspired by what he considered God's betrayal of Joan of Arc.

Gilles de Rais left his wife, vowed never to have sexual intercourse with another woman, and secreted himself in his castle at Tiffauges. He surrounded himself with profligates, broken-down courtiers, sycophants, and wastrels and embarked on several rounds of lavish orgies. After what seemed to a tireless series of marathon days and nights of debauchery, even the vast wealth of his estate began to diminish. It was then that Gilles decided to try his hand at alchemy, the dream of transmuting base metals into gold, as a means of replenishing his fortune. Within a short time, he had converted an entire wing of his castle into a series of extensive alchemical laboratories.

Alchemists and sorcerers from all over Europe flocked to Tiffauges. Some came to freeload on the young nobleman's lavish feasts and to fleece him out of a few bags of gold. Others were sincere in their desire to achieve the final answer to the ancient alchemists' quest. Gilles de Rais joined the magicians and the alchemists in work sessions that went nearly around the clock, but all of their experiments counted for naught.

It was the great sorcerer Prelati who counseled de Rais that mortal man could not hope to achieve the transmutation of base metals into gold without the help of Satan. And no alchemist could hope to arouse the interest of the Prince of Darkness unless he was willing to dedicate the most abominable crimes to his name.

Under Prelati's direction, de Rais lured a young peasant boy into the castle, slashed the boy's throat, gouged his eyeballs from their sockets, ripped out his heart, and caught the **blood** in inkwells so that he might utilize it for the writing of magical evocations and alchemical formulas. Satan did not appear, and no base metals were transmuted into gold, but Gilles de Rais no longer cared. He had discovered an enterprise far more satisfying to him than the alchemist's quest. He had aroused the latent werewolf within him and taken great sadistic satisfaction in the murder of a child.

In their *Perverse Crimes in History*, R. E. L. Masters and Eduard Lea tell of de Rais's own testimony of how he enjoyed dramatizing his murder of the children. He would have one of his servants kidnap a child from the village or countryside, carry him off to the castle, then tie him up and leave him in a room. Some time later, Gilles would enter, feign shock and surprise at seeing the lad so woefully treated, and cut him free from his bonds. He would then hold the child on his knees, speak softly to him, assure him that all would be well and that he would soon be back in his mother's arms—then he would slit the boy's throat in one swift movement and violate the spasmodically twitching corpse. After he had obtained sexual gratification in this manner, the child would be dismembered and certain of the remains put away to be utilized for magical purposes.

Etienne Corrillaut, one of de Rais's personal servants, later testified at his master's trial when de Rais was accused of having slain more than 800 children. According to Corrillaut, de Rais took special pleasure in masturbating on a child's stomach while the boy was being decapitated. The monster kept the heads of handsome children on upright rods and employed a beautician to curl their hair and rouge their lips and cheeks. When he believed that he had accumulated enough heads, he would summon the staff of the entire castle and conduct a perverse kind of beauty contest, demanding that everyone vote on which boy's head was the most attractive.

Because of his high position in the court of France, Gilles de Rais was granted the mercy of being strangled before being burned. The tribunal conveniently looked the other way after his execution, however, and the de Rais family was permitted to remove his corpse after it had been given only a slight singeing. The mass murderer of nearly 1,000 children was interred in a Carmelite churchyard after a Roman Catholic ceremony.

The fiendish Prelati and the other professing Satanists who resided in Gilles de Rais's castle were given at most a few months in prison for their part in the sadistic murders. Masters and Lea speculate that this was their reward for testifying against de Rais. It is thought likely that both ecclesiastical and civil authorities were far more interested in obtaining Gilles's money and properties, which were still considerable, than in punishing him for his despicable crimes.

SOURCES:

Masters, R. E. L., and Eduard Lea. *Perverse Crimes in History.* New York: The Julian Press, 1963.

Steiger, Brad. *Demon Lovers: Cases of Possession, Vampires, and Werewolves.* New Brunswick, NJ: 1987.

de Sade, Donatien Alphonse Francois (1740–1814)

Donatien Alphonse Francois de Sade, son of the Comte de Sade, was born in Paris on June 2, 1740, but he did not share as many of the details of his childhood as did **Leopold von Sacher-Masoch.** When he was 14, de Sade's uncle sent him off to join the aristocratic cavalry regiment of the *Chevaux Legers* accompanied by a valet, a somewhat older boy, selected from the peasants who served his family. Within less than two years, the teenage officer and his regiment were sent with the contingent of the French army to fight in the Seven Years War against England and Prussia.

As a nobleman, de Sade was exempt from corporal punishment, but during the war (1756–1763), he witnessed common soldiers being forced to run the gauntlet for minor offenses against the strict military discipline. Whenever a village was occupied, he saw young and old women raped, and men, women, and children tortured to disclose the hiding places of any objects of value. Without question, these cruel wartime experiences left deep impressions on the psyche of a young man who was promoted to captain by the time he was 18. It should not be surprising to discover that a person so young given so much power in the midst of butchery and debauchery would feature torture and cruelty in his daydreams and his erotic experiments. What will be surprising to many is that the Marquis de Sade expressed his desires primarily through his writings, such as *The Bedroom Philosophers* (1795) and *The Story of Juliette* (1797). He was not at all a **Gilles de Rais,** the monstrous Marshal of France as he was called, the mass murderer of hundreds of children. De Sade found himself in legal difficulties most often because of who he was, a member of the aristocracy when aristocrats were falling out of fashion.

He was accused of having taken a common prostitute into a pavilion in his garden, undressing her, spanking her, and pricking her with a knife. The marquis denied the charges, and the woman agreed to drop her complaint for an agreed-upon sum of money. The social ostracism he incurred from his peers as a result of the sordid lawsuit was worse than the monetary loss. Soon after, a second lawsuit was brought against him, charging that he had poisoned a group of prostitutes at a banquet. Doctors who examined the women a few days later found none of them to be ill or weakened by the alleged experience, but once again de Sade was treated like an outcast by his fellow nobles. De Sade had already become an outspoken opponent of the abuses of the church and the judicial establishment, and he suspected the whole lawsuit had been a device fashioned by his enemies and his wife's family, who had made no secret of their objection to his taking their daughter as his bride. Since they had turned his wife's affections against him, he eloped with his sister-in-law,

Fredric March (here as Mr. Hyde) won a Best Actor Oscar for his efforts in the 1931 version of *Dr. Jekyll and Mr. Hyde.*

who returned his love, and they left France. Later, he was forced to return and he was imprisoned in the fortress of Vincennes on the strength of accusations levied by his powerful in-laws.

De Sade spent seven years, from 1777 to 1784, in the prisons of the Chateau de Vincennes and five more years, until July 6, 1789, in the Bastille. Freed when the notorious prison was destroyed, he was imprisoned again by Napoleon I in Sainte-Pelagie from 1801 to 1803 and at Charenton from 1803 until his death in December 1814. De Sade had spent half of his 74 years in prison. In his will, he requested that he be buried in the densest forest-thicket on his estate and that his grave be strewn with acorns.

Marquis de Sade had come to praise the natural human. He was not persecuted because of the sexual content of his novels, but because of his political views. He was an aristocrat who had come to despise his class, the church, the high-ranking judges, and the officials of the government; and he portrayed them all in his writing—dukes, bishops, judges, priests, presidents—as contemptible monsters of ugliness, sexual perversion, and greed.

"What need has man to live in society?" de Sade pondered. "Return him to the wild forests where he was born. Savage man knows only two needs—copulation and food. Both are natural, and nothing which he can do to obtain either can be criminal. All that produces in [man] other passions is the work of civilization and society. . . . How tempted I am to go and live among bears."

While some have decreed the works of de Sade as the most lascivious in all of literature, the erotic excesses, the voluptuous enjoyment of libertine acts, torture, murder, and sexual perversions can be interpreted as an indictment against the abuses of the aristocracy of his time. The novels were written quite likely as a form of release and a method of dealing with those he deemed the true villains of the world. The imaginary sufferings of the virtuous heroes and heroines at the hands of the sadistic monsters he created may well have been his method of retaining his sanity during his 37 years of what many deem unjust imprisonment.

SOURCES:

Eisler, Robert. *Man into Wolf.* London: Spring Books, n.d.

Hunt, Morton M. *The Natural History of Love.* New York: Grove Press, 1959.

Demons

When Socrates spoke of consulting his "daimon," he was not referring to an evil spirit or a fallen angel, but to his tutelary spirit. The ancient Greeks believed that everyone had an attendant entity to whom he or she might turn for advice in dealing with life's problems. The Romans called their "daimon," their guardian angel, a "genius," which could also be interpreted as roughly

Movie poster from the 1941 version of *Dr. Jekyll and Mr. Hyde,* which starred Spencer Tracy as the tortured doctor.

analogous to the soul. Since those days of antiquity, however, "demon" has come to refer only to the fallen angels who seek to work harm against humankind and a "genius" is a mortal human being of high intelligence.

Demons are the ultimate shapeshifters, for they can appear in any form they choose. They are unlikely to appear as slit-eyed, reptilian monsters, however, for then they would be easily recognized as evil-doers. They are more likely to appear to their potential victims in as an attractive, seductive, and alluring a manner as possible.

The main task of demons, the fallen angels, is to disseminate errors among humankind and to deceive mortals into committing evil deeds. The Middle Ages in Europe was a devil-infested period, and perhaps the demon horde's greatest accomplishment lay in deceiving officials of the church that there were millions of witches, werewolves, vampires, and other shapeshifters that required the torture chamber and deserved death by burning at the stake.

Throughout the centuries, the wisest priests among their flocks have acknowledged that it is very difficult to develop an adequate litmus test that will unfailingly distinguish between good angels and bad ones. Unless one is pure in heart, mind, and soul it is an exceeding complex task to discern accurately the true nature of spirits. It is generally known that good spirits will never attempt to interfere with a human being's free will or possess one's physical body. And, on the other hand, it is acknowledged that demons, the evil ones, desire the physical body of the human. In fact, they must have it in order to experience earthly pleasures and to work evil against other humans.

Demonic entities are credited with will and intellect that are directed toward evil as they exert their malevolent powers. When these evil spirits penetrate the world and the circumstances of human life, they conceal themselves in every aspect of earthly existence. Their ultimate intent is to bring about the death of the good creation of God.

According to Christian tradition, there was a great outburst of demonic activity upon the occasion of Jesus coming to earth in order to attack the material kingdom of Satan. Certain church scholars believe that another such outburst of demonic power will manifest just before the Second Coming of Jesus. Some clerics would say that time has already begun.

Professor Morton Kelsey, an Episcopal priest, a noted Notre Dame professor of theology, and the author of *Discernment: The Study of Ecstasy and Evil*, states without equivocation that demons are real and can invade the minds of humans.

"Most people in the modern world consider themselves too sophisticated and too intelligent to be concerned with demons," he comments. "They totally ignore the evidence around them. But in 30 years of study, I have seen the effects of angels and demons on humans."

Professor Kelsey insists that a demon is not a figment of the imagination. "It is a negative, destructive spiritual force. It seeks to destroy the person and everyone with whom that person comes into contact. The essential mark of the demon—and those possessed by demons—is total self-interest. A possessed individual is dominated by this self-interest to the exclusion of everyone and everything else."

Like so many other contemporary members of the clergy, Professor Kelsey is afraid that most people today offer little challenge for demons. "Demons find it easy to enter and operate in the unconscious part of the mind, taking control of the person and his character." He agrees with other authorities who have studied demonic attacks when he states that the most severe cases of **possession** can trigger suicide, because the demon is trying to destroy people any way it can. "Such a form of depression—or any other form—is caused by possession by demons, and it is only through religious means that you can properly deal with it."

In offering advice for those who may fear themselves to be in danger of being possessed, Professor Kelsey says that they should not be depressed: "You must think of the creator, the supreme being. Try to reach out for him and find his light. When you touch this light, it will be like punching a small hole in a dike—the light and the angels will flow in. The angels will drive out the demons, and you will be delivered. It is within every human to have the ability to seek the angels."

Monsignor Corrado Balducci, who lives in the shadow of St. Peter's Basilica in Rome, is assigned to assess thousands of cases of demonic possession each year. In the early 1990s, in order to assist those who asked how they might identify the demon possessed, the priest prepared the following checklist of symptoms:

- They are able to "see past events."
- They have incredible powers of extrasensory perception.
- They can move objects with their mind.
- They can levitate.
- They can speak in languages they didn't know before the possession.
- They know about events happening miles away.
- They do things that defy scientific analysis.

Lest one comes to believe that only the clergy believe in demonic possession, pay attention to the comments of Dr. Ralph Allison, senior psychiatrist at the California state prison in San Luis Obispo: "My conclusion after 30 years of observing over 1,000 mentally disturbed individuals is that some patients act in a bizarre fashion due to possession by spirits. The spirit may be that of a human being who died. Or it may be a spirit entity that has never been a human being and sometimes identifies itself as an agent of evil."

SOURCES:

Oesterreich, T. K. *Possession: Demoniacal and Other.* Translated by D. Ibberson. New Hyde Park: University Books, 1966.

Ruehl, Franklin R., "Many Mental Patients Are Really Possessed by Demons," *National Enquirer,* 15 October 1991.

Steiger, Brad, and Sherry Hansen Steiger. *Demon Deaths.* New York: Berkley Books, 1991.

Detecting Werewolves Among Us

It's not as easy detecting the werewolves among us as it is to hunt down the vampires lurking in the shadows. Perhaps the most essential difference between the two creatures of the dark side is the fact that the werewolf is not

Dr. Jekyll and Sister Hyde, **which starred Ralph Bates and Martine Beswick in the title roles, presented a new twist on the old legend.**

a member of the undead. When lycanthropes are not in the throes of transformation precipitated by the rays of the **full moon** or the wearing of the magic **wolf belt,** they walk about the bustling streets of the city or the pleasant country lanes appearing as any normal human. Werewolves have no need to scamper off to a coffin before the rays of the rising sun begin to burn welts into their hide. Werewolves can don shades, lie out on the sunny beach, and work on their tan if that should that be their pleasure.

Mirrors offer no problem for werewolves. They can straighten their neckties or apply lipstick without worrying if they are casting a reflection.

Crucifixes are of no concern. Werewolves might even wear the sign of the cross themselves, attend church services, and perhaps even serve as members of the clergy.

Some old traditions do offer certain advice when it comes to detecting the werewolves among us. As early as the seventh century, Paulos Agina, a physician who lived in Alexandria, described the symptoms of werewolfism for his fellow doctors:

- Pale skin.

- Weak vision.

- An absence of tears or saliva, making the eyes and tongue very dry.

- Excessive thirst.

- Ulcers and abrasions on the arms and legs that do not heal, caused by walking on all fours.

- An obsession with wandering in cemeteries at night.

- Howling until dawn.

Many old traditions insist that the hands may provide the biggest giveaway. Check the palms of a suspected werewolf, and if his or her palms are covered with a coarse, stiff growth of hair, you had better avoid his or her company on the nights of the full moon. And while you would rightfully argue that any reasonably intelligent werewolves would be careful to shave their palms—especially female lycanthropes—if you are reasonably observant you would be able to notice that the flesh of their palms is rough, perhaps even a bit scaly from repeated razor scrapings.

According to a vast number of ancient traditions, another certain sign of the werewolf is the extreme length of the index finger. If you should notice a man or woman with an index finger considerably longer than the middle finger, you have quite likely spotted a werewolf.

Then there is the matter of the eyebrows growing together. If they should meet in the center of the forehead, there is cause for genuine concern that you have encountered a werewolf. Once again, if it is obvious that the area is regularly shaved, beware of walks in the moonlight with this individual.

A good many traditions regard the **pentagram,** the five-pointed star, as a symbol of witchcraft and werewolves. Some werewolf hunters of old believed that the sign of the pentagram would be found somewhere on a lycanthrope's body, most often on the chest or the hand. It was also an aspect of that belief structure that the shadow of the pentagram would manifest on the palm or forehead of the werewolf's next victim and would be visible only to the monster's eyes.

And speaking of the eyes of the werewolf, while they appear normal at all other times, when the curse is upon them, their eyes glow in the dark, most often with a reddish hue.

Perhaps with tongue firmly in cheek, the following test for detecting the werewolves was posted on Tina's Humor Archives on the Internet. Although some of the items on the list are actually traditional determinants in the folklore of werewolves, others are a bit off the wall. Allegedly compiled by a scholar who has been studying werewolves for 50 years, here, edited and condensed, is Dr. Werner Bokelman's test for determining if your friend or neighbor is a werewolf:

- Werewolves have extra glands that emit unpleasant odors. Therefore, if your friend or neighbor smells like a mixture of stale hay and horse manure, he or she could be a werewolf.

- Doctors in Denmark have declared that a certain mark of the werewolf is evidenced when he or she possesses eyebrows that meet in the middle of the forehead.

- The arms, legs, and bodies of werewolves are extremely hairy, especially the backs of their hands and the tops of their feet.

- Werewolves reach sexual maturity five years ahead of normal humans, so keep an eye on that neighbor's child who seems unusually attracted to children of the opposite sex at the age of seven or eight.

- Check the ring finger of both of the suspected werewolf's hands. Experts have determined that a long ring finger is a certain sign of a werewolf.

- Does your neighbor own large pets that are always disappearing, only to be replaced by others? Because werewolves have demanding appetites that require large amounts of raw flesh, they may be devouring their pets.

- If you hear strange howling and moaning sounds at night in the neighborhood where there is a full moon but no dogs around, you are quite likely living next to a werewolf.

- Have you noticed his or her skin slowly changing color? It may take a few hours for a werewolf to transform from human to animal form, and the first sign of the coming metamorphosis is a gradual darkening of the skin.

- If you spot your neighbor wandering around graveyards and mortuaries and often appearing at the scene of fatal accidents, he or she may be a werewolf scouting for fresh corpses.

- If you have the courage to be near a werewolf in the daylight, you might follow him into a public restroom to see if his urine is a deep purple color—another sure sign of a werewolf.

SOURCES:

Douglas, Drake. *Horror!* New York: Collier Books, 1966.
Hurwood, Bernardt J. *Vampires, Werewolves, and Ghouls.* New York: Ace Books, 1968.
Noll, Richard. *Bizarre Diseases of the Mind.* New York: Berkley Books, 1990.

Diana, the Huntress

Throughout the Middle Ages, Diana, the goddess of the wilderness and the hunt, ruled all the dark forests of Europe. Some scholars have declared that the Inquisition was instituted to stamp out all worship of Diana in Europe. In the Bible, the book of Acts is filled with the struggles of the early apostles to counteract the influence of Diana, whose temple was one of the Seven Wonders of the World. "Great is Diana of the Ephesians," the tradespeople of Ephesus shouted at Paul and his company, setting in motion a riot (Acts 19). To the members of the Christian clergy, Diana was the Queen of the Witches. To the infamous witchhunter and grand inquisitor Torquemada, Diana was Satan.

From ancient times Diana was the Queen of Heaven, the Mother of Creatures, the Huntress, the Destroyer. To the Greeks, she was Artemis. While the early Christian fathers felt great satisfaction when the peasantry bent their knee to worship Mary as the Queen of Heaven, in truth, the majority believed that they were really worshipping Diana, the great and powerful goddess of old.

Diana, with her pack of hunting dogs, her stature as the Mother of Animals, the Lady of Wild Creatures, was the patron goddess of those who chose the life of the outlaw werewolf and all others who defied conventional society. She has remained the goddess of the wild woodlands and hunting throughout most of the Western world.

SOURCES:

Hazlin, W. E. *Dictionary of Faiths & Folklore*. London: Studio Editions, 1995.

Spence, Lewis. *An Encyclopedia of Occultism*. New Hyde Park, NY: University Books, 1960.

Walker, Barbara G. *The Woman's Encyclopedia of Myths and Secrets*. San Francisco: Harper & Row, 1983.

Dientudo

El Dientudo (Big Teeth) is a commonly reported Bigfoot-type creature in the region around Buenos Aires, Argentina. Many people have reported seeing this half-bear, half-man beast in the wooded areas near El Gato Creek and outside the city of Toloso.

SOURCES:

Picasso, Fabio. "South American Monsters & Mystery Animals." *Strange,* December 1998.

Dr. Jekyll and Mr. Hyde

The ghost of the man who inspired the story of the questing scientist and his violent, monstrous dark side personality is said to haunt a tavern more than 200 years after he was hanged for his crimes. Despite his death in the late 1700s, the Deacon Brodie Tavern in Edinburgh, Scotland, is plagued by eerie sounds, mysterious lights, and unexplained occurrences. By day, William

Screen legend John Barrymore, right, was one of the first to to take on the dual role of Dr. Jekyll and Mr. Hyde in 1920.

"Deacon" Brodie was a respected businessman, but by night he emerged as a hard-drinking gambler who burglarized private homes to support his multitude of vices. An accomplice turned him in for a reward, and Brodie was hanged on the very gallows that he had helped design.

Eighty years after Brodie swung on the gallows, Robert Louis Stevenson visited the tavern and heard the tale of the man with the strange double life, and it is said to have inspired him to write "The Strange Case of Dr. Jekyll and Mr. Hyde." And now today, over 100 years after Stevenson wrote his classic story in 1886, bartender Gert Pranstatter of the Deacon Brodie Tavern says the ghost of Brodie still haunts the place—and the terrible vision of Dr. Henry Jekyll transmutating into the evil Edward Hyde still haunts the rest of the world.

When Stevenson seized upon the account of the businessman/thief in Edinburgh and transformed that germ of a story into the tale of Dr. Jekyll and Mr. Hyde, little did he know he would be creating a masterpiece that explores the potential power of the beast within the human psyche. The concept of man to beast as portrayed in Stevenson's story has reached archetypal status, and there seems little doubt that the early dramatic and cinematic versions of the story greatly influenced the manner in which the transformation of humans into werewolves were portrayed in motion pictures.

Although in our own time we are familiar with an instant novelization appearing in the bookstores to accompany the latest Hollywood epic, it seems astonishing that in 1887, within a year after the publication of Stevenson's novella, Thomas Russell Sullivan had adapted *The Strange Case of Dr. Jekyll and Mr. Hyde* for the Boston theater. Richard Mansfield was the first actor to transform himself from the humanitarian scientist to the evil Hyde in a dramatic performance.

In 1908, William N. Selig, the first film producer to establish a studio in Hollywood, released the first motion picture version of Stevenson's story, its title now shortened to the more familiar *Dr. Jekyll and Mr. Hyde*. In 1909, a Danish film company released its version of the London doctor who experiments with a drug that frees the beast within to wreak chaos and death.

Carl Laemmle filmed the third production of the story in the United States in 1912, starring King Baggot and Jane Gail. By the time the great John Barrymore distorted his fabled matinee idol features to play the dual role of research chemist and monster in 1920, his interpretation was the seventh cinematic representation of *Dr. Jekyll and Mr. Hyde* —and four other film versions of the tale were released that same year.

An old Hollywood story has it that Barrymore, well known for his bawdy sense of humor, so loved his grotesque Mr. Hyde makeup that he decided to wear it while house hunting in Beverly Hills. He was concerned that property owners would raise their prices once they recognized his handsome profile, but if they encountered Mr. Hyde, they wouldn't be likely to spend a great deal of time bargaining.

The 1932 screen translation of Jekyll and Hyde starred the great actor Fredric March in the dual role, aided in the on-camera transformations by the genius of Wally Westmore's cosmetic magic. March won an Academy Award for his portrayal of Jekyll and Hyde, and in 1998, *Entertainment Weekly* listed this classic film, directed by Rouben Mamoulian, as number 73 on its assessment of the "Top 100 Science Fiction Movies."

Although Spencer Tracy was one of Hollywood's most dynamic actors and he was supported by an all-star MGM cast, including Donald Crisp, C. Aubrey Smith, Lana Turner, and the young Ingrid Bergman, the 1941 film doesn't quite reach the high-water mark in horror achieved by the March/Mamoulian motion picture.

Fredric March's portrayal of Mr. Hyde seems almost comic now, but it terrified audiences when the film came out in 1931.

Since the golden years of Barrymore, March, and Tracy, the classic Stevenson tale continues to fascinate audiences with its morality play of a decent man struggling to control the primeval monster within. Some of the recent efforts have included role reversals (*Dr. Jekyll and Sister Hyde*, 1972; *Dr. Jekyll and Ms. Hyde*, 1995), a musical (*Dr. Jekyll and Mr. Hyde*, made for television, 1973), spoofs (*The Nutty Professor*, 1963; *Dr. Heckyl and Mr. Hype*, 1980), a story told from the point of view of Dr. Jekyll's maid (*Mary Reilly*, 1996), and even one version wherein Dr. Jekyll becomes a werewolf (*Dr. Jekyll and the Werewolf*, 1971).

SOURCES:

Claren, Carlos. *An Illustrated History of the Horror Film.* New York: Capricorn Books, 1968.
Katz, Ephraim. *The Film Encyclopedia.* New York: Perigee, 1979.
Ruehl, Franklin, "Real-Life Jekyll & Hyde Haunts Pub," *National Examiner,* 22 October 1996.
Skal, David J. *The Monster Show.* New York: W.W. Norton, 1993.

Dracula

Bram Stoker's description of Count Dracula in his famous novel of the same name sounds as much like a member of the decadent aristocracy as a bloodthirsty member of the undead:

> His face was a strong—a very strong—aquiline, with a high bridge of the thin nose and peculiarly arched nostrils; with lofty domed forehead and hair growing scantily round the temples but profusely elsewhere. His eyebrows were very massive, almost meeting over the nose, and with bushy hair that seemed to curl in its own profusion. The mouth, so far as I could see it under the heavy mustache, was fixed and rather cruel-looking, with peculiarly sharp white teeth; these protruded over the lips, whose remarkable ruddiness showed astonishing vitality in a man of his years.

It is fascinating that, with such an accurate and detailed description of the immortal count provided by Stoker, no cinematic portrayal has ever really cast an actor that really looked like the Dracula that originally lurked in the dark side of the author's imagination. Many Dracula fans find it particularly strange that the "heavy mustache" has always been completely ignored. Of all the screen Draculas—and some of the portrayals have been creepily masterful—only John Carradine and **Lon Chaney Jr.** wore mustaches, though neither upper-lip adornment was at all a "heavy"one. Christopher Lee did not add the mustache to his otherwise extremely convincing physical impersonation of Dracula.

Bela Lugosi must be placed in a special category of achievement for his unique, aristocratic, formally attired Count Dracula. In a very real sense, in the collective unconscious of horror buffs, Lugosi's visage and demeanor will always be the archetypal image of the **vampire.** I would have to name Francis Ford Coppola's *Bram Stoker's Dracula* (1992) with Gary Oldman as Count

The legends of the Wolf Man and Dracula have intersected many times in Hollywood, as this scene from 1944's *Return of the Vampire* illustrates.

Dracula as the most accurate presentation of Stoker's original concepts—and for his depicting Dracula as a true shapeshifter, assuming the form of bat, wolf, demon, and varying stages and ages of his human self—including one characterization with a mustache!

"Historically, the werewolf is entwined with vampire beliefs," David J. Skal writes in *The Monster Show*. "Bram Stoker's Dracula, for instance, was unabashedly a werewolf as well as a blood-drinker. The werewolf theme was largely eliminated from *Dracula* stage adaptations, due to the difficulties of convincingly presenting such a total physical transformation in the theater. The vampire and the werewolf became discrete in the public mind."

While numerous books have been written in recent years demonstrating various proofs that the fifteenth-century Romanian ruler Vlad the Impaler served as the historical antecedent for Dracula, the impetus for the creation of the eternal count lies in the genius of Bram Stoker's imagination. Dracula is the quintessential vampire, the dark embodiment of hundreds of ancient fears and dreads compacted in one compelling and sinister figure. Werewolfdom has no such quintessential figure. There is no "Dracula" that comes instantly to mind as the essence of all werewolves.

Lawrence Talbot, of course, comes closest to fulfilling such a role—and horror buffs would undoubtedly name him as the first of the werewolf figures to capture the mass public's imagination. But Talbot and most of the other werewolves of popular culture are victims, helpless to combat the horror of the curse that has turned them into monsters. Perhaps there is no "Dracula" in werewolfdom because the werewolf can never attain the romantic and openly sexual fantasies associated with the vampire. Dracula doesn't whimper and complain over his dominion over the night. The sophisticated, elegant count does not search for a cure for his vampirism. The vampire of popular culture is in control of his fate, not its victim.

There is no such commanding Dracula figure in the popular depictions of the werewolf because those truly seized by the power of lycanthropy are drenched in the **blood** of real people— they are the mass murderers, the serial killers, the true monsters among us. The werewolf represents the beast within, the savagery, the bloodlust, the ripper, the slasher, the sadist that too many of us are aware lies too near the surface of the psyche. While we may be amused with the children on Halloween who drape cloaks around their little shoulders and declare themselves vampires or with those who stick cotton "fur" balls on their cheeks and howl at the moon like Lawrence Talbot–type gentle werewolves, there would be little tolerance for the children who, enacting true lycanthropes, brandish rubber knives dripping stage blood and become make-believe serial killers on All Hallows' Eve.

SOURCES:

Clarens, Carlos. *An Illustrated History of the Horror Film.* New York: Capricorn Books, 1968.

Melton, J. Gordon. *The Vampire Book: The Encyclopedia of the Undead.* Farmington Hills: Visible Ink Press, 1998.

Skal, David J. *The Monster Show.* New York: Boulevard, 1997.

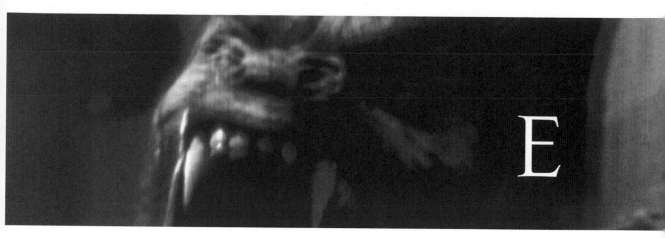

E

Eisler, Robert (1904–1949)

Robert Eisler, author of *Man into Wolf* (c. 1950), had a distinguished and tragic life. Born in Vienna in 1904, educated there and in Leipzig, he gained his degrees and his doctorates *summa cum laude*. He was a Fellow of the Austrian Historical Institute, traveled widely, and visited the excavations at Ephesus, Miletus, and Knossos.

From 1925 to 1931, Eisler worked with the League of Nations in Paris and lectured at the Sorbonne University on the origins of Christianity. He returned to his native Austria and spent the next six years doing research. In 1938, he had just received a position teaching comparative religion at Oxford when he was arrested by the Gestapo.

After 15 months in Buchenwald and Dachau, he was released and permitted to travel to England to accept the position at Oxford. Although he lectured at the university for nearly two years, the terrible results of the treatment that he had endured in the concentration camps began to take their toll on his body. By now the war was in full fury, and he remained in England, continuing to research and write, until his death in 1949.

The author of many works in German, Eisler's final achievement was *Man into Wolf: An Anthropological Interpretation of Sadism, Masochism, and Lycanthropy* in which he sought to demonstrate that all violence, from individual rape and murder to collective organized war, stems from an ancestral memory of humankind's prehistoric descent from timid vegetarian to savage, meat-and-blood eating lycanthrope. Eisler was convinced that humankind's collective consciousness—and conscience—had expressed its guilt all over the world in its legends, myths, and psycho-religious rites.

SOURCES:

Eisler, Robert. *Man into Wolf*. London: Spring Books, n.d.

El Sisemite

In the mythology of the Guatemalan Indians the monster known as *El Sisemite* is said to be taller than the tallest man and is described as being a cross between a man and a monkey. El Sisemite is believed to be strong enough to break down the biggest trees in the forest and to sprout hair thick enough to withstand a hunter's bullet. The Guatemalan tribes accuse El Sisemite as having designs of their women and there are numerous accounts of village females being carried off by the man-beast. Male tribe members may be crushed and pummeled to death if they are unfortunate enough to encounter one of the giants when it feels like a bit of fresh **blood** and sport.

Tribal folklore says that El Sisemite kidnaps children and takes them to the privacy of his cave, where he hopes they will teach him how to speak. Legend also has it that the jungle giant envies the tribal peoples' mastery of fire, for hunters have found much evidence to indicate that El Sisemite warms itself by campfires that have been deserted by humans.

SOURCES:
Norman, Eric. *The Abominable Snowmen.* New York: Award Books, 1969.

Elementals

The elementary spirits, the so-called elementals, are the unseen intelligences who inhabit the four basic elements of the material plane. The creatures of the air are known as sylphs; of the earth, gnomes; of fire, salamanders; and of water, the nymphs or undines. According to ancient occult tradition, before the Fall from Grace, Adam had complete control over these entities. After the Fall, in the Garden of Eden, Adam lost his easy access to the elementals, but he was still able to command their obedience by means of certain incantations and spells. That same ancient tradition suggests that such communication with the unseen entities can be established by the sincere magician who seeks out the old spells. Others say that the ancient incantations are not necessary at all. All that is required to gain the support of the elementals is to recognize their presence and powers and to live openly in a manner that indicates that the magician is respectful, but unafraid, of the forces of nature.

When discerned by the human eye, the elementals appear as attractive males and beautiful females. Because they are created from the pure essences of their element, they may live for centuries; but because they were fashioned from terrestrial elements, their souls are not immortal, as are those of humans. If, however, an elemental should be joined in marriage to a human, their union can transform the creature's soul into a spirit that may enjoy eternal life. Some of the greatest figures of antiquity, such as Zoroaster, Alexander, Merlin, and Hercules, were reported to have been the children of elementary spirits.

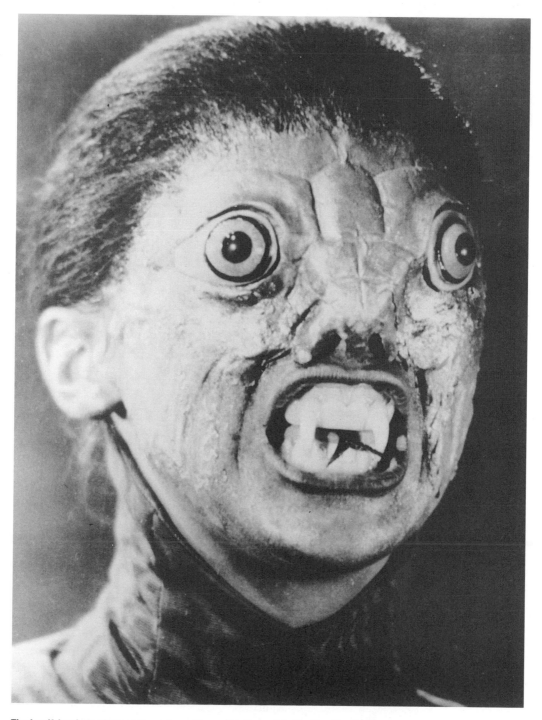

The horrifying face of the snake woman (Jacqueline Pearce) in the film *The Reptile*.

While most traditions hold the elementals to be friendly to humans and in general benignly disposed to providing assistance to righteous endeavors, whether or not they are seen or unseen, some authorities warn that each of the four elements contains a number of mischief makers and entities that tend more toward the demonic than the angelic.

SOURCES:

Hazlitt, W. C. *Dictionary of Faiths & Folklore.* London: Studio Editions, 1995.

Spence, Lewis. *An Encyclopedia of Occultism.* New Hyde Park, NY: University Books, 1960.

Endore, Guy (1900–1970)

When Guy Endore attended Columbia University in the early 1920s and his classmates first began to perceive his literary talents—together with his aureole of blond hair—they began to describe him as the present incarnation of the young English poet Percy Shelley. Although Endore preferred the sciences, he excelled in the humanities and was a member of a group of young intellectuals who included such future literary luminaries as Clifton Fadiman, Mortimer Adler, Edgar Johnson, and Henry Morton Robinson. It is unlikely, though, that any of his classmates in Columbia's class of 1924 knew that Endore's childhood had known desperate poverty.

When he was just a small boy in Brooklyn, New York, his mother died, and his father sent him, with his brother and three sisters, to a Methodist orphanage in Ohio. Later, family circumstances dramatically improved to the point where their father took them to Vienna, Austria. Here, however, rather than discovering comfort and peace of mind, Endore's father left his children with a French governess and then mysteriously disappeared.

For five years, the governess fulfilled her responsibility to her vanished employer and saw to it that the young Americans were trained in scholarly ways in the rigorous elementary schools and *gymnasia* of Vienna. And then the funds ran out. The governess appealed to the United States consulate to intervene and the Endore children were restored to their father who had taken residence in Pittsburgh, Pennsylvania. Guy enrolled in Schenley High School and the Carnegie Institute of Technology in Pittsburgh before his acceptance at Columbia.

Soon after his graduation, he married his wife Henrietta and managed to support himself, his wife, and eventually a child by doing translations from French and German. His first book, published in 1929, was a biography of Casanova. His second was a study of Joan of Arc. In 1933, he published the famous horror tale, *The Werewolf of Paris.*

Endore, his wife, and two daughters Marcia and Gita survived the Great Depression by answering Hollywood's call to come to Los Angeles and write scripts for motion pictures. Endore subsequently wrote scripts for all the major studios and worked on a number of horror films, including *The Mark of the Vampire* (1936). Although Endore's werewolf novel is credited as the inspiration for *The Werewolf of London* (1935) and *Curse of the Werewolf* (1961), it actually bears very little resemblance to either one of the cinematic treatments. Endore's wolfman is based on the actual case of **Sgt. Francois Bertrand,** who was truly more ghoul than werewolf.

Endore wrote a number of novels after his stint at the studios, including *Methinks the Lady* (1945) and *The King of Paris* (1956).

SOURCES:

Endore, Guy. *The King of Paris.* New York: Simon and Schuster, 1956.

Melton, J. Gordon. *The Vampire Book: The Encyclopedia of the Undead.* Farmington Hills: Visible Ink Press, 1998.

Enkidu

Perhaps our earliest written record of a man-beast appears on a Babylonian fragment c. 2000 B.C. that tells the story of King Gilgamesh and his werewolf-like friend, Enkidu. *The Epic of Gilgamesh* remains to date the oldest known literary work in the world. Although it comprises 12 cantos of about 300 verses each, ancient records indicate that the original epic was at least twice as long as its present length.

Pieced together from 30,000 fragments discovered in the library at Ninevah in 1853, the story tells of Gilgamesh, the legendary Sumerian king of Uruk, and his quest for immortality. At first perceiving the physical aspect of his quest to lie in perpetuating his seed, Gilgamesh becomes such a lustful monarch that no woman in his kingdom is safe from his advances. The goddess Aruru, assessing the situation, decides to take matters into her own hands, and she forms the man-beast Enkidu from clay and her spittle in order to create an opponent powerful enough to challenge Gilgamesh.

Gilgamesh soon learns of this hairy wildman of the desert who protects the beasts from all those who would hunt in his desolate domain, and the king begins to have uncomfortable dreams of wrestling with a strong opponent whom he could not defeat. Gilgamesh sends a woman into the wilderness to seduce the wild man-beast and to tame him. She accomplishes her mission, teaching him such social graces as wearing clothing and other amenities of civilization as they wind their way to Uruk. When Enkidu eventually arrives in the city, the two giants engage in fierce hand-to-hand combat. The king manages to throw the man-beast, but instead of killing him, the two become fast friends, combining their strength to battle formidable giants and even the gods themselves. It is the jealous goddess Ishtar who causes the fatal illness that leads to Enkidu's death.

Ghoulish cast of the camp horror classic *The Rats Are Coming! The Werewolves Are Here!*

Gilgamesh finally abandons his search for immortality when the goddess Siduri Sabitu, dispenser of the wine of immortality to the gods, confides in him that his quest will forever be in vain—the cruel gods have decreed that all mortals shall die. Each day should be treasured, she advises, and one should enjoy the good things of life—a wife, family, friends, eating, and drinking.

SOURCES:

Brown, Calvin S., ed. *The Reader's Companion to World Literature.* New York: New American Library, 1956.

Gordon, Stuart. *The Encyclopedia of Myths and Legends.* London: Headline Books, 1993.

Ethnology of the Werewolf

In the beginning of the thirteenth century, Gervase of Tillbury wrote in Latin in his *Otia Imperialia* that "In English they say *werewolf,* for in English *were* means man, and *wolf* means wolf." In Medieval Latin, werewolf was written *guerulfus.*

In Scandinavia, the Norwegian counterpart to werewolf is *vargulf*, which, literally translated, is "rogue wolf." In Swedish, *varulf*; in Danish, *vaerulf*. The Norse words *ulfhedhnar* ("wolf-clothed") and *ber-werker* (in German, *baren-hauter*) refer to the skins worn by the dreaded Northern warriors when they went berserk, war-mad, running amuck among their opponents.

In other regions of Europe, there is the Medieval Norman, garwalf; in Norman-French, **loup-garou**; in Portugal, *lobarraz*; in Italy, *upo-manaro*; in Calabria, *lupu-minaru*; and in Sicily, *lupu minaru*.

In the Slavonic languages, the werewolf is called *vlukodlak*, literally, "wolf haired" or "wolf-skinned." In Bulgaria, *vulkolak*; in Poland, wilkolak; in Russia, *olkolka* or *volkulaku*; in Serbia, *vulkodlak*.

In modern Greek, the word *brukolakas* or *bourkolakas* can apply to vampires as well as werewolves, since it is adapted from a Slavic word for a creature that flies or attacks by night.

SOURCES:

Eisler, Robert. *Man into Wolf.* London: Spring Books, n.d.

Simek, Rudolf. *Dictionary of Northern Mythology.* Translated by Angela Hall. Rochester, NY: Boydell & Brewer, 1993.

Spence, Lewis. *An Encyclopedia of Occultism.* New Hyde Park, NY: University Books, 1960.

Exorcism

During his Sunday, March 4, 1990, sermon at St. Patrick's Cathedral in New York City, Cardinal John O'Connor stated that diabolically instigated violence is on the rise around the world, and he disclosed that two church-sanctioned exorcisms had been performed in the New York area within that past year.

Cardinal O'Connor went on to say that William Peter Blatty's novel *The Exorcist* by was a gruesomely authentic portrayal of demonic **possession**:

> Perhaps the only exposure that most people have to the concept of exorcism is derived from that popular novel and motion picture—and perhaps the majority of those who read the book or shuddered through the chilling cinematic version believe that such demonic manifestations and such rites of exorcism exist only in the lively imagination of authors of horror novels. Those people could not be further from the truth.

Ed and Lorraine Warren of the New England Society for Psychic Research revealed that they had been present during the two violent exorcisms referred to by Cardinal O'Connor. The first exorcism involved a woman who howled like a wolf, vomited vile fluid from her mouth, and levitated about a foot off the floor while the priests and their assistants tried to hold her down. The second case was that of a woman who had been into drugs and who joined a satanic cult. She spoke in the deep, rough voice of a vulgar, profane man, and she struggled against her exorcists with such strength that seven

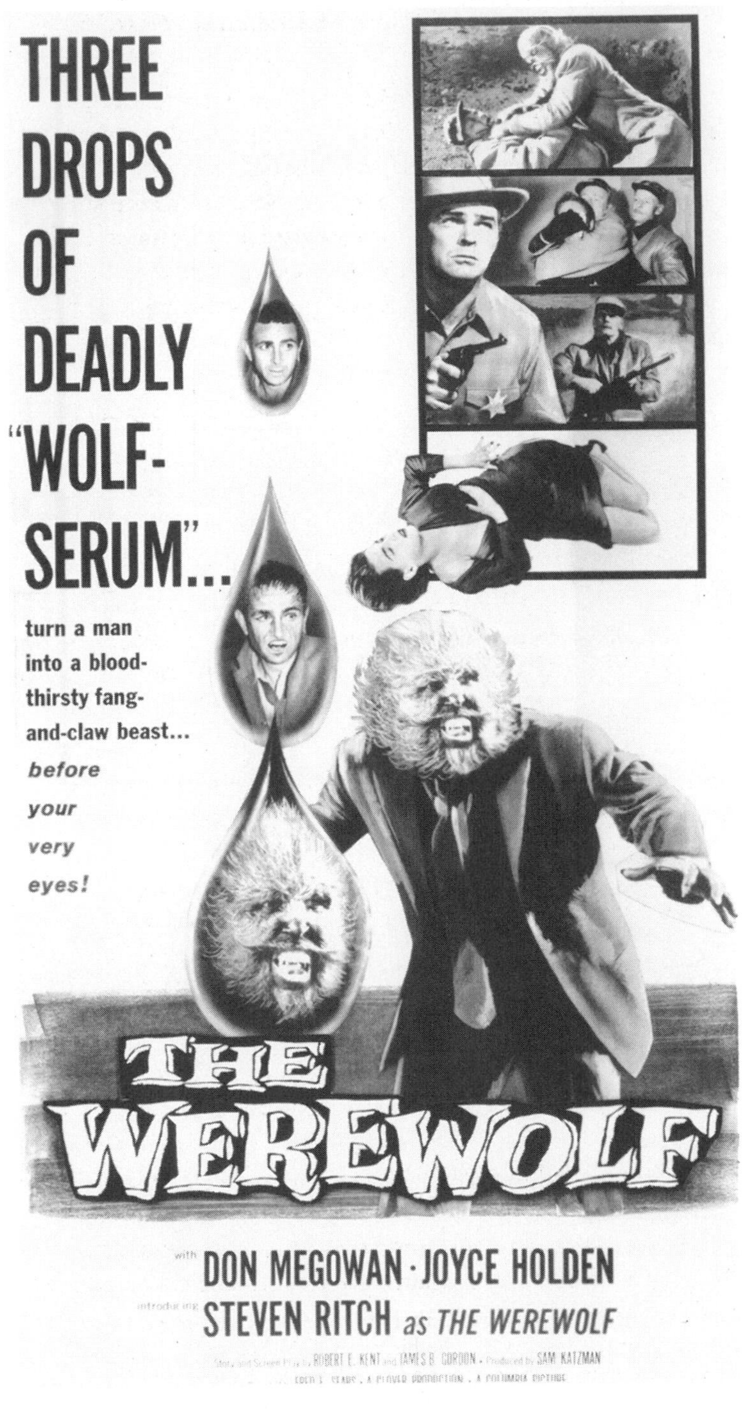

Movie poster from the film *The Werewolf*.

people could not restrain her. She, too, snarled like some monstrous beast, levitated, and vomited vile fluids.

On December 30, 1998, *The Guardian* (London) reported that Christian clergy are increasingly being called upon to conduct exorcisms to rid people of evil spirits. The Church of England and the Roman Catholic Church declined the opportunity to make an official comment, but they did admit that every diocese has dedicated staff experienced in dealing with exorcism. While some clerics are embarrassed by critics who claim the entire subject hearkens back to the Middle Ages, priests throughout the Western world are coping with steadily growing demands for exorcism and requests to drive away evil spirits from the afflicted.

Rev. Peter Irwin-Clark, an evangelical Anglican priest in Brighton and a former lawyer, brushes off criticism of such work by reminding his detractors of the frequent references in the New Testament to demonic possession and the commandments of Christ to his followers to cast out evil spirits.

The Church of England has established the Christian Deliverance Study Group for the purpose of examining the issues of exorcism and demon possession. In order to divert criticism by mental health professionals that evil spirits are more likely to have their origin in psychiatric disorders than Satan, the church has issued guidelines that advise priests to work in close cooperation with medically trained professionals.

Rev. Tom Willis, an authorized Church of England exorcist for more than 30 years in the York diocese, told *The Guardian* that his experiences have convinced him that about one in 10 people see a ghost in their lifetime:

> People see apparitions, objects moving around, they experience being tapped on their shoulder, doors opening or strange smells. I've seen objects disappearing and reappearing in a neighboring room. It's not clear to me whether this is an offshoot of the human mind—some sort of stress leaking out—or if it is something using human energy. I've had the experience of poltergeists reading my mind. It can be quite frightening.

In their remarkable book, *Werewolf: A True Story of Demonic Possession*, Ed and Lorraine Warren recount the exorcism of **Bill Ramsey,** a man possessed with the spirit of a werewolf, by Bishop Robert McKenna. The Warrens were in attendance, along with a number of journalists and four off-duty policemen, especially hired by the bishop to defend him from the werewolf's violent attacks. They report the following scenario during the course of the exorcism, when Bishop McKenna placed his crucifix against Ramsey's forehead:

> . . . the werewolf inside him went berserk. He came up from his chair, snarling and growling at the bishop . . . the bishop had no choice but to retreat beyond the altar gate. [Ramsey] spittle flying from his mouth, eyes wild, began to rush through the gate . . . But the priest stood absolutely still now, holding his cross up once again and beginning to speak in Latin . . .

> [Ramsey] felt suddenly weak . . . he felt his desire to attack the Bishop begin
> to fade . . . the werewolf's power was slipping quickly away. A faint roar
> sounded in [Ramsey's] chest, then faded. He brought up his hands, but they
> were no longer clawlike. They were merely hands. . . .

Father Pellegrino Ernetti, an exorcist with the Vatican, has stated that
some people actually do make pacts with Satan in order to become powerful
werewolf-like creatures and to gain material success on earth. He tells of a
young French boxer who made such a pact after his career in the ring had
proven to be very disappointing. After he allowed the beast to come into him,
he was soon winning bout after bout— but then he still had the conscience to
realize that his opponents very often were severely injured or disabled after
fighting with him.

Father Ernetti said that the young boxer had the courage to come to him
for help, and after a difficult series of exorcisms he was able to drive the beast
from his body. Now the man leads a happy, normal life as a garage mechanic
in Paris.

For the first time since 1614, the Vatican issued new guidelines for exorcism in January 1999. The new rite of exorcism is written in Latin and contained in a red, leather-bound, 84-page book, and it very much reflects Pope
John Paul II's efforts to convince a skeptical, materialistic generation that
Satan is alive, well, and very much in the world. As Cardinal Jorge Medina
Estevez, a Vatican official put it, "The existence of the devil isn't an opinion,
something to take or leave as you wish."

Although the revisions do not drastically alter the words or the gestures
to be used by the exorcists, the update does provide optional texts that may be
utilized by the priests. And the new guidelines stress that the priest must be
certain that the afflicted is not suffering from a mental illness or the excesses
of his or her own imagination.

SOURCES:

D'emilio, Frances. "Vatican Updates Rules for Exorcisms." Associated Press. January 26, 1999.

"Clergy Responds to an Increasing Demand for Exorcisms." *The Guardian* (London), December 30, 1998.

Steiger, Brad, and Sherry Hansen Steiger. *Demon Deaths*. New York: Berkley Publishing, 1991.

Warren, Ed, and Lorraine Warren. *Werewolf: A True Story of Demonic Possession*. New York: St. Martin's Press, 1993.

Explanations for Lycanthropy

Quite understandably, contemporary medical professionals seek to offer rational explanations for the werewolves that have scourged the past and haunted
the present. The word *lycanthropy* (from the Greek, literally, wolfman) was
used by Reginald Scot in his *The Discovery of Witchcraft* (1584) to denote an
extreme form of violent insanity in which the individual may imitate the

behavior of a wild beast, especially a wolf. Scot argued against the church and the Inquisition and its institutionalized program of torturing and burning of witches, werewolves, and other shapeshifters; and he nearly ended up bound to a stake for his heretical efforts on behalf of reason. Scot used the term in the same manner as a modern health professional when referring to the mental disease that manifests itself in ways applicable to werewolfism.

The term lycanthropy was also applied to those individuals afflicted with a form of dark melancholy, a deep depression that gave rise to a violent form of insanity. In his *Anatomy of Melancholy* (1621), Robert Burton writes that those men and women who are suffering from an advanced form of melancholy that graduates into werewolfism lie hidden throughout the daylight hours, then "go abroad in the night, barking, howling, at graves . . . they have unusually hollow eyes, scabbed legs and thighs, very dry and pale."

Dr. Mary Matossian, professor of history at the University of Maryland, viewed such statistics as those from France which proclaim that 30,000 individuals were condemned as werewolves between the years of 1520 to 1630 and wondered how such a mental aberration could possibly have been so widespread. As she researched the phenomenon, she derived a theory that the peasants were eating a rye bread that was contaminated by a fungus that acted as a powerful hallucinogenic. In essence, Dr. Matossian suggested that thousands of men and women were suffering from "bad trips" from a potent fungus that caused them to have delusions that they were magical beings capable of transforming themselves into werewolves.

According to Dr. Matossian:

> The fungus was ergot, a parasite that attacks rye. The ergot produces *sclerotia* which grow on the rye plant, taking the place of its natural seeds. The wind blows and the fungus latches onto other rye plants. . . . During harvesting, the ergot was collected along with the grain and became part of the bread. Since ergot is like today's LSD, some individuals suffered bad trips and imagined themselves being transformed into animals, such as **wolves.** Others saw themselves with special powers, like flying on a broomstick. They were the witches.

> The ergot caused them to act in other bizarre ways, even committing murder and injury. As a result, numerous victims of ergot poisoning were tried as wolves and werewolves—and executed. With the advent of modern methods of cleaning and processing grain, ergot was eliminated—along with **the appearance of werewolves** and witches.

An interesting theory, but Dr. Matossian should take a better look around the contemporary scene if she believes there are no witches gathering in covens in the 1990s. And she had better look carefully over her shoulder if she believes that werewolves no longer prowl the night—whether in the embodiment of the mentally ill, serial killers, or true lycanthropes.

Sherilynn Fenn is visited by a werewolf-like beast in the 1990 film *Meridian: Kiss of the Beast*.

In the *Canadian Psychiatric Association Journal* in 1975, psychiatrists Frida Surawicz and Richard Banta of Lexington, Kentucky, published their paper "Lycanthropy Revisited" in which they presented two case studies of contemporary werewolves.

Their first case, that of Mr. H., obliquely supported Dr. Matossian's hallucinogenic hypothesis in that Mr. H had ingested LSD before he saw himself changing into a werewolf. He saw fur growing over his hands and face, and he craved flesh and **blood.** Even after the effects of the drug had supposedly worn off, Mr. H. still believed he was a werewolf. He was treated as a paranoid schizophrenic, treated with antipsychotic medication, and after about five weeks, released from a psychiatric unit.

Surawicz and Banta's second case study was that of a 37-year-old farmer, who, after his discharge from the navy, began allowing his hair to grow long and began sleeping in cemeteries and howling at the moon. Although there was no indication of drug abuse or misuse in Mr. W.'s case, he was freed from his delusion after treatment with antipsychotic medication.

Psychiatrist Harvey Rosenstock and psychologist Kenneth Vincent discuss their case history of a 49-year-old woman who underwent the metamorphosis into a werewolf in their paper, "A Case of Lycanthropy," published in the *American Journal of Psychiatry* in 1977. Although she finally was admitted to a locked psychiatric unit and received daily psychotherapy and antipsychotic drugs, she still beheld herself as a wolfwoman with claws, teeth, and fangs and believed that her werewolf spirit would roam the earth long after her physical death. Medical personnel would manage to get the woman under control until the next **full moon.** At that time, she would snarl, howl, and resume her wolflike behavior. She was eventually discharged and provided with antipsychotic medication, but she promised to haunt the graveyards until she found the tall, dark, hairy creature of her dreams.

And speaking of hairy creatures, according to Brian K. Hall, a developmental biologist at Dalhousie University in Nova Scotia, Canada, a team of scientists recently discovered a gene that may make certain people extra hairy and appear very much like the classic Hollywood werewolves. Doctors at the Baylor College of Medicine in Houston, Texas, took blood samples from 19 people whose faces and upper bodies were entirely covered with thick, dark hair. The samples spanned five generations of a single family and revealed that their DNA includes a mutant gene that was responsible for a condition known as congenital generalized hypertrichosis.

While all humans possess the "hairy gene," Hall maintains, it is dormant in most people. The tendency to produce hair that covers the entire face and upper torso may be "an evolutionary trait left over from our **animal ances-**

tors." The discovery that the gene still exists in a dormant state in all people and manifests as super hairiness in a small number, Hall says, "tells us that our body stores a lot of genetic information for a long time."

In his *Bizarre Diseases of the Mind*, Dr. Richard Noll lists the traditional traits of lycanthropes:

- The belief that they are wolves or wild dogs.
- The belief that they have been physically transformed into animals with fur and claws.
- Animal-like behavior, including growling, howling, clawing, pawing, crawling on all fours, and offering oneself in the sexual postures of a female animal.
- The desire to assault or kill others.
- Hypersexuality, including the desire to have sex with animals.
- Use of a hallucinogenic substance to achieve the metamorphosis of human into wolf.
- A desire for isolation from human society (stalking the woods, haunting cemeteries).
- The belief that "the devil" has possessed the afflicted werewolf and provided the power that causes the transformation from human to wolf.

The March 1999 issue of *Discover* magazine reported the hypothesis of neurologist Juan Gomez-Alonso of the Xeral Hospital in Vigo, Spain, who suggests that tales of vampires and werewolves could be inspired by people who suffered from rabies. He traced the connection between a rabies outbreak in central Europe in the early eighteenth century shortly before tales of the undead and shapeshifters began circulating. According to Gomez-Alonso: "Some of the symptoms, such as aggressiveness and hypersexuality, would not have been seen as manifestations of a disease. Uneducated people could have thought all this was the work of a malign being. Moreover, the bizarre rejection of some stimuli—odors, light, water, and mirrors—shown by rabid humans must have been quite puzzling."

SOURCES:
Jones, Linda. "Werewolf Gene Found." *Science World,* October 20, 1995.
Noll, Richard. *Bizarre Diseases of the Mind.* New York: Berkley Books, 1990.
Ruehl, Franklin, "Real Reason Werewolves and Witches Haunted Europe," *National Examiner,* April 6, 1997.

F

Familiars

How bizarre that in one culture it is perfectly acceptable for everyone to acknowledge a totem animal or a spirit guide, while in another an individual can be burned at the stake for professing a similar concept. During the same historical period when all good little European children said their prayers and beseeched 14 angels to keep watch over them while they slept, innocent men and women were being tortured to death for being suspected of calling upon other spirit entities to help them cure their neighbors of diseases.

The concept of certain spirit beings who assist a magician or a witch undoubtedly hearkens back to the totem animal guides that attended the ancient **shamans,** for the familiars express themselves most often in animal forms. The black cat, for instance, has become synonymous in popular folklore as the traditional companion of the witch. Attendant upon such a sorcerer as the legendary Cornelius Agrippa is the **black dog** or the dark-haired wolf.

The ancient Greeks called upon the *predrii,* spirit beings who were ever at hand to provide assistance to the physicians or magicians. In Rome, the seers and soothsayers asked their *familiares* or *magistelli* to lend a little supernatural assistance. In many lands where the Christian missionaries planted their faith, various saints provided an acceptable substitute for the ancient practice of asking favors or help from the totem animal. Interestingly, many of the saints of Christendom are identified by an animal symbol, for example, the dog with St. Bernard; the lion with St. Mark; the stag with St. Eustace; and the crow with St. Anthony. However, in those regions where the country folk and rural residents persisted in calling upon their familiars, the church decreed the spirit beings to be **demons** sent by Satan to undermine the work of the clergy. All those accused of possessing a familiar or relying on it for guidance or assistance were forced to recant such an association or be in danger of the torture chamber and the stake.

While the wolf became the symbol for such Christian spiritual illuminaries as St. Francis of Assisi and St. Edmund of East Anglia, for the common folk, to maintain the wolf as one's personal totem was proof of their desire to be transformed into a werewolf.

SOURCES:

Hazlitt, W. C. *Dictionary of Faiths & Folklore*. London: Studio Editions, 1995.

Spence, Lewis. *An Encyclopedia of Occultism*. New Hyde Park, NY: University Books, 1960.

Steiger, Brad. *Totems: The Transformative Power of Your Personal Animal Totem*. San Francisco: HarperSanFrancisco, 1997.

Fenrir

When Garmr, the hound of hell, breaks free and begins its awful baying, Fenrir, the wolf child of the giantess Angrboda and the god Loki, will snap its fetters and devour the father of the gods, Odin, before Vioarr can protect him. All of these events signal the onset of Ragnarok (in Old Norse, "the final destiny of the gods"), the destruction of the old world and the old gods. Vioarr, the strongest of the gods after Thor, appears soon after Odin has been killed by Fenrir, and he avenges him by grasping the wolf's jaws in his hands and ripping its mouth apart. Fenrir dies, and Vioarr joins the generation of gods who will live in the new world.

In some accounts of the myth of Ragnarok, Loki fathered three children by his dalliance with the giantess Angrboda—Fenrir, the wolf-child, the Midgard serpent, and Hel. The gods decided to rear the wolf, but when Fenrir grew too strong for them to handle comfortably, they decided to bind him. The werewolf easily broke his fetters until dwarfs at last managed to create a chain that he could not shatter until he regained his freedom at Ragnarok, the end of the old world.

In certain tellings of the onset of Ragnarok, Gamr and Fenrir become one wolf that rips free of its chains and kills Odin. In other accounts, Gamr is also a wolf, and when Fenrir is freed, one of them swallows the sun, the other, the moon. Still other versions allow Gamr and Fenrir to assume their traditional roles in the drama and assign the names Skoll and Hati to the two **wolves** who devour the sun and the moon.

SOURCES:

Davidson, Ellis H. R. *Gods and Myths of the Viking Age*. New York: Barnes & Noble, 1996.

Simek, Rudolf. *Dictionary of Northern Mythology*. Translated by Angela Hall. Rochester, NY: Boydell & Brewer, 1993.

Carl Schell is about to burst out of his suit as he transforms into a werewolf in the 1961 film *Werewolf in a Girl's Dormitory*.

Fish, Albert (1870–1935)

Albert Fish was a sadistic werewolf, a cannibal, and a **vampire** who was believed to have killed, eaten, and drunk the **blood** of between eight and 15 children. He also castrated a number of small boys, somehow believing in his demented rationale that he was paying homage to Abraham's near-sacrifice of his son, Isaac. In addition, official estimates tallied that Fish had molested more than 100 children before his criminal career was finally terminated.

Born in 1870 in Washington, D.C., Fish came from a family were nearly every member was mentally unbalanced. Systematically whipped and abused as a small boy, Fish grew to become erotically stimulated by the cruel treatment. Later, he justified his murders by proclaiming himself to be Christ returned, administering God's vengeance upon a sinful and depraved humanity. His killings, he explained, were really sacrifices that spared the chosen children from living a life of depravity and sin that would have led to their eternal damnation.

For six years after one of his most heinous crimes—the murder, dismemberment, and eating of 10-year-old Grace Budd—Fish continued to send obscene letters to the girl's parents, describing in perverse detail the sadistic acts that he had performed upon their daughter. It was this series of profane correspondence that led to Fish's eventual capture.

The monster died in the electric chair without showing any signs of fear of his own mortality. It was witnessed that he even helped the attendants adjust the straps and apparatus as he sat in the chair awaiting the moment when the warden pulled the lever.

SOURCES:
Masters, R. E. L., and Eduard Lea. *Perverse Crimes in History.* New York: The Julian Press, 1963.

Dion Fortune's Werewolf

Dion Fortune, the author of the occult classic *Psychic Self-Defense* (1957) defines the "psychic parasitism" and "psychic vampirism" that can result from any relationship in which one of the partners "feeds" upon the energy of the other. Such a psychic drain may occur between friends or lovers, marriage partners, parents and children, and supervisors and employees in the workplace. Ms. Fortune was a pupil of J. W. Brodie-Innes, one of the leaders of the Golden Dawn, and she later formed The Fraternity of the Inner Light.

In her book *Psychic Self-Defense*, she tells how on one occasion she inadvertently created a werewolf with a powerful projection of her will. She had been lying in bed in that familiar altered state of consciousness wherein one is half-awake and half-asleep, brooding over her resentment against someone she was convinced had deliberately slandered her. In an interesting flow of thought progression, she considered throwing off all restraints and going berserk, like the Viking warriors of old. Then came the thought of **Fenrir,** the powerful and evil "judgment day" wolf of Norse mythology.

"Immediately I felt a curious drawing-out sensation from my solar plexus," she writes, "and there materialized beside me on the bed was a large wolf."

When she appeared about to move, the wolf snarled at her; and she admitted that it required all of the courage she could muster to order it off her bed. At last, the creature went meekly from the bed, turned into a dog, and vanished through the wall in the northern corner of the room. The next morning, Fortune said, someone else in the house spoke of dreaming of **wolves** and having awakened in the night to see the eyes of a wild animal glowing in the dark.

SOURCES:
Cavendish, Richard. *The Powers of Evil.* New York: G. P. Putnam's Sons, 1975.

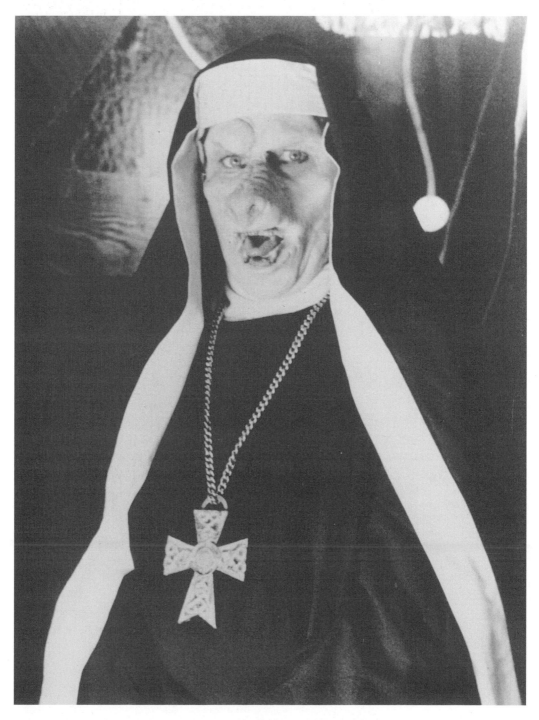

A disturbing scene featuring an odd werewolf in *The Howling 3: The Marsupials.*

Fox Maidens of Japan

The seventeenth-century scholar P'u Sung Ling devoted his life to collecting and recording accounts of the fox maidens of Japan. One such story is that of the encounter of a young man named Sang.

Late one night Sang heard a knock at his door. When he allowed the unexpected visitor to enter his home, he was astonished to behold a girl of such great beauty that his heart began immediately to pound. When she identified herself as Lien Shiang, a singing girl from the red light district of the village, Sang allowed his passion to take full control of his senses and he made love to the beautiful girl until dawn. Lien Shiang left at sunrise, but she promised to return to him every fourth or fifth night.

On one of those nights when Sang was not expecting Lien Shiang, he sat alone, deeply engrossed in his studies. When he glanced up from his work, he was startled to see that a very young, very elegant girl with long, flowing hair stood watching him. For a nervous moment, Sang wondered if she might be one of the fox maidens about whom he had so often heard eerie tales. The lovely girl laughed and promised him that she was not such a creature. Her name was Lee, and she came from a very honorable family.

When Sang took her proffered hand and led her to a comfortable cushion, he could not help noticing how cold she felt. She quickly explained that she had been chilled by the evening frost as she walked to his house. Lee went on to astonish Sang by her admission that she had fallen in love with him from afar and that she had decided to sacrifice her virginity to him that very night. Hardly able to believe his good fortune, the young student enjoyed an evening of rapture with the beautiful and highly responsive girl.

Before she left the next morning, she forthrightly asked Sang if there were any other women in his life. The student admitted his liaison with Lien Shiang, and Lee became very serious when she stated that she must be careful to avoid the other girl, because they were of very different classes. Then she presented Sang with one of her shoes, whispering that whenever he touched it, she would know that he was thinking of her. But before she left in the mist of dawn, she admonished him never to take the shoe out when Lien Shiang was there with him.

The next evening, when he paused in his studies, Sang took the shoe from its hiding place and began to stroke it lovingly, his thoughts filled with the memory of the lovely Lee. Within moments, she was at his side. After their embrace, Sang wondered aloud how she had come to his home so quickly, but Lee only smiled and evaded the question.

A few nights later, when Lien Shiang was visiting Sang, she looked at her lover carefully and bluntly told him that he did not appear to be well. When the student replied that there was nothing wrong with him, Lien told him that she would not return for 10 nights.

During that period, Lee came to Sang's home every night; and on the tenth night, she hid herself nearby to see what her rival, Lien Shiang, looked like. And she was near enough to the house when Lien told Sang that he looked terrible, that he must be suffering from spirit sickness. She could perceive that he had been making love to a ghost.

And now the two different classes of spirit entities are revealed. Lee appears and warns Sang that Lien Shiang is a fox maiden. Lien admits the charge, and she confidently informs Sang that there is no danger in a human making love to a fox maiden every four or five days. On the other hand, if he were to make love to a ghost, his health would soon be debilitated and he would eventually die. Lee, Lien Shiang accuses, is a ghost—and Sang's life is in great danger.

Sang, who truly has weakened his body by making love to both a fox maiden and a ghost, collapses and falls desperately ill. But this story from old Japan is not a tale in which the werefox and the ghost gleefully claim their victim. Both of the supernatural women set about nursing the young student back to health. Lee confesses that even though she is a ghost, she has fallen deeply in love with Sang. Because she realizes that her presence is detrimental to her lover, she will make the great sacrifice and leave his house forever.

The story by P'u Sung Ling has a happy, if somewhat bizarre, ending. Lee comes upon a household in which a beautiful young girl has just died. She takes over the body and returns to Sang as a flesh and **blood** woman. As soon as Sang is fully recovered, he marries Lee. Lien Shiang remains in the household until she bears a son. Once she has delivered the child, she dies and returns to her true form of a fox. Ten years later, though, following Lee's example, Lien Shiang's spirit finds the suitable body of a young woman and she returns to Sang and Lee—and the three of them live happily ever after.

SOURCES:
Hurwood, Bernardt J. *Vampires, Werewolves, and Ghouls*. New York: Ace Books, 1968.
Larousse Dictionary of World Folklore. New York: Larousse, 1995.

Fox People

Northern China has a tradition of werefoxes who inhabit the netherworld between the material plane and the unseen dimensions. In their human form they appear as very attractive girls and young men—occasionally betrayed by their tails popping out of their clothing. The male werefoxes and the female werevixens can mate with human partners, but for a man or woman to do so may result in a zombie-like servitude. The werefoxes animal shape is often revealed as they sleep or when they have had too much alcohol to drink.

In Japan, the werefox, *nogitsone*, is a shapeshifter that can assume any form that suits its nefarious purposes. The werefox is always betrayed by its reflection in a mirror or a pool of water. Some werefoxes, however, manage to keep their identity secret for quite some time.

A favorite Japanese folktale tells of Abe No Yasuna, a poet and hero, who rescued a white fox from a hunting party and allowed it to go free. Not long after this humane act, he met and fell in love with the beautiful Kuzunhoa, who professed her admiration for him and agreed to marry him. Tragically, a year later, she died giving birth to their son, Abe No Seimei, who would one day become magician and astrologer to the emperor. Three days after her death, Kuzunhoa came to her grieving husband in a dream and revealed herself as the white fox that he had so nobly saved from the hunters.

In many Native American tribes, the fox is the form most favored by shapeshifting sorcerers who are on their night rounds to do evil to their enemies. Consequently, among many tribes, the fox is regarded as an instrument of negativity and witchcraft. While a werefox may not slash, rip, or eat those who get in its path, it would most certainly place a terrible curse upon their heads.

SOURCES:

Larousse Dictionary of World Folklore. New York: Larousse, 1995.

Steiger, Brad. *Totems: The Transformative Power of Your Personal Animal Totem.* San Francisco: HarperSanFrancisco, 1997.

Fox Strap

It was widely believed that certain sorcerers and witches possessed a strap of wolf or fox hide that could transform them into the beast of their choice. In the village of Dodow near Wittenburg, Germany, there lived a witch who owned such a strap, and through its magic she could transform herself into a fox whenever she wished and keep her larder well stocked with geese, ducks, and chickens. One day, her grandson, who knew that his grandmother was a witch and was fully aware of why it was that their table never lacked for tasty poultry— even though they owned none of their own— sneaked the fox strap from its hiding place and brought it with him to school.

As it so happened, the schoolmaster that day happened to be discussing magic and witchcraft, and the eager child volunteered that his grandmother was a witch and that he had her fox strap with him. Amused by such childlike belief, the schoolmaster politely asked to examine the strip of animal hide. Unfortunately, as he strode back and forth in front of the class, gesturing broadly to make his points, the strap brushed against his forehead, adhered to his flesh, and instantly transformed him into a fox.

The children began to scream loudly in terror at what their young eyes had beheld, and the schoolmaster, a mild-mannered gentleman who was unaware of his transformation, became frightened at whatever it was that had so terrified his students. As they all ran screaming from the classroom, the schoolmaster's new animal nature assumed command and he found himself jumping out the open window in a single leap.

Confused and bewildered to find himself running across the countryside on all fours, the schoolmaster had no choice but to make the best of a most peculiar situation. Trusting in his newfound instincts, he found a suitable hill and made himself a den.

Several days later, a group of local sportsmen organized a hunt, and the confused schoolmaster found himself among the other animals running to escape the hunters. A bullet struck him in the heart. Another bullet had severed the fox strap and returned the schoolmaster to his human form. The stunned sportsmen found themselves staring at the meek schoolmaster lying bleeding on the ground.

SOURCES:

Bartsch, Karl. *Sagen, Marchen und Gebrauche aus Meklenburg.* Translated by D. L. Ashliman. Wien: Wilhem Braumuller, 1879.

Frankenstein Meets the Wolf Man

It seemed inevitable that someone at Universal would come up with the idea of pairing two of their famous monsters in a single feature. Of course to do so meant that the creatures who had been so effectively killed off in their previous respective cinematic outings would have to be miraculously resurrected.

Once again **Lawrence Talbot (Lon Chaney Jr.)** is tormented by the lycanthropic curse that has afflicted him. He does not revel in its **full moon** power, and he takes no delight in mauling human beings when he is under its spell. Because he genuinely wishes to be free of the demonic beast within, he seeks out the old gypsy woman Maliva (**Maria Ouspenskaya**) in an effort to gain more knowledge of the ways of werewolfdom. She counsels that there is only one man she knows that learned enough to free him of the taint of the beast and that man is Dr. Frankenstein, the same scientist who created the Monster.

Talbot and Maliva set out from Wales in her horse-drawn cart, and the audience crosses the sea with them until they arrive in the mystical village of Vasaria, that quaint little town that combines touches of Transylvania and Germany and has a lot of folks who speak in British accents. Here Maliva and Talbot learn that Dr. Frankenstein and his Monster were destroyed in a fire set

Lon Chaney Jr. poses as the Wolf Man in a publicity photograph from the film *Frankenstein Meets the Wolf Man*.

by the angry villagers. Talbot undergoes one of his unfortunate werewolf transformations, and now it is his turn to be pursued by the angry villagers of Vasaria.

As he runs from their torches and pitchforks, he stumbles into the ruins of Dr. Frankenstein's famous laboratory—where he is astonished to discover the Monster (**Bela Lugosi**) frozen in a block of ice. Talbot manages to thaw him and revive the creature, but he soon realizes that the mute creation of the scientist will be of no assistance in removing the curse of the werewolf.

Later, in his human form, Talbot meets Frankenstein's daughter (Ilona Massey), who happens to be visiting Vasaria. He pleads with her to assist him, but only after the Monster disrupts a village festival does she agree to furnish Talbot's London friend, Dr. Mannering (Patric Knowles), with her late father's laboratory notes. The Baroness wants it clearly understood, however, that Dr. Mannering will first use the knowledge contained in those notes to destroy the Monster and redeem the Frankenstein name before any efforts are applied to removing the werewolfism that afflicts Talbot.

The opportunity to work with such godlike powers and to restore a man-made humanoid monster to full strength proves too tempting for Mannering, and he concentrates on such an application of Dr. Frankenstein's knowledge at the expense of his friend Talbot. The Monster breaks loose just as the full moon exerts its spell upon the Wolf Man, who meets the challenge of the rampaging creature with full lycanthropic fury. As the two monsters battle, Mannering and the Baroness flee to safety just in time to avoid the destruction of the laboratory by the villagers, who blow up the village dam in order to sweep the curse of Frankenstein and the werewolf away in its flood waters.

Frankenstein Meets the Wolf Man (1943) proved so popular that Universal added Dracula to the mix in *House of Frankenstein* (1944) and *House of Dracula* (1946). In his book *The Monster Show*, David J. Skal writes that *Frankenstein Meets the Wolf Man* "elicited some immediate, if facetious, war parallels on the part of reviewers." *The Hollywood Reporter* observed that "Roosevelt meets Churchill at Casablanca. Yanks meet Japs at Guadalcanal—and yet these events will fade into insignificance to those seemingly inexhaustible legion of horror fans when they hear that *Frankenstein Meets the Wolf Man.*"

SOURCES:

Skal, David J. *The Monster Show*. New York: W.W. Norton, 1993.
Stanley, John. *Creature Features*. New York: Boulevard, 1997.

Full Moon

Since the very earliest accounts of werewolves, those who would seek to explain the onset of such frightening behavior have stated with authority that

An illustration by J. C. Dollman showing two wolves howling at the moon, the light of which supposedly is the catalyst that changes a human into a werewolf.

it is the light of the full moon that serves as the catalyst for the transformation of human into wolf. The ancient Greeks and Romans associated the moon with the underworld and those human and inhuman entities who used the night to work their dark magic. Witches, werewolves, and other shapeshifters received great power from the moon—and just as the moon changed its shape throughout the month, so could these servants of the underworld transform their shapes into bats, **wolves,** dogs, rats, or any creature they so chose. In addition, they could also change their hapless victims into animals.

The moon goddesses—Hecate, **Diana,** or Selene—surveyed the world below them and awaited the summons from their disciples who wished to draw down the power of the moon (i.e., the goddess). The moon is nearly always associated with the feminine vibration. Egyptians gave the moon a prominent role in the act of creation, naming her Mother of the Universe. The Babylonians gave the moon dominance over the sun, and numerous Asian cultures worshipped the moon over the sun, for the goddess of the moon gave her light at night when humankind really needed it, while the sun chose to shine only by day.

There have been a number of studies that indicate that the full moon does make people more violent. The most recent was conducted in 1998 when researchers observed prisoners in the maximum-security wing at Armley jail, in Leeds, England. Prison officer Claire Smith carried out the psychological study of all 1,200 inmates for more than three months, and the researchers found that there was a definite rise in the number of violent and unruly incidents recorded during the first and last quarter of each lunar cycle, the days on either side of a full moon.

Smith expressed her opinion to journalist David Bamber that she believed her study to have proved that there is a link between the moon and human behavior. Smith says, "The best theory I have heard to explain why this happens is that we are made up of 60 to 70 percent of water. And if the moon controls the tides, what is it doing to us?"

As with every theory regarding human behavior, there are other points of view. While some researchers agree that there is more crime during a full moon, they attribute the rise in antisocial statistics to the simple fact that there is more light out by which to commit mischief. As for dogs and wolves howling wildly at the full moon, animal control officers and park rangers disagree. They say that a full moon appears to calm the canines because they can see more of their surroundings on those nights when there is a full moon.

It is quite interesting that *The Werewolf Book* was written during a most remarkable period of time in which there occurred two "blue moons," that is, twice within the space of three months. In January and again in March 1999, there were two full moons per month. According to Geoff Chester of the U.S. Naval Observatory, two blue moons within three months had not been seen since 1915.

And talk about strange events occurring during the Blue Moon periods: Residents of Bastrop, Louisiana, reported a bizarre mass death of birds. An out-of-place Siberian tiger was shot in New Jersey. A Western coyote appeared in New York City's Central Park and was finally captured in Memorial Grove near 69th Street. And residents of Juba, a city on the upper Nile River, were startled to discover thousands of fish and dozens of crocodiles and hippopotami floating dead in the water.

SOURCES:

"Coyote Corralled in Central Park," *New York Post*. 2 April 1999.

Gaskell, G. A. *Dictionary of All Scriptures and Myths*. Avenel, NJ: Gramercy Books, 1981.

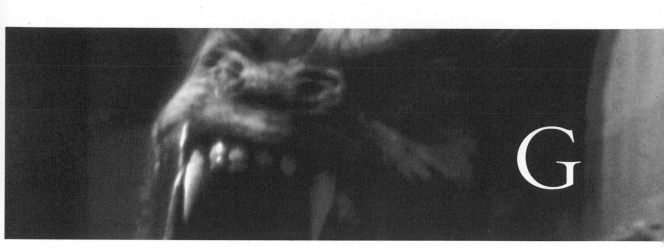

Gargoyles

Those eerie-looking, somewhat grotesque creatures staring out from certain cathedrals and private residences are not **demons.** Quite the contrary, gargoyles are entities whose mission is to protect the weak and the unwary from demonic attack. While it is true that some gargoyles look very much like werewolves and other shapeshifting entities, they are supposed to look as fearsome and powerfully threatening as possible to ward off demons, vampires, and werewolves. After all, the bloodthirsty monsters of darkness would hardly be frightened off by a sweetly smiling, curly-haired nymph in a pastel robe.

Garlic

Use garlic to ward off vampires, witches, or the evil eye. Use garlic to ward off hunger by putting it on toast and eating it with your spaghetti. Use garlic for health reasons, such as improving your circulation and building your immune system. But don't think it does anything to ward off werewolves or shapeshifters. They'll probably even join you in a hearty Italian meal with lots of garlic—before they start looking at you for dessert.

There are some areas in southern Europe in which garlic is believed to be effective against werewolves, as well as vampires. It is possible that the tradition of garlic as an agent capable of warding off creatures of the night grew out of the simple fact that heavy consumers of garlic are never welcome in any kind of intimate contact. In the ancient mystery religions, which emphasized the goddess and fertility rites, those who had eaten heavily of garlic were ostracized from worship.

Garnier, Gilles (d. 1573)

Over a period of several months in 1572, the small French village of Dole lost two boys and two girls to the attacks of a pitiless werewolf. Each of the four children had been found nude and gruesomely mutilated. One of the boys had one of his legs completely ripped from the torso, and all those villagers who dared to look could see the teeth marks on the arms and legs of all the victims.

The mystery of the werewolf's identity was quickly solved, for more than 50 witnesses claimed to have seen the peculiar vagrant that everyone referred to as the Hermit of Dole in various stages of committing the perverse acts on the children. Gilles Garnier was arrested on the grounds that he was a **loup-garou,** a werewolf, and that he had been seen tearing apart the bodies of the murdered children with his teeth, gulping down pieces of raw flesh.

Before he "freely confessed" his crimes and was executed in 1573, Garnier told how shortly after the feast of St. Michael, "being in the form of a wolf," he seized a 10-year-old girl in a vineyard and "there he slew her with both hands, seemingly paws, and with his teeth carried some of her flesh home to his wife."

Eight days later, after the Feast of All Saints, Garnier attacked another young girl at about the same place. "He slew her, tearing her body and wounding her in five places on her body with her hands and teeth, with the intention of eating her flesh, had he not been hindered and prevented by three persons."

Seven days later, the wolfman seized yet another child, a boy 10 years old. The sickened court recorded that upon the Friday before the Feast of St. Bartholomew, Garnier captured and assaulted a young boy of 12 or 13 under a large pear three and "had he not been hindered and prevented, he would have eaten the flesh of the aforesaid young boy, notwithstanding that it was a Friday."

In view of the heinous crimes, coupled with Garnier's free confession, the court was quick to decree that the werewolf should be handed over to the master executioner of high justice and directed that, "the said, Gilles Garnier, shall be drawn upon a hurdle from this very place unto the customary place of execution, and that there by the aforesaid master executioner he shall be burned quick and his body reduced to ashes."

SOURCES:

Masters, R. E. L., and Eduard Lea. *Perverse Crimes in History.* New York: The Julian Press, 1963.

Steiger, Brad. *Demon Lovers: Cases of Possession, Vampires, and Werewolves.* New Brunswick, NJ: Inner Light, 1987.

Gein, Ed (1907–1984)

In 1957, Ed Gein, an unwed, middle-aged farmer from Plainfield, Wisconsin, confessed to stealing a dozen female bodies from fresh graves in the commu-

Doctor Keiserperg von den werwölffen.

A sixteenth-century woodcarving from a book by Johann Geller von Kaiserberg showing a werewolf attacking a man at the entrance to a house.

nity cemetery. Although the necrophagic (a fancy name for a ghoul) returned most of the body parts after he had dismembered the bodies, he kept a collection of sex organs and noses in a box.

Like a true ghoul, Gein was disposed to nibble at some of the choicest bits and pieces that he carved from the dead, and he also saved 10 of the skulls as his special companions. Not one to waste anything, Gein upholstered some of his furniture with human skin.

Gein progressed from grave-robbing to murder by killing at least two local women. When the sheriff entered the bachelor's farmhouse to investigate some local complaints, he was horrified to find one of the victims strung up by her heels, decapitated and eviscerated.

The ghoul's neighbors later recalled with great unpleasantness and queasiness of stomach that he was forever bringing them portions of "venison." Later, while undergoing psychiatric examination, Gein told the analyst that he had never shot a deer in his life.

SOURCES:
Steiger, Brad. *Bizarre Crime.* New York: Signet, 1992.

Ghosts

The classic definition of a ghost is a nonmaterial embodiment or the spiritual essence of a human being. Many people would argue that animals also have a spiritual essence that survives physical death and may later appear as ghosts. A letter to the author from a correspondent who went simply by the initials J. E. D. recounted his experience with a ghost wolf:

> I have been told many times that there absolutely are no **wolves** in the vicinity of Missouri where I live. Yet I and people with a certain sensitivity have heard a wolf moving in the brush and have seen and heard the ghost wolf. And always, the authorities insist that there are no wolves in the area. Once my eyes were drawn to lights moving among the trees. I felt uncomfortable and walked away. When I had gone about 150 feet, I heard the unmistakable howl of a wolf.

In addition to the spirits of animals prowling the darkened forests, it may well be that there are a host of multidimensional beings that masquerade as ghosts or are perceived to be the spirits of the dead when they are actually entities of quite a different nature—some benevolent, some malevolent. Some may even appear as grotesque, werewolf-like monsters.

In one particularly vivid account, three young couples, all close friends, decided to economize and decrease their debts by temporarily renting an immense three-story house on the outskirts of a medium-sized city on the West Coast. Mrs. M., an avid student of antiques, was overwhelmed by the splendid treasures that had been left in the house. A few days later, they received their first eerie clue as to why the house had so long stood deserted with all its valuables left untouched. They all heard the unmistakable sounds of someone clomping noisily up the stairs, then running the full length of the upstairs hallway. In addition, there were slamming doors, cold breezes blowing past them, and the sight of the huge sliding doors being pushed open by an invisible hand.

Then, one night, Mrs. N. was attacked in bed by an invisible assailant that attempted to smother her. At last she freed herself, only to be thrown to the floor with such force that her ankle twisted beneath her and her head hit the wall. Throughout the incredible attack, her husband could only sit helplessly by, his face ashen with fear.

The three couples held a council to decide whether or not they should move, but they voted to bear the frightening phenomena and continue to save their money. And so they endured foul, nauseating odors, the sound of something sighing and panting in a darkened corner of the basement, and a remarkable variety of ghostly clanks, creaks, and thuds.

They received some insight into their haunted home when Mrs. M.'s grandparents came for a visit. Grandmother W. was a tiny woman who possessed great psychic abilities. She told the couples that the blond woman in the portrait that hung above the living room fireplace had been poisoned in one of the upstairs bedrooms. After a few days of getting to feel the atmosphere of the old mansion, Grandmother W. said that the place was haunted by something inhuman. She stated that she was not easily frightened, but the creature had terrified her.

As the elderly couple were preparing to leave, some invisible monster threw Grandmother W. to the floor in front of the fireplace and began to choke her. Grandmother W. was turning blue when her husband called upon the name of God and wrenched her free of the unseen beast and into his arms.

Her voice barely a whisper after the attack, Grandmother W. said that she had been "speaking" with the blond lady in the portrait when she saw an awful creature creep up behind her. It was as big as a large man, but like nothing that she had ever seen before. It had stiff, wiry orangish-colored hair standing out from its head, its arms, and its torso. Its hands curved into claws, like that of a wolf. The beast had threatened to kill her, and it had left cuts on her neck where its claws had gouged her flesh. Grandfather W. proclaimed the mansion a place of evil and urged the three couples to move.

They made their final decision to move a few days later after a night in which a huge black bat had crept under the covers and clamped its teeth onto Mrs. N.'s foot. It took two men to beat and pry the monstrous bat off her foot—and even after it had been clubbed to the floor, it managed to rise, circle the room, and smash a window to escape.

The encounters with the grotesque, werewolf spirit being did not end with their vacating the haunted mansion. Ten years after Grandmother W.'s death, some of her family members were living in her old ranchhouse. One night Uncle J. came downstairs, trembling with fear, claiming that he had seen a monster with orangish-colored bristly hair poke its head out of a storage room, then shut the door. Although the family teased him when he began to claim that "something" was entering his room at nights, the laughter ceased when Uncle J. died after about a week of such nocturnal visitations.

A decade later, Mr. and Mrs. M., one of the three couples who had occupied the haunted mansion, were now themselves grandparents, and they decided to spend their vacation on Grandmother W.'s old ranch. They had their nine-year-old grandson with them, and they were looking forward to a comfortable stay in the old homestead. But on their very first night, Mrs. M. was awakened by something shuffling toward her grandson.

Looking the creature full in the face, she saw a grinning mouth with huge, yellow teeth. Its eyes were nearly hidden in a series of mottled lumps. It brushed Mrs. M. aside and lunged at her grandson, who was now wide awake and screaming. She grabbed a handful of thick, long hair and desperately clutched a hairy, scaly arm with the other hand. In the moonlight which shone through the window, she could see huge hands that curved into long claws.

At last her husband was alerted to the terrible struggle taking place and turned on the light. The monster backed away, seemingly irritated by the sudden illumination, but it still gestured toward their grandson. In the light, they could see that the beast wore a light-colored, tight-fitting one-piece suit of a thin material that ended at the knees and elbows. Thick, bristly orangish-colored hair protruded from its flattened and grossly misshapen face; and thick, bulbous lips drew back over snarling yellow teeth. It gestured again toward their grandson, then turned and shuffled through the doorway, leaving behind a sickening odor of decay.

To the M. family, it had been demonstrated that a ghostly entity that haunts one house can follow the family to another domicile. Perhaps Grandmother W. had thrown down a psychic gauntlet and a challenge that the grotesque, werewolf-like entity had accepted. Whatever the explanation for the frightening manifestation, they razed the old ranchhouse shortly thereafter.

Ghouls

The ghoul is linked with both the **vampire** and the werewolf in the traditional folklore of the frightening, but there are a number of somewhat different entities that are included in the category of ghoul. There is the ghoul that, like the vampire, is a member of the unrelenting family of the undead, continually on the nocturnal prowl for new victims. Unlike the vampire, however, this ghoul feasts upon the flesh of the deceased, tearing their corpses from cemeteries and morgues. The ghoul more common to the waking world is that of the mentally unbalanced individual who engages in perhaps the most disgusting of aberrations, necrophagia, eating or otherwise desecrating the flesh of deceased humans. Yet a third type of ghoul would be those creatures of Arabic folklore, the *ghul* (male) and *ghulah* (female), demonic jinns that hover near burial grounds and sustain themselves on human flesh stolen from graves.

Sgt. Bertrand, the infamous werewolf of Paris, is literally an all-purpose monster, for rather than ripping and slashing the living, he suffered from the necrophilic perversion of mutilating and sexually abusing the dead. In their *Perverse Crimes in History,* R.E. L. Masters and Eduard Lea tell of a similar necrophilic, the ghoul Ardisson, who exhumed the corpses of females ranging

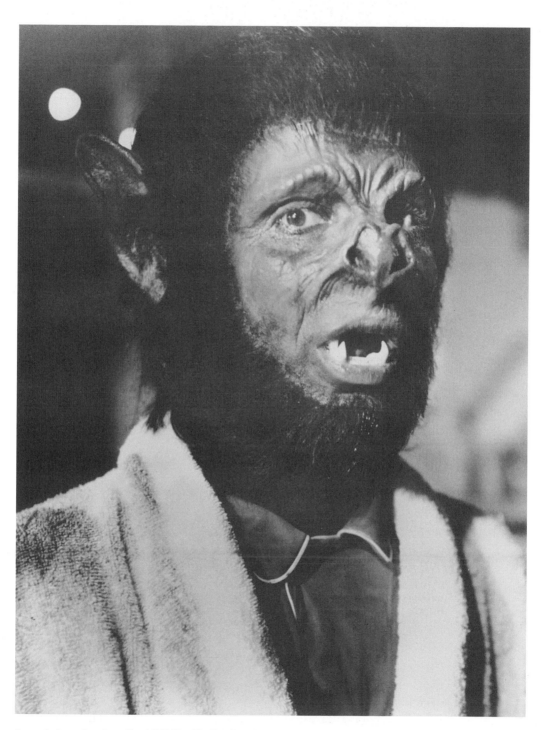

A man-bat creature from the 1974 film *The Bat People.*

in age from three to 80. On one occasion he removed a woman's head from its body and took it home with him to be his "bride."

It is quite easy to envision how the legend of the ghoul began in ancient times when graves were shallow and very often subject to the desecrations of wild animals seeking carrion. Later, as funeral customs became more elaborate and men and women were buried with their jewelry and other personal treasures, the lure of easy wealth circumvented any superstitions or ecclesiastical admonitions that might have otherwise kept grave robbers away from cemeteries and disturbing the corpses' final rest.

Then, in the late 1820s, surgeons and doctors began to discover the value of dissection. The infant science of surgery was progressing rapidly, but advancement required cadavers—and the more cadavers that were supplied, the more the doctors realized how little they knew, and thus the more cadavers they needed. As a result, societies of grave robbers were formed called the resurrectionists. These men made certain that the corpses finding their way to the dissecting tables were as fresh as possible. And besides, digging was easier in unsettled dirt.

Ghoulish practices continue well into our own times. Jilted lover Michael Schinkel of Herald, California, was so obsessed with his girlfriend, Sandra Lee Crane, that he stabbed her to death in September 1986 and placed her body in a freezer. For the next five years, until the corpse was accidently discovered by a landlord in 1991, Schinkel kept the body with him wherever he moved. He even continued to cherish the mummified corpse after he was married.

In 1994 in Rochester, New York, Jeffrey Watkins, 24, a self-proclaimed sorcerer who named himself the Grinch, was found guilty of 19 charges of stealing corpses, digging up graves, and vandalizing mausoleums. Watkins slept in coffins with corpses, desecrated cemeteries, and kept a human skull at his bedside. He explained to police that he felt safe with the dead because he could trust them. He needed their company to enable him to feel peaceful inside.

SOURCES:

Hurwood, Bernardt J. *Vampires, Werewolves, and Ghouls.* New York: Ace Books, 1968.

Masters, R. E. L., and Eduard Lea. *Perverse Crimes in History.* New York: The Julian Press, 1963.

Gill Man

Perhaps one of the reasons why the idea of a gill man is so appealing to monster lovers is the theory that all life began in the great Mother Ocean and that there may be a link between some prehuman, bipedal aquatic humanoid and our present-day species. After all, amphibians provide living proof that creatures can exist both in water and on land.

In *Creature from the Black Lagoon* (1954), scientists Richard Carlson, Julia Adams, and Richard Denning believe that they have found such a survivor of a prehistoric half-aquatic, half-man creature. Riccou Browning and Ben Chapman shared the role of the gill man and made audiences forget that there had to be an actor inside that rubber suit in all those remarkable underwater shots. Perhaps the movie has become a classic because it tickles certain ancient memories in our reptilian brains that have continued to resurface in the perpetuation of legends of merman and mermaids. The pursuit of the gill man—and his pursuit of his human captors and antagonists—continues in *Revenge of the Creature* (1955) and *The Creature Walks Among Us* (1956).

The theme of the aquatic or amphibious werecreature has also been featured in such motion pictures as *The Alligator People* (1959), *The Monster of Piedras Blancas* (1959), *The Hideous Sun Demon* (1959), *The Amphibious Man* (1961), and *War Gods of the Deep* (1965).

SOURCES:
Stanley, John. *Creature Features.* New York: Boulevard, 1997.

Gordon, Harry (?–1941)

William Johnston, alias Harry Meyers, alias Harry Gordon—the sadistic killer of three women—did not claw or bite his victims to death, but he earned the title "The Werewolf of San Francisco" with a straight razor. In the manner of London's Jack the Ripper, Johnston chose prostitutes for his victims.

On the night of April 6, 1935, Betty Coffin turned a corner and started to walk down San Francisco's Market Street. It was 2:30 A.M., and her feet hurt. It was time to call it a night.

Then she saw him. She walked right up to the heavy-set, slightly drunk man, who was dressed like a seaman, and propositioned him. Fifteen minutes later, "Mr. and Mrs. Harry Meyers" had registered in a cheap waterfront hotel.

Two hours later, Meyers came down alone and asked the sleepy night clerk where he could get a beer and a sandwich. The clerk directed him to an all-night greasy spoon diner on the corner.

At eight o'clock the next morning, the maid entered the Meyers's room using her passkey and found the nude, bloody, and battered body of Betty Coffin sprawled on the bed. Her face had been beaten savagely. Her mouth was taped shut. Her body had been ripped open again and again with gaping wounds in regular pattern, as if she had been raked over and over again by the claws of a wild beast, a werewolf. Bloodstained fragments of clothing were strewn about the room.

Inspector Allan McGinn of the San Francisco police told the press that the kind of monster who murders in such a fashion is the type to strike again and again. Newspapers headlined stories of the Werewolf of San Francisco and his brutal and bloody savagery. But the most arduous of police work failed to turn up any clue of the murderer.

Five years passed without another werewolf murder in San Francisco, but Inspector McGinn had been correct about the sadistic human monster working according to some inner cycle of bloodlust. On June 25, 1940, the moon was right for the San Francisco Werewolf to strike again.

The body of Irene Chandler was found in another waterfront hotel in the same condition as that of Betty Coffin. Official causes of death were listed as strangulation and loss of **blood,** but the corpse bore the same terrible beastlike slashings. The victim was known to the police as a "seagull," a streetwalker who catered to seafaring men. And this time the werewolf had left his "claws" behind—a rusty, bloodstained razor.

The Sailors' Union of the Pacific supplied the police with a picture of the man whom they felt fit the werewolf's general description. On July 8, 1940, a detective confronted Harry W. Gordon at a sailors' union meeting. Gordon was a big, blond man, and the manner in which he had mutilated the two women indicated that he was bestial, cruel, and most likely a psychopath. The detective braced himself for a struggle.

Keeping his voice quiet, hoping to avert violence and to defuse the situation, the detective told Gordon that the police wanted to talk with him at headquarters. Amazingly, the brute who had so hideously carved up two women slumped his shoulders and offered no resistance. Later, after intense questioning, he broke down and confessed to the murders of Betty Coffin and Irene Chandler. The officers were unprepared for Gordon's next confession: "And I killed my first wife in New York, too!"

On September 5, 1941, Harry W. Gordon took his last breath in San Quentin's lethal gas chamber. The savage hunger of the Werewolf of San Francisco was quieted at last.

SOURCES:

Steiger, Brad. *Demon Lovers: Cases of Possession, Vampires, and Werewolves.* New Brunswick, NJ: Inner Light, 1987.

Green Wolf

The celebration of the green wolf marks an ancient custom that commemorates the times past when outlaws, **wolves,** and werewolves would hide in the fields, sometimes camouflaged with green leaves and moss. At harvest time, farmers would come upon "werewolves' nests," where the creatures had trampled down the crop to make a more comfortable sleeping spot. In many sections of France, the children were warned about the **loup-garou** (werewolves) that crouched in the fields.

In the Normandy region of France, *le loup vert*, the green wolf, is chosen each year to dance at the head of the other members of the farming community during the harvest festival. The climax of the dance comes when a group of husky farmers make a pretense of tossing the green wolf—the man who has been selected to masquerade as the wolf at next year's observance—into the roaring bonfire. The burning of the werewolf clothed in leaves and moss symbolizes the farmers' triumph over hidden menaces in their land which might threaten their families or their crops.

SOURCES:
Eisler, Robert. *Man into Wolf*. London: Spring Books, n.d.

The Greifswald Werewolves

According to old records, c. 1640 the German city of Griefswald became overrun with werewolves. The lycanthropic population had become so large that they literally took over the city, working outward from their principal hovel in Rokover Street. Any human who ventured out after dark was in certain danger of being attacked and killed by the large company of werewolves.

As the story goes, at last a group of bold students decided that they had had enough of living in fear and staying indoors at night, cowering before their hearths. One night they banded together and led a charge against the monsters. Although the students put up a good fight, they were virtually helpless against the powerful werewolves.

But then a clever lad suggested that they gather all their silver buttons, goblets, belt buckles, and so forth, and melt them down into bullets for their muskets and pistols. Thus reinforced, the students set out once again to challenge the dominance of the werewolves—and this time they slaughtered the creatures and rid Greifswald of the lycanthropes.

SOURCES:
Temme, J. D. H. *Die Volkssagen von Pommern und Rugen*. Translated by D. L. Ashliman. Berlin: In de Nicolaischen Buchhandlung, 1840.

Grenier, Jean (c. 1589–1610)

In 1610, Pierre de Lancre, a noted judge of Bordeaux, France, visited the Monastery of the Cordeliers personally to investigate a werewolf that had been confined to a cloister cell for seven years. The werewolf, Jean Grenier, had viciously attacked several victims, and eyewitnesses to the assaults had sworn that Grenier had been in the form of a wolf when he made the attacks.

Noted horror actors John Carradine (right) and Frank Moran (as the Ape Man) teamed up in the 1944 film *Return of the Ape Man*.

In his *L'inconstance* (1612), Lancre writes of Grenier that he possessed glittering, deep-set eyes, long, black fingernails, and sharp, protruding teeth. According to the jurist's account, Grenier freely confessed to having been a werewolf, and it was apparent that he walked on all fours with much greater ease than he could walk erect. The judge writes that he was horrified when Grenier told him that he still craved human flesh, especially that of little girls, and he hoped that he might once again savor such fine meat.

The nights and days as a werewolf began for Jean Grenier in the spring of 1603 in the Gascony region of France when small children began to disappear. Then, during a **full moon,** witnesses watched in horror as a 13-year-old girl named Marguerite Poirer was attacked by a monstrous creature resembling a wolf.

When the fear of a stalking werewolf was reaching fever pitch in the villages of Gascony, a teenage boy whom everyone had believed to be mentally deficient began to boast of having the ability to transform himself into a wolf. As if that announcement was not disturbing enough to his neighbors, 13-year-old Jean Grenier also confessed to having eaten the missing children and having attacked Marguerite.

When he was questioned by the authorities, Grenier told of having been given the magical wolf's belt that could transform him into a wolf. This awesome gift had been presented to him by the Master of the Forest, who revealed himself as a large man dressed entirely in black. Although Grenier was content merely to accomplish such a powerful transformation, the very act of doing so caused him to crave the tender, raw flesh of plump children. He tried to stifle the perverse hunger by killing dogs and drinking their warm **blood,** but such measures were only temporary. He was driven to steal children and eat their flesh.

What is perhaps most remarkable about the case of Jean Grenier is that the court elected not to have him burned at the stake for being a werewolf, but, instead, assessed his claims as the result of his being mentally defective. They decided that his supposed powers of transmutation were but lycanthropic delusions, and because the young man was therefore insane, could not be held accountable for his terrible crimes. Rather than enduring the **tortures of the Inquisition** and the usual transformation into ashes at the stake, Grenier was given a life sentence to a cell in a monastery in Bordeaux.

SOURCES:
Eisler, Robert. *Man into Wolf*. London: Spring Books, n.d.
Hurwood, Bernardt J. *Terror by Night*. New York: Lancer Books, 1963.

Gypsies

Considered as the traditional companions of werewolves and other creatures of the night, gypsies have not been well regarded since they began their migration to Europe around the year 1000. At best they were considered thieves, fortune tellers, and cheats. At worst they were condemned as witches who worshipped **Diana,** the chief nemesis of the Christian clergy in the Middle Ages. In the common mind it was believed that all gypsies were descended from the union of the first gypsy woman with Satan. In 1500, the Diet of Augsburg ruled that Christians could kill gypsies without legal penalty. The same ruling decreed that gypsies had no legal rights whatsoever.

During the Middle Ages, thousands of gypsies were burned at the stake as witches and in punishment for the popular belief that it was gypsy smiths who forged the nails that bound Christ to the cross. Gypsies fared no better in the twentieth century when the Nazis identified them as "nonhuman" and killed an estimated 400,000 of them in the death camps.

Although even today many gypsies prefer to treat their true origins with mystery, most scholars agree that they are likely of Hindu roots, rather than Egyptian, as many nongypsies suppose. Generally, gypsies believe in past lives, the concept of karma, and the triune goddess of fate. Gypsy fortune tellers are known as *Vedavica*, literally, a reader of the Vedas, for they seem to regard the tarot cards as their own interpretation of the sacred Hindu writings.

SOURCES:

Walker, Barbara G. *The Woman's Encyclopedia of Myths and Secrets.* San Francisco: Harper & Row, 1983.

H

Haarmann, Fritz (1879–1925)

Some years ago, an examination of the terrible crimes of Fritz Haarmann, otherwise known as the Hanover Vampire, led experts to conclude that his acts were those of a sadist, a werewolf, since they involved his biting his victims to death and cannibalistically eating their flesh. In their *Perverse Crimes in History*, R. E. L. Masters and Eduard Lea agree, stating that in a book about vampires, such as Summers' *The Vampire: Its Kith and Kin*, it is permissible to characterize Haarmann as one of that breed, but it is "somewhat more accurate to regard him as a homosexual sadist and lust murder—and of course as a cannibal." Haarmann had at least a six-year reign of terror, from 1918 to 1924, before he was apprehended by the authorities.

Some of his posthumous analysts and biographers have characterized him as a dull and stupid youth who served a number of jail sentences for child molestation, indecent exposure, and homosexuality. Haarmann's antisocial acts graduated from the petty to the perverse when he became enamored with a young male prostitute, Hans Grans, who also appeared to give evidence of werewolfism. Haarmann, then in his forties, had made a token effort to work at gainful employment and had opened a small combination butcher shop and restaurant. With the gleeful urging of Grans, Haarmann would lure a young man to his shop, overpower him, and begin biting and chewing at his throat. In some instances, he did not cease his bloody attack until he had nearly eaten the head away from the body.

After Haarmann had satisfied his werewolfism and both men had been erotically stimulated by the brutal murder, the body of the victim would be butchered and made into steaks, sausages, and other cuts of meat. Both Haarmann and Grans ate regular meals from their private stock of human flesh.

What they didn't eat, Haarmann sold in his butcher shop. His patrons never questioned how it was that his shop always had choice cuts of meat for sale when fresh meat became scarce in other stores throughout the city. When the sensational news of Haarmann's werewolfism and butchery came to light, there were no doubt a large number of Hanover citizens who had cause to wonder if by their patronage they had become unwitting cannibals.

After his conviction at about the age of 46, Haarmann was beheaded with a sword and his brain removed from its skull and delivered to Goettingen University for study. Hans Grans received a sentence of life imprisonment, which was later commuted to 12 years. The estimated total of Haarmann's victims ranges from 24 to 50. But the newspapers of the city noted that during the year 1924, when the monster's crimes were first revealed, some 600 boys had disappeared in Hanover, at that time a city of about 450,000 population.

SOURCES:

Masters, R. E. L., and Eduard Lea. *Perverse Crimes in History.* New York: The Julian Press, 1963.

A Hammer to Strike Witches

The terrible sexual repressions of the medieval church placed special emphasis on women as the source of all fleshly evil. In the Dark Ages, women had been largely regarded as property; in the Middle Ages, they were held responsible for all sexual guilt. It was women who had precipitated the Fall by tempting man, who would otherwise surely have remained pure. The mere presence of a woman was liable to attract evil.

St. Chrysostom of Constantinople, who was decidedly more tolerant than his clerical descendants of the Middle Ages would be, declared that women were a "necessary evil, a natural temptation, a desirable calamity, a domestic peril, a deadly fascination, and a painted ill." But in 1486, James Sprenger and Henry Kramer set forth inflammatory guidelines regarding the true nature of women in their *Malleus Maleficarum (A Hammer to Strike Witches)*:

> A woman is beautiful to look upon, contaminating to the touch, and deadly to keep . . . a foe to friendship . . . a necessary evil . . . a liar by nature . . . . Since [women] are feeble both in mind and body, it is not surprising that they should come under the spell of witchcraft [more than men would succumb] . . . A woman is more carnal than a man . . . . All witchcraft comes from carnal lust, which in is women insatiable.

> [Witches] satisfy their filthy lusts not only in themselves, but even in the mighty ones of the ages, of whatever sort and condition, causing by all sorts of witchcraft the death of their souls through the excessive infatuation of carnal love.

The text of the *Malleus Maleficarum* was a powerful force in the Middle Ages in making "witch" and "woman" largely synonymous. St. Augustine had

Veteran actor Chuck Connors starred in the short-lived television show *The Werewolf.*

declared that humankind has been sent to destruction through one woman (Eve) and has its salvation restored to it through another woman (Mary). Woman had to become the medieval man—and even the so-called enlightened Renaissance man—become almost completely dualistic. As Morton Hunt observes in his *The Natural History of Love:* "She was not Woman—she was either Lady or Witch, Blessed Virgin or Sinful Eve, object of adoration or vessel of abominable lust."

Hunt also points out the incongruity of the "golden Renaissance" during which time "the burning of witches was never more prevalent than at the time when woman was being glorified by Botticelli, Giorgione, and Titian."

It seems ironic that in the early days of Christianity, women were offered equal roles. The early church fathers permitted women to preach, cure, exorcise, and to baptize. By the Middle Ages, women had lost nearly all vestige of any legal rights whatsoever. Writing in his *Witchcraft* of the work that became the handbook for professional witch hunters, Charles Williams states:

> As an intellectual achievement the work is almost of the first order. . . .
> They deal with sex, of course, as any examination of a great part of life must,
> but there is no sign that they were particularly interested in sex. They were
> interested in the Catholic faith and its perpetuation, and they were, also
> and therefore, interested in the great effort which it seemed to them was
> then in existence to destroy and eradicate the Catholic faith.

Williams is of the belief that Sprenger and Kramer proceeded with great care in the *Malleus Maleficarum* to examine the nature of witchcraft and to analyze the best methods of operating against its menace to the Roman Catholic Church. They took extreme pains to correct error, to instruct against ignorance, and to direct careful action. "In spite of all this," Williams declares, "the book is one of the most appalling that has ever been written."

Sprenger and Kramer make it clear that one of the chief activities of the witches was the interference with normal sexual intercourse between man and wife in marriage. They perceived the witches as making use of their unholy alliance with Satan to corrupt the generative powers of men. In addition, witches sought to depopulate Christendom by sacrificing children and babies to Satan and shapeshifting into werewolves and other monsters that especially craved the flesh of children.

Although the authors of the *Malleus Maleficarum* may not have been "particularly interested in sex," the Grand Inquisitors unfailingly directed their tortures against the private parts of the female body. The judges of the great tribunals examined, tried, and tortured females at a ratio of—depending on the authority—10 to one, 100 to one, or 10,000 to one. Once an accused woman found herself in prison through the testimonies of witnesses who had seen her evil powers at work (these could be a neighbor woman jealous of her beauty, a suitor disappointed at her rejection of his love, or a relative who sought her inheritance) she was as good as dead. At the height of the witch mania, an accusation was the equivalent of guilt in the eyes of the judges. And no lawyer would dare defend an accused witch for fear that he would himself be accused of heresy if he pled her case too well.

SOURCES:
Hurwood, Bernardt J. *Terror by Night.* New York: Lancer Books, 1963.
Masters, R. E. L., and Eduard Lea. *Perverse Crimes in History.* New York: The Julian Press, 1963.
Steiger, Brad. *Demon Lovers: Cases of Possession, Vampires and Werewolves.* New Brunswick, NJ: Inner Light, 1987.

Harpies

The Harpies may have had their origin in Greek legend as goddesses of the four winds, but they evolved into repulsive, winged female beings that became associated with cruel attacks on hapless wayfarers that usually ended in death. In some accounts, the Harpies appear to be acting as agents of retribution, bringing justice to those who would exploit others. Generally speaking, it might be said that the Harpies are members of a worldwide tradition of winged, taloned, vulturelike feminine beings, such as the Valkyries.

SOURCES:
Larousse Dictionary of World Folklore. New York: Larousse, 1995.

Hitler, Adolf (1889–1945)

Adolf Hitler was deeply enamored of **wolves** and werewolves. The very title "Fuhrer" denotes the leader of a pack of hunting wolves. And Hitler's name, Adolf, means "Father Wolf."

It was as werewolves that Hitler envisioned German youth when he dictated in his program for the education of the *Hitler Jugend* (Hitler Youth) that they must learn to become indifferent to pain. They must have no weakness or tenderness in them. When he looked into their eyes, Hitler said that he wanted to see "once more in the eyes of a pitiless youth the gleam of pride and independence of the beast of prey." It was his wish that he might somehow "eradicate thousands of years of human domestication" and allow the werewolves once again to run free and to work their destruction upon the weak and those unsuited to be members of the new world order that he was creating.

Numerous stories have been widely circulated about the rages that would possess Hitler to the point where he fell to the floor and literally began chewing the carpet. "If the stories about Hitler's rages are true," states Robert Eisler, "they would appear to have been manic lycanthropic states and not melancholic bouts of repentance. If the accounts were invented, they have sprung from the archetypal depths of the storytellers' unconscious race-memory and not from the archetypal minds of the doubtless paranoic subjects of the stories in question."

Robert G. L. Waite, the psychobiographer, states that Hitler was always fascinated with wolves. At the beginning of his political career, he had chosen Herr Wolf as his pseudonym. He named his headquarters in France *Woflsschlucht* (Wolf's Gulch) and in the Ukraine, *Werwolf*. He demanded that his sister change her name to Frau Wolf. He renamed the Volkswagen factory Wolfsburg and decreed himself Conductor Wolf. His favorite tune for whistling in his carefree moods was "Who's Afraid of the Big Bad Wolf?"

SOURCES:
Eisler, Robert. *Man into Wolf.* London: Spring Books, n.d.
Waite, Robert G. L. *The Psychopathic God: Adolf Hitler.* New York: Basic Books, 1977.

The Howling

Horror buff Joe Dante peppered *The Howling* (1981) with inside jokes that enriched the film for fellow devotees of monster movies. His former boss, the legendary Roger Corman of New World Pictures, has a cameo as a "guy just hanging out"; Forrest J. Ackerman, the longtime editor of *Famous Monsters of Filmland*, can be glimpsed as a customer in a bookstore with a stack of *Famous Monsters* magazines under his arm; and even *The Howling* scriptwriter John Sayles gets a minor part as a morgue attendant.

But Dante's biggest coup for horror buff insiders lies in naming a good many of the film's main characters after werewolf or horror movie directors—Patrick McNee portrays Dr. George Waggner (George Waggner, **The Wolf Man,** 1941); Christopher Stone is William Neill (Roy William Neill, **Frankenstein Meets the Wolf Man,** 1943); Belinda Balaksi is Terry Fisher (Terence Fisher, *Brides of Dracula,* 1960); Kevin McCarthy is Fred Francis (Freddie Francis, *Legend of the Werewolf,* 1975); John Carradine is Erle Kenton (Earle Kenton, *Island of Lost Souls,* 1932); Slim Pickens is Sam Newfield (Sam Newfield, *Ghost of Hidden Valley,* 1946); Noble Willingham is Charlie Barton (Charles Barton, **Abbott and Costello Meet Frankenstein,** 1948); Jim McKrell is Lew Landers (Lew Landers; *The Raven,* 1963).

Dante admitted later in an interview that some fans were turned off by such in-jokes and certain other tongue-in-cheek touches in the film. Some reviews in the fanzines took him to task for making fun of a serious genre.

At the time that he was creating werewolves for *The Howling*, Rob Bottin, at 21, was the youngest special effects expert working in Hollywood. Remarkably, when he was only 14 years old, Bottin began as an apprentice to his hero, Rick Baker, the makeup master on such films as *King Kong* (1976)

Eddie the werewolf (portrayed by Robert Picardo) was one of the stars of *The Howling*.

and *Star Wars* (1977). Before creating his groundbreaking werewolf makeup and special effects for *The Howling*, Bottin had contributed to such diverse films as *The Fog* (1980) and *Rock and Roll High School* (1979). After work on *The Howling* was completed, Bottin said, "This was, for me, a once-in-a-life-time opportunity to put some of my best ideas on the screen. It was painstaking, difficult, often back-breaking work, but I loved every single second of it. Besides, werewolves are my very, very favorite creatures."

Joe Dante said that he changed a great deal of the novel *The Howling* with the assistance of screenwriters Terry Winkless and John Sayles, because they wished to make the story resonate more with contemporary audiences. According to Dante, "The studio wanted us to use *real* **wolves** and base it strictly on the book. Ultimately, though, I still wasn't satisfied with the final version. But considering what *The Howling* was and what we had to work with, I'm still proud of it."

In *Cut! Horror Writers on Horror Film*, the novel's author, Gary Brandner, expressed his mixed feelings when he saw for the first time what Dante and his crew had done with his work of fiction. Although he had not been involved in the writing of the screenplay, he had assumed that he might be consulted for his opinions regarding the essence of his werewolf story. When he heard nothing more of *The Howling* until his agent wrangled an invitation to a screening of the finished picture for exhibitors, he sat unrecognized in the darkness, feeling quite certain for a time that his name spelled correctly in the opening credits would be the only things about his novel that he himself would recognize:

> Whereas my book opened with the rape of a young suburban wife, the movie jumped off with a female television reporter going into a bookstore to trap a psycho killer. . . . A couple of the character names were mine, but not much else. It took me a while for me to see that my basic story line—a troubled woman menaced by a village of werewolves—remained. I was at least gratified that a sex scene by firelight between a male and female werewolf was transferred nearly intact from page to screen. My feelings were mixed when the lights went up. The basic story and the lead characters were mine, but there were long stretches of the movie where I recognized nothing.

Brandner notes with satisfaction that when screen rights to *Howling II* were sold, he did manage to win the assignment to write the screenplay.

Among Joe Dante's perks in directing the motion picture was working with the legendary John Carradine, who numbered *The Howling* as his 361st film. Among his frustrations with *The Howling* were his attempts to get full use of a number of the technical effects:

> One of Rob's [Bottin] last makeup effects didn't get into the film until one day before the mix. That was the shot of Dee Wallace at the end of the picture looking like a Pekinese. When we originally contracted Dave [Allen] to do [scenes of stop-motion, animated werewolves] we had no idea

The classic 1981 werewolf film *The Howling* was followed by three sequels that never matched the quality of the original. Shown above is a scene from *The Howling 3: The Marsupials.*

of just how much werewolf we were going to get on film. . . . The problem was, the footage never really matched with what we did afterward. We just kept . . . making it shorter and shorter until finally we had to make it so short that there was no point anymore in having the animated werewolves in the picture.

SOURCES:

Golden, Christopher, ed. *Cut! Horror Writers on Horror Film.* New York: Berkley Books, 1992.

Mandell, Paul. "Dante's Inferno Blazes Again." *Fantastic Films,* August 1981.

Mitchell, Blake, and Jim Ferguson. "The Howling." *Fantastic Films,* August 1981.

Walker, John, ed. *Halliwell's Filmgoer's Companion, 12th Edition.* New York: HarperCollins, 1997.

Howls

"Howls" are conventions of werewolves—or rather, those men and women who enjoy role-playing as werewolves. The first Howl was the 1994 Harvest Howl organized by Smash Grewolf in Ohio. According to a posting on alt.horror.werewolves (AHWW) a Howl is "basically a gathering flesh (or fur) of readers of AHWW to socialize, get to know about one another, howl at the moon, leap over raging bonfires, and share the camaraderie that exists among members of the cyberpack."

Human Sacrifice

The February 1990 issue of *Omni* magazine's "Explorations" section carried the following quote from a 74-year-old Aymara Indian, an admitted practitioner of human sacrifice: "If a person *comprehends*, if he's really convinced, and has faith enough to carry out a human sacrifice, only then does good luck really come to him—cars, houses, everything."

Using the alias "Maximo Coa," the man described how he cut his victims' throats, filled a crystal goblet with their **blood,** and presented it to the patron of the sacrifice. Proud of at least 12 human sacrifices, Coa offered author Patrick Tierney unique discourses on the Bible, which he believes promises hidden knowledge.

Interestingly, Coa's interpretation of the Genesis story of Cain and Abel reaches the same conclusion as that of Biblical scholar Hyam Maccoby in his book *The Sacred Executioner* when he deduces that Cain was the hero in the original telling of Genesis. Cain built the first city and became the patriarch of metallurgists, musicians, and pastoralists. Cain's killing of his brother was not a senseless homicide, but the primeval sacrifice that secured the civilization of the human race.

Rites of human sacrifice go back to the very dawn of time. An extremely ancient Hittite cylinder seal from the second millennium B.C. depicts a human sacrifice in intricate detail. Although the living God of the Hebrews did demand blood sacrifices, He strictly forbade his people from imitating their heathen neighbors in the offering of human sacrifices.

In the Mosaic laws there were three basic reasons for animal and grain sacrifices to the living God: consecration, to dedicate oneself; expiation, to cover one's sin or guilt; propitiation, to satisfy divine wrath. Consecration sacrifices were vegetable or grain offerings, but they could not be brought to God unless they were preceded by an expiatory blood sacrifice. There was no consecration or commitment to God apart from expiation. Man could not approach God and be right with Him without the shedding of blood.

The surrender of Jesus to the will of God and his acceptance of the ignoble death of crucifixion serves, in the Christian cosmology, as the ultimate sacrifice and forever puts the issue of blood sacrifice to rest. The *Upanishads* of the Hindu sages, the *Bhagavad Gita* of Lord Krishna, the *Koran* of Mohammed, the teachings of the Buddha, the utterances of Zoroasters, the sayings of Confucius—all contain admonishments to their followers to resist the demands of the flesh and to exult the spirit.

But even though none of the major world religions permit human sacrifices, the compulsion to appease a higher power through the spilling of human blood appears to exert a powerful hold on those members of humankind who seek to strike a bargain with gods or **demons** that will insure their earthly, materialistic successes.

On June 3, 1970, a hitchhiker found the body of Mrs. Florence Nancy Brown off Highway 74 midway between San Juan Capistrano and Elsinore, California. Her right arm had been severed at the shoulder and her heart and lungs had been removed. As if that were not enough grisly desecration, three of the victim's ribs had been removed and a large strip of flesh and been sliced from her upper right leg.

Toward the end of June, three young men were arrested as suspects in the murder of a gas station attendant in Santa Ana, California, and one of them, Steven Hurd, confessed to the mutilation of Brown. According to Hurd's testimony, the victim's right arm, heart, and lungs had been removed as a sacrifice to Satan.

On January 5, 1990, authorities searching an Ohio farm commune found the slain bodies of a family of five—all victims of human sacrifice. Jeffrey Lundren, a defrocked minister of the reorganized Church of Jesus Christ of the Latter Day Saints who had declared himself the prophet of his own religion, was charged with instigating the ritual murders. Incredibly, other cult members enigmatically credited the motive for the sacrificial rites as a cleansing for the group so they might be better able to seek a mystical gold sword.

SOURCES:

Steiger, Brad, and Sherry Hansen Steiger. *Demon Deaths*. New York: Berkley Publishing, 1991.

Hyena People

The Berbers of Morocco believe in the *boudas,* men who have the ability to transform themselves into hyenas at nightfall and resume their human shape at dawn. In Abyssinia, people believe that the transformation is achieved through a special concoction of herbs.

Added to the belief in the hyena people is the common fear that ordinary hyenas have the ability to so faithfully imitate the human voice that hundreds of people are lured to their deaths each year. A number of African tribes also maintain that the hyena is a favorite form for shapeshifting witch doctors to assume when they are out after midnight exacting revenge on their enemies.

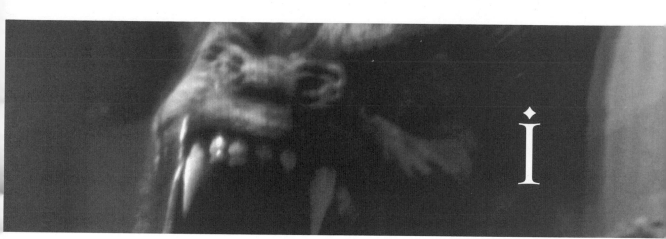

I

Incubus

According to ancient tradition, there are two main classifications of **demons** that lust sexually for humans—the incubi that assault women and the succubi that seduce men. Both sexual predators are said to have been born as a result of Adam's sexual intercourse with **Lilith,** a beautiful devil, often said to have been his first wife—or in same traditions, a fantasy wife created to assuage his great loneliness before the advent of Eve. If Lilith were but the personification of our First Father's erotic imagination, then his intercourse with her would really have been nothing more than masturbation. In such an interpretation, the incubi and the succubi would have been born of Adam's spilled semen. Modern occultists theorize that the lustful human imagination, when excited by powerfully erotic daydreams and fantasies, ejaculates an ethereal sperm that provides the seed for succubi and incubi.

In the Middle Ages, theologians warned against masturbation on the grounds that waiting demons stood ready to transport the spent semen for their own nefarious purposes. Nocturnal emissions were interpreted as the work of succubi, who excited sleeping males to the point of ejaculation.

The lusty incubi often seduced unsuspecting women by appearing to them in the guise of their husbands or lovers, and as one might suspect, the incubi played an important role in the history of the Inquisition. We might suppose that the tribunal listened with commingled attitudes of disgust and fascination as a female witch told of the pain of having intercourse with her incubus's large cold penis that set her belly aflame. Even pious nuns appeared before the Inquisition, attesting to their affliction by persistent incubi that tried to persuade them to break their vows of chastity. The epidemics of demon **possession** and erotomania that swept such convents as those of Loudon, Louviers, Auxonne, and Aixen-Provence have become classic cases of sexual hysteria.

In his *Eros and Evil,* R. E. L. Masters remarks on the scant amount of records from the Inquisition concerning the experiences of men who succumbed to seductive succubi in contrast to the enormous number of recorded instances in which women yielded to the sexual attentions of the incubi: "This did not, of course, imply that succubi were less seductive than incubi, and in fact the reverse seems to have been the case. The stories rested on the belief that women, ragingly lustful and naturally inclined to vice, would always put up defenses more feeble than those offered by males."

The incubus could prove to be a very jealous lover. In April 1533, according to old church records, an incubus became enraged when he discovered his human mistress in the arms of the son of the tavernkeeper at Schilttach, near Freiburg. In his furious state of mind, the incubus not only set the tavern ablaze, but he burned the entire village to the ground.

An often repeated case to demonstrate the sexual possessiveness of the incubus is that of the mother of Guibert of Nogent in the eleventh century. The good woman was possessed of an incubus, but she spurned her demon lover and married a human husband. This act of disobedience caused the incubus to become so furious that he cursed her husband and made him impotent for seven years. During those years when her husband was unable to perform his marital duties, the demon sat on the marriage bed and either laughed at the incapacitated human male or obscenely volunteered to perform in his stead.

It is recorded that the good Christian husband managed to break the demon's curse by nightly prayers and devotions; but shortly, thereafter, he was sent off to war and was forced to leave his wife vulnerable. The incubus wasted no time. On the very first night of her husband's absence, the demon was trying to resume his sexual hold on the woman. With the help of fervent prayers to the Holy Mother, the good woman was able to keep her demon lover at bay until her husband returned to the marriage bed.

Church authorities dealt with the corporeal condition of the incubus by advancing such theories as these: incubi fashion temporary bodies out of water vapor or gases; they have no actual physical bodies, but they possess the power to create an illusion of corporeality; they inhabit recently deceased corpses and animate them for the purpose of sexual intercourse with the living; they actually have material bodies which they can shapeshift into any shape they desire.

Father Montague Summers, that indefatigable pursuer of witches and werewolves, theorized that such demons as the incubi might be composed of that same substance known as ectoplasm from which the spirits of the dead draw their temporary body during materialization seances. He reasoned that

Werewolves on film know no cultural boundaries—here Paul Naschy portrays the tortured werewolf in the 1970 Spanish film *The Werewolf vs. The Vampire Woman.*

such a psychic drainage could occur if a frustrated young person encouraged the attentions of an evil entity by longing thoughts and concentrated willpower.

SOURCES:

Masters, R. E. L. *Eros and Evil.* New York: The Julian Press, 1962.

Spence, Lewis. *An Encyclopedia of Occultism.* New Hyde Park, NY: University Books, 1960.

Steiger, Brad. *Demon Lovers: Cases of Possession, Vampires, and Werewolves.* New Brunswick, NJ: Inner Light, 1987.

Indochina's Vicious Swamp Demons

Author Ed Bodin tells of the **possession** by a vicious, ripping, biting swamp demon of the beautiful Yvonne Marchand, the daughter of Col. Marchand, the French officer who had been sent to take command of the French detachment in Indochina in 1923. The lovely blond 18-year-old had become the belle of the military colony, and Col. Marchand's troubles seemed few. Although he was of the old military school and contemptuous of native beliefs concerning jungle monsters and **demons,** the native people, for the most part, tolerated him.

The colonel's principal error in public relations lay in the area of what he adjudged native trespassing on military property. A native corporal did his best to explain to the officer that the reason for such regular trespassing could be found in the people's desire to avoid going through a certain demon-inhabited swamp to get to the hills beyond. According to native legend, those who passed through the swamp at night would be in extreme danger of becoming possessed by fiendish demons. As an intelligent Frenchman educated in the best schools, Col. Marchand found only amusement in such tales.

One day a native thief surrendered to the authorities rather than risk escaping capture by running into the accursed swamp. Col. Marchand saw this as an opportunity to demonstrate the qualities of French justice, so rather than shooting the man, he ordered him cast into the midst of the swamp so that he would have to wade through the very area that he so feared.

The terrified felon begged the colonel to reconsider, and he attempted to throw himself at the feet of the colonel's daughter to beseech her intercession. All he accomplished by such a gesture was to trip Yvonne. In a rage, the colonel had the man forced into the swamp at bayonet point.

Late that night, Yvonne's maid rushed to the colonel with the news of the thief's terrible revenge. He had managed to creep back into the military camp, and he carried off the colonel's daughter. A search was organized immediately, but the native corporal feared the worst when the trail led to the swamp.

The search party was met by a soldier at the edge of the swamp. The thief had been found bleeding to death, his face and body covered with teeth marks and scratches, his jugular vein torn open. With his dying words he gasped that the beautiful Yvonne had wrenched herself free of his grasp and had turned on him with her teeth and nails. The colonel took some satisfaction that his daughter had escaped from her kidnapper—but who or what had ripped open the man's jugular vein?

The men searched an hour with powerful spotlights and lanterns before they caught sight of something white moving ahead of them in the swamp. It was Yvonne, naked except for a strip of cloth about her thighs. The searchlights caught the streaks of **blood** on her body, but her father was most horrified by the fiendish grin that parted her lips. Yvonne stood there before them, her teeth flashing as if she were some wild thing waiting for prey to fall within reach of her claws and fangs. To the astonishment of the entire search party, the girl rushed the nearest soldier, ready to gouge and bite.

Col. Marchand ran to his daughter's side. She eluded his grasp, seemed about to turn on him, then collapsed at his feet. Her shoulders and breasts were splotched with the indentations of dozens of tooth marks. The colonel covered his daughter's nakedness from the curious gaze of the soldiers, and he called for a litter to carry Yvonne home.

Later, when the girl regained consciousness, she told a most bizarre and frightening story. The thief had clamped a rough hand over her mouth and dragged her into the swamp. When they stopped to rest, Yvonne became aware of hideous, fanged demonic faces bobbing all around them.

"A terrible sensation came over me," she said. "Never before have I felt anything like it. I wanted only to kill the man, to bite his throat, to tear at his face. I have never had such strength before. I ripped and slashed at the man and mangled him as if he were but a small child cowering before me. I gloried in tearing away his flesh, in hearing him scream, in seeing him drop to the ground and crawl away. Then the faces summoned me on into the swamp. I tore off my clothes and began to bite myself. The faces laughed at me, and I laughed too."

When Yvonne had seen the lights of the searchers, she became furious and had wanted to kill them. "And, Father," she went on, "I knew you, but I wanted to kill you too. I kept trying to think of you as my father, but something terrible kept tearing at my brain. Then, when you reached out to touch me, the awful fire that was burning inside me seemed to fall away."

After that horrible incident, Col. Marchand was much more sympathetic to the hill people who trespassed across a small portion of military property to avoid the swamp. His daughter had said over and over again that if there were truly a hell, that swamp must be it. Eventually the swamp was completely filled in by earth and stone. Yvonne Marchand bore no lasting ill effects of her awful ordeal and she later married and produced healthy children. But when she recalled for others her night of possession in the Indochinese swamp, few walked away as skeptics.

SOURCES:
Bodin, Ed. *Scare Me!* New York: Orlin Tremaine Company, 1940.

Isawiyya

One of the most remarkable examples of structured lycanthropic behavior in contemporary times is found in the fanatical Moslem sect known as the Isawiyya, whose adherents are spread out across North Africa, the Middle East, and the Sudan. Founded in the early sixteenth century by the fakir and mystic Sheikh Abu Abd Allah Sidi Muhammed ben Isa as-Sofiani al Mukhteari (Ibn Isa), his followers vow to love God above all else, to fight His enemies wherever they are to be found, and to take unto themselves the name of an animal. Because Ibn Isa had the ability to communicate with all creatures, the religious gatherings of the sect require that each individual member wear a mask that represents one of seven animals—camel, cat, dog, panther, jackal, boar, or lion.

Ibn Isa, "the son of the Hairy One, Isa (Esau)," slept and prayed on two panther skins. Like the Biblical Esau, he had the gift of catching wild animals and rendering poisonous snakes harmless. In the *qasida At-Taiya* which he composed, Ibn Isa defined his powers by writing: "Men as well as the jinns are all devoted to me, also the venomous reptiles and the beasts of the desert."

Before embarking on a pilgrimage, the followers of Isawiyya sacrifice a bull or a calf in honor of Ibn Isa. Before the ritual, the calf or bull is dressed in women's clothing, thus becoming an obvious substitute for a human victim. As the rites progress, the brothers and sisters work themselves into such a frenzy that the sacrificial animal is torn to bits and its flesh eaten raw. When they begin their journey homeward after the pilgrimage, they dye their hands and feet red to represent fresh **blood.**

European witnesses to an Isawiyya initiation rite told of watching the initiates dancing and whirling faster and faster until they reached a point of violent ecstasy. Then, as they were writhing in the dust, bowls of live snakes, lizards, toads, and scorpions were set before them. Immediately, the initiates seized the bowls and began stuffing the wriggling creatures into their mouths, biting and tearing at them until there was nothing left but bloodstains.

SOURCES:

Eisler, Robert. *Man into Wolf.* London: Spring Books, n.d.

Hurwood, Bernardt J. *Vampires, Werewolves, and Ghouls.* New York: Ace Books, 1968.

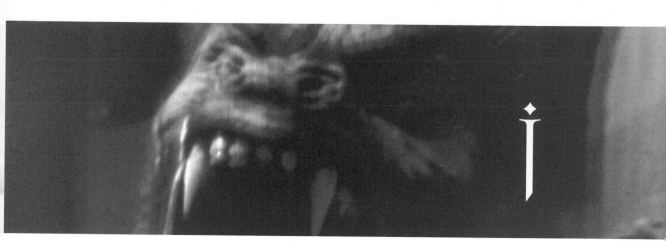

Jack the Ripper

The true identity of one of the most famous of the werewolf-type rippers of the past century and a quarter remains unknown. No one knows for certain whether Jack the Ripper was a man or a woman—a Jane the Ripper. There is even disagreement over how many victims were ripped and slashed by the monster's maniacal blade. What is generally agreed upon is that in 1888, during the black hours before dawn, the Ripper butchered at least five women in London's East End.

The newspapers gave him his notorious nickname, and it caught on quickly among the Londoners who shuddered behind locked doors on those foggy autumn nights. But there were always those women who went out at night in spite of the malignant presence of lurking death. The victims were all streetwalkers, but that fact didn't make the job of catching the Ripper any easier for the London police. Although some historians of crime place the number of deaths attributed to the Ripper as high as 15, there is a consensus that the series of slayings began with the murder of Mary Ann Nichols on the night of August 31, 1888, and ended nine weeks later with the gruesome slaughter of Mary Jeanette Kelly.

Mary Ann Nichols was found lying across a gutter. She had been repeatedly slashed by someone with a long-handled knife and a general knowledge of anatomy. A week later, Annie Chapman was found in a backyard, her head nearly severed from her neck. Certain other "horrible mutilations" were hinted at in the papers. The Ripper had taken two brass rings from her pockets and carefully arranged them at her feet.

A few nights later, the Ripper was interrupted in his attack on a local celebrity known as Long Liz by a man who drove a pony cart into the yard.

The pony shied at the fleeing figure of Jack, and the driver jumped down from his seat to lift the woman's head. The **blood** poured from the open wound in her throat, and it was evident that she was not going to survive.

Apparently the intrusion so annoyed the Ripper that within an hour he had lured Catherine Eddows into a lonely alley were he could indulge his perverse and deadly passions at his leisure. After the preliminary slashing of the throat, Jack extracted the left kidney, certain other organs, and wiped his hands and knife upon her apron.

The London newspapers ran countless stories speculating about the Ripper's true identity. Perhaps he was a demonic butcher, a Polish Jew, an American sailor, a Russian doctor, and a host of other suspects—anyone, it seemed, so long as he was not English. Jack, who was obviously following his press quite carefully and enjoying every inch of ink in the papers, countered with this famous quatrain which he sent to the *Times*:

> I'm not a butcher; I'm not a Yid,
> Nor yet a foreign skipper;
> But I am your own true loving friend,
> Yours truly—Jack the Ripper.

The Ripper corresponded with Scotland Yard as well as the London newspapers in a monstrous yet grimly humorous manner. He once wrote, "Next time I shall clip the lady's ears off and send them to the police, just for jolly." To a persistent police officer, whose investigation was evidently well known to the Ripper, he sent part of a human kidney. "I have fried and eaten the other part," he stated in an accompanying note.

Jeanette Kelly was the only victim killed indoors, and she was the only lady of the streets who might have been considered quite attractive. She had been heard by someone singing "Sweet Violet" during the evening and she had seemed to be in high spirits. Her horribly mutilated corpse was discovered the next morning by a passerby who could look directly into her ground-level apartment.

Sir Melville Macnaghten, a Scotland Yard official, reported that the Ripper must have spent at least two hours over his hellish work: "A fire was burning low in the room, but neither stove nor gas were there. The madman made a bonfire of some old newspapers and of his victim's clothes, and by this dim irreligious light, a scene was enacted which nothing witnessed by Dante, in his visit to the infernal regions, could have surpassed."

Although most of Kelly's internal organs had been scattered about the room, the Ripper had carried away no part of the body. This break in his *modus operandi* seems to puncture the theory that the murders were committed for the purpose of gathering anatomical specimens.

The only possible description that we have of Jack the Ripper came from someone who saw Jeanette Kelly in the company of a man who may well have been the monster himself: "A man about 35 years old, five feet six inches tall, of a dark complexion, with a dark mustache turned up at the ends."

Abruptly the murders ceased, but theories about the now-romanticized Ripper continued to afford morbid pleasures for amateur detectives at the local pubs and painstaking police work for tough-minded Scotland Yard inspectors. Someone with a knowledge of surgery always ranked first in the theoretical list of suspects. The second favorite was a midwife who had both familiarity with her victims and a knowledge of elementary surgery. A journalist reported the death of a diabolical doctor in Buenos Aires who allegedly made a deathbed confession that he had been Jack the Ripper, but his claim was impossible to document.

The notorious Dr. Neill Cream, convicted for poisoning four women, shouted, "I am Jack the . . ." just as the executioner pulled the lever on the hangman's platform and dropped the doctor to the end of his rope. Eager devotees of the Dr. Cream/Jack solution to the Ripper legend were disappointed when their investigation yielded the results that Cream had been in Joliet Prison in Illinois throughout the period of the East End murders.

More recent theories to Jack's identity have even included HRH Prince Albert Victor, Duke of Clarence, the grandson of Queen Victoria. And then there are those who say that Jack the Ripper is still among us—traveling first in one country to rip and to slash, then moving to another. These individuals see him as an evil, restless spirit, condemned to go on killing forever, like a Flying Dutchman of Death, a monster that seeks the life blood of women to rekindle his strength to wield a deadly butcher's blade.

SOURCES:

Masters, R. E. L., and Eduard Lea. *Perverse Crimes in History.* New York: The Julian Press, 1963.

Steiger, Brad. *Ghosts, Ghouls and Other Peculiar People.* Chicago: Merit Books, 1965.

Jackal People

Since the days of ancient Egypt and because of their close association with **Anubis,** god of the souls of the dead, jackals have been regarded as entities somehow connected with the underworld. In Hebrew tradition, jackals became symbols of destruction, and throughout a good portion of Asia, a jackal represents cowardice. Indian folklore dictates that if one hears the howl of a jackal and it appears to be coming from somewhere over the person's left shoulder, he or she has been given an omen of very bad luck.

In many parts of Africa, the jackal is very often regarded as a not very brave, but very wise, trickster figure. Those who become werejackals do so by wearing a strip of its hide across the forehead or about the waist. A witch doctor who has the ability to shapeshift will often choose the form of a jackal in order to travel secretly at night.

SOURCES:

Larousse Dictionary of World Folklore. New York: Larousse, 1995.

Steiger, Brad. *Totems: The Transformative Power of Your Personal Animal Totem.* San Francisco: HarperSanFrancisco, 1997.

Jacko

The native people of northwestern Canada have known about Sasquatch and Bigfoot for centuries and have included the mysterious monsters in their myths and legends. Stories from the early European explorers and settlers about Canada's Sasquatch have been cropping up since the 1850s, and on July 3, 1884, it appears that someone might actually have captured one of the elusive creatures. According to the *Daily British Colonist*, datelined Yale, British Columbia, dated July 4, 1884:

> In the immediate vicinity of No. 4 tunnel, situated some 20 miles above this village, are bluffs of rock which hitherto have been unsurmountable, but on Monday morning last were successfully scaled by Mr. Onderdonk's employees on the regular train from Lytton. Assisted by Mr. Costerton, a number of gentlemen from Lytton and points east of that place, after considerable trouble and perilous climbing, captured a creature who may truly be called half-man and half-beast.

> "Jacko," as the creature has been called by his captors, is something of the gorilla type standing about four feet seven inches in height and weighing 127 pounds. He has long, black, strong hair and resembles a human being with one exception: his entire body, excepting his hands (or paws) and feet are covered with glossy hair about one inch long. His forearm is much longer than a man's forearm, and he possesses extraordinary strength, as he will take hold of a stick and break it by wrenching or twisting it, which no man living could break in the same way.

> Since his capture he . . . only occasionally utters a noise which is half-bark and half-growl. He is, however, becoming daily more attached to his keeper, Mr. George Telbury . . . who proposes shortly to start for London, England, to exhibit him. [Jacko's] favorite food, so far, is berries, and he drinks fresh milk with relish. By advice of Dr. Hannington, raw meats have been withheld from Jacko, as the doctor thinks it would have a tendency to make him savage.

> The mode of capture was as follows: Ned Austin, the engineer, on coming in sight of the bluff at the eastern end of the No. 4 tunnel saw what he supposed to be a man lying asleep at close proximity to the track, as quick as thought blew the signal to apply the brakes . . . .At this moment the supposed man sprang up, and uttering a sharp quick bark, began to climb the steep bluff. Conductor R. J. Craig and Express Messenger Costerton, followed by the baggageman and brakeman, jumped from the train, and knowing they were 20 minutes ahead of time, immediately gave chase.

> After five minutes of perilous climbing, the then supposed demented

In Hollywood, werewolves are often teamed up with other monsters. Here, the Wolf Man joins forces with Dracula and the Mummy in the 1987 film *The Monster Squad*.

Indian was corralled on a protruding shelf of rocks where he could neither ascend or descend. The question of how to capture him alive . . . was quickly decided by Mr. Craig, who crawled on his hands and knees until he was 40 feet above the creature. Taking a small piece of loose rock, he let it fall . . . rendering Jacko incapable of resistance for a time at least. . . . Jacko was now lowered to terra firma. After binding him and placing him in a baggage car. . . . the train started for Yale. . . .

Although there were a rash of news stories after Jacko's capture, the creature seems to have vanished. Perhaps George Telbury did take him to England for exhibition and Jacko died there—or perhaps at sea, during the journey. In 1959, an elderly resident of the area verified the old newspaper stories. He remembered that some kind of "apeman" had been captured by the crewmen of a train, but he forgot whatever had happened to Jacko.

SOURCES:

Norman, Eric. *The Abominable Snowmen.* New York: Award Books, 1969.

Johnson, Liver-Eating (?–1899)

Talk about a major bit of Hollywood mistypecasting! Liver-Eating Johnson is the same man that ruggedly handsome and slender Robert Redford portrayed in *Jeremiah Johnson* (1972), that beautifully photographed tribute to the mountain men. The real Johnson had flaming red hair and beard, stood over six feet tall, and weighed a solid 250 pounds.

The plot of the movie was fairly accurate. In 1847, Johnson married Swan, a girl from the Flathead tribe, and took her with him to his cabin on the Little Snake River in northwestern Colorado. After making certain that Swan was comfortable and had plenty of food and firewood, Johnson left for his winter trapping grounds with his .30 caliber Hawken rifle, his tomahawk, knife, and backpack. He was unaware that Swan was pregnant with his child.

When he returned as soon as the spring thaws permitted, he was horrified to see vultures circling over his cabin. Inside he found the bones of Swan scattered by birds and animals. Beside her lay the skull of an unborn baby. The markings on a feather lying among the skeletal remains told him that the assassins had been members of the Crow tribe. At that same moment of recognition and rage, Johnson vowed a vendetta to the death—a personal feud that would take the lives of 300 Crow braves.

As portrayed in the Redford film, during all the years of Johnson's one-man war against the Crow, they never once managed to catch him unaware. What they did not show in the motion picture was Johnson's method of revenge. Whenever he triumphed over a Crow warrior, he would slash open the fallen brave's chest with his knife, rip out the warm liver from within, and eat it raw. Johnson had peeled away centuries of civilization and allowed the unbridled lycanthrope within his psyche to assume control. Such savagery inspired great terror among the Crow tribe, for it seemed as though they were dealing with a wild beast, something much more terrible than a mere man.

Once Johnson was captured by a group of Blackfeet who saw a chance to sell him to the Crow and receive a rich reward. Bound with leather thongs and placed under guard in a tepee, Johnson managed to gnaw through the straps, disarm one of his captors and amputate one of his legs. Fleeing into the deep snows and freezing cold of winter, it required superhuman strength and endurance to survive. But he had food in the form of the Blackfoot brave's leg to sustain him until he reached the cabin of a fellow trapper.

Johnson finally made peace with the Crow and lived to a ripe old age, passing away in a Los Angeles veterans' hospital in 1899.

SOURCES:

Hurwood, Bernardt J. *Vampires, Werewolves, and Ghouls.* New York: Ace Books, 1968.

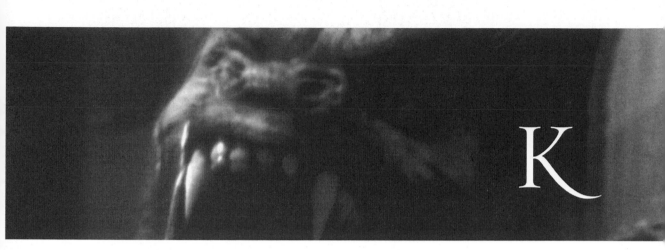

K

Dr. Stephen Kaplan Tracks Werewolves

For many years the late Dr. Stephen Kaplan (d. 1995) and his wife Roxanne Salch Kaplan conducted worldwide research on the number of real-life vampires and werewolves. When he served as the consultant on the cable television series *Werewolf,* more than half a million telephone calls were received on their "werewolf hotline." According to Kaplan, "People were invited to call in if they thought they knew a real werewolf or if they felt they had ever seen one in real life. They were also invited to call if they *were* werewolves."

Most of the callers simply requested additional information, but Kaplan said that 5,000 insisted that they had seen actual werewolves apart from the motion picture or television screen. An astonishing number of callers claimed that they, themselves, were real werewolves, with some describing very convincingly how they had killed their victims. Others claimed to be "latent werewolves," the result of werewolves who had mated with normal humans.

"It was great," Kaplan laughed at the memory. "Television was helping me research werewolves!"

Kaplan reports that he had actually had his first encounters with real werewolves—both females—in the late 1970s, but he chose not to go public with this aspect of his research until 1985. He maintains that he was always very cautious in conducting interviews with self-professed werewolves: "Many of them have spent time in mental institutions. Many have killed as teenagers and were committed. And the **full moon** really does affect them."

Although he says that he had never observed an actual metamorphosis from human to werewolf or to wolf in the manner of **Lon Chaney Jr.** or David Naughton in *An American Werewolf in London* (1981), many of the self-professed werewolves do have unusually long canine teeth. "Many of them said that they are affected about two days before the full moon," Kaplan says. "Then it's two days during the full moon and two days after—so for six days, they are werewolves."

Because of their obsession with becoming **wolves,** Kaplan reports, male werewolves may go for those six days without shaving, thus adding to their hairy effect. A six-foot male may walk on his toes—wolf-style—thus adding to his height and appearing three or more inches taller. Kaplan explains that, "The voice, the posture, the personality changes. In some cases, even eye color changes. They become full-blown schizoids. Some of them will actually use artificial hair to give a stronger emphasis to their werewolf appearance."

Kaplan says that he had received angry threats from werewolves: "A couple of werewolves in Pittsburgh were disturbed because I had maligned their kind. They took exception to hearing me on a radio talk show state that werewolves ripped, mutilated, raped, and sometimes devoured a portion of their victims. How dare I say such terrible things? So they threatened to kill me as an object lesson."

Stephen Kaplan has a theory that werewolves may be the genetic result of the more aggressive Yeti—the so-called **Abominable Snowman**—who came down from the mountains and eventually crossbred with humans. Werewolfism may skip a generation, but it may lie latent in many people.

"One of the most common causes of accidents on the playgrounds, in nursery schools, in primary schools, is kids biting each other," he comments. "How many latent werewolves do we have out there among us?"

SOURCES:
Steiger, Brad, and Sherry Hansen Steiger. *Hollywood and the Supernatural.* New York, St. Martin's Press, 1990.

Kappas

The *kappa* is the traditional water demon of Japan, most frequently described as having the body and shell of a turtle, the legs of a frog, and the head of a monkey. Among its favorite items on its bill of fare are tasty parts of human beings.

In more recent times, certain researchers have theorized that the origin of the folklore surrounding the kappas may actually be ancestral memories of the Japanese people recalling ancient interactions with aliens from other worlds. Japanese archaeologist and historian Komatsu Kitamura suggests that these **alien beings** visited Japan sometime between the ninth and eleventh centuries and that the ancient peoples mistook their breathing gear, antennae, diving suits, and so forth, for actual monsterlike appendages.

Movie poster from the 1970 film *Cry of the Banshee*.

Other researchers deny the alien beings theory and champion an indigenous monster hypothesis, because, they maintain, the kappas still live in Japan and are still being sighted. In 1978, two local construction workers were fishing one evening off a rock sea wall in the Japanese port city of Yokosura. According to one of the men, Makoto Ito, they saw a *kappa* come out of the water: "It just popped up from beneath the surface and stood there. It was not a fish, an animal, or a man. It was about three meters in height and was covered with thick, scaly skin like a reptile. It had a face and two large yellow eyes that seemed to be focused on us."

Researcher Sergio Morega added that such strange creatures were often sighted near the U.S. Navy base in Yokosura and that the local residents called the being *Masunta* and compare its appearance to that of the gill man in *Creature from the Black Lagoon* (1954).

Author-researcher Fabio Picasso states that similar *kappa* beings have been sighted in rivers and bodies of water throughout Argentina.

SOURCES:
Morega, Sergio. "U.S. Navy Base Under Siege by UFOs." *Ideal's UFO Magazine,* March 1979.
Picasso, Fabio. "Infrequent Types of South American Humanoids." *Strange,* fall 1991.

Kasha

Kasha is the name for the Japanese ghoul. This cannibalistic spirit entity hovers near crematoriums and tries to feed off human corpses before they can be properly cremated. Many Japanese families maintain a vigil over the bodies of their dearly departed to ward off the kasha by making loud noises on bells, gongs, and drums.

SOURCES:
Larousse Dictionary of World Folklore. New York: Larousse, 1995.

Khaki besar

Tribespeople in the jungles of Malaysia burn twigs and dry leaves, bang tin cans and gongs, and perform ritual dances to drive away the *Khaki besar* from their villages. The creature, said to be around eight feet tall, is the Malaysian "Bigfoot," and whether natural beast or werebeast, the big brute frequently leaves behind four-toed, 18-inch-long footprints in the soft soil of the undergrowth.

In January 1995, after a number of close encounters and the discovery of footprints had been reported, a massive search for the monster was conducted by wildlife experts, army and police units, and local tribesmen. Several thousand square miles of dense jungle surrounding Tanjung Piai in Johor state were trod in an effort to find Khaki besar and to capture it alive. The Malaysian tribespeople believe the creature was created by evil forces.

SOURCES:
Scripps Howard News Service. January 13, 1995.

The Klein-Krams Werewolf

In earlier times there were extensive forests rich with game in the vicinity of Klein-Krams near Lugwigslust, Germany. Great hunts were held in the area by sportsmen who came from all over Germany to test their prowess at bringing down their choice of game. For years, however, the hunters had been stymied by the appearance of a great wolf that seemed impervious to any bullet. Sometimes the beast would taunt them by approaching within easy shooting distance, on occasion even adding to the mockery by snatching a piece of their kill, then dash away without a bullet seeming to come anywhere near it.

Now it happened during one great hunt that one of the participants, a young cavalry officer, was traveling through the village when his attention was captured by a group of children running screaming out of a house. Seeing nothing pursuing them that would cause such panic, he stopped one of the youngsters and inquired whatever could be the matter. The child told him that no adult from the Feeg family was at home except for their young son. When he was left alone, it was his custom to transform himself into a werewolf and terrorize the neighborhood children. They all ran from their playmate when he achieved such a transformation because they didn't want him to bite them.

The officer was bemused by such a wild play of the children's imagination, and he assumed that they were playing big bad wolf after the sheep or some such game. But then he caught a glimpse of a wolf in the house—and in the next few moments, a small boy stood in its place.

Now greatly intrigued, the officer approached the boy in the house and asked him to disclose more about his game of wolf. At first the boy refused, but the young cavalry officer was persistent. Finally the boy confessed that his grandmother possessed a wolf strap, and that when he put it on he became a werewolf. The officer begged for a demonstration of such a remarkable transformation. After much persuasion, the boy agreed if the officer would first climb into the loft and pull the ladder up after him so he would not be bitten. The officer readily agreed to the conditions.

The boy left the room and soon returned as a wolf, once again chasing away his little playmates who had gathered in the doorway to watch. After a few minutes of pleasuring himself by frightening his friends, the werewolf disappeared for a few moments and then returned as the boy. Although the astonished cavalryman carefully examined the magic wolf strap, he could not discover any such properties of transformation in the strip of wolf hide.

Not long after his experience at the Feeg house, the officer told a local forester about the demonstration. Perhaps the child had fooled him with a large dog of wolflike appearance. The forester said nothing, but he thought at once of the large wolf that could not be brought down during any of the great hunts. He resolved to test both the bizarre tale told by the cavalry officer and the strength of the wolf by making a bullet of silver for the next hunt.

A few weeks later, during the hunt, the wolf showed itself in its usual taunting manner. Many of the hunters were determined to bring the beast down, but their bullets appeared to miss the mark or to have no effect on the great wolf. Then the forester fired his rifle. To everyone's astonishment the wolf spun wounded to the ground, then scrambled back to its feet and ran off toward the village.

A print from the fifteenth-century book *Leaves from the Golden Bough* in which a man turns into a wolf.

The huntsmen followed the trail of **blood** to the Feeg household where they found the wolf lying bleeding in grandmother's bed. In her pain she had forgotten to remove the wolf strap, and she was at last revealed as the werewolf.

SOURCES:

Bartsch, Karl. *Sagen, Marchen und Gebrauche aus Meklenburg.* Translated by D. L. Ashliman. Wein: Wilhelm Bramuller, 1879.

Kornwolf

In those days in Europe when **wolves** were numerous, they would run through the corn fields after hares and other small game completely hidden by the tall stalks. Because of the possibility of coming upon a hunting wolf or a wolf nest without warning, farmers warned their children to stay out of the fields and the way of the corn wolves. And in those same days of old when wolves were plentiful, so were escaped prisoners of war, fugitives from justice or injustice, and outlaws—all of whom took refuge in the temporary safety of the corn-fields. Until the harvest, someone on the run could remain out of sight for days—and not go hungry with the ripening grain and peas and beans from the garden.

In some rural areas of France, Germany, Lower Hungary, Estonia, Latvia, Poland, and other countries, festivals celebrating the harvest are often structured around the corn wolf (*kornwolf*) and the disposing of his corpse in a ritual bonfire. While some folklorists speak of the commemoration of a vegetation spirit, most experts agree that *le loup est dans les bles* refers to the real wolves and werewolves (outlaws) who once haunted the cornfields.

SOURCES:

Eisler, Robert. *Man into Wolf.* London: Spring Books, n.d.

Kung-lu

In the native Tibetean dialect *Kung-lu* means "great hulking thing," and the creature that merits such a title is also known as the Ggin-sung, Tok, or Dsu-teh. This legendary beast is indigenous to the Tibetan plateaus and has seldom been sighted beyond the boundaries of those mountains. According to those who have encountered the Kung-lu, the monster stands as tall as nine feet, weighs many hundred pounds, and is covered with black shaggy fur. Tibetan legends are filled with frightening claims that packs of these shaggy-haired monsters have lurked in ambush to abduct small children. Young, pretty native girls have allegedly disappeared during Kung-lu raids on native villages.

According to one account, when the famous mountain climber Huerta led the Argentinean Mountaineering Expedition in 1955, the group was stunned when one of their native porters was killed by a Kung-lu. Tales of these hairy monsters lurking in the Asian wilderness and bizarre legends of ancient Tibetan tribes battling aggressive hordes of howling Kung-lu are said to be found in ancient Asian manuscripts. Numerous venerable Chinese scholars linked these creatures to the "time of the dragon," the presumed genesis of Asian civilization. Many early Europeans to the courts of the khans were alarmed by tales of apelike creatures that raided caravans, murdered humans, and stole women and supplies during midnight ambushes.

SOURCES:

Norman, Eric. *The Abominable Snowmen.* New York: Award Books, 1969.

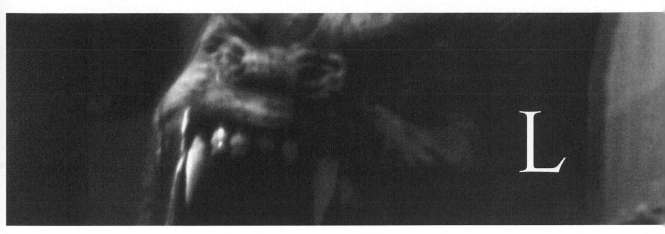

L

Lamia

In Greek Mythology, Lamia became a monstrous shapeshifter because of the jealousy of Hera, the consort of Zeus, the father of the Greek hierarchy of gods. Lamia was a beautiful woman who, like so many before and after her personal amorous encounter with Zeus, bore a number of his children. The furious Hera kidnapped those hybrid offspring and bundled them off to Olympia, far out of the reach of their mother's arms. Distraught with grief and helpless in her wrath, Lamia knew that she was powerless to combat the wiles of Hera and to win back her children. In desperation, she began to entice any mortal child to serve as substitute for her own progeny. Regretfully, such wrongful actions transformed her into a beast with the head and breasts of a woman and the writhing, scaly body of a great serpent. And rather than mothering the human children she lured into her presence, she began to feast upon them.

In time, Lamia reproduced and gave life to other creatures such as herself, beautiful women with the power to seduce and to suck the vital essence from those men who fell under their spell. In certain applications of the ancient legend, the lamiae become very much like vampires or succubi, stealing the life force from their victims.

SOURCES:
Gordon, Stuart. *Encyclopedia of Myths and Legends.* London: Headline Books, 1993.
Larousse Dictionary of World Folklore. New York: Larousse, 1995.

Lawton, Texas's, Werewolf

On the evening of February 27, 1971, 35-year-old Donald Childs of Lawton, Texas, suffered a heart attack as he looked out in his front yard and saw a wolfen creature on its hands and knees attempting to drink out of an empty fish pond. When he was released from the hospital two days later, Childs told police officer Clancy Williams that the werewolf had been tall, "with a lot of hair all over his face . . . and dressed in an indescribable manner."

Childs was not the only one who saw the werewolf of Lawton, Texas. Other witnesses who viewed the incredible creature told police investigators that the thing was wearing pants "which were far too small for him."

The first reports of the werewolf came from west Lawton. Police officer Harry Ezell said that they received calls describing "something monstrous" running down the street, dodging cars, hiding behind bushes, then getting up and running again.

Twenty minutes after the initial reports, Officer Ezell stated that they received a call from a man who had seen the monster sitting on a railing outside of his apartment. According to Ezell, the man told him that he saw the thing when he opened his curtain about 11:15 P.M.:

> He thought it was all a practical joke because the thing was perched on the railing. It looked like some monkey or ape. He thought it was a joke until it turned its head and looked at him. then jumped off its perch on the second floor railing and onto the ground 17 feet below.

> Once it hit the ground, it ran from the area on all fours, running something like the man thought an ape or monkey would run. He described it as wearing only pants, which covered its leg to its knee, as if it had outgrown them. He said that it had a horribly distorted face, as if it had been in a fire. It had hair all over its face, the upper parts of its body, and the lower parts of its legs.

A group of soldiers from Ft. Sill encountered the werewolf 15 minutes later, and they freely admitted that the beast had frightened them.

The monster was sighted on Friday and Saturday nights in Lawton. Sunday night was quiet, and on Monday night, Maj. Clarence Hill, commander of the police patrol division, sent out an alert, ordering his men to be on careful watch for the wolfman.

But the nightmarish creature—whoever or whatever it might have been—had already moved back into the strange dimension from which it had come—or else it traveled north to make its den under an old farmhouse near Fouke, Arkansas.

On May 1, 1971, Bobby Ford, 25, moved into the old Crank place outside of Fouke. He had lived in the home for less than five days when he had a face-to-face encounter with a six-foot-tall, hairy monster. An Associated Press release quoted Ford as saying that the hideous creature had frightened him so badly that he had run "right through the front screen door—without opening it."

SOURCES:

Steiger, Brad. *Monsters Among Us*. New York: Berkley Publishing Group, 1989.

A female skeleton creature from the medieval fantasy world of the 1985 film *Company of Wolves*.

Leopard Men

In ancient Egypt, the leopard was regarded as an aspect of divinity and associated with the god Osiris, the judge of the dead. For many African tribes, the leopard is a totem animal that is believed to guide the spirits of the dead to their rest.

A deadly cult whose members express their wereleopard lust for human **blood** and flesh has been in existence in West Africa for several hundred years. Particularly widespread in Nigeria and Sierra Leone, its members regularly eat human flesh in their religious ceremonies. Those who aspire to become initiates in the cult must bring back a bottle of their victim's blood and drink it in the presence of the assembled members. The cult killed as did the leopard, by slashing, gashing, and mauling their victims with steel claws and knives. They prepared a magical elixir known as *borfima*, brewed from their victim's intestines, which they believed gave them superhuman powers and allowed them to become leopards.

After a serious outbreak of systematic murders and **human sacrifice**s by the cult shortly after World War I, the authorities believed that they had rounded up its leaders and broken the strength of the leopard men. In spite of the executions of numerous key cult members, the leopard men only went underground and conducted sporadic human sacrifices. The cult's principal executioner in its ritual sacrifices was known as the *Bali Yeli*. This grim individual wore the ritual leopard mask and a leopard skin robe, and after the selected victim had been dragged to the jungle shrine, he performed the act of ritual murder with a deadly, two-pronged steel claw.

In 1948, there were 48 instances of murder that the police knew they must attribute directly to an upsurge in the leopard cult. After two decades of lying relatively low, the leopard men had returned to work savage, full-scale carnage on the people of Sierra Leone and Nigeria. During the first seven months of 1947, there were 43 known killings that bore the bloody, unmistakable marks of the leopard men.

When the police fired upon a cult member in the act of murdering a victim and killed him with their bullets, the people of the region began to accept the reality that the leopard men were only vicious humans, not supernatural beings. Witnesses began to come forward with clues to the identity of cult members and the possible location of their secret jungle shrine.

The shrine itself was discovered deep in the jungle, cunningly hidden and protected by a huge boulder. The cult's altar was a flat stone slab that was covered with dark bloodstains. Human bones were strewn over the ground. A grotesque effigy of a wereleopard, half-man, half-beast, towered above the gore-caked altar.

During February 1948, 73 initiated members of the cult were arrested and sent to prison. Eventually, 39 of them were sentenced to death and hanged in Abak Prison, their executions witnessed by a number of local tribal chiefs.

SOURCES:
Lefebure, Charles. *The Blood Cults.* New York: Ace Books, 1969.

Francis Leroy—The Werewolf of the Dordogne

On June 24, 1989, court officials in Paris sentenced Francis Leroy, the "werewolf of the Dordogne," to life imprisonment. Leroy had previously been imprisoned for the **full moon** rape and murder of a woman, but he was freed in 1973 after having served nine years of a 20-year sentence.

Leroy acknowledged that he was unable to control his bloodlust during the full moon, and he wished that he had been able to convince doctors to experiment on him to determine why he was compelled to murder when the moon madness seized him. He was convicted of murdering one woman and raping two others in the Paris area. He was also convicted of eight other attacks in southwest France.

Prosecutor Gerard Aldige told the court at Perigreux that Leroy was a "jackal who prowled by night, seeking his prey."

SOURCES:

Commercial Appeal (Memphis), 25 June 1989.

Lilith

In the Jewish tradition, Lilith was a beautiful fallen angel who was Adam's wife before God created Eve as his mate. The incubi and succubi, lustful male and female **demons,** were the children of Adam's sexual intercourse with Lilith.

Other mystics believe that Lilith was only a "fantasy wife" for Adam as he existed in his loneliness before God separated him from one of his ribs and presented with an acceptable mortal wife. If Lilith were nothing but the projection personification of Adam's lustful imagination, these mystics argue, then his sexual relationship with her was nothing more than masturbation accompanied by erotic fantasy. The incubi and succubi, therefore, were born of Adam's spilled semen—which serves as a warning that the human imagination that dwells upon sexual daydreams and forbidden erotic fantasies may cause a man to ejaculate an ethereal sperm which contains the psychic seed for such demon lovers.

Lilith is also the name of an Assyrian **succubus** who visits men at night in their dreams.

SOURCES:

Gordon, Stuart. *The Encyclopedia of Myths and Legends*. London: Headline Books, 1993.
Spence, Lewis. *An Encyclopedia of Occultism*. New Hyde Park, NY: University Books, 1960.

Lion Men

Few animals inspire as much awe as the lion, the "King of Beasts," for centuries linked with royalty, strength, and courage. As might be supposed, the lion is a favored totem animal for many African tribes, and its flesh is considered a potent food and a medicinal cure of a host of illnesses. From time to time, however, there will be those individuals who so identify with the lion that they will believe that they can achieve the power to shapeshift and become a lion.

In 1947, London newspapers carried accounts of lion men in Tanganyika who claimed the lives of more than 40 victims before their killing spree was stopped by the authorities. Twenty-six men and women were arrested in Tanganyika in connection with the lion men murders.

While the film *Fright Night 2* was primarily about vampires, it also featured this werewolf.

According to law enforcement officers, the lion men believed that their ritual murders would help to obtain such blessings as good weather. They wore lion skins and left wounds on their victims that resembled the marks of a lion's claws. The London *Evening Standard*, January 10, 1948, stated that three women have been hanged in Tanganyika for the first time in the country's recorded history. They died with four men for their part in the lion men murders in the Singida district . . . when more than 40 natives were slaughtered by people dressed in lion skins.

SOURCES:

Daily Telegraph (London), 9 April 1947.

The Evening Standard (London), 10 January 1948.

Little Red Riding Hood

Most people are very familiar with the story of Little Red Riding Hood, the young girl who walks through the deep, dark forest with a basket of goodies for her grandmother. "My, what big teeth you have, Grandma!" is the line that made most folks shudder as children, for they knew that a wicked wolf had taken Grandma's place under her nightcap and her blankets.

The popular nursery tale "Little Red Riding Hood" was first recorded in Perrault's *Petit Chaperon Rouge* (1697), which ends with both grandmother and Red Riding Hood being eaten by the wolf. Later, the brothers Grimms retold the story in *Rotkappchen* and provided the happier, more familiar ending that incorporated the woodsman who rescues Red Riding Hood and frees the grandmother from the wolf's belly. We know, however, that the tale is much older than the literary version and that it originated far back in the oral tradition of western Europe.

With what folklorists have learned of the werewolf and witchcraft traditions of Europe, they can recast the story of Little Red Riding Hood as it might have been told around the fireplace long before it was written down as a nursery tale. Witches were said to put on red caps or hoods before they went riding on their familiars to visit the magic circle deep in the woods where they could pay homage to the horned god, the Dark Woodsman. As they danced the Witches Round, the witches would be joined by vampires, werewolves, and other shapeshifting entities, all who wished to summon the Dark Woodsman to receive his blessing.

Therefore, the ancient oral tradition of Little Red Riding Hood could well be the tale of a young initiate who wishes to become a fully accepted member of a witch cult that meets deep in the forest. She puts on a red hood, places the gifts she brings for sacrifice in her basket, and summons her familiar, a wolf, to bear her to the secret meeting in the dark forest. On the way, she encounters an older witch, an aged crone, a grandmother figure, who wishes to become a werewolf as a reward for her years of service to the cult. Later, when the Dark Woodsman appears, he grants the crone a magical wolf strap that enables her to transform herself into a wolf whenever she wishes, and he accepts the sacrifice of the young red-hooded initiate and receives her as a member in good standing in the coven.

Lobizon

The legend of the werewolf or the wolfman is well-known in nearly all the provinces of Argentina and in parts of Brazil, Uruguay, and Paraguay. Throughout South America, the werewolf is known as *lobizon*.

SOURCES:
Picasso, Fabio. "South American Monsters and Mystery Animals." *Strange,* December 1998.

Loup-garou

Loup-garou is the traditional French name for the werewolf, and struggles with the man-beast were a standard of French folklore as early as the sixth century. Most often the werewolves in these stories were horrid monsters that ripped and tore their victims to bloody shreds. Occasionally, however, someone would enter an account into the records in which the werewolf was not all that bad. One such popular story of a werewolf that used his lupine talents for good is that of the Abbot Guilbert.

Guilbert was the abbot of a monastery on the banks of the Loire River who had one day granted himself the indulgence of saddling his horse and riding into a village to attend a fair. While he was there inspecting the fruits of a bountiful harvest, he also granted himself the indulgence of drinking rather too many glasses of good French wine. As he rode home to the monastery, the effects of the wine and the warm sun made him groggy, and he fell from the saddle.

Quickly regaining a few more of his senses after the shock of the fall, Abbot Guilbert realized that he had cut himself quite badly when he struck the ground—and that the scent of fresh blood had attracted a pack of wildcats. As the snarling, hissing cats surrounded him, he felt all was lost and he crossed himself and awaited a cruel demise.

Just as the moment seemed darkest, however, a ferocious werewolf appeared and attacked the cats with his flashing fangs and savage claws. The creatures were driven off, but the werewolf's victory was not without price, for the abbot saw that the beast had received a number of bloody wounds. Guilbert did not dare approach the werewolf for fear the monster might turn on

An 1857 illustration by Maurice Sand showing a man being attacked by a *loup-garou,* or werewolf.

him, so he managed to get back into the saddle and spur his horse back to the monastery. He was curious to note that the werewolf followed him right up to a waiting group of monks, who eagerly dressed the beast's wounds after they heard of Abbot Guilbert's frightening encounter and the daring rescue.

The next morning, Abbot Guilbert and his fellow monks were astonished to see that the werewolf had resumed its normal human shape, and they beheld the person of a very well-known, high-ranking official of the church. Then, to Guilbert's humiliation, the dignitary proceeded to give him a severe tongue lashing for having besotted himself with wine the day before when he attended the village fair. The werewolf ordered the abbot to do such harsh penance that he resigned from his position and left the monastery.

SOURCES:
Hurwood, Bernhardt J. *Terror by Night*. New York: Lancer Books, 1963.

Lucas, Henry Lee (1936–)

If law enforcement officers can ever completely substantiate the grisly claims of Henry Lee Lucas, then he would certainly be in the running for the most ruthless and vicious werewolf in history—for his victims would number over 200. The provocative, graphic, and generally unpleasant motion picture *Henry, Portrait of a Serial Killer* (1990) was loosely based on the life and the savage exploits of Lucas.

Finally charged with 11 murders, Lucas has changed his stories many times since he was arrested in May 1983. Demands by the authorities to prove his estimate of a likely 200 victims were often shrugged off by the 47-year-old psychopath with the comment that once he had committed such an act, he simply forgot about it. His first murder, he claims, occurred when he was only 13 and he killed a young female school teacher who rejected his adolescent advances. It is known for certain that he stabbed his mother to death in January 1960 when he was 24.

Lucas was confined to the Ionia State Psychiatric Hospital after being sentenced to 40 years for second-degree murder. Psychiatrists who interviewed him learned that he had been regularly beaten and abused as a child. Henry Lee did, in fact, suffer from frequent dizziness and blackouts because of cruel blows to the head delivered by his mother. Also in his childhood, he had lost his left eye when his brother accidently pierced it with a knife. When doctors ordered X rays of Lucas's skull, they detected extensive damage to the areas of the brain that control behavior and emotion. In assessing the results of their tests of the young outcast, doctors diagnosed Henry Lee Lucas as a psychopath, a sadist, and a sexual deviant.

Then, in spite of such a frightening diagnosis, Lucas was released after he had served only six years of the 40-year sentence. Henry Lee warned them that he should stay locked up. He just knew that it was his nature to kill again. As if to prove his point in the most dramatic way possible, he murdered a young woman within walking distance of the hospital on the same day that he was let loose upon society.

Lucas figured that he had given the authorities a fair warning. But, rejected once again, he began a savage and brutal campaign of systematic murder and rape that would continue for 17 years and would touch nearly every state in North America. Toward the end of that terrible run, he teamed up for one year with Otis Elwood Toole, a pyromaniac, and Toole's 13-year-old mentally challenged niece Frieda. While Henry Lee raped and killed, Otis would burn, and little Frieda would always be there to service them both during the lulls in their travels.

Serial killer Henry Lee Lucas, who claims to have killed more than 200 people.

Lucas was finally apprehended when Otis left to follow his own pyromaniac impulses and he and Frieda decided to settle in the small Texas town of Stoneburg. Lucas got a job as a general handyman to an elderly woman named Kate Rich. Unable to still his perverse instincts to kill, it wasn't long before he had enough of domesticity and regular employment. Suspicious neighbors notified the sheriff that Mrs. Rich and the handyman's "wife" seemed to have disappeared without a trace.

Faced with arrest after his 17-year spree of murder and rape, Lucas showed the police where he had hidden the remains of Mrs. Rich and Frieda. Then, sadly shaking his head, Henry Lee Lucas confessed that he had done some pretty bad things. For at least some of those "pretty bad things," he was sent to Death Row in Huntsville, Texas.

SOURCES:
Lane, Brian, and Wilfred Gregg. *The Encyclopedia of Serial Killers.* New York: Berkley Publishing, 1994.

Luceres

The *Luceres* were one of three possible tribes of lycanthropes that roamed the region near Rome and who were considered as wild or mad people by their neighbors. *Lucumones* may be translated as "mad people," and a derivative, *loco*, in Spanish and in American slang means "crazy." Numerous scholars have theorized that the original Luceres or Lucumones consisted of tribes of lupine werewolves with powerful, brutal chiefs that systematically terrorized the native people of the area.

Some authorities on the subject have connected the Luceres with *Lokroi*, whose legend may well have been brought to ancient Italy by Greek colonists. *Lokroi/Lokros* was said to be the son of Zeus and Maira, one of the she-wolves in the pack of the great hunter god and goddess, Hermes and Artemis.

SOURCES:
Eisler, Robert. *Man into Wolf.* London: Spring Books, n.d.

Lugosi, Bela (1884–1956)

Perhaps even more popular among amateur mimics and impressionists than James Cagney's phrase "You dirty rat" (which Cagney never said in any of his movies), is Bela Lugosi's "Good evening, I vant to suck your **blood**" (which Lugosi never said in any of his movies, either). While everyone thinks of Bela Lugosi in his formal evening attire and swirling cape as the quintessential **vampire** in *Dracula* (1931), the Hungarian-born actor also portrayed a number of lycanthropic characters in his extensive motion picture career.

Bela Lugosi, most famous for his film portrayals of Dracula, also took on other monster roles. As Frankenstein's monster, he battled Lon Chaney Jr.'s Wolf Man in *Frankenstein Meets the Wolf Man*.

Two years after he had achieved fame as the immortal Count **Dracula,** Lugosi appeared in the brilliant *Island of Lost Souls* (1933) as a man-beast, completely covered with hair and unrecognizable to any but the most perceptive fan. In this film, he had only a few lines, but they were integral to the plot. As the Sayer of the Law, he reminded the other animals that they must not shed blood or they would return to the house of pain.

In *Son of Frankenstein* (1939) Lugosi is once again almost unrecognizable as Igor, the hunchbacked assistant to the new Baron Frankenstein. It is a rather sad commentary on the bane of Hollywood typecasting that Lugosi could not escape roles in horror films, but even sadder that his fame as Dracula did not elevate him to a greater status in the monster movie-pecking order. In *Ghost of Frankenstin* (1942), he is once again hidden under hunchback, bowl haircut, and grimacing makeup as the mostly mute Igor. In **Frankenstein**

Meets the Wolf Man (1943), at least he graduated from the servile Igor to the mighty Monster himself, grunting and snarling at the growling and teeth-baring Wolf Man, played by **Lon Chaney Jr.**; but his facial features are completely masked under the trademarked monster makeup. Only his Count Dracula smile remains discernable.

In the werewolf classic *The Wolf Man* (1941), Bela Lugosi is Bela, the gypsy lycanthrope who bites **Lawrence Talbot** and becomes the agent whereby the **full moon** curse is passed to the unsuspecting scion of the Talbot estate.

Lugosi was born Bela Ferenc Dezso Blasko in Lugos, Austria-Hungary (now Lugoj, Romania), and he took his professional name from his native city. Playing Dracula became both a blessing and a curse for the actor who had enjoyed a distinguished stage career in his native Hungary. Typecast as vampires, monsters, and mad doctors, Lugosi's film career deteriorated to such roles as "Dr. Zabor," frightening the Bowery Boys in *Bela Lugosi Meets a Brooklyn Gorilla* (1952), and "Ghoul Man" in Ed D. Wood Jr.'s classic bad movie, *Plan 9 from Outer Space* (1958). Martin Landau won an Academy Award for impersonating Lugosi in *Ed Wood* (1994), and the film has made the tragic life of Bela Lugosi, from respected actor to drug-addicted pauper, more familiar to millions of moviegoers.

SOURCES:

Siegel, Scott, and Barbara Siegel. *The Encyclopedia of Hollywood.* New York: Avon Books, 1990.
Stanley, John. *Creature Features.* New York: Boulevard: 1997.

Lupercali

The annual Lupercali festival of the Romans was a perpetuation of the ancient blooding rites of the hunter in which the novice is smeared with the **blood** of his first kill. The god Lupercus, represented by a wolf, inspires men to act as **wolves,** to be thus as werewolves during the festival on February 15. A sacrificial slaying of a goat—representing the flocks that supported early humans in their attempts at establishing permanent or semipermanent dwelling places—is followed by the sacrifice of a dog, the watchful protector of a flock that would be the first to be killed by attacking wolves.

Once the blood of the she-goat and the dog are mixed, a bloodstained knife is dipped into the fluid, then drawn slowly across the foreheads of two noble-born children. Once the children have been "blooded," the blood is wiped off their foreheads with wool that has been dipped in milk. As they are being cleansed, they are expected to laugh, demonstrating their lack of fear of blood and their acknowledgment that they have received the magic of protection against wolves and werewolves.

Certain scholars believe this ritual of protection derived from a much earlier version of the Lupercali in which the smearing of the blood on the forehead indicated that the recipient had been "wolf-blooded" and would now forever be a solitary outlaw, a lycanthrope, a wolfman.

SOURCES:

Eisler, Robert. *Man into Wolf*. London: Spring Books, n.d.

Luperci

The exact meaning of *Luperci* remains in dispute. *Lupus* itself is not an authentic or original Latin word, but was borrowed from the Sabine dialect. *Luperca* or *lupa romana*, the she-wolf who suckled **Romulus and Remus,** may have given rise to secret fraternities known as the Luperci, who sacrificed she-goats at the entrances to their "**wolves**' dens." For centuries, the Luperci observed an annual ritual that found them chasing women through the streets of Roman cities and beating them with leather thongs. Scholars generally agree that such a violent expression of eroticism celebrated the ancient behavior of hunting tribes corralling captive women. In certain instances, the packs of early hunters, envisioning themselves as wolves, may even have practiced **cannibalism** on some of their captives. Perhaps, as some scholars theorize, this yearly rite of lashing at women with leather thongs became an acceptable societal substitute for the bloodlust of the Luperci's latent werewolfism that in days past had seen them tearing the flesh of innocent victims with their teeth.

SOURCES:

Eisler, Robert. *Man into Wolf*. London: Spring Books, n.d.

Lupicinus

Among the ancient Greeks and Romans, the wolf enchanter, the wolf charmer, was called the *lupicinus*. Perhaps hearkening back to prehistoric times, the lupicinus may well have been an individual tribesman who had a particular infinity for communicating with **wolves.** As the tribes became somewhat more sophisticated and developed agriculture and small villages, it was still necessary to have a person skilled in singing with the wolves and convincing them not to attack the domesticated animals. The lupicinus had the ability to howl with the wolves and lead them away from the livestock pens. In some views, because he also wore the pelt of a wolf, the luicinus also that the power to transform himself into a wolf if he so desired.

SOURCES:

Eisler, Robert. *Man into Wolf*. London: Spring Books, n.d.

Lupo, Michael (1953–)

Michael Lupo took great delight in the fact that his last name in Italian meant "wolf," and he boasted that he truly was the "wolfman." Lupo also bragged that he had taken over 4,000 homosexual lovers and that he had murdered four of them.

In May 1986, the London police realized that a serial killer was stalking the homosexual communities. Twenty-four-year-old Tony Connolly's body had been found on April 6 by children playing near a Brixton railway embankment in South London. Connolly was determined to be HIV positive, and the police soon linked his death to that of another gay man who had been strangled in West London, as well as another attempted murder in the same area.

On May 18, police arrested Michael Lupo, an Italian-born ex-commando who now worked as a makeup artist and the manager of a fashion shop in Chelsea. The 33-year-old Lupo had not been all that discreet in boasting of the murders and his prowess as the wolfman and he had been heard to state that he would continue killing until the police were able to catch him. Lupo was charged with the murder of Tony Connolly, as well as that of railway guard James Burns. Police also accused him of the attempted murder of a man in South London.

Three days after his arrest, the police were able to add the death of Damien McClusky, a 22-year-old hospital worker, to the wolfman's list of murders. Before Lupo was brought to central criminal court, a new murder charge, that of an unidentified man in his sixties, strangled near Hungerford Bridge, brought the tally to four murders and two attempted murders.

On July 10, 1987, Lupo pleaded guilty to all charges, and he was sentenced to life imprisonment on each of the murder charges, and to consecutive terms of seven years on each of the counts of attempted murder.

SOURCES:

Lane, Brian, and Wilfred Gregg. *The Encyclopedia of Serial Killers.* New York: Berkley Publishing, 1994.

Maenads

Worshippers of the horned god **Pan** and devotees of the wine god Dionysus, the cult of female acolytes known as Maenads held drunken orgies in the Arcadian mountains, whipping themselves into such frenzies that they would rip both animals and humans to shreds. Greek vases depict Maenads rending and devouring snakes and fishes. A red-figured vase from Cumae shows a Maenad brandishing a fish while sitting astride a panther.

The ancient writings of Galen the physician tell of witnessing Maenads tearing snakes to pieces and eating them raw. Other accounts describe the women, fired by wine and whirling, ecstatic dances, cavorting with human heads and bits and pieces of dismembered animals. In his *Bacchae*, Euripides saw the Maenads expressing their lycanthropic desires by lifting wolf pups to their breasts to suck on their nipples.

SOURCES:
Gordon, Stuart. *The Encyclopedia of Myths and Legends*. London: Headline Books, 1993.

Magnus, Olaus (?–?)

Bishop Olaf Magnussen, who signed his treatise *History of the Goths, Swedes, and Vandals* (1555) with his Latinized name Olaus Magnus, declared that the residents of Prussia, Lithuania, and Livonia often lost their livestock to bands of roving **wolves,** but their losses from the creatures of nature were not nearly as severe as those they suffered from the depredations of the werewolves.

According to Olaus Magnus, large numbers of werewolves prowled the outlying districts, attacking humans, as well as livestock. The monsters besieged isolated farms, broke into homes, and devoured every living thing.

An illustration from Book 18 of the *Historia Gentibus Septentrionalibus* by Olaus Magnus.

Their favorite haunt was said to be a ruined castle near Courland, a place avoided by all reasonable people, a place where the werewolves were equally ferocious with their own kind, slaying their weaker fellows.

The bishop also asserted that in Scandinavia devils came nightly to clean the stables and feed the animals. Devils also worked the mines, enjoying a work environment so like the labyrinths of their own hellish habitation. According to Olaus Magnus, Scandinavians learned to pay little attention to the devils working among them. Those indiscreet who might insult or molest the devils are in danger of having their heads twisted backward.

Many a practical sea captain has gainfully employed a devil as a navigator; for a devil, possessing control over the elements can always induce favorable sailing weather. Bishop Magnussen was clear that those who made such profitable deals with devils were in danger of losing their souls in the bargain.

SOURCES:
Seligmann, Kurt. *The History of Magic.* New York: Pantheon Books, 1948.

Mambu-mutu

Those eyewitnesses who claim to have seen the *mambu-mutu* in Lake Tanganyika in the small East African country of Burundi describe the creature as half-human and half-fish. Although the mambu-mutu sounds very much like the charming mermaids and mermen of classic folklore and myth, this were-fish grabs hold of people with the sole intention of killing them, eating their brains, and sucking their **blood.**

SOURCES:

Shuker, Dr. Karl P. N. "Managerie of Mystery." *Strange,* spring 1995.

Manson, Charles (1934–)

On the night of August 8, 1969, an evil sorcerer sent his pack of werewolves out to brutally and sadistically sacrifice victims to his cult of fear and chaos. The spellbinding magician was called Sweet Daddy-O by his young female disciples, but after that terrible evening of slaughter in the Hollywood Hills, the world would know the malevolent sorcerer of the dark side as Charles Manson and his vicious pack of werewolves as Charles "Tex" Watson, Susan Atkins, Linda Kasabian, and Patricia Krenwinkel. Their sacrificial victims that night were actress Sharon Tate, Jay Sebring, Abigail Folger, Voityck Frokowsky, and Steven Parent.

Today, watching flim clips and interviews of Charles Manson in prison, it is difficult to imagine how this wild-eyed, disheveled, incoherent little man could have been capable of casting a spell that would bend young men and women to his murderous will. As baffling as it might seem to rational minds, the antisocial ravings of this silly, illiterate, hostile malcontent set in motion one of the most brutal and senseless crimes in Los Angeles's history.

When 35-year-old Manson was indicted for the terrible murders in the Hollywood mansion, he had already spent 22 years of his life in state or federal prisons. Uneducated, untrained, and barely able to read, the only things that he had learned in his years of confinement were how to steal cars, how to pass bad checks, and how to pimp. On those rare occasions when he was out of prison and free on parole, he exhibited an obsession with sex.

In the early 1960s, Charles Manson stole and cashed two U.S. Treasury checks. He was promptly apprehended and sent to the federal prison at McNeil Island, Washington. It was here that he began to explore offbeat religious philosophies and the occult. Interestingly, it was also here that he began to work seriously to develop his singing voice, to play the guitar, and to write his own songs.

When the slender, brown-eyed, brown-haired Manson walked out of prison in March 1967, he found that a whole new world had been created while he had been behind bars. The flower children had launched the hippie movement, and the Haight-Ashbury section of San Francisco had become a golden gloryland of naive and gullible young people. Charlie got himself a hillside pad and began to collect his followers.

One of his first disciples was an attractive, long-haired, 19-year-old brunette named Patricia Krenwinkel, a 1966 graduate of Los Angeles High. She had always been considered a reserved and conservative young woman, but the magic of Manson soon transformed her into a cult camp follower. The teenager fell under Charlie's spell so quickly that she abandoned her car in a parking lot, left work without picking up her paycheck, and wrote her family a brief note that she was going off to "find" herself.

A few young men joined the Manson family, but many more women were drawn to the mystical minstrel by some weird power. Charlie was a magical man to those desperate young people who came to sit at his feet. He led them in weird chants and mystical rites, freely adapted from other traditions and reshaped through his own unique personality. Anyone who questioned or doubted Sweet Daddy-O was threatened with explusion from the group.

In May 1968, with the hippie scene fading in San Francisco, Manson and his subservient family headed south toward Los Angeles. Led by their mystical guru, the flock of young disciples converted an old schoolbus into a rolling pad and headed for the City of Angels. It was there in the movie capital, the bearded, long-haired Manson declared, that he would make a fortune as a songwriter and a musician.

Boyd Rice, San Francisco's "King of Noise Music" and a passionate Mansonophile, claims to be in possession of nearly nine hours of Charlie's music, which he recorded in his cell at Vacaville in the early 1980s. The songs are known collectively as *Charlie Manson's Good Time Gospel Hour*. Rice also refers to a Wade Williams documentary of Manson singing his song "Mechanical Man." According to Rice, film director Roman Polanski and actor Warren Beatty bought up all the original copies of the documentary and destroyed them.

For a time the family and Sweet Daddy-O moved in with 34-year-old Gary Hinman, a musician, who kept a place, labeled the "pig farm," for druggies and other assorted weirdos. A year later (c. 1968), Hinman was murdered by the Manson family when he tried to toss them off his property. The musician was discovered slashed to death, the bloody legend "political piggy" scrawled on the walls of his home. Hinman's death is believed to be the first murder perpetrated by Manson and his cultists.

Then came the terrible night of carnage in the mansion of Sharon Tate and her husband Roman Polanski. The house had once belonged to Terry Melcher, actress Doris Day's son. Although Melcher no longer lived there, the mission on which Manson sent his pack of werewolves was supposed to be part of a plan to frighten him for having failed to get Charlie a big-money record deal.

Tex Watson, one of Manson's subchiefs in the cult, relayed the master's orders to the girls, Susan Atkins, Linda Kasabian, and Pat Krenwinkel, who were commanded to bring knives and to change into their "creepie crawlie" black clothes. Watson, armed with a gun, drove the she-wolves to the Tate-Polanski mansion.

After they pulled up in front of the house, Watson snipped the telephone wires and motioned the women to follow him. The family members were surprised when Steven Parent emerged from the caretaker's cottage and began walking down the driveway. Watson fired twice, killing the young man instantly.

Watson forced open a window, crawled inside, and opened the door for the three women. Voityck Frokowsky, a friend of Polanski's, was asleep on a couch in the living room. Awakened by the invaders, he stared in drugged disbelief at their bizarre outfits and demanded to know who they were. When one of the girls told him that they wanted money, Frokowsky said that he would give them all that he had. Watson warned him not to make a false move or he would die. "I am the devil," Watson said, "and we're here to do my business."

The disturbance alarmed Sharon Tate and the other guests, Abigail Folger and Jay Sebring, who were brought into the living room. Tate, who was several months pregnant, wanted to know what the intruders were going to do with them. Watson did not hesitate to decree their deadly mission: "You're all going to be killed!"

Sebring, a celebrated hairstylist, took a good look at the five armed strangers and decided to fight for his life. He was shot, stabbed, and collapsed dead in the living room.

Although Frokowsky had been bound on the couch, he managed to break the nylon cords that tied him. One of the girls stabbed him again and again as he ran from the house, screaming for help. Watson also pursued him, clubbed him with the pistol, then shot him in the back.

Abigail Folger, heiress to the Folger coffee fortune, was stabbed as she tried to run toward the caretaker's house on the southern edge of the grounds. She was slashed to death on the lawn.

Sharon Tate battled two of the girls, but she was overpowered and forced back on a couch. She pleaded with them that all she wanted to do was to have her baby. "Kill her!" the girls chanted—and they continued to stab and to slash at her body even after she lay dead on the floor. Someone in the family dipped a towel in the **blood** that flowed from Sharon Tate's breasts and painted PIG on the mansion door.

The multiple murders were discovered by Winifred Chapman, a maid at the home, when she walked up to the Hollywood mansion early on the morning of August 9. A Los Angeles police official stated that the bodies of the victims had been mutilated as if "by an insane butcher." The bodies of Tate and Sebring had been placed in weird positions, suggestive of perverted sex practices. Sebring's face was covered by a dark, grotesque mummer's mask. All of the victims had their faces frozen into twisted death masks of absolute terror.

Sharon Tate had been considered one of the most beautiful women in Hollywood. Modest, reserved, and unwilling to be cast as a sex symbol, she met Roman Polanski when she accepted a role in his movie *Fearless Vampire Killers* (1967), and she married him shortly thereafter. When she was not making films, Sharon often joined coffee heiress Abigail Folger and actress Mia Farrow for philosophical discussions.

While the Los Angeles police frantically searched for clues, rumors of drug-induced satanic orgies in the Hollywood hills began to surface in the media. Journalists speculated that the brutal massacre was triggered in some way by Hollywood's bizarre, kinky preoccupation with offbeat sex, heavy drugs, and the dark side of the occult.

To dispel such suggestions that their mansion had hosted drug parties, sex orgies, or satanic rituals, Roman Polanski made a sorrowful appearance on national television. He explained that the reason that his wife had not accompanied him to Europe was because of discomfort with her pregnancy. He had last spoken with her by telephone only a few hours before the tragedy. "Sharon not only did not use drugs," he said firmly, "she didn't take alcohol, and she didn't smoke."

On the night following the murders at the Tate-Polanski mansion, Patricia Krenwinkel and Leslie Van Houten tripped out on LSD, then went for a ride with Linda Kasabian and Tex Watson. Somehow they ended up in front of the home of Leno and Rosemary LaBianca, wealthy Los Angeles business owners. The family grabbed the couple, tied them up, and stabbed them to death. They had now brought seven new bloody bodies to lay on the sacrificial altar of their mad messiah.

Throughout the lengthy ordeals of their arraignment and trials, Manson's female disciples insisted that their guru was innocent of any blame in the gruesome slayings. On April 19, 1971, Charles Manson, Patricia Krenwinkel, Susan Atkins, and Leslie Van Houten were convicted and sentenced to death, subsequently reduced to life imprisonment, for the Tate/LaBianca murders. Tex Watson was tried separately, found guilty, and sentenced to life imprisonment. Linda Kasabian turned state's evidence and no charges were brought against her.

In the cosmology of Charles Manson, he and all of humanity are both God and the devil at the same time. He also professed that every human was a part of all others, which, in his philosophy, meant that individual human life was of no consequence. If you killed someone, you were just killing a part of yourself, so that justified the murder.

SOURCES:

Lane, Brian, and Wilfred Gregg. *The Encyclopedia of Serial Killers.* New York: Berkley Publishing, 1994.

Schreck, Nicolas. "An Interview with Charles Manson." *Blitz,* September 1988.

Steiger, Brad, and Sherry Hansen Steiger. *Demon Deaths.* New York: Berkley Publishing, 1991.

Mapinguary

In the dense jungle growth of the Matto Grosso, the natives fear the monstrous *mapinguary*, a creature so powerful that it kills oxen by pulling out their tongues. In his book *On the Track of Unknown Animals*, Dr. Bernard Heuvelmans repeats an account of a mapinguary that was sent to him from a respected Brazilian writer. In the report, the principal, Inocencio, was on an expedition to the Urubu watershed when he left the main party to pursue a group of black monkeys with the intention of shooting one of them. Then, as it grew dark, he was surprised to hear what he believed to be a man shouting—a horrible, deafening cry.

Inocencio heard the sound of heavy footsteps, as if a large animal was running toward him, then he saw a silhouette the size of a man of middle height appear in the clearing. The figure remained where it stood, looking suspiciously at the place where Inocencio crouched quietly.

When the creature roared again, Inocencio fired at it, and he was terrified to see the wounded monster charging toward him. He fired another bullet, and the mapinguary leaped behind a barricade of undergrowth and brush. Inocencio himself took refuge in a tree and later observed that the roars from the creature that he heard that night were far more terrible and deafening than those of a jaguar.

He did not venture down from his perch until dawn. He found **blood** splashed around the clearing, and he noticed a sour smell that permeated the entire area. His companions began firing shots so that he might find them, and Inocencio rejoined the expedition, convinced that he had survived an encounter with a mapinguary.

In British Guiana and Venezuela, mapinguary, the jungle wildman, is known as the *didi*. According to the native inhabitants, the creature is a short, thickset, and powerful beast that sounds like a human when it signals its fellows with its plaintive howl or whistle.

In 1931, during an expedition to British Guiana, Nico Beccari, an Italian anthropologist and professor, received an account of the didi from no less a personage than the British resident magistrate, who told of encountering

A dinner party goes bad when some of the guests are turned into animals in the film *The Company of Wolves*.

two strange animals walking on their hind feet. The puzzling creatures had human features but were completely covered with reddish-brown fur. They retreated slowly back into the jungle, never once taking their eyes off the magistrate, who stood, baffled by what he had seen, on the narrow trail.

Miegam, the guide for the Italian expedition, told of his own experience with the didi in 1918 when he had been traveling up the Berbice with three other men. A bit beyond Mambaca they spotted two men on the riverbank and called to them to ask if the fishing was good. The fisherman appeared startled by Miegam and the other men in the boat and ran away into the forest.

When Miegam and his party landed to investigate the strange behavior of the fishermen on the bank, they were startled to find that the footprints the "men" had left in the sand resembled the tracks of apes more than the footprints of humans.

SOURCES:
Norman, Eric. *The Abominable Snowmen*. New York: Award Books, 1969.

Mars

Mars and Saturn are the two planets in astrological tradition that are considered "malefic." Mars, like the Roman god of the same name (the god Ares to the ancient Greeks), is representative of violent energy, aggressiveness, destruction, hostility, and war. According to astrological determinations, when Mars and Saturn achieve significant relationships in the heavens, bad things are certain to occur on earth. A conjunction of Jupiter, the planet of health, with Mars and Saturn in the sign of Aquarius in 1345 heralded the onset of the Black Death that decimated Europe. The conjunction of Mars and Saturn in Pisces in 1496 marked the appearance of syphilis on the European continent.

In the Middle Ages, Christian scholars interpreting astrological symbols deemed those with Mars in their sign to be highly susceptible to demonic influences. When the god Mars later became equated with the Master of Animals, the horned god of the North, he was also identified as Silvanus, a woodland god, very much like Pan. The horned god became synonymous with Satan in the eyes of the church fathers, the god of the witches, werewolves, and other shapeshifters.

SOURCES:
Gaskell, G. A. *Dictionary of All Scriptures and Myths.* Avenel, NJ: Gramercy Books, 1981.

Moeris

The Roman poet Vergil's *Alphesiboeus* sang of Moeris the werewolf in 39 B.C., one of the earliest lycanthropic references to appear in western literature: "These herbs and these poisons, culled in Pontus, Moeris himself gave me— they grow plenteously in Pontus. By their aid I have often seen Moeris turn into a wolf and hide in the woods, often call spirits from the depth of the grave, and charm sown corn away to other fields."

SOURCES:
Eisler, Robert. *Man into Wolf.* London: Spring Books, n.d.

Montvoisin, Catherine (?–1680)

The character of Catherine Montvoisin, known as La Voisin, serves as an example of the type of individual who stood ready to cater to the demand of the jaded nobility for secret and sensual satanic rites. When she went to the stake on February 23, 1680, she boastfully shrieked that she had sacrificed over 2,500 infants to her lord Satan.

In 1647, Catherine Deshayes was a barefooted beggar girl who had been sent out into the streets to tell fortunes. By propitious circumstances, many of the waif's predictions came true, and she cultivated a clientele who swore by the child's "God-given powers." When she was 20, she married a ne'er-do-well named Antoine Montvoisin and began to establish herself as a midwife, a beautician, and a herbalist.

It was when the enterprising La Voisin included palmistry, prophecy, and astrology among her stock-in-trade that she incurred the wrath of the church. But somehow the bright-eyed and vivacious young woman accomplished a miracle seldom achieved by others. Instead of being flayed alive by a grand inquisitor, she managed to convince a learned tribunal composed of the vicars-general and several doctors of theology from the Sorbonne that her particular approach to astrology was completely acceptable to church doctrine.

The effect that her release from the inquisitors had upon her already flourishing trade as a herbalist and her ever-increasing reputation as seer was fruitful beyond her dreams. Surely, people reasoned, La Voisin had secured the church's blessing on her magic. And rather than giving her thanks to God for deliverance, Catherine decided that it was Satan who had brought her unharmed from the **tortures of the Inquisition.**

La Voisin began to receive her clients in a darkened chamber wherein she appeared in an ermine-lined robe emblazoned with 200 eagles embroidered in gold thread on purple velvet. She was now a satanic high priestess and, for a properly weighted bag of gold, she would officiate at a special black mass for the troubled seeker of wealth and power. She kept a secret list of more than 50 Roman Catholic priests who would celebrate the black mass at her bidding.

La Voisin's favorite among the heretical clergymen was Abbe Guilborg, who, in spite of the fact that he held a number of high-ranking public and private ecclesiastical offices, was always in need of extra money to maintain the stable of mistresses that he kept closeted around Paris. His skill as a chemist was also put to good use by La Voisin, who had a number of clients who had use for special poisons.

Babies for sacrifice cost La Voisin a good deal of money, but she had learned to economize when she was a starving waif in the Paris streets. She established a home for unwed mothers, which saw the girls through their pregnancies, then relieved them of the responsibility of caring for an unwanted child. Girls without financial means were provided for at no charge. The bills presented to the women of the nobility were large enough to cover the operating expenses for the entire home.

La Voisin's black mass rituals were conducted deep in the bowels of her high-walled house in the region lying south of St. Denis, which, in seventeenth-century Paris, was called Villeneuve. Although Abbe Guilborg wore vestments of an orthodox shape made of white linen, the chasuble and possibly the alb were embroidered with black pine cones, ancient Greek symbols of fertility. The prayer book was bound in human skin; the "holy water" was urine; the "host" was usually a toad, a turnip, or, on occasion, true host stolen from a church and desecrated with filth. When it was time for the sacrifice, Guilborg raised aloft a squalling child, silenced its cries by slashing its throat, and allowed its **blood** to flow over the naked bodies of the supplicants who beseeched Satan to fulfill their desires. Once enough of the sacrificial blood had been caught in a silver chalice, it was mixed with wine and drugs for the ceremonial drinking. The pathetic little corpse was handed to La Voisin, who tossed it into the roaring mouth of the waiting oven.

A police official named Desgrez had been closing in on La Voisin and her obscene black sabbats, but when his informants reported the number of high-ranking and high-born nobility who were frequenting the subterranean chambers, he found himself faced with an ethical issue. It could be very unpleasant for him to anger so many important people by suggesting that the activities in which they were engaging were both heretical and illegal. Even the arrest of La Voisin would, at least indirectly, be criticizing the members of the aristocracy who regularly attended her sabbats and who openly relied upon her talents as a seeress.

Desgrez was about to place service to the law above servility to the aristocracy when one of his officers told him that one of the coaches waiting before the high walls of La Voisin's mansion belonged to none other than Madame de Montespan, the mistress of King Louis XIV. The detective's head must have been sent spinning as his officer said that he had learned through an informant that the lovely royal mistress had herself served as a naked, living altar at one of La Voisin's Sabbats. What was more, de Montespan had ordered the sacrifice of a child and had bathed in its blood in order to insure her place in the king's heart.

It was too much for Desgrez. He brought his evidence and the list of names of La Voisin's aristocratic supplicants to his superior, La Renie, head of the *Chambre Ardente*. King Louis had pledged himself to support the *Chambre*, but when he saw the list of names and considered their high ranking, including that of his own mistress, he realized that he was in a politically explosive situation. His advisors cautioned him that a hasty exposure of the decadence of court life could lead to revolution—or even encourage England to launch an invasion against a morally sick and internally torn France.

It took the Sun King nearly a year to make his first move. La Voisin was arrested, and thereafter a few carefully planted rumors caused large numbers of the court favorites to decide to take extended trips aboard. Once these nobles and their ladies were out of the country, a program was instituted that managed to suppress all incriminatory evidence against highborn figures and

Madame de Montespan. La Voisin was treated to a pleasant stay in jail until King Louis was confident that all those of high position had been protected. Then she was handed unceremoniously into the hands of the grand inquisitor.

Catherine Montvoisin endured four six-hour ordeals in the torture chamber before she was delivered to the stake on February 23, 1680. By the king's order, only testimony concerning those satanists who had already been condemned was allowed to be recorded. The former little barefooted fortune-teller from the streets of Paris went to her death singing ribald songs and cursing the priests who sought her final confession.

SOURCES:
Steiger, Brad. *Demon Lovers: Cases of Possession, Vampires, and Werewolves.* New Brunswick, NJ: Inner Light, 1987.

The Morbach Monster

According to legend, Wittlich was the last town in Germany where a werewolf was killed, but it would appear that something very much in the werewolf tradition still stalks the area.

D. L. Ashliman, author of *Werewolf Legends from Germany,* received the following account from a respondent who first learned of the legend while he was stationed at Hahn Airforce Base c. 1988. Morbach is a munitions site just outside the village of Wittlich:

> There is a shrine just outside of town where a candle always burns. Legend has it that if the candle ever goes out, the werewolf will return. One night a group of security policemen were on the way to their post at Morbach when they noticed that the candle was out at the shrine. They all joked about the monster.
>
> Later that night, alarms were received from a fence-line sensor. When the security policemen investigated the call, one of them saw a huge "dog-like" animal stand up on its back legs, look at him, and jump over the seven-and-a-half-foot chain-link fence. A military working dog was brought to the area where the creature was last seen, and the dog went nuts, not wanting anything to do with tracking the creature.

SOURCES:
E-mail dated October 6, 1997, to D. L. Ashliman from a respondent who wishes to remain anonymous.

Mowgli

Although he was in no way a werewolf, Mowgli, the jungle boy, was reared by **wolves** in the classic Rudyard Kipling story, *The Jungle Book.* And just as Tarzan, who was reared by apes, could speak the language of all creatures, so did Mowgli share this extremely useful survival skill.

Two werepigs and a werecat combine to form one of many odd scenes from the classic 1922 silent Swedish film *Haxan (Witchcraft Through the Ages).*

Kipling's highly romanticized tale has proven to have lasting power to fire the imagination of each succeeding generation since its publication in 1895. Scholar **Robert Eisler** terms the advent of the "wolf cubs" in the Boy Scouts to be a "curious and harmless revival of atavistic lycanthropic ideas," inspired by the wolf-child Mowgli. Eisler attributes the worldwide success of Kipling's stories to the appeal they make to "archetypal ideas of the human race."

Eisler speaks of such legendary figures as **Romulus and Remus,** but states that there are a number of cases of exposed Hindu children who were cared for by she-wolves with their cubs. He is also familiar with the two wolf sisters rescued by the Rev. J. A. L. Singh and with numerous other cases.

Mowgli was first portrayed in motion pictures in 1942 by Sabu, a former stable boy from Karapur, Mysore, India, who went on to play numerous exotic roles in British and American films. In 1967, the Walt Disney Studios applied the magic of animation to *The Jungle Book*. In 1998, they released a direct-to-video sequel entitled *The Jungle Book: Mowgli's Story*. Four years prior to their second animated treatment of Mowgli, Disney released a live-action film, *Rudyard Kipling's The Jungle Book*, with Jason Scott Lee as an excellent personification of the wolf-boy grown to young adulthood.

SOURCES:

Stanley, John. *Creature Features*. New York: Boulevard; 1997.

Msomi, Elifasi (?–1956)

Beginning in August 1953 and continuing for nearly two years, Elifasi Msomi killed 15 men, women, and children under the alleged control of the *Tokoloshe*, the South African equivalent of the Bogeyman. A witch doctor in Richmond, Natal, Msomi turned lycanthrope when he deemed it a requirement of his magic to sacrifice the flesh and **blood** of humans. To prove the power of the Tokoloshe, Msomi summoned his mistress, then raped and stabbed a young girl to death in her presence. Rather than being impressed by his spiritual guidance, the woman ran straight to the police, who immediately arrested Msomi. But the Tokoloshe had been impressed by Msomi's obedience to its demands, and the entity, in Msomi's view, enabled him to escape from police custody.

In April 1955, after the stabbing deaths of at least five children were attributed to his bloody handiwork, Msomi was once again arrested and placed in custody. But almost as soon as he was behind bars, he had again made his escape due to the power of the Tokoloshe.

A month later, he was recaptured with some of his victims' property in his possession and the same bloody knife that had by now claimed the lives of 15 men, women, and children. Msomi did not hesitate to show the police where he had disposed of some bodies that had remained undiscovered, for, after all, he was not to blame. The Tokoloshe did it.

The court, however, viewed it differently and in September 1955 sentenced Elifasi Msomi to death for the murders. The local populace was so terrified that the Tokoloshe would once again free the witch doctor and allow him to go on killing that the prison authorities permitted a deputation of chiefs and elders to view Msomi's corpse after his appointment with the hangman at Pretoria Central Prison on February 10, 1956.

SOURCES:

Lane, Brian, and Wilfred Gregg. *The Encyclopedia of Serial Killers*. New York: Berkley Publishing, 1994.

Munster, Eddie

In 1964, CBS television presented monster fans with a entirely new look at the creatures of the night that for so many years had terrified theater audi-

The cast of the television show *The Munsters,* which included little werewolf Eddie (second from right).

ences. *The Munsters* television show portrayed a family of wholesome, clean-living, socially responsible monsters made up of a hulking, good-humored father who bore a strong resemblance to the Frankenstein Monster (Fred Gwynne); a beautiful, but spooky mother, who was unmistakably a **vampire** (Yvonne De Carlo); a grandfather, who was also a vampire and dressed formally, **Dracula**-style (Al Lewis); a son, who bore the pointy ears, coarse hair, and sharp teeth of a werewolf (Butch Patrick); and a lovely niece who was perfectly normal in every way (Pat Priest).

By presenting the Big Three of Monsterdom—the Frankenstein Monster, vampires, and a werewolf—in a wholesome, next-door neighbor environment, the classic creatures of the late-night features were humanized in a comical and appealing manner. Quite likely inspired by the success of *The Addams Family*, the Munsters were never the slightest bit cynical or sinister, and their plots struck very different chords with viewers.

When Butch Patrick portrayed the werewolf son, Eddie, he was only 11 years old, stood 51 inches tall, and weighed 80 pounds—but he was already established as a veteran of motion pictures and television. To suggest that a monster created in a laboratory and a member of the undead could marry and produce a werewolf boy suggested the very harmony and wholeness of monsterdom. A Frankenstein-type monster assembled from assorted body parts stolen from graveyards would still be, essentially, a human being. A member of the undead was once a human and still manifests in human form. A werewolf is a human being transformed into a personification of the primeval beast within. In the old traditions, such creatures were horrible, evil beings exploiting humankind. By humanizing them in *The Munsters*, we met the ancient nightmares and once again discovered that they are us.

SOURCES:
Hollywood Screen Legends 1 (May 1965).

Nagas

In the Hindu and Buddhist traditions, the Nagas are a proud, handsome race of **serpent people** who dwell in Naga-Ioka, their splendid, underground bejeweled kingdom. Although an ancient race of serpent people figure in the myths and traditions of many cultures, in the Hindu and Buddhist traditions, the Nagas are semidivine beings with many supernatural powers. Because both the male and female members of the Naga are physically attractive, legends of intermarriage with surface humans abound; and in the past, many noble families of India claimed a Naga ancestor.

SOURCES:
Larousse Dictionary of World Folklore. New York: Larousse, 1995.

Nagual

In ancient Aztec lore, the *nagual* is essentially the form that shapeshifting **shamans** assume in order to perform their secret assignments—good or evil. The term can also be applied to a shaman's familiar spirit or an individual's guardian spirit. In a fashion similar to the vision quest of the North American tribes, the traditional youth of Central America leave their villages to spend a night in a solitary place away from all other tribal members. The animal that appears to them in their dreams is their *nagual*, or guiding totemic spirit.

SOURCES:
Bierhorst, John. *The Mythology of South America.* New York: William Morrow & Company, 1988.

Nakh

Shapeshifting water **demons** who appear most frequently as handsome men or beautiful women, the *nakh*, like the Greek Sirens, lure their victims into the river or sea with the sound of their sweet, seductive singing. Very often, according to old Estonian folklore, the spirits of the drowned may also become *nakhs*, seeking to entice the living into watery graves. Even if one should escape the enchantment of their singing, the very sighting of a *nakh* is a bad omen, usually a sign that either the witness or someone dear to him will die soon in river, lake, or ocean.

SOURCES:
Larousse Dictionary of World Folklore. New York: Larousee, 1995.

Nasnas

The *nasnas* is a shapeshifting demon that often appears to its victims as a frail old man or woman. The nasnas's favorite environment is that of a riverbank where, in its guise as an elderly person in need, it asks to be helped or carried across the water. Once a kindhearted passerby agrees to help the demon in disguise, the *nasnas* overpowers the traveler and drowns him or her.

SOURCES:
Larousse Dictionary of World Folklore. New York: Larousse, 1995.

Necrophilia

Necrophilia, defined as "love of death or of the dead," includes a number of extremely distasteful practices, including sexual intercourse with corpses. A classic case of necrophilia is that of **Sgt. Francois Bertrand,** a soldier in the French army in the mid-1800s, who was only 25 at the time of his arrest for his ghoulish work in the cemeteries of Paris. Eventually he was placed under the care of Dr. Marchal de Calvis.

During his first meeting with the doctor, Bertrand portrayed himself as a successful Don Juan, a claim frequently made by impotents and deviates. Dr. de Calvis soon determined that the young soldier mostly fantasized about torturing women or making love to them after they were dead. His first sexual experiences with corpses were with those of dead animals that he found along the roadside.

It was in 1847 at a cemetery near Bere that Bertrand had his first actual sexual contact with the corpse of a 17-year-old girl. He told Dr. de Calvis that the joy that he experienced when he possessed a living woman was nothing compared to the passion that he felt when he mutilated the corpse of the young woman. The Ghoul of Paris told the doctor that he believed the motivating force behind his foul deeds was the urge to destroy. The urge to dismember the bodies, he stated fervently, was incomparably more violent in him than the urge to violate the bodies sexually.

A giant werewolf/monster was one of the stars of the 1959 film *Horrors of Spider Island.*

Other cases of necrophilia involve absolutely no violence and no dismemberment. Like the Norman Bates character in Alfred Hitchcock's classic horror film *Psycho* (1960), there are people who actually live with the dead bodies of their loved ones.

When Anna's husband passed away when they were both in their late fifties, she couldn't bear to part with him—so she placed him in their bed, kept him dressed, sat by his side to talk with him, and continued to cook him his meals. In a futile effort to slow the process of decomposition, she left the windows of the bedroom open to the cold. Since the couple had no children or many close friends, it was months before the gruesome situation was discovered by a gas company repairman who had come to the house to fix the home's heater. The nauseating odor of decay that permeated the house prompted the man to locate the rotting body on the bed.

When his mother died, Harold, the 49-year-old obedient son, kept to his routine of going to work, buying the groceries, and watching television with his mother in the evenings. At first he attempted to keep his mother's corpse clean and fresh, but after a while he just ignored the stench of decaying flesh coming from his mother's room. When government investigators arrived to determine why the mother had not been cashing her pension checks, they found only a note tacked on the door that advised them that she had gone away on a long holiday. Suspicious, they called police, who broke in and found the son curled up on a bed next to the decomposed corpse of his mother on the bed nearby.

Angel Rivera didn't really want to kill his girlfriend, 30-year-old Trudy Poley. It was just that he'd lost his job and she kept needling him about how she was paying all the bills, so that morning in Lawrence, Kansas, Rivera stabbed her six times. Once he saw the terrible thing that he had done, he was frightened and confused. He didn't just want to dump Trudy's body somewhere where wild dogs and other animals would eat her. He loved her, truly, madly. Killing her had just been a stupid macho thing.

In the next two days, the remorseful killer drove 2,000 miles in two days with his dead girlfriend lying on the seat beside him. He headed first to Denver, Colorado, then turned around and headed the car east for New York City. When he walked into the 48th Precinct, he freely confessed to the crime. New York police captain John Dillon said that Rivera had tilted the seat back on the passenger side and covered Trudy with his jacket: "It looked like she was taking a nap until you looked down at the floor. She had bled to death from six stab wounds, and the smell was overpowering."

SOURCES:

Kuncl, Tom, "Killer Drives Halfway Across America with Dead Girlfriend in His Front Seat," *National Examiner,* 19 November 1996.

Ruehl, Franklin R., "There Are People Who Live with Dead Bodies," *National Enquirer,* 28 April 1992.

Steiger, Brad. *Demon Lovers: Cases of Possession, Vampires, and Werewolves.* New Brunswick, NJ: Inner Light, 1987.

Nelson, Earle Leonard (1897–1928)

Earle Leonard Nelson, the Gorilla Man, was also referred to as a wolfman during a year-long rampage during which he murdered 22 female victims—one a 14-year-old girl, another an infant of eight months—by strangling them with his large, oversized hands. When he was a boy, Earle believed God had made his hands so big so he could better hold his Bible. He was a pious lad—until a trolley car put him in the hospital for six weeks.

His aunt, who cared for the boy, offered prayers of thanks for the miracle that had healed his body, but she had no way of hearing the voices inside

Earle's head that told him his new mission was to deal harshly with "Jezebels" and "Delilahs." Within a short time, Nelson was convicted of attempted rape and sentenced to the state penal farm for two years. In less than a week, he broke free, but was soon recaptured. Six months later, he escaped again.

This time when he was recaptured as he stood leering through the bedroom window at his cousin Rachael, he was transferred to the state penitentiary. Three months later, on December 4, 1918, Nelson managed to crawl over a 20-foot wall without being seen by prison guards. It would be nine years before he would be behind bars again—nine years and 22 murdered and sexually violated victims.

On August 12, 1919, under the assumed name of Roger Wilson, he married a lovely young schoolteacher and might have lived happily ever after if the **demons** inside his head had not continued to torment him. He began to accuse his innocent wife of promiscuous behavior, and he beat her savagely when she pleaded her innocence. When he went berserk in the hospital, he fled into the night and was not seen again by his battered and bewildered wife. Eight years later she would learn how fortunate she was that she managed to survive her life with "Roger Wilson."

On February 20, 1926, Nelson followed Mrs. Clara Newman up three flights of stairs as the San Francisco landlady showed the new boarder to his room. When they reached the room on the top floor, the demon voices told him to take his big, powerful hands and strangle her. The season of death had begun.

On March 2, Mrs. Laura Beale was found strangled and raped in her rooming house in San Jose, California. On June 10, the ravished body of Mrs. St. Mary was discovered beneath the bed of an unoccupied room in her boarding house. A Santa Barbara, California, landlady fell victim to the monster's insatiable appetite for murder and perverted sex on June 26.

And so it went. The vicious strangler claimed two victims in two days in Portland, Oregon. By November, 10 landladies on the West Coast had been murdered and violated, and the journalists across the country were warning their readers about the Gorilla Man who hunted landladies. On December 23, he murdered Mrs. John Berard of Council Bluffs, Iowa. Five days later, in Kansas City, he raped and strangled a woman and her eight-month-old daughter.

By April 1927, Nelson had moved east. On April 27, he strangled Mary McConnell of Philadelphia, Pennsylvania; and Jennie Randolph of Buffalo, New York, fell victim to his monster's hands on May 30. In Detroit, Michigan, he killed two adult women on the same day. Mrs. Mary Sietsome of Chicago became his eighteenth victim on June 3.

And then the demon voices told him to travel to Canada. On June 8, the very night that "Mr. Wilson" moved into Mrs. Hill's rooming house in Winnipeg, a pretty teenager named Lola Cowan, who supported her family by selling artificial flowers, disappeared. A few nights later, William Patterson came home from work to find the naked and ravished body of his wife shoved roughly underneath their bed.

It seemed to the constables in Winnipeg that the Gorilla Man had left the United States to continue his murderous path north of the border. When police officers began making routine checks of all recent arrivals to their city, they found the three-day-old corpse of Lola Cowan under the bed of a "Mr. Wilson."

Two days later, Constables Grey and Sewell, working out of Killarney, just 12 miles north of the international border, stopped a man walking on the highway who identified himself as Roger Wilson. They handcuffed him, locked him in an interrogation room, and went to call the chief of detectives in Winnipeg. When they returned 15 minutes later, they found to their horror that the likely murderer of 22 females had picked the lock on his handcuffs and escaped.

The entire female population of Killarney was locked up in the town hall and kept under armed guard. And while a 500-man posse scoured the area for him, Earle Nelson slept peacefully in a barn just a block away from the jail where he had escaped the two constables. The next morning he calmly boarded a train out of town and probably would have made good his escape if fate had not dictated that he got on the very train that was bringing the Winnipeg chief of detectives and several police officers to Killarney.

No one heard the vicious Gorilla Man utter a single word throughout the entire course of his trial. Rather, he appeared to be listening to voices that remained unheard by others. On January 12, 1928, he quietly ascended the 13 steps of the gallows—and just before the hangman dropped the black hood over his head, Earle Nelson broke his silence to say that he forgave all those who had wronged him.

SOURCES:
Steiger, Brad. *The Mass Murderer.* New York: Award Books, 1967.

Nix

In American slang, "nix," adapted from the German *nichts,* means to stop what you are doing or to be aware that someone is approaching who might not like what you were doing. Although the term is not widely used today, it became a popular slang word in the 1870s and remained in common parlance through the 1940s. In German folklore the nixes are particularly nasty shapeshifting entities who generally have little love for humans. Like the fairy folk of Great Britain, the nixes take great delight in music and they are danc-

A animal/human hybrid creature from 1932's *Island of Lost Souls*.

ing fools. In fact, they may be drawn down into a village if they hear the music of a festival or a dance drifting into their forest homes. If they should venture into the company of humans to join in the party, they will appear as beautiful women or handsome men.

Once the merriment of the music and the dance has fired their passions, the nixes are not at all opposed to a romantic dalliance with a human man or woman. Pity the person who makes love with a nix, however, for the shapeshifter will undoubtedly wait until after the passion has subsided to reveal itself as an ugly, wizened, green-skinned creature—and then the hapless human lover will discover that all liaisons with a nix ends with their sacrificing their victims by drowning them in the nearest body of water.

SOURCES:

Larousse Dictionary of World Folklore. New York: Larousse, 1995.

The Northumberland Werewolf

In Northumberland County, Pennsylvania, c. 1899, many rural residents had their suspicions about a reclusive old man being a werewolf. While some scoffed at such stories as nonsense and superstition, the Paul family became uneasy when they noticed that the old fellow had taken an apparent liking to their 12-year-old daughter, May.

Although they had never seen the man do the slightest thing that anyone could consider improper, it made them uncomfortable when he would sit some distance from May while she tended the family's sheep. They knew that their little girl was a lovely, cheerful child who seemed to lift the spirits of all those she encountered, and the elderly gent simply seemed to gain pleasure from watching her performing her daily tasks with the flock. From all they could ascertain, he never even spoke to her or disturbed her duties in any manner whatsoever.

Other shepherds found it strange, though, that while the **wolves** in the area were so bold that they could attack flocks of sheep in broad daylight, they never bothered the sheep that were tended by little May. Some had witnessed the wolves approaching her flock, then turn tail and run away. Such bizarre behavior on the part of the beasts only increased the gossip about the old man being a werewolf that frightened normal wolves away.

One night when the moon was full, a hunter spotted a gaunt old wolf skulking out of the underbrush. Thinking of the 25-dollar bounty on wolves, he took aim and fired. He could tell from the yelp of pain that his bullet had struck home, but the wolf staggered into the thicket. Deciding it was too dark for pursuit of a wounded wolf in such tangled growth, the hunter went home, resolving to return at the first light.

Many people thought Jack Nicholson was perfectly cast as the businessman-turned-werewolf in the 1994 film, *Wolf*.

RIGHT: The 1981 film *An American Werewolf in London* set a new standard in werewolf films for the special effects used to show David Naughton's transformation. Viewers watched in horror as Naughton's hands and teeth began to change... BELOW: ...and remained transfixed as his entire body underwent the painful metamorphosis. BOTTOM: One of the main myths involving werewolves is that the primary cause of lycanthropy is being bitten by a wolf. That is exactly what caused Jack Nicholson to change into a werewolf in the movie *Wolf*, as this attack scene demonstrates.

ABOVE: **Werewolf fans finally got their wish when a sequel was made to the popular film, *An American Werewolf in London*. Here, Phil Buckman endures being tied to a cross during a key scene in the follow-up, *An American Werewolf in Paris* (1997).**

RIGHT: **Albert Finney in the film *Wolfen*.**

CLOCKWISE FROM TOP RIGHT: **Alien shapeshifters are an important part of the film world's treatment of lycanthropy. Jeff Bridges, with Karen Allen, stars as an alien who takes on human form when he comes to Earth in the '80s film *Starman*. • The story of Dr. Jekyll and Mr. Hyde is one of the most popular tales in the shapeshifting mythology. John Malkovich starred as the tortured doctor in the 1995 film *Mary Reilly*. • Wolves are most commonly represented in the world of shapeshifting, but other animals have been featured also. Here, Sondra Locke stands behind Robert Townsend in the title role in the film *Ratboy*. • Susan Strasberg is terrorized by a werewolf in the film *The Manitou*.**

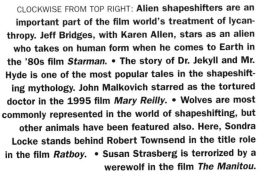

CLOCKWISE FROM TOP LEFT: **Since the 1950s, Hollywood has often used the idea of teenager-as-werewolf as a metaphor for how difficult the teenage years can be. Here, Michael J. Fox takes his turn as a mixed-up young werewolf in the 1985 movie** *Teen Wolf*. • **Kurt Russell had his hands full fighting vicious alien shapeshifters in the 1982 remake of the horror classic** *The Thing*. • **Famed horror writer Stephen King tackled the werewolf myth in his novelette** *Cycle of the Werewolf*, **which was later adapted into the 1985 film** *Silver Bullet*, **starring (l. to r.) Megan Follows, Gary Busey, and Corey Haim.** • **Nastassia Kinski starred in the 1982 cult classic** *Cat People*.

RIGHT: **Foreign film makers have always been attracted to the werewolf myth. Jannie Fauerscuou keeps a wolf on a tight leash in the film** *Ulvetid.* BOTTOM: **Jens Okking prepares to butcher a cow in the film** *Menneskedyret.*

LEFT AND BELOW: **Unlike vampires, which have been featured on television many times, the only series to feature werewolves was the short-lived show** *Werewolf*, **which starred actor Chuck Connors, of** *Rifleman* **fame. In the shot at the left, Connors, fully transformed, tries to exit a burning building. Below, he exhibits the early stages of his transformation into a werewolf.** BOTTOM: **Alex Stevens as a werewolf in the gothic 1970s soap opera** *Dark Shadows*.

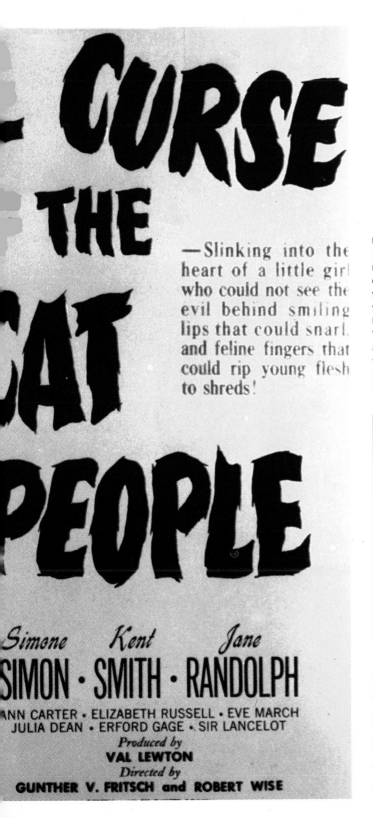

CURSE
THE
CAT
PEOPLE

—Slinking into the heart of a little girl who could not see the evil behind smiling lips that could snarl... and feline fingers that could rip young flesh to shreds!

Simone *Kent* *Jane*
SIMON · SMITH · RANDOLPH

ANN CARTER · ELIZABETH RUSSELL · EVE MARCH
JULIA DEAN · ERFORD GAGE · SIR LANCELOT
Produced by
VAL LEWTON
Directed by
GUNTHER V. FRITSCH and ROBERT WISE

LEFT AND BELOW: **With the success of such classics as** *The Wolf Man* **and** *Dracula*, **Hollywood learned that horror movies were a huge hit with audiences. As a result, dozens of low-budget horror flicks were made during the 1940s and '50s, including many featuring werewolves or other shapeshifting animals. Second in popularity to wolves were cats, as these two posters show. They also show that, as always in Hollywood, sex appeal sells. To the left, Simone Simon stars as a sultry cat woman in 1944's** *The Curse of the Cat People*. **Below, Lenore Aubert is menaced by the evil** *Catman of Paris.*

RIGHT: *The Wolf Man*, which was released in 1941, remains the most famous werewolf movie of all time. It made a star out of Lon Chaney Jr., who played the title role, and also provided veteran character actress Maria Ouspenskaya with one of her most memorable roles as the prophetic Gypsy woman. In this poster from the film, Ouspenskaya is shown talking to Claude Rains.

BELOW: Original poster art from the 1957 film *I Was a Teenage Werewolf*, in which Michael Landon made his screen debut as the troubled teen.

CLOCKWISE FROM RIGHT: **While many werewolf movies, such as *An American Werewolf in London* and its sequel *An American Werewolf in Paris*, have used some of the greatest special effects ever seen on film to show how a person transforms into a werewolf, other films have been a little less spectacular. In fact, werewolves have a long history of appearing in some truly low-bud-get—and sometimes downright cheesy—films. In the photo at right, a not-so-scary werewolf carries off a victim in the 1973 film *The Boy Who Cried Werewolf*. • Apparently, a hairy mask is enough of a transformation for some werewolf films, as shown in this shot from the 1972 film *Wolfman*. • In movies aimed at a young audience, the werewolf is often inten-tionally made to appear less frightening, as this scene from the 1987 film *The Monster Squad* illustrates.**

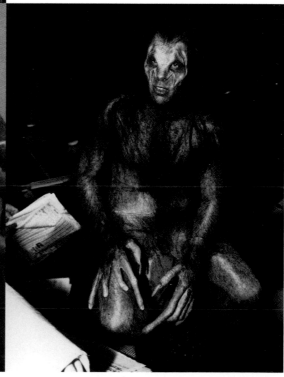

CLOCKWISE FROM LEFT: **While the film *Fright Night II* primarily dealt with vampires, it also featured some very scary werewolf scenes. To the left, the werewolf after he has undergone a full transformation. • A behind-the-scenes shot shows a werewolf character between shots in what had to be some rather hot and uncomfortable make-up. • A werewolf that has undergone a nearly complete transformation. Since it was a vampire film, note the extremely long and sharp canine teeth that this werewolf exhibits.**

Based on the 1896 novel by H. G. Wells, *The Island of Dr. Moreau* dealt with shapeshifting in a unique way. Instead of humans changing into wolves or other creatures, the story features a mad scientist who combines the DNA of animals and humans to form weird hybrid creatures. These two scenes are from the 1996 film adaptation of Wells's story. Above, actor Mark Dacascos portrays a cat creature. In the inset, David Thewlis is terrorized by one of the creatures after they take over the island.

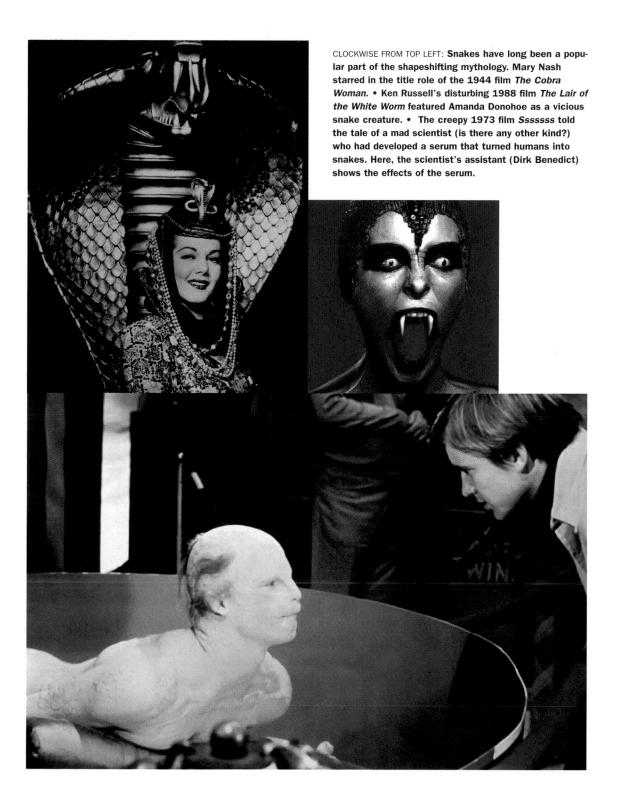

CLOCKWISE FROM TOP LEFT: **Snakes have long been a popular part of the shapeshifting mythology. Mary Nash starred in the title role of the 1944 film *The Cobra Woman*. • Ken Russell's disturbing 1988 film *The Lair of the White Worm* featured Amanda Donohoe as a vicious snake creature. • The creepy 1973 film *Sssssss* told the tale of a mad scientist (is there any other kind?) who had developed a serum that turned humans into snakes. Here, the scientist's assistant (Dirk Benedict) shows the effects of the serum.**

The 1981 film *The Howling* is one of the favorites among werewolf afficionados. This publicity still from the movie shows a werewolf ripping through fabric, while the inset photo shows the results of one werewolf attack—a severed head.

The next morning, he returned to the spot, followed the trail of **blood,** and instead of the carcass of a wolf, he found the body of May Paul's elderly admirer lying stiff and cold—thus confirming the rumors about his being a werewolf. According to regional tradition, he was buried on the spot, which became known as *die Woolfman's grob* (the wolfman's grave).

As the story goes, May Paul continued to tend her family's flocks in the same area for the next 25 years. Although wolves and other predators continued to harass the flocks of the neighboring farmers, May's sheep were never troubled. She claimed that the spirit of her werewolf protector still watched out for her and drove away the beasts of prey.

SOURCES:

Hurwood, Bernhardt J. *Vampires, Werewolves, and Ghouls.* New York: Ace Books, 1968.

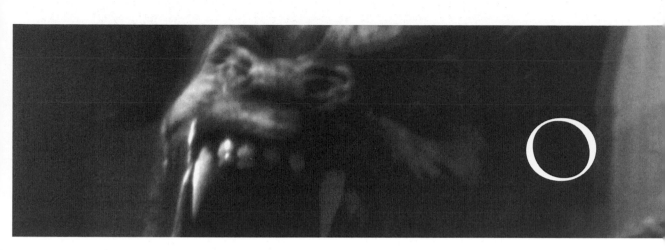

Orang Pendek

Sumatra has an ancient tradition of apemen known as *orang pendek* ("little man") or *orang utan* ("man of the woods"). While many naturalists regard the tales of the orang pendek as native folklore, in 1916, Dr. Edward Jacobson wrote in a Dutch scientific journal of his encounter with one of the creatures. Since Dr. Jacobson's sighting, there have been many accounts of people seeing the orang pendek.

Most witnesses describe the creature as standing about five feet tall and as being covered with short dark hair. It is definitely bipedal, and its arms are proportioned more like that of a human, rather than the extended arms of the ape. Most remarkably, the orang pendeks have been heard conversing with one another in some unintelligible language.

Debbie Martyr, former editor of a London newspaper, went in search of the elusive Sumatran apeman and returned in March 1995 with numerous consistent eyewitness accounts of the orang pendek and plaster casts of its footprints. She stated that she even saw the creature for herself on three different occasions. She remarked that "he is wonderfully camouflaged. If he freezes, you can't see him."

SOURCES:
Fortean Times 85 (October–November 1995).
Western Daily Press, February 1995.

Organization Werewolf

In 1923, a secret terrorist group known as Organization Werewolf was organized in Germany by Fritz Kappe. Their banner was essentially that of the pirates' old Jolly Roger—a black flag with a skull and crossbones in stark white contrast. At first the movement spread rather quickly across Germany, but as a result of a number of arrests by the Weimar government, the Werewolves never became a force that caused any real threat to the establishment. Quite likely, the more ruthless members of the organization responded to **Adolf Hitler**'s summons for malevolent men to join his Nazi party and to his admonition that Germany's youth should be like werewolves, cruel and pitiless, prepared to erode thousands of years of human domestication.

Toward the end of World War II when the collapse of Nazi Germany appeared imminent, Josef Goebbels revived the Organization Werewolf after Heinrich Himmler's rabid speech in 1945 calling for a new *Volkssturm* to harass the allied lines of communication in occupied Germany. The organization took as their insignia a black armband with a skull and crossbones and a silver S. S. Their main function was to assassinate and terrorize anti-Nazi Germans and to harass advancing allied troops. In Leipsig, female werewolves poured scalding water from the windows of houses onto the heads of allied soldiers passing below. In Baden, they killed a number of French soldiers by ambushing them as they were resting.

Even after hostilities had ended and the war was officially over, the werewolves continued their terrorist activities. At the Nuremburg trials, several Nazi leaders testified that the werewolves were now under the control of the notorious Martin Bormann, who had somehow managed to escape capture by the allies.

The Werewolves resurfaced in 1994 when Steven Spielberg's masterpiece film about the Holocaust, *Schindler's List* (1993), was scheduled to open in Russian theaters. Members of the group who were arrested by Russian security forces confessed their plans to firebomb Moscow cinemas showing the film. The Werewolves, estimated at about 100 members strong, acknowledged that they took their name from the Nazi secret police operation that went underground once the allies defeated Hitler's troops in World War II.

SOURCES:

Eisler, Robert. *Man into Wolf*. London: Spring Books, n.d.

Singer, Natasha, "'Schindler' vs. the Werewolves: Spielberg Opus Stirs Controversy in Moscow," *Forward: Ethnic News Watch*, 22 July 1994.

Ouspenskaya, Maria (1876–1949)

In the film **The Wolf Man** (1941), it became the destiny of the diminutive, soft-spoken Maria Ouspenskaya to speak the most famous lines in all of the cinematic werewolf tradition:

> Even the man who is pure in heart
> And says his prayers by night

May become a wolf when the wolf-bane blooms
And the moon is clear and bright.

Madame Maria Ouspenskaya was a distinguished Russian actress who came to the United States in 1923 with the Moscow Art Theater and remained to play on Broadway and to run a New York acting school before she headed for Hollywood in 1936. In addition to her role as the gypsy soothsayer in *The Wolf Man*, Madame Ouspenskaya appeared in such horror films as *The Mystery of Marie Roget* (1942) and **Frankenstein Meets the Wolf Man** (1943). A forceful and popular character actor with her dark eyes and thick Slavic accent, she was featured in a number of Hollywood classics, such as *The Rains Came* (1939), *Waterloo Bridge* (1940), and *Kings Row* (1942).

SOURCES:

Walker, John, ed. *Halliwell's Filmgoer's Companion, 12th Edition*. New York: HarperCollins, 1997.

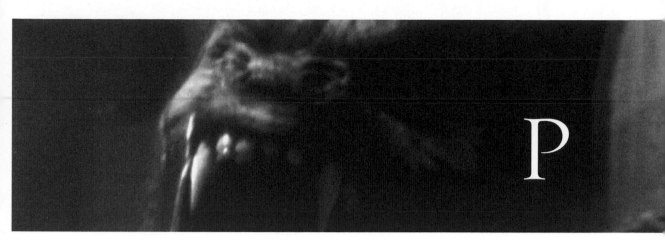

P

Pan

So many paintings and woodcuts from medieval times picture the horned god Pan as a devil that few contemporary men and women understand that the lusty, goat-footed god of everything pastoral originally had nothing to do with evil. In truth, Pan was more closely aligned with ancient fertility rites. But as many wise observers of humankind have observed, the god of the old religion often becomes the devil of the new.

For the most ancient of witch cults in Greece, Pan, son of the god Hermes, was a symbol of fertility. The evolution of the horned god has seen him progress from a pantheistic nature god, essentially concerned with the fecundity of his followers to a demonic, evil enemy of church and State, essentially concerned with sexual indulgence and materialistic gain (and in the church's view, with seizing souls for his fiery underworld kingdom). Contemporary witches, for the most part, see Pan on a much more spiritual plane than he was in ancient times. While witchcraft may have begun as a fertility cult, today's witches strive more for the fertility of the mind and the soul.

SOURCES:

Larousse Dictionary of World Folklore. New York: Larousse, 1995.

Steiger, Brad. *Demon Lovers: Cases of Possession, Vampires and Werewolves.* New Brunswick, NJ: 1987.

Paulin, Thierry (1962–1989)

Between the years 1984 and the end of 1987, a modern werewolf sought his prey among older women—suffocating, strangling, stabbing, or beating to death a toll of victims that may have reached as high as 50. For three anguished years, women over 65 in France's capital city lived in terror as the

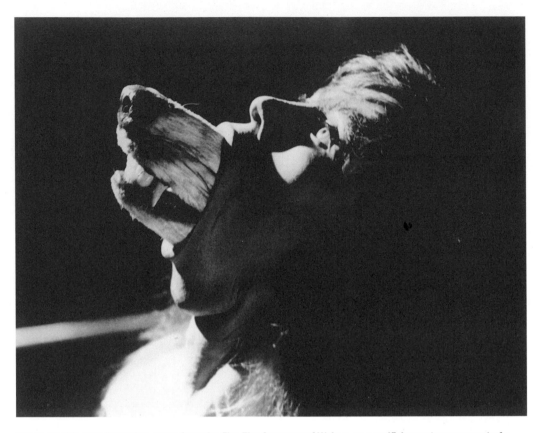

A very graphic transformation scene from the film *The Company of Wolves,* as a wolfish snout appears out of a man's mouth.

Monster of Montmarte struck again and again, torturing and murdering for the sake of a few francs.

At last in December 1987 the Monster inadvertently left one of his victims, a 70-year-old widow, with a spark of life remaining in her cruelly beaten body. She provided the police with a detailed description of the beast who had attacked her, and the police recognized Thierry Paulin, a petty thief who already had a record of theft and drug offenses. When his fingerprints matched many of the 150,000 prints the police had accumulated during the three-year death prowl of the werewolf, there could be no mistake—Paulin was the Monster of Montmarte.

When arrested, the 25-year-old, tall, athletic Paulin readily confessed to the brutal murders of 21 women in a manner the police found chillingly detached. While he was confined to Fleury-Merogis prison to await trial, Paulin's health rapidly began to deteriorate. It soon began apparent that his drug abuse and homosexual lifestyle had placed his health at risk. Transferred to the prison hospital at Fresnes, Paulin died on April 16, 1989, from the tuberculosis and meningitis which his AIDS-impaired immune system could not combat.

SOURCES:

Lane, Brian, and Wilfred Gregg. *The Encyclopedia of Serial Killers.* New York: Berkley Publishing, 1994.

Pentagram

In true magic, the pentagram, the five-pointed star, represents the sign of the microcosm and is considered the most powerful symbol of conjuration in any magical rite. As a symbol of the microcosm, the pentagram may represent evil as well as good. If one point is held in the ascendant, it assumes the character of Christ. Some traditions maintain that it was such a star that led the three magi to the birthplace of the infant Jesus. However, if two points are in the ascendant, the pentagram is the sign of Satan. By such a simple alteration, the pentagram may be used to summon the powers of light or the powers of darkness.

In the werewolf tradition, it is said that the sign of the pentagram is to be located somewhere on the person of the lycanthrope, most often on the chest or the palms of the hand. It is also stated in some traditions that the werewolves choose their next victim when the sign of the pentagram appears to their vision alone on either the person's palm or forehead.

SOURCES:

Spence, Lewis. *An Encyclopedia of Occultism.* New Hyde Park, NY: University Books, 1960.

Petronius (?–66)

The Roman satirist Gaius Petronius Arbiter, the Arbiter of Elegance, was well known among his contemporaries as an intimate companion to the Emperor Nero. In his classic work *The Satyricon* (c. 50), Petronius deals with the seamier side of Roman life, in which he chronicles a series of loosely based episodes detailing the adventures of three young men as they wander through southern Italy. In one of those picaresque episodes, one of the young narrators describes a man transforming himself into a werewolf:

> Niceros tells of his soldier friend [who] stripped off his clothes and addressed himself to the stars. Then he [removed his vestments] and all at once became a wolf, which ran howling into the woods. Niceros next heard from a widow whom he visited that a wolf had been worrying her cattle and had been wounded in the neck. On his return home [he] found his friend bleeding at the neck, and he knew then that he was a *versipellis* [werewolf].

SOURCES:

Eisler, Robert. *Man into Wolf.* London: Spring Books, n.d.

Porphyria

Porphyria is a group of rare genetic disorders caused by an enzyme defect. Because of the affliction, the human body accumulates and excretes one or more of the natural pigments that combine with iron to form aspects of the oxygen-carrying proteins hemoglobin and myoglobin. Such a process causes the individual's urine to turn a reddish-purple color, thus prompting earlier medical consultants to term porphyria as the "royal disease," naming Mary Queen of Scots, James I, and George III among those who passed purple urine.

In addition to the discoloration of urine, porphyria causes abdominal discomfort, extreme nervousness, high blood pressure, and can lead to psychotic disorders, epilepsy, and general physical weakness. Another pronounced effect of porphyria is an extreme hypersensitivity to light, a factor that has prompted a number of scientists to theorize that those individuals beset with vampirism in ancient and medieval times may really have been suffering from the disease. In 1964, L. Illis, in the article "On Porphyria and the Aetiology of Werewolves," set forth his hypothesis that the disease could also account for the old reports of werewolves.

SOURCES:

Webster's Concise Encyclopedia. Helicon Publishing Ltd. 1994.

Melton, Gordon J. *The Vampire Book: Encyclopedia of the Undead.* Farmington Hills, MI: Visible Ink Press, 1998.

Possession

Skeptics say with finality that the evil thoughts and emotions of the living or the dead cannot overpower the healthy brain of a normal person. The mind cannot be subdued unless by physical distortion or disease.

There are, however, intelligent men and women who feel otherwise. They are convinced that they have felt the touch of **demons.** In their experience, the admonition, "Get thee behind me, Satan," is by no means a fanciful directive. Serious individuals claim to have undergone fearsome ordeals in which either they or their loved ones became the targets of vile entities that sought the possession of physical bodies and minds in order that they might enjoy the sensations of demonically aroused mortals who yield to ungodly temptations.

The cynic and the materialists dismiss such stories as examples of psychological disorders, but certain mental health care professionals and those who have been victimized argue that demonic possession is not insanity, for in most cases the possession is only temporary. The individual who has become possessed is unable to control himself, but, at the same time, he or she may be entirely conscious of the fiendish manipulation of his or her mind and body—and in many instances, the possessed may actually see grotesque and devilish faces before him.

In ancient times, people suspected of being werewolves were often branded as heretics and violently punished, as the man on the wheel is learning the hard way.

Dr. Wilson Van Dusen has served as chief psychologist at Mendocino State Hospital in California and has published more than 150 scientific papers and books detailing the research that has led him to believe that there are entities that can possess the human mind and body. In a landmark research paper, Dr. Van Dusen notes the "striking similarities" between the hierarchy of the unseen world described by the Swedish inventor-mystic Emanuel Swedenborg and the alleged hallucinations of his patients in a state mental hospital. Dr. Van Dusen began to seek out those from among the hundreds of chronic schizophrenics, alcoholics, and brain-damaged persons who could distinguish between their own thoughts and the products of their hallucinations.

"I would question these other 'persons' directly," Dr. Van Dusen states, "and instruct the patient to give a word-for-word account of what the voices answered or what was seen."

On numerous occasions, Dr. Van Dusen found that he was engaged in dialogues with "hallucinations" that were above the patient's comprehension. He found this to be especially true when he contacted the higher order of hallucinations, which he discovered to be "symbolically rich beyond the patient's own understanding." The lower order, on the other hand, Dr. Van Dusen found to be consistently antireligious, and some actively obstructed the patient's religious practices. Occasionally they would refer to themselves as demons.

The demons, Dr. Van Dusen notes, would suggest lewd acts to their host bodies, then scold them for considering them. "They find a weak point of conscience and work on it interminably," he says. "They invade every nook and cranny of privacy; work on every weakness and credibility; claim awesome powers; lie, make promises, and then undermine the patient's will."

These demonic entities, he learned, could take over a person's eyes, ears, and voice, just as the traditional accounts of demon possession maintain. The entities had totally different personalities from his patients, which indicates that they were not simply products of his patients' minds. Some of the beings had extrasensory perception and could predict the future. To his great concern, Dr. Van Dusen discovered that some of the entities knew far more than he did, even though he tried to test them by looking up obscure academic references.

One of his conclusions was that the demons found it easier to take over the minds of people who were emotionally or physically at a low ebb. The entities were able to leech on those particular individuals because they had been weakened by strains and stresses with which they could not cope.

Other researchers have found that such demonic beings frequently move into the mind and body of drug and alcohol users and actually encourage their unwitting hosts to use more drugs or alcohol, for humans are more easily controlled while they are under the influence of mind-altering substances.

Professor Ian Currie of Toronto's Guelph University states that he has often come across cases of discarnate entities that wanted to make slaves out of humans, and he readily concedes that mental illness could be caused by possession by spirits. A fellow psychotherapist in Toronto, Dr. Adam Crabtree, a former priest and Benedictine monk, notes that although the reasons for possession vary, sometimes the dead simply do not realize that they have changed planes of existence and wish to maintain their relationship with friends and relatives by occupying one of their bodies.

Quite understandably, since ancient times possession by demons has been strongly considered by many wise investigators and learned church officials as the principal reason why certain men and women consider themselves to be werewolves. The snarling, growling, grotesque behavior evidenced by so many of those who exhibit signs of lycanthropy would certainly suggest that a ravenous and raving demon had possessed an otherwise normal human being.

SOURCES:

Steiger, Brad, and Sherry Hansen Steiger. *Demon Deaths.* New York: Berkley Publishing, 1991.

Van Dusen, Wilson. *The Natural Depth in Man.* New York: Harper & Row, 1972.

Puck

Puck, the mischievous fellow who crows about what fools we mortals be in Shakespeare's *A Midsummer's Night Dream*, is one of the most accomplished shapeshifters in all of folklore and legend. Because of his ability to appear as anything from a horse to will-o'-the-wisp, Puck was thought in medieval times to be a demonic spirit. Later, as we foolish mortals became more perceptive and learned to take ourselves less seriously, we began to perceive the rascal as a good-natured prankster.

Certain scholars feel that rather than one omnipresent entity, Puck must actually be the generic for an entire tribe or type of being. Witness in the following countries extremely similar names for the same type of slightly troublesome shapeshifter, who almost always turns out to be a merry fellow, rather than a malicious monster: in Scandinavia—*Puke*; in Germany—*Spuk*; in Holland—*Spook*; in Ireland—*Pooka*; in Wales—*Pwca*; and amongst Native American tribes—*Puck-wudjini* ("little vanishing person").

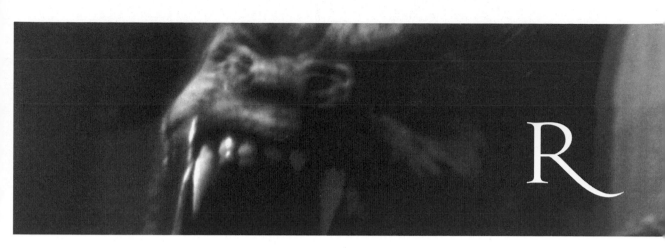

Rains, Claude (1889–1967)

The distinguished British actor Claude Rains, who played the role of Sir John Talbot in **The Wolf Man** (1941), had journeyed into the shadowy world of horror many years before he entered into werewolf country. Rains began his acting career at the age of 11; and before his death in 1967 at the age of 78, he had been nominated four times for an Academy Award as best supporting actor. Although he never won an Oscar, Rains became the very essence of the debonair villain—a likable bad guy with a ready wry comment to ease the pain of his skullduggery.

Rains came to the United States in 1914 when he was 25. His distinctive, well-modulated baritone voice made him quite successful both on the stage and in radio. He did not become a film star until he assumed the title role in the film classic *The Invisible Man* (1933), a part in which his true features were scarcely seen at all. After the starring role in *Crime without Passion* (1934), there followed a series of rather undistinguished parts in such motion pictures as *The Clairvoyant* (1934), *The Man Who Reclaimed His Head* (1934), and *The Mystery of Edwin Drood* (1935). With his portrayal of the wicked King John in the robust Errol Flynn epic, *The Adventures of Robin Hood* (1938), Rains received wide public notice and critical acclaim.

He received his first Academy Award nomination for his portrayal of the corrupt senator in *Mr. Smith Goes to Washington* (1939). The next year after his portrayal of Sir John Talbot in *The Wolf Man* (1941), he received his second Academy Award nomination for one of his most famous roles, Captain Louis Renault in *Casablanca* (1942), the recipient of Humphrey Bogart's tagline: "Louie, I think this could be the start of a beautiful friendship."

Rains also received Academy Award nominations for his roles in *Mr. Skeffington* (1944) and *Notorious* (1946). He had prestigious starring roles in

The Phantom of the Opera (1943), *Deception* (1946), and *The Unsuspected* (1947). He was Julius Caesar in *Caesar and Cleopatra* (1946), Professor George Edward Challenger in *The Lost World* (1960), King Herod in *The Greatest Story Ever Told* (1965), and the devil in *Angel on My Shoulder* (1946).

SOURCES:

Maltin, Leonard. *Leonard Maltin's 1999 Movie & Video Guide*. New York: Signet, 1998.

Siegel, Scott, and Barbara Siegel. *The Encyclopedia of Hollywood*. New York: Avon Books, 1990.

Raku-nene

Among the native inhabitants of the Gilbert Islands, women must be wary of *Raku-nene*, an evil spirit that disfigures, perhaps even kills, those ladies who have cruelly rejected their suitors. Raku-nene was once a mortal man who was known as a great lover, a kind of Casanova of the South Sea islands. When he died, young men began to invoke his name and he became the collaborating spirit of men courting female hearts. As time passed, however, his specialty became that of an avenging spirit for those suitors who had received great pain and humiliation due to the machinations of a fickle or thoughtless female.

Should a man be rejected by the one he loves, he must follow a prescribed rite to solicit the terrible supernatural aid of Raku-nene. First he must manage to obtain a single strand of hair from the unresponsive lady's head. Once this hair is procured from a brush, a comb, or some other source, the rejected lover must bind it around his thigh for three days. On the fourth day, he removes it and burns it in a fire of leaves. As he watches the hair burn, he invokes the spirit of Raku-nene.

That night, Raku-nene visits the unfortunate girl in a dream—and this visitation marks the end of her sanity. By morning, her body has begun to swell, and she mumbles constantly about bad dreams. Thereafter, she falls into a moody silence and refuses to don clothing. Before long, she begins to moan, quietly at first, but with gradually increasing strength and volume. By the next morning, the sixth day after the spell has been cast, the girl is quite mad, tearing at her own flesh and snapping at all who approach her. This disturbing behavior continues until the next day, when the girl suddenly cries out, "Raku-nene! Raku-nene!" some half-dozen times. The cries fade; the girl becomes rigid, and, sometimes, unless she truly had an innocent heart or if she repents of her cruel treatment of the suitor, she dies.

SOURCES:

Steiger, Brad. *Monsters Among Us*. New York: Berkley Books, 1989.

Ramirez, Richard (1960–)

In September 1985, Los Angeles police were at last able to end one of the largest manhunts ever conducted in the area when they arrested Richard

Richard Ramirez, the infamous Night Stalker killer who terrorized southern California in the mid-1980s.

Ramirez, the Night Stalker, who had committed a series of brutal nighttime killings and sexual attacks, primarily in the San Fernando and San Gabriel Valleys of Southern California, during the period of June 1984 to August 1985. Left behind him, scrawled in the homes of some of his victims, were inverted **pentagrams,** the traditional symbol associated with satanic rituals and werewolves. When he was being arraigned on charges of having murdered 14 people, Ramirez shouted, "Hail, Satan!" and displayed a pentagram that he had tattooed into his own hand, the sign of the werewolf.

During his trial, Ramirez would place his forefingers to the sides of his temples, as if they were horns, and chant, "evil. . .evil. . . ." Other times he would sit in sullen silence, as if he were totally uninterested in the court proceedings. Then, suddenly, he would explode, spitting at the court, calling all those around him maggots, flashing the pentagram on his palm, and warning the jury of Lucifer's vengeance upon them. Today Ramirez resides on Death Row, the recipient of 19 death sentences.

SOURCES:

Lane, Brian, and Wilfred Gregg. *The Encyclopedia of Serial Killers.* New York: Berkley Publishing, 1994.

Steiger, Brad, and Sherry Hansen Steiger. *Demon Deaths.* New York: Berkley Publishing, 1991.

Bill Ramsey—The Real-Life Werewolf of London (c. 1950)

The first time the eerie sensation overcame him, Bill Ramsey was only nine years old, playing in the backyard with his toy airplane. Suddenly he felt a strange coldness move through him, as if he had walked from the warmth of a summer's afternoon into a frigid meat locker. Later he remembered the sensation as if he had somehow stepped into another dimension, some unearthly place with a terrible, foul odor to it.

Then the peculiar feeling passed, but the boy felt different, as though something frightening had happened to him. He began to perceive himself as a wolf, and he suddenly felt himself filled with a monstrous rage. To his parents' horror, their little boy began to growl and snap his teeth. He pulled a large fence post out of the ground as if it were a stick, and he tore at the wire fencing with his teeth, pulling it free of the posts. And then the bizarre incident was over. At least for that night. From time to time the "wolf seizures" would take him, but most of the time, Bill was in control.

In 1983, Bill Ramsey was a London carpenter with a wife and a family. It was on a Monday evening, December 5, when he headed for his second job with the taxi cab company. He had scarcely pulled away from the curb when he felt a severe pain in his chest. He tried to get his breathing under control, but the pain got worse. He had a sense that he was dying, that his entire system was shutting down.

Ramsey ended up in the emergency room at Southend Hospital. He clutched at his chest, feeling disoriented and in awful pain. The image of a wolf kept reoccurring in his thoughts, and he prayed that he wasn't having another one of *those* seizures.

Two nurses were pushing him on a gurney when Ramsey suddenly began to growl and roar, his hands curling into powerful pawlike claws. Before he could check himself, he had bitten one of the nurses just below the elbow.

When a policeman arrived, Ramsey was crouched in a corner, growling like a wolf and holding the two nurses captive. The policeman attempted to intervene, and Ramsey attacked him, trying to bite his arm, growling fiercely all the while. After an intense struggle, the policeman and an intern managed to force Ramsey onto a gurney and restrain him with straps until a doctor arrived to inject the wolfman with Thorazine.

Bill Ramsey remembered how he regained consciousness in the ambulance that was transporting him to Runwell, the mental hospital. He was terrified. He had no memory of what he had done.

At last the strange case of the modern day Werewolf of London came to the attention of **Ed and Lorraine Warren,** directors of the New England Society for Psychic Research, experts on the supernatural and demonologists, who assessed Bill Ramsey's plight as that of **possession** by a werewolf-like demon. Once contact had been made with the Ramseys and the proper authorities, the Warrens suggested that they arrange an **exorcism** for Bill with Bishop Robert McKenna, a cleric who had performed more than 50 exorcisms. *The People*, a London newspaper, paid the fares for Bill and his wife Nina to fly to the United States, accompanied by David Alford and John Cleve, a writer and a photographer from their staff.

During the ancient rite of exorcism, holy water, a crucifix, and a relic of a saint are applied to various parts of the victim of the demon while the priest prays in Latin in a strong and loud voice. In addition to the instruments of his holy office, Bishop McKenna had added four off-duty policeman—just in case the werewolf took control of Bill Ramsey's body.

Ramsey remembers that the demonic spirit within him began to trouble him the moment they walked into the church. It made him feel very negative toward the bishop and convinced him that such an absurd old ritual would end in failure. He mumbled something to Nina about the whole business being a bunch of mumbo jumbo.

Bishop McKenna, on the other hand, felt immediately that the exorcism would be successful, but he could sense that the demonic spirit within Ramsey was going to put up a fight. Thirty minutes into the ritual, Bishop McKenna took Ramsey's head in his hands and ordered the werewolf spirit to be banished forever.

The demon within Ramsey caused him to shake and writhe and to curl his hands into claws to attempt to rip the bishop's face. Two of the burly policemen restrained the werewolf, and the clergyman pushed a crucifix against Ramsey's forehead. The sight of the cross caused the werewolf within Ramsey to go berserk, snarling, growling, and grasping at the bishop. The priest stood his ground, and Ramsey suddenly staggered back to his chair and collapsed.

As the Bishop continued his admonitions in Latin, Ramsey felt the demon leaving him. The poison that had been within him was leaving. The werewolf's power was slipping away. A faint roar rose from his chest, then faded away. Bill Ramsey felt purified. The curse of the werewolf had been lifted from his soul.

SOURCES:
Zaffis, John. "Report from the New England Society for Psychic Research," 1998.

Rancho Santa Elena

In April 1989, Mexican police officials followed a member of a drug-demented satanic cult who led them to a large black cauldron in which a human brain, a turtle shell, a horseshoe, a human spinal column, and an assortment of human bones had been boiled in **blood.**

The first day of digging on the grounds of Rancho Santa Elena outside of Matamoros, Mexico, brought up a dozen mutilated human corpses. Each of the victims had been slashed, beaten, shot, hanged, or boiled alive. Each had suffered ritual mutilations.

The human monsters responsible for such ghastly acts were Adolfo de Jesus Constanzo, a drug smuggler/high priest, and Sara Maria Aldrete, an attractive young woman who led a bizarre double life as a high priestess of the satanic cult and as an honor student at Texas Southmost College in Brownsville. The essence of the "evil for evil's sake" cult of Adolfo and Sara was **human sacrifice.**

Although it seems certain that the ritual executions were used as a disciplinary tool for Constanzo, the drug lord, the murders must never be dismissed as a grisly motivational object lesson designed to enforce absolute obedience among the members of the gang. As in all instances of ritual sacrifice from the Aztecs to the pagan altars of Astarte, the high priest, Constanzo, promised his followers that they would be able to absorb the spiritual essence of the victims.

The cruel murders were performed in accordance with prayers for strength, riches, and protection from physical harm and the police.

Constanzo's mother was a practitioner of Santeria, a religious amalgamation that evolved from the blending of African slaves' spirit worship with their Roman Catholic masters' hierarchy of intercessory saints. Far from an obscure cult, Santeria may have as many as 100 million followers, most of them in the Caribbean and South America. While the rites of Santeria may include the blood sacrifice of fowl or small animals, it is essentially a benign religion.

It was in the late summer of 1988 that Constanzo decided to create a religious amalgam of his own. Beginning with his mother's faith of Santeria, he tossed in some of the elements of **voodoo.** Next he began adding the violent practices of *Palo Mayombe*, a harsh Afro-Caribbean cult, and combining them with *santismo*, a particularly bloody Aztec ritual. But however Constanzo mixed the ingredients of his terrible religious expression, the blood-drenched altar of sacrifice remained central to his cruel cosmology.

On May 5, 1989, police in Mexico City engaged Constanzo and members of his gang in a gun battle that lasted about 45 minutes. The high priest of the cult and his homosexual-bodyguard-cum-lover Martin Quintana were killed at Constanzo's orders, which he preferred to being taken captive by the authorities. Three cult members and the high priestess Sara Aldrete were still alive when police entered their hideout. In August 1990, Sara Maria Aldrete was sentenced to six years' imprisonment for criminal association.

SOURCES:

Lane, Brian, and Wilfred Gregg. *The Encyclopedia of Serial Killers.* New York: Berkley Publishing, 1994.

Steiger, Brad, and Sherry Hansen Steiger. *Demon Deaths.* New York: Berkley Publishing, 1991.

Red Coyote

In 1887 a savage red coyote was terrorizing the miners in Saskatchewan, Canada, in the section just north of Montana. A mining engineer who lived in New York City (c. 1940) told writer Ed Bodin that he could graphically remember the fear of the monster he had experienced as a small boy, and that his mother and father never allowed him outdoors after dark. According to the engineer, the red coyote had killed so many men, women, and children by slashing their throats with its fangs that numerous miners had sworn to take their revenge on the beast. And it wasn't long before talk of a werecoyote chilled the mining camps for miles around. Men who had tried to track the deadly creature said that its tracks always disappeared in the vicinity around the cabin of Red Morgan, an older miner who pretty much lived a hermitlike existence.

One night when the moon was full, a young miner spotted the dangerous beast slinking behind a hill less than half a mile away. He reached for his rifle, an old-style cap and ball model that his uncle had carried in the Civil War. Then he remembered that there was plenty of powder in the horn, but he was out of molded balls. Desperate, because he knew lives were at stake and he had a chance to kill the savage coyote, he ran his fingers over the nuggets in his pan until he found one that was close enough to the caliber of his rifle's muzzle. He pushed the nugget down the barrel with the ramrod and started after the monster.

There was a light snowfall, so he was easily able to track the coyote for several miles. As he came around a small hill, the miner and the killer coyote saw each other at the same time. The miner had never experienced anything like the fury of the snarling, gnashing coyote as it lunged at his throat. Fortunately, his nerves held steady, and he fired his rifle directly at the rearing coyote's heart. The golden slug stopped the beast, but it didn't fall. Wounded, it turned and ran into the forest.

The young miner followed the trail of **blood** left by the coyote, but soon the wind had covered most of the tracks and he lost them in the denseness of the trees. But he knew the shot had been true. Sooner or later, the dreaded red coyote would breathe its last. The miner returned to camp and told everyone the good news.

Two days later, it appeared the young miner had not just been telling a tall tale. The dreaded red coyote had not been seen for several nights. A group of miners were gathered in the general store when one of the local tribesmen came in with the news that Red Morgan had been found shot to death in his cabin with a bullet hole in his heart.

"But here is the strange thing that no one was able to explain," the mining engineer told Bodin, "the doctor found a gold bullet in Morgan's body. And from that day on, no one ever saw the red coyote again."

SOURCES:

Bodin, Ed. *Scare Me! A Symposium on Ghosts and Black Magic*. New York: Orlin Tremaine Company, 1940.

Reed, Oliver (1938–1999)

When 23-year-old British actor Oliver Reed played the role of Leon in **The Curse of the Werewolf** (1961), he had the perfect scowl and muscular build to be extremely convincing as an enraged young werewolf. A nephew of famed film director Sir Carol Reed, Oliver dropped out of school when he was 17 and supported himself as a Soho nightclub bouncer, a boxer, and a cab driver. After military service with the Medical Corps, the burly young man began playing

Oliver Reed played the part of Leon, the enraged young werewolf, in the 1961 film *The Curse of the Werewolf*.

extra and bit parts in British films. He was a "Teddy Boy" in *The Bulldog Breed* (1960), a nightclub bouncer in *The Two Faces of Dr. Jekyll* (1960), and an artist in a cafe in *The Rebel* (1961). And then came the title role in *The Curse of the Werewolf*, also known as *The Curse of Siniestro*.

In his *Horror!* author Drake Douglas describes Reed as a "handsome young actor of powerful and impressive physique." He continued, "In makeup he was probably the most interesting of the screen's lycanthropes. He was covered, chest and back included, with a mass of gleaming silvery hair, and technicolor made excellent use of blood-dripping fangs and burning red eyes. All in all, *Curse of the Werewolf* is probably the most satisfying and intelligent of all werewolf films.

As so often occurs in the cinema, a successful interpretation of a particular role tends to typecast an actor. For awhile, Reed was saddled with roles in which he did not transform into a werewolf, but he was just as sullen, scowling, and potentially violent. After serving a "bad guy" apprenticeship in such films as *Pirates of Blood River* (1962), *Paranoiac* (1963), and *The Shuttered Room* (1967), Reed was able to display his considerable versatility and range of thespian talents as the crafty and cruel Bill Sikes in *Oliver* (1968), the tormented Urbain Grandier in *The Devils* (1971), and the dashing swordsman Athos in *The Three Musketeers* (1973) and *The Four Musketeers* (1974). Reed's most recent films include *Funny Bones* (1995), *Marco Polo* (1998), and *Gladiator* (1999). In May 1999, while in Malta filming *Gladiator*, Reed died after falling ill following a night on the town.

SOURCES:

Douglas, Drake. *Horror!* New York: Collier Books, 1966.

Katz, Ephraim. *The Film Encyclopedia.* New York: Perigee, 1979.

Romulus and Remus

Romulus and Remus, the legendary founders of Rome, were twin brothers suckled and reared by a she-wolf who filled them with her lycanthropic powers. The jealous Romulus killed his brother, just as Cain slew Abel, thus giving us a cross-cultural myth of two great patriarchies being established through an act of fratricide.

In his *Man into Wolf* (c. 1950), **Robert Eisler** links the Roman she-wolf (*Lupa Romana*) with the **Luperci,** whose priests each year sacrificed a goat at the traditional entrance of the old *Lupercal* (**wolves'** den), and establishes the original founders of Rome as members of a tribe that bore the name of wolf. Pursuing even deeper reaches of history in his research, Eisler points out that a *lupanar*, a she-wolves' den, was an old Roman term for a brothel. He maintains the classical poets Livy and Ovid said that the "she-wolf" who gave suck to the abandoned twins Romulus and Remus was really a harlot who dressed in wolf skins. As Romulus matured into the leader of his tribe, he wore a *galea lupina*, a helmet shaped like a wolf's head, and his warriors outfitted themselves as did he, wearing wolf's head helmets and the hide of wolves or dogs.

SOURCES:

Eisler, Robert. *Man into Wolf*. London: Spring Books, n.d.

Rusalki

The Slavic people have a legend that beautiful girls who use their physical charms to work wickedness and who are damned for their sins get another chance to be even nastier when they cross over to the other side. It is at that time that they may choose to become a *rusalki*, a sultry shapeshifter who can appear along the river banks as an innocent young maiden, singing sweet, seductive songs to smitten young men—before she drowns them.

Some *rusalki* are a bit nicer to their victims. They first make love to the men they've seduced and permit them to die happy before they pull them into the water and drown them. In Bulgaria, the *rusalki*, known as *samovily*, are made up of the souls of unbaptized baby girls or of brides who died on their wedding night. They, too, are allowed another opportunity to manifest as tempting shapeshifters who lure men to their watery deaths.

SOURCES:

Larousse Dictionary of World Folklore. New York: Larousse, 1995.

St. Patrick

According to legend, St. Patrick once humbled the Welsh king Vereticus by changing him into a wolf. While in Ireland, Patrick became so disgusted with certain tribes who continued to resist his efforts to convert them to Christianity that he cursed them and condemned them to become werewolves. The spell took effect, and the tribes would turn into **wolves** at a certain time every seven years, and would remain wolves for seven years. During their seven-year werewolf period, they were not denied the sacraments or the offices of the church. In his *Topographia Hibernica* (c. 1191), **Giraldus Cambrensis** recorded the testimony of a priest who vividly recalled giving the sacrament to a werewolf.

Early travelers to Ireland also insisted that they had met entire families of werewolves and had witnessed certain individuals transform themselves into wolves. Up until the end of the eighteenth century, Ireland was known as Wolfland, and werewolf stories abounded in the land.

SOURCES:

Hurwood, Bernardt J. *Vampires, Werewolves, and Ghouls*. New York: Ace Books, 1968.

Walker, Barbara G. *The Woman's Encyclopedia of Myths and Secrets*. San Francisco: Harper & Row, 1983.

Santu sakai

The Malaysian legends of the *santu sakai* have always sounded like something from a Hollywood monster movie to those who doubted the monsters' existence. According to the old stories, the santu sakai are werebeasts, half-humans, half-monsters, that the native people refer to as the "mouth men," because of their large fangs and their craving for fresh, red meat. When hordes of these savage creatures attack a village, they capture, kill, and eat their victims.

In June 1967, a hunter named Henri Van Heerdan claimed to have his skepticism about the santu sakai removed completely after a near-fatal close encounter with the beasts during a hunting trip near Kuala Lumpur. According to his account, he had bagged a number of birds for his dinner and was about half of a mile from his vehicle when he began hearing "ugly growls and strange screams" coming from the other side of the trail. He decided to make a run for his vehicle. When he stopped at one point to look behind him, he saw "two absolute monstrosities" running toward him. They were tall, very large, and they looked "like **demons** from hell."

Van Heerdan reached his vehicle, and he could hear that the beasts were close behind him. He turned and raised his shotgun, intending to fire, but it was too late. The hideous "mouth men" were on top of him. One of them bit his arm with its fangs, forcing him to drop his weapon. Somehow Van Heerdan managed to pick up a good-sized rock and use it to pound one of the monsters on the skull, causing it to fall in a daze. He struck another in the face and got inside his car.

The santu sakai closed around the vehicle, growling, roaring, pounding at the sides and the windows. Van Heerdan's shaking hand at last got the key in the ignition just as one of the "mouth men" was smashing the back window and another was crouched on the hood, banging its fist against the windshield. The car's wheels spun into motion, leaving the santu sakai to chase after him. When Van Heerdan got up speed, he slammed on the brakes, sending the man-beast on the hood flying off the car and into a patch of weeds.

The hunter reported the incident to the police, but they only laughed and told him to go home and sleep it off. The next afternoon Van Heerdan talked a number of his friends into accompanying him back to the scene of the attack. Those who had initially doubted his word revised their thinking when they found a number of strange humanlike footprints and splotches of **blood** in several places. Van Heerdan's expensive shotgun was never recovered, and he speculated whether or not one of the beasts might eventually pull the trigger and blow a hole in one of his fellow "mouth men."

SOURCES:

Norman, Eric. *The Abominable Snowmen*. New York: Award Books, 1969.

Satanism

Satanism is essentially a perversion of both the old religion and formal, orthodox church worship—especially and specifically Christianity. Satanism mocks both the old religion's rituals and the dogma, priestcraft, and liturgies of the Church of Christ. In a very real sense, the church "created" the Satan of satanism, and the decadent aristocracy of certain European cities converted

An anonymous engraving of a wolflike creature that was included in the *Nurnberg Chronicle* in 1493.

the primitive beliefs of their serfs into an obscene and jaded perversion of the ritualistic aspects of Christianity and witchcraft. Although traditional witchcraft has no "devil" or "Satan," witches and satanists have been confused in the popular and ecclesiastical mind since the Middle Ages. Witchcraft is the ancient search to control natural forces through human thoughts and deeds. Satanism is the rendering of ancient rituals into debased and demeaning orgies and is symptomatic of sexual unrest and moral rebellion. While witchcraft originated among earlier cultures as a force intended to be complementary to primitive society, satanism has never pretended to be other than an enemy of the civil and religious establishment, and unrelenting foe of the orthodox church and the very antithesis of the precepts of white magic.

In its fervent desire to stamp out the worship of **Diana** and **Pan** and all other expressions of the old religion, the medieval church lumped all devils into one and called them Satan, enemy of Christ's work on earth. To the common people, who could not really care about the philosophical dualism of an evil adversary for the church and the lords of the church, the old ways of the nature religions offered release from oppression and unrelenting drudgery.

The church and the lords of the feudal establishment united to combat the "evil" influence of the gods and goddesses of fertility, nature, and freedom. Church scholars consulted ancient manuscripts to determine how best to deal with the formidable adversaries of witches, **demons,** werewolves, and the like, and the feudal lords began to lose all patience with the rebellious serfs and set about to slay them as methodically as a farmer sets out to remove noxious weeds from his grain field.

In *The History of Magic,* Kurt Seligmann offers an astute analysis of the situation:

> With the devil's establishment of his power, the ancient survivals, the amusements of serfs, the most innocent stories, were henceforth satanic, and the women who knew about the old legends and magic traditions were transformed into witches. . . . . The traditional gatherings, the Druid's Festival on the eve of May Day, the Bacchanals, the Diana feasts, became the witches' sabbath . . . the broom, symbol of the sacred hearth . . . became an evil tool. The sexual rites of old, destined to stimulate the fertility of nature, were now the manifestations of forbidden carnal lust.

While the fires of the Inquisition sought to burn out all traces of the demonic machinations of Satan on earth, the satanism that most people recognize as the blasphemous rituals, the worship of a demonic force or Satan himself, and the practice of **human sacrifice** began to raise its horned head in fifteenth-century France. Unrestrained immorality was the order of the day as Parisians followed the hedonistic example of their sun king, Louis XIV. Satanism was developed to its highest estate as the jaded aristocrats began to adapt certain of the ancient witchcraft rituals and the rites of the Roman Catholic Church to suit their own sexual fantasies. The enlightened sophisticate's mockery of primitive customs had been converted to a serious interest by the tension and insecurity of the times, and lords and ladies began to pray in earnest to their holy Satan to grant them high office and wealth. Although the fires of the Inquisition still consumed its quota of men and women accused of being witches and shapeshifters, the France of King Louis XIV was a high-living, low-principled era. Such human monsters as **Gilles de Rais, Catherine Montvoisin,** Abbe Guilborg, and many others were bringing the black mass and other obscene rites to their peaks of perversity.

Even as the world approaches the year 2000, people are generally lured into satanic groups because they are going through a rebellious phase in their lives, and they see the trappings of satanism as a way of demonstrating their opposition to the traditional authority that has alienated them. Others become members of satanic covens because they have failed to fit in or to be accepted in other more conventional groups.

Those individuals who are attracted to the mysterious, the bizarre, and the Dark Side may join such cults because they feel that they are somehow imitating their favorite heavy metal or rock star. Still others are pressured into membership because of their own superstitious beliefs and their general dissatisfaction with life.

Satanism continues to find its way into sensational headlines. In June 1998, Luke Woodham, the 17-year-old high school boy accused of killing two students and wounding seven others in Pearl, Mississippi, said that the shootings occurred after he had become involved in satanism. Woodham testified that he joined a group that worshipped Satan: "You can send demons to go and do things. I've seen them. I know what I was dealing with. I felt like I had complete power over things. I know it's real in spite of what people think."

Anton Szandor LaVey, the Black Pope, founder of San Francisco's Church of Satan, died on Halloween 1997. In the late 1960s, LaVey was the subject of a great deal of media attention, often allowing reporters to attend certain rituals that he conducted over the living altar of a lovely woman's naked body, explaining: "An altar shouldn't be a cold, unyielding slab of sterile stone or wood. It should be a symbol of enthusiastic lust and indulgence."

In 1972, LaVey defined the role of satanism in the modern world. He spent a good deal of time defending satanism from the charges of being an evil cult, and he carefully explained that the Church of Satan did not condone any acts of violence against anyone. He chose, it seemed, to regard satanism more as an expression of true magic:

> Magic has always been with us, and it is a very real force. It is not supernatural; it is, rather, supernormal. I have always felt that the supernormal is just beyond the realm of one's normal existence. . . . There are 25-watt minds and 250-watt minds. [The larger] mind is able to conceive of greater forces.

When LaVey was asked to define evil, he replied:

> Things that hurt people who don't deserve to be hurt are evil. Vandalism is a terrible thing, ripping up fine paintings in museums, even toppling over potted plants in front of apartment houses. Evil is not as much a force as a human behavioral factor that is independent of any satanic motivation. Wrongs can be righted by magical means. By getting your adrenalin up and getting those thought waves out and to the proper place and the proper time and to the proper condition with the proper imagery. You might have an enemy to whom you level a curse, and it might be that you are totally justified. This man may have robbed you of a contract, may have stolen an idea, may have taken something that is very valuable to you. He deserves his just desserts.

Anton LaVey and his Church of Satan never won any popularity contests with members of the Christian clergy, but he was serious about the path that he had chosen and the manner in which he shaped his lifestyle. And he never condoned the indulgent, perverse, and destructive types of satanic disciples. LaVey lost ownership of the famous "Black House" in San Francisco in 1991 when a judge ordered him to sell the satanic temple, along with such mementos as a shrunken head and a stuffed wolf, and split the proceeds with his estranged wife, Diane Hagerty. In January 1999, the satanic high priest's last consort, the high priestess Blanche Barton, was struggling to raise enough donations to keep the Black House from being demolished to make way for the construction of condominiums.

SOURCES:

"Has Church of Satan Gone to Hell?" Reuters, January 22, 1999.

Seligmann, Kurt. *The History of Magic.* New York: Pantheon Books, 1948.

Steiger, Brad. "A Conversation with Anton S. LaVey." In *The Devil Is Alive and Well and Living in America Today,* edited by Jason Michaels. New York: Award Books, 1973.

"Woodham Testifies He Was Involved in Satanism." *CNN Interactive,* June 11, 1998.

Selkies

The selkies are the seal people who can shapeshift and appear in human form, resuming their true forms only when they wish to travel through the sea. The selkies are among the small number of gentle shapeshifters, desiring to live harmoniously with the fisherfolk of the Orkney and Shetland Islands. They often take human spouses and produce children who occasionally have webbed hands and feet and who are always born with a love for the sea. John Sayles, one of the screenwriters of **The Howling** (1981), wrote and directed an enchanting film about the selkies in *The Secret of Roan Inish* (1994).

SOURCES:

Larousse Dictionary of World Folklore. New York: Larousse, 1995.

Serpent People

Nearly every known earth culture has its legends of wise serpent people who ruled the planet in prehistoric times and assisted humankind in rising in status from hairless ape to the lords of the planet. Many of these serpent kings were said to come from the sky to promulgate the beneficent and civilizing rule of the sons of the sun, or the sons of heaven, upon earth. Quetzacoatl, the "feathered serpent," the culture-bearer of the Aztecs, was said to have descended from heaven in a silver egg. Ciuacoatl, Great Mother of the Gods for the ancient people of Mexico, was represented as a serpent woman. Among many African tribes, it is Aido Hwendo, the rainbow serpent, that supports the earth.

The Babylonian priest-historian Berossus chronicled the legend of Oannes, an entity described as a serpentlike half-man, half-fish, who surfaced

In 1966's *The Reptile,* Jacqueline Pearce suffered from an ancient curse that caused her to turn into a snake.

from the Persian Gulf to instruct the early inhabitants of Mesopotamia in the arts of civilization. Before the advent of the serpent master Oannes, Berossus stated, the Sumerians were savages, living like the beasts, with no order or rule.

Like so many accounts of the serpent people, Oannes appeared to be some kind of amphibious master teacher endowed with superior intelligence, but possessed of an appearance that was frightening to behold. Oannes had the body of a fishlike serpent with humanlike feet and a head that combined the features of fish and human. Berossus explained that the creature walked about on land during the day, counseling and teaching the Sumerians, but returned to the ocean each evening. The amphibious master gave the once-primitive Sumerians insight into letters and sciences and every kind of art. He taught them to construct houses, to found temples, to compile laws, and explained to them the principles of geometrical knowledge. He made them distinguish the seeds of the earth and showed them how to harvest fruits. In short, Oannes instructed them in everything that could tend to soften the manners and humanize humankind.

Because of the respect for the great serpent masters of prehistoric times, the collective unconscious of humankind both fears and reveres the snake. In ancient Egypt the serpent was regarded as both a symbol of immortality and of death, and the pharaoh wore a snake emblem on his headdress as a mark of royalty and divinity. Apollo, the Greek god of healing and medicine, was originally invoked and worshipped as a serpent. Aesculapius, another deity associated with medicine, often materialized as a serpent, and his crest of the double snakes remains today as a symbol of the medical profession.

In the Hebrew account of the Fall from Grace, the serpent was the king of beasts, walking on two legs, who became jealous when he saw how the angels honored Adam. For his part in the seduction of Eve, the serpent is punished by having his limbs removed and being forced to crawl on his belly. In the Moslem tradition, it is Michael the archangel who chops off the serpent's limbs with the sword of God. In many Native American legends, the great hero Manabozho must battle many serpent people to free his people from bondage.

Father Charlevoix, an early French missionary to the eastern tribes of North America, recorded in his journals that there was no image that the tribespeople marked on their faces or bodies more than that of the snake. According to many tribal legends, in the beginning of time, humans and snakes could converse freely. **Shamans** and others who were powerfully attuned to the spirit level, it was believed, could still communicate with the serpent and learn the secrets of the future and powerful healing medicines.

Serpent people remain popular as shapeshifting entities in the local folklore of many areas around the world. Some serious-minded researchers have even suggested that an underground race of reptilian beings secretly control all the major events of life on this planet. Other UFO investigators have theorized the serpent people of prehistoric times are the same beings who today visit the earth in spaceships as overlords surveying the evolution of humankind.

SOURCES:

Steiger, Brad. *Totems: The Transformative Power of Your Personal Animal Totem.* San Francisco: HarperSanFrancisco, 1997.

Shaitan

For centuries there has been a popular belief among the people of the Caucasus that the mountains are haunted by gigantic evil spirits called *shaitans*. According to legend, these restless mountain spirits once dared attempt to climb into heaven at some period in prehistory, a misdeed for which Allah has condemned them to wander the remote mountain passes forever. The legend goes on to say that if true believers in God should ever encounter one of these terrible spirits, they would do well to make a quick and cautious retreat lest they anger the shaitan into taking revenge on them for Allah's punishment and deliver misfortune to their household. If the creature should request food of a true believer, he should satisfy the demand and circumvent the spirit's wrath.

SOURCES:

Steiger, Brad. *Monsters Among Us.* New York: Berkley Books, 1989.

Shamans

In order to be able to pass through the portal of the Great Mystery that will lead them into another dimension of time and space, shamans must seek the assistance and guidance of their spirit helpers, who appear in the form of their totem animals. To more effectively explore this spiritual dimension, shamans may even assume the shape of their totemic animal and become for a time a wolf, a raven, an owl, or whatever creature has granted its power to their quest.

Among the characteristics that the popular culture has come to associate with shamans is their ability to enter into a kind of divine frenzy or ecstasy, very often achieved by the act of dancing and chanting. Once shamans have managed to separate themselves from mundane, ordinary existence, they enter a state of heightened awareness. To the observer, shamans lose their outward consciousness and become inspired or enraptured. While in this altered state of consciousness, they hear voices, see apparitions of spirits, and receive visions. Very often, they undergo a dramatic out-of-body experience that enables them to perceive physical events actually happening great distances away from the place where they have undergone their trance state.

In perhaps the majority of cases, those who become shamans have previously suffered a severe and sudden illness or accident that precipitated a near-death experience in which their spiritual essence left their physical body and

A king cobra prepares to strike in a scene from the 1961 film *The Snake Woman,* in which a young woman had the power to turn into a snake.

traveled for a time to a higher spiritual plane. Many shamans have also been beset by other natural interventions in their lives, such as spells of fever or epileptic seizures.

The shamans' robes or costumes are covered with animal shapes and magical symbols. From the beginning of time, shamans have employed their animal totems to assist them in communicating with spirits, so the tradition of bedecking their robes with feathers, fur, claws, and the like has remained constant throughout the centuries. The robe of the shaman is, in essence, a spiritual microcosm, a reflection of the greater cosmic system that reaches beyond the stars. When shamans wrap their robes about them, they are allowing their spirits to step across the physical dimension and begin at once to establish contact with the world of spirits. The great ethnologist Ivar Lissner observed that a shaman is one who knows how to deal with spirits and influence them:

> He is thus a magician. Every shaman is a magician, but not every magician is a shaman. A magician may also be a sorcerer. The essential charac-

teristic of a shaman is his excitement, his ecstasy and trancelike condition. It is because so many scholars have applied the word shaman to the magicians of primitive tribes, who are usually sorcerers and nothing more, that the idea of shamanism has become so vague and distorted.

SOURCES:
Lissner, Ivar. Translated by J. Maxwell Brownjohn. *Man, God, and Magic.* New York: G. P. Putnam's Sons, 1961.

Sidhe

If you should ever have an encounter with a fairy and wish to survive basically intact, there are two rules you must remember: Don't you dare ask its name; and don't you dare call it a fairy. According to those who speak the Gaelic tongue of Scotland and Ireland, the wee folk prefer to be known as *sidhe* (also spelled *sidh, sith, sithche,* and pronounced "shee"). There is disagreement as to the exact meaning of sidhe. Some say that it refers to the mounds or hills in which the supernatural folk abide. Others say that it means "the people of peace," and that is how the sidhe generally behave toward humans—except for those seemingly incurable elfin traits of kidnapping human children and shapeshifting into a seemingly endless variety of forms in order to work mischief.

SOURCES:
Spence, Lewis. *The Fairy Tradition in Britain.* London: Rider and Company, 1948.

Sirens

The **selkies,** the seal people of the Orkney and Shetland Islands, may wish to live harmoniously with the humans who love the sea as much as they do, but the sirens have no interest in creating anything but death and chaos for seafarers. In Greek lore, there were at first only two sirens, large birdlike beings with the heads of beautiful women and the gift for singing so soothingly and sweetly that no sailor could resist their enchanting duets. As the popularity of the legend grew, storytellers increased the number of sirens to three. Later, with the passing of time, the sirens became an entire chorus of mesmerizing female voices. They also evolved in their appearance, from the large birdlike entities with human heads to creatures more in the style of the mermaid tradition. In Homer's *Odyssey,* Odysseus foils the sirens by ordering his men to stuff their ears with wax so they cannot hear their fatal songs.

SOURCES:
Larousse Dictionary of World Folklore. New York: Larousse, 1995.

Skin Walkers

To many Navajo tribespeople, a werewolf is called a "skin walker." In the magic of the Navajo, Hopi, and Pueblo, the principal reason that a **shaman**

A cobra-worshiping cult led by Mary Nash (left) was the subject of the well-received 1944 film *The Cobra Woman*.

might shapeshift into a wolf is to traverse great distances in a much shorter time than he or she could walk the miles in human form. Those who cover themselves in the skin of a wolf are therefore known as *yee naaldlooshii* (those who trot about with it).

In January 1970, four Gallup, New Mexico, youths claimed to have encountered a werewolf on their way to Zuni, near Whitewater. All four swore that they saw a two-legged, hairy thing run alongside their car as they were traveling 45 miles per hour. When Clifford Heronemus later told reporters that he accelerated their vehicle to 60 miles per hour and the creature still paced them, he got scared. The highway section where the werewolf appeared is full of sharp turns, and Heronemus was concerned that the car could skid off the road and they would be easy prey for the monster.

According to Heronemus, one of the four finally got out a gun and shot it. "I know it got hit and it fell down—but there was no **blood.** It got up again and ran off. I know it couldn't have been a person, because people cannot move that fast."

Heronemus and his three friends were convinced that they had been chased by a werewolf, and they said that they were going looking for the creature with a camera. If he could obtain a photograph of the werewolf, "People won't think I'm half-cracked."

In 1936, anthropologist William Morgan wrote about the werewolf beliefs of the Navajo in Arizona and New Mexico, and he recorded one of his conversations with a Navajo who told him that the *Yee Naaldlooshii* could run very fast. They could get to Albuquerque in an hour and a half, the anthropologist was informed. Morgan noted that in those days it took four hours to drive the distance by automobile.

SOURCES:
Coleman, Loren. "Werewolves of the Southwest." *Strange,* April 1991.

Slaying the Werewolf

Teenager Buffy Summers is a chosen slayer of vampires, a guardian of an unsuspecting world that cannot perceive the magnitude of the evil that threatens it in veritable legions of the undead. When she sinks a wooden stake in the chest of a **vampire,** the creature disintegrates before our eyes; and each week on the popular television series, *Buffy the Vampire Slayer,* the diminutive high school senior effectively fulfills her ancient legacy as the one chosen to be a slayer, a protector of us all.

Oz (Seth Green), one of Buffy's friends and fellow high school students, is a werewolf that she and her small circle of teenaged accomplices keep under lock and key whenever the moon is full. Other than those occasional lunar spells, it seems as though Oz is a friendly and domesticated high school student. And if he weren't, well, one of Buffy's wooden stakes in the chest would probably make him really mad—but it wouldn't kill him. Slaying a werewolf is no easy accomplishment.

There are some notable examples in the literature of the vampire where slayers of the undead have laid in wait with stakes in hand to attack the night stalkers when they return to a victim's bedroom for their nightly feast of **blood.** Vampires depend upon such regular sustenance for their existence, and they can be vulnerable to an ambush by fearless vampire slayers as they revisit their current blood supply. Werewolves, however, have no need to stash away victims for nightly feedings. Lycanthropes do not kill to exist. Werewolves most often attack their victims for the sheer joy of the slaughter—the ripping, tearing, and biting at the flesh. True, werewolves may on occasion devour parts of their victims, but such butchery is not because they are starving for sustenance. In their human form, werewolves may eat very well, indeed. Remember, they do not lie in coffins during the day, but they walk about freely in human form, partaking, no doubt, of regular meals of great variety.

And because a werewolf is never lying somewhere dormant during certain hours of the day, as a vampire must do to survive, there is really no time when a slayer might catch the beast unaware, momentarily helpless, or off guard. When the werewolf attacks, it does so as a great beast attacks, tearing at its victim's jugular vein with claws or fangs. Its strength is superhuman—and terminally foolish and suddenly dead would be the slayer who seeks to go *mano a mano* with a werewolf.

If one has evidence that a werewolf is on the prowl, some traditions still insist that the creatures really don't like the smell of **garlic** blossoms or garlic oil, so they recommend liberally sprinkling the scent of garlic on all window sills and doorsteps. Wearing a crucifix around your neck won't protect you from a werewolf, but a sprig of garlic worn at the throat just might turn it off from going for your jugular.

Since there is no time when a werewolf is really vulnerable in animal form, over the centuries slayers have learned to wait until the lycanthrope has shifted back to its human shape. That was when the Inquisition seized both witches and werewolves for its torture machines and death by burning at the stake. Some judges at the various tribunals insisted that those suspected of being werewolves be executed by beheading with a double-edged sword.

What about the silver bullet? According to some legends, shooting the werewolf with a silver bullet is the only infallible method of slaying a werewolf. While some scholars state that such an "ancient tradition" actually began with Universal Studios' *Wolf Man* series in the 1940s, historians know for certain that in 1767 the notorious **Beast of Le Gevaudan** was said to be killed by silver bullets made from a chalice that had been blessed by a priest, and it is likely that the belief in slaying werewolves with bullets or other weapons made of silver predates that event by many years.

In assessing the limited means of destroying a werewolf, unless one is an accomplished wizard with a multitude of spells that are certain to dispense evil and keep werewolves at bay, it is not recommended by those who study werewolves that one adopts the role of werewolf slayer—even with an entire clip of silver bullets in hand. A clip might not be enough if a savage, roaring, slashing werewolf suddenly leaps out from the dark recesses of a midnight forest. In the popular television series *Buffy the Vampire Slayer*, when Oz is about to shapeshift into a wolf, he is voluntarily locked up by his friends. If the opportunity to cage him passes them by, they shoot him with a tranquilizer dart and let him sleep off his lycanthropic rage. Now that sounds like really good advice.

SOURCES:

Douglas, Drake. *Horror!* New York: Collier Books, 1966.

Steiger, Brad. *Monsters Among Us.* New York: Berkley Books, 1989.

An unlucky human about to transform into a werewolf in the film adaptation of Stephen King's *Silver Bullet.*

Solis, Magdalena (c. 1938–)

While the number of female murderers, sexual predators, and serial killers are minuscule compared to the number of men who perpetrate such heinous offenses against society, when a woman such as **Elisabeth Bathory** or **Catherine Montvoisin** comes on the scene, they seem determined to tip the scales of **blood** and cruelty—at least temporarily—toward the reality that history has had a number of very lethal ladies. In 1963, the federal police learned that a former prostitute from Monterrey, Mexico, had created a cult that had ripped the hearts out of the chests of 12 living victims in sacrifice to ancient Incan gods.

It was in the summer of 1962 that the Hernandez brothers, Santos and Cayetano, devised their ingenious plan to supplement the sex cult that they had established in the village of Yerba Buena. They needed a beautiful blonde goddess and her consort to help them control the villagers. Magdalena Solis had always believed she was born for better things than selling herself for a few pesos to the patrons of Monterrey's bars. And her brother Eleazor, who worked as her pimp, would enjoy the country life.

The Hernandez brothers told their new god and goddess that they had been living in a cave for several months, holding mystic rites, and promising the farmers who brought them regular offerings of food and money that they would continue to pray to the cave gods to yield the hidden Inca treasure in the mountains. None of the villagers questioned the fact that the Incas lived in ancient Peru, not Mexico. Nor did the farmers question the two mystics when they said that sex with the priests was necessary to rid their bodies of **demons.** But finally, the simple folk had become impatient and were weary of having their bodies purged of demons. They now wanted to have their share of the Inca treasure.

In order to keep their scam progressing, the Hernandez brothers promised the villagers that they would manifest the reincarnation of a local faith healer who had been dead for 50 years. They explained to the country folk that the woman had advanced to the status of a goddess and that she would return in the company of an Incan god. Magdalena and Eleazor would impersonate the two deities, and the four of them could continue to fleece the farmers of their money and exploit them sexually.

Magdalena found that she had a real flair for being a goddess. She and Eleazor appeared in the cave in the midst of billowing smoke, and the villagers fell to their knees in awe before the goddess and the god from the mountains. In an imperiously manner, she told her trembling congregation that before she could accomplish any healings or reveal the location of the Inca treasure, there must be a serious purging of their bodily demons. Then she led the assembled villagers through a series of weird chants, bizarre dances, the sharing of a bowl that had been filled with chicken blood and marijuana leaves, and climaxed the evening with uninhibited group sex.

Eventually the day came when extra portions of marijuana leaves and group sex rites could no longer distract the poor farmers from their hopes of ending their poverty with the Inca treasure. Incredibly, with cool efficiency and goddesslike detachment, Magdalena told her disciples that the doubts and demands of certain villagers had constituted blasphemy. Those who questioned the gods must be destroyed or the treasure would never be revealed. To the astonishment of Eleazor and the Hernandez brothers, the villagers, high on marijuana and greed, obeyed the goddess and stoned to death the two men who had protested their impatience the loudest. At her command, their blood was collected in basins and used later that night in the group communion.

By May 28, 1963, at least eight villagers had been slaughtered by Magdalena's primitive manner of cult purification. But also by that time, those men and women who feared they might be marked for sacrifice had begun fleeing the village of Yerba Buena.

In order to keep the cultists under her spell of sex, lies, greed, and fear, Magdalena performed an elaborate sacrificial ritual in which each of the cult members participated in the clubbing to death of a young woman. As the once-beautiful Celina was being beaten to a bloody, faceless corpse by the ceremonial clubbing, a teenage boy named Sebastian Gurrero happened to pass the cave entrance and witnessed a scene out of humankind's primordial past. Gurrero knew nothing of the group sex and ritual sacrifices being conducted in the cave. A serious-minded young man, he had been too immersed in his studies to pay attention to the rumors of gods and goddess living in the village, but now he ran from the scene in wide-eyed horror after he witnessed a man being hacked to death for protesting Celina's sacrifice.

Sebastian Gurrero walked 17 miles to Villa Gran, the nearest station of the federal police. Patrolman Luis Martinez did not doubt the teenager's incredible story. He had been hearing some very strange rumors about a pagan cult flourishing in Yerba Buena. He returned to the village with Sebastian Gurrero to investigate for himself. Tragically, as the patrolman and the boy approached the cave, the cultists fell upon them with machetes and added their corpses as sacrifices to the Inca gods.

When Martinez did not return to the station, Inspector Abelardo G. Gomez arrived in Yebra Buena with backup. Although the cultists resisted arrest and attacked Gomez and his officers, they dropped their weapons when a bullet from a policeman's rifle killed Santos Hernandez, one of the "immortal priests."

On June 13, 1963, only 11 days after their arrest, Magdalena and Eleazor Solis were brought to trial along with 12 members of the cult. The Mexican state of Tamaulipas had abolished capital punishment, but each of the 14 cultists received the maximum sentence of 30 years in the state prison at Victoria. Cayetano Hernandez, the man who had originally conceived the scheme of milking the villagers of Yerba Buena for sex and money, had been murdered by a disgruntled follower during the killings of Luis Martinez and Sebastian Gurrero.

SOURCES:

Lane, Brian, and Wilfred Gregg. *The Encyclopedia of Serial Killers.* New York: Berkley Publishing, 1994.

Steiger, Brad. *The Mass Murderer.* New York: Award Books, 1967.

Sorcery

In the ancient traditions, there were two basic ways by which a person became a werewolf—and they both involved sorcery. Either one deliberately sought to become a shapeshifter by employing a number of spells, invocations, and secret rituals so that he or she might have the power and strength of a lycanthrope to perform nefarious deeds, or one was cursed by a powerful sorcerer who used his magic to turn his victim into a werewolf to live the life of the damned. In other words, there were voluntary and involuntary werewolves. The notion that a victim of a werewolf attack became him- or herself a lycanthrope because of a bite or a scratch from the beast is largely the invention of motion pictures, quite probably beginning with **The Wolf Man** (1941). In all of the accounts of werewolf attacks throughout Europe in earlier times, we never read of the victims returning as lycanthropes. If the thousands of victims of **the Beast of Le Gevaudan** had returned as werewolves, all of France would have been overrun by an army of conqueror lycanthropes. In point of actual fact, the victim of a werewolf attack is almost always mangled, mutilated, and murdered—not merely bitten and "infected" with the werewolf curse.

Sorcery involves the manifestation of supernatural powers granted by spirits who have been summoned by a skillful magician or sorcerer. Many believe that such manipulation of psychic energy can only manifest evil spirits, who seize such an opportunity to enter the physical dimension in order to work evil against humankind and the true God of the universe. The French jurist **Jean Bodin** insisted that only Satan can change the shape of one body into that of another—and only because God grants him that power in the elemental world.

Those who voluntarily became werewolves through sorcery did so most frequently through the use of special ointments, the wearing of the magical **wolf belt,** and the chanting of various spells and invocations to summon the

Amanda Donohoe transforms into a serpent-like creature in the 1988 film *Lair of the White Worm.*

demonic beings that would implement the shapeshifting process. Those who involuntarily became werewolves were the victims of such incantations, curses, and the sinister work of **demons** summoned to do the evil work of sorcerers who had given themselves to the dark side.

SOURCES:
Spence, Lewis. *An Encyclopedia of Occultism*. New Hyde Park, NY: University Books, 1960.

Speck, Richard (1942–1991)

On that terrible after-midnight massacre on July 14, 1966, nine student nurses had been marked for death by Richard Speck. Miraculously, one of them escaped and lived to tell the world of the awful ordeal of the bloody hours of horror in which a human werewolf had slashed and murdered her friends one by one.

The nurses had all been students at the South Chicago Community Hospital. Three were graduate nurses from the Philippines. The other six were

Americans. Eight of the young women lived in a townhouse on the South Side of Chicago in a pleasant neighborhood known as Jeffrey Manor. Everyone who knew the young nurses regarded them as quiet, serious, and well mannered.

Earlier on the evening of Wednesday, July 13, Philippine exchange student Luisa Silverio had stopped by the dormitory and had been invited to stay for dinner by Valentina Paison and Corazon Amurao, both 23 years old and also Philippine nurses. On any other night, Luisa later told reporters, she would have readily have accepted the invitation of her friends—especially since Valentina had prepared a special Philippine dish—but she had a strange intuition that something terrible was about to happen. On this particular night, there seemed something strange and foreboding about the dormitory rooms that bothered her. Luisa Silverio made her apologies, then returned to her own dormitory—and to life.

When Richard Speck broke into the kitchen around midnight, he crept downstairs to the front bedroom where Corazon Amurao was sleeping. Puzzled when she heard a knock at her door, she opened it and was shocked to see a man standing there. She noticed the strong odor of alcohol before she saw the gun in his hand. He forced her down the hallway as he awakened the other women and herded them into one bedroom. In a soft, quiet voice, he promised them that he would not hurt them. He just needed some cash to get to New Orleans.

Speck used a knife to cut bedsheets so that he could bind the young women. As he bound and gagged each of them, he would ask her where she kept her money.

Outside the townhouse, Suzanne Farris, 21, was riding around in the car of her future sister-in-law, Mary Ann Jordan, 20, a fellow student nurse. They had been discussing plans for the forthcoming wedding of Suzanne and Mary Ann's brother, and they had lost track of time. Suzanne invited Mary Ann to sneak into her townhouse and spend the night so they could chat more about the wedding. At 12:25, the two nurses met Gloria Jean Davy, 22, another dormitory resident, who was also rushing toward the entrance of the townhouse. The three of them giggled about just missing the 12:30 curfew, then they stepped inside to meet their destiny at the hands of a monster.

Speck bound and gagged the three latecomers and made them lie down on the floor with the six other young women. For a time he sat on the floor in the midst of them, saying nothing, only fingering the knife that he had used to fashion their bonds. Then he stood up and took one of the girls out of the room.

When he returned after a few minutes and took another of the nurses away, Corazon Amurao thought it was obvious what was on the mind of the tall, blond man with the soft voice. She and 22-year-old Merlita Gargulla set about attempting to loosen their bonds. Corazon whispered to the others that once she got free, she would untie them, then pick up a steel bunk ladder and hit the intruder over the head with it. The seven of them could easily overpower him if they all jumped him at once.

But the other nurses said it was best to lie still. The man had promised not to hurt them if they cooperated and gave him money. It was best not to start anything that might make him go crazy.

Corazon argued that if the intruder was so harmless, why hadn't the two women he had taken from the room been returned to them? When she saw it was useless to debate the matter, she rolled under one of the bunk beds and hid. There she cringed and prayed while the tall blond man took the girls one by one out of the room. Later, she remembered that none of the nurses uttered more than "a little scream."

In the frenzy of the horrible atrocities that he was committing, Richard Speck either lost track of the number of his victims or else he had known prior to his invasion of the townhouse that the dormitory housed eight nurses. If such were the case, he was unaware that there were nine nurses present that night, since Suzanne Farris had invited Mary Ann Jordan to stay the night.

At 5:00 A.M., Corazon Amurao heard an alarm clock go off. Summoning her courage, she crept out from under the bed, crawled out on a balcony ledge, and began to shout for help, screaming that all of her friends were dead.

Patrolman Daniel Kelly and police officer Leonard Ponne entered the townhouse through the back door that Speck had left unlocked. They found bodies strewn all over the place. **Blood** was everywhere.

On the couch in the downstairs living room, the officers found the naked and lifeless body of one of the nurses. She had been strangled and mutilated. In the middle bedroom, the blood from three bodies had drenched nightgowns. In the other bedroom were the corpses of three more young women. One of the nurses found in a bathroom had been stabbed nine times and strangled. Despite his own shock, Patrolman Kelly managed to calm Corazon Amurao and obtain a description of the killer.

Homicide commander Francis Flanagan lived in Jeffrey Manor and had been able to walk to the scene of the grisly murders in about five minutes. A veteran of 3,000 homicide investigations, the detective was appalled at the beastlike savagery with which the nurses had been slain. Flanagan agreed with other officers on the scene that the murderer was likely a seaman because of the expert square knots in which the nurses' hands had been tied. The fact that he had continued to mention that he needed to get to New Orleans, long an ideal port from which an itinerant seaman on the lam could ship out, also indicated a seaman with a police record who needed to leave Chicago. Offi-

Serial killer Richard Speck, who murdered eight student nurses in Chicago on July 14, 1966.

cers were dispatched to the seaman's union with a description of the murderer provided by Corazon Amurao.

While Amurao was going through a stack of mug shots of men in their twenties who had records of crimes against women, an investigating officer slipped a copy of the photograph of Richard Speck that he had obtained from the seaman's union hiring hall. It was the same man.

At the same time, on North Clark Street, a team of detectives followed Speck's trail through a string of seedy bars that he had patronized in the company of local prostitutes. They found a bartender who had nearly thrown him out for horsing around with a knife, demonstrating to willing and unwilling patrons how best to kill someone with a knife. The creep had even boasted that his knife had killed many people.

At 12:30 Sunday morning, July 17, 1966, Dr. LeRoy Smith, resident surgeon on trauma duty at Chicago's Cook County Hospital, hastily appraised a bloodied derelict who had just been brought in from a skid-row flophouse on West Madison Street as a botched suicide. The semiconscious man was bleeding from cuts on the arm and a slash across the right wrist. Then, as Dr. Smith looked more closely at the derelict, he recognized him as the man in the photograph the newspapers and television stations had been displaying as the suspected murderer in the ghastly slaughter of eight young nurses.

When Dr. Smith asked his name, the man answered in a weak whisper: "Richard Speck. Do you collect the 10,000-dollar reward they're offering for me, Doc?"

During the trial and after Richard Speck's subsequent imprisonment, a great deal of investigation suggested that he may have committed many other stranglings and stabbings of women in various parts of the United States. On September 11, 1990, Illinois prison officials at Stateville Correctional Center near Joliet denied parole for the *seventh* time to Richard Speck. The Illinois Prisoner Review Board stated that the then 48-year-old killer would continue to serve his sentence of up to 1,200 years. Somewhere along his bloody path to committing one of the most brutal mass murders in the annals of crime, Speck had obtained a tatoo that declared, "Born to Raise Hell." With his vicious and cruel slashing knife, the motto might as well have read, "Born to Be a Werewolf."

SOURCES:
Steiger, Brad. *The Mass Murderer.* New York: Award Books, 1967.

Spells to Ward Off Werewolves

A practitioner of magic who had set up a retail outlet in order to supply witches, sorcerers, and magicians with the genuine articles needed for occult research admitted to duplicating and disseminating ancient potions and spells. The practitioner, who shall remain anonymous, had completed worldwide travel and an enormous amount of research and experimentation over more than 20 years, Because of his extensive research, he was able to offer potions and mixtures that were absolutely identical to the ancient, original formulas.

In his opinion, superstition and ignorance had given ceremonial magic a bad name:

> If one approaches the occult from a strictly objective viewpoint, it will prove to be one of the most fascinating subjects which one can study. There are so many ramifications and complexities that no one person could master the occult in one lifetime. In our coven, we had each member specialize in certain aspects of magic, while, at the same time, maintaining a general knowledge of the entire field. In this way, we always have an expert at hand.

> **Sorcery** does not have to be evil. Sorcery and ceremonial magic does involve the summoning of beings and forces from other planes. As a general rule, sorcery is used for self-gain, but it can serve other purposes just as well. We feel that it is the purpose that counts, assuming no harm is attendant. The most ideal usage of magic is the gaining of knowledge. Those who are sincere follow this path. Naturally there are pitfalls and dangerous areas, but is this not also true of everyday, mundane life?

For whatever the following may be worth—as werewolf repellents or entertaining curiosities—such spells as these have been used traditionally to keep one's household safe from lycanthropes when the moon is full.

An Invocation to **Diana,** *the Moon Goddess, to Keep One Safe from Evil Entities—Specifically Werewolves*

'tis _____(Name the date) now, and at an early hour
I fain would turn good fortune and safe passage to myself,
Firstly at home and then when I go forth.
With the aid of the beautiful Diana, Goddess of the Moon,
Great Huntress with her pack of she-wolves,
I pray for protection from evil werewolf fang and claw
ere I do leave this house! May her guiding and protective hand kept me safe
  until my return.

Three drops of oil are now required to be slowly fed to the flame of a candle in propitiation to Diana with the supplication that she remove any evil influence that might be lurking about in the shadows of the night.

A Spell to Repel Werewolves

Well-protected may I be as I go forth to roam,
for Diana, beautiful, Diana, I walk abroad with thy blessing.
I do implore thee to keep all evil from me;
I do beseech thee to drive all werewolves away from my path.
May you change deadly wolf intent and savage heart

back to the human form of gentle man or woman.

May you quench the lust for **blood**

And transform it into love for thee.

At this point, slowly drip three drops of oil into the flame of a candle in propitiation to Diana.

A Prayer to Ask Light Beings for Protection

As you recite the following, be prepared to sprinkle drops of perfume over the flame of a candle or a small tin of burning oil.

> I dedicate to you, o ye Angels of Light and all heavenly spirits, these drops of aromatic perfume to send a sweet smell that will inspire all goodness. Receive the prayer from my heart to keep me safe from evil and from those beings who transform their human flesh into the unholy bodies of **wolves** and monsters. Receive these drops as perfume from my heart to quelch the foul stench of **demons** and shapeshifters who would do evil to me and to others whom I love. Receive these drops of heavenly perfume to cover the putrid odor of evil and to cleanse my household from demonic influences. Keep our home safe from evil, O Living God of the Universe and all Angelic Beings of Light. Amen and amen.

Spiritual Shapeshifting

Among the stone etchings and 416 Paleolithic paintings recently discovered in a cavern in the Ardeche Gorge in southeast France are a number of depictions of creatures with animal heads and human legs. The team of archaeologists examining the ancient artworks in 1998 felt that rather than representing monstrous beings, the bipedal wereanimals indicated that the people of 32,000 years ago sought to incorporate the animals' spiritual and physical strengths within themselves.

Decades ago, when the ethnologist Ivar Lissner entered the caves that sheltered the paintings of the Franco-Cambrian artists of over 20,000 years ago, he also pondered the mystery of two-legged beings with animal heads. Lissner suggested that the Stone Age artists were portraying themselves in the guise of intermediary beings who were something more than ordinary humans and able to penetrate more deeply into the great mysteries of existence. He wondered if the ancient cave painters might not be saying that the path to supernatural power is easier to follow in animal shape and that the spirits can best be reached with an animal's assistance.

Lissner also believed that the shamans and creative thinkers of long ago were not trying to turn themselves into wereanimals, but were seeking to shapeshift on a spiritual level. Rather than transforming themselves into monsters, these ancient wise ones wished to absorb the strength, agility, nobility, and spiritual power of the animals that they most admired and respected. As it is written in the Book of Job (12:7-8): "Ask the animals, and they will teach you, or the birds of the air, and they will tell you . . . or let the fish of the sea inform you."

When traditional Native American supplicants receive their totem animal in a vision quest, they acquire the spirit helper that will steadfastly serve as their guide on the path that the Great Mystery perceives as their destiny. I received my principal totem animal of the wolf in August of 1972 when Twylah Nitsch, the Repositor of Wisdom for the Wolf Clan of the Seneca nation, adopted me into the clan and granted me the honor of being initiated into the Wolf Clan Medicine Lodge. I have always felt very comfortable with the wolf as my personal totem, and I have tried to emulate the animal's sense of loyalty and devotion to other members of the pack, as well as its independent spirit and sense of personal responsibility. Wolf as the Great Teacher is a strong guiding force in my life, and images of wolves or dogs have often appeared to me in signficant dreams to warn me of impending crises or to present me with symbols that have aided me in solving troublesome problems.

Many men and women experience vivid dreams that they have become wolves. Others sense their spiritual essence blending with that of a wolf and becoming one entity, and they have received powerful visions in which they perceive themselves as wolves. These individuals do not see themselves becoming wolves in order to attack or to harm others. They experience the transformation in order to glory in the sense of strength and personal freedom of the animal as it runs through the forest trails and the mountain paths. Just as the ancient artists respected the physical prowess of their totem animals and immortalized their representations on the walls of caves, and just as traditional shamans revere the wisdom and inspiration given to them by their totem animals, in like manner do these contemporary spiritual shapeshifters desire to incorporate the power and the insights of the pure wolf spirit into their own psyches.

For many years now at various seminars and Medicine gatherings, I have conducted a guided visualization in which serious students may achieve insights into how they can absorb the truly commendable facets of the wolf persona and accomplish spiritual shapeshifting into the essence of a wolf. This is not the sorcery that sought to turn dark magicians of old into vicious werewolves that would kill and maim, but a spiritual technique that can accentuate the methods by which those who cherish the true wolf spirit may rise to higher levels of awareness and may learn better how to assist and aid fellow members of their human pack.

In order to accomplish this exercise in spiritual shapeshifting, you will need a time and place in which you are certain to be undisturbed for at least 40 minutes. The technique requires you to be in as relaxed a state as possible in order to receive suggestions and to act upon them with maximum effect. For that purpose I am providing a relaxation process.

You may wish to have a family member or friend read the relaxation process and the guided visualization to you in a soft, soothing voice. I have found the use of Native American flute music softly playing in the background to be a most effective aid in achieving exceptional results in this exercise. If you do use music as background, be certain that it contains no lyrics, for they will be certain to distract you from attaining the full benefit from the technique.

Through the years, some people have told me that they like to record the relaxation process and the guided visualization using their own voice to guide them through the exercise. Either method can be effective, and your success with the process depends upon your willingness to visualize in your mind the conditions of your spiritual shapeshifting.

The Relaxation Process

Assume a comfortable position, either sitting or lying down, that you can maintain for 40 minutes and not be interrupted. Release all worries . . . all tensions . . . all problems. Take a comfortably deep breath...and begin to relax.

With every breath you take, you find that you are becoming more and more relaxed. With every breath you take, you find that you are becoming more and more peaceful.

Any sound that you might hear—a barking dog, a slamming door, a honking car horn—will not disturb you. Any sound that you hear will only help you to relax . . . relax . . . relax.

Visualize that at your feet there lies a soft rose-colored blanket. The color rose stimulates natural body warmth and helps to induce sleep and relaxation. The color rose also provides a sense of well-being and a marvelous feeling of being loved.

Imagine that you are mentally moving the rose-colored blanket slowly up over your body. Feel it moving over your feet, relaxing them. Feel it moving over your legs, relaxing them. Feel it moving over your stomach, removing all tensions . . . over your back, removing all stress. Feel the rose-colored blanket moving over your chest . . . your arms, relaxing them.

As the rose-colored blanket moves over your neck, relaxing all the muscles, visualize the blanket transforming itself into a hood that covers your head like a cowl. Now you are completely enveloped in the beautiful rose-colored blanket, and you feel the color of rose permeating your psyche, permitting you to relax . . . relax . . . relax.

With every breath you take, you find that you are becoming more and more relaxed. With every breath you take, you find that you are becoming more and more peaceful. Any sound that you might hear will not disturb you. Any sound that you hear will only help you to relax . . . relax . . . relax.

Now imagine that there lies at your feet a soft blanket the color of green, the color of Mother Earth. The color green is a cleanser, a healer, that will help you to relax even deeper. Visualize yourself beginning to pull the green blanket slowly over your body.

Feel it moving over your feet, relaxing them, healing them of any pain or discomfort. Feel the lovely green blanket moving over your legs, relaxing them, healing them of any pain or discomfort. Feel the green blanket moving over your stomach, ridding it of all tensions. Feel the green blanket of Mother Earth moving over your chest, your arms . . . relaxing, healing, relaxing.

With every breath you take, you are becoming more and more relaxed . . . more at peace . . . more and more at one with your body, mind, and spirit. With every breath you take, you are becoming more and more relaxed . . . more at one with Mother Earth.

Feel the healing color of green moving over your back, relieving all stress along the spine. Feel the healing color of green relaxing, healing, relaxing your entire body.

As you move the green blanket over your neck, relaxing all the muscles, visualize the green blanket of Mother Earth transforming itself into a hood that covers your head like a cowl. As you pull the green blanket over your head, feel it calming all your nerves, your anxieties, your stresses. You are now completely enveloped in the healing color of green, the healing energy of Mother Earth, and you feel it permeate your psyche, relaxing you . . . calming you . . . healing you.

Nothing will disturb you, nothing will distress you. All concerns are being left behind . . . as you become more and more relaxed . . . relaxed . . . relaxed.

Visualize now at your feet a blanket the color of blue, the color of the Sky Father. Blue prompts psychic sensitivity. The color of blue will aid you greatly in receiving dream or vision teachings of a positive and helpful nature. The color of blue will aid you greatly in achieving your spiritual shapeshifting into a wolf.

Imagine now that you are willing the blue-colored blanket to move slowly up your body. Feel it moving slowly over your feet, relaxing them. Feel it moving over your legs, your hips, relaxing them . . . relaxing them.

With every breath you take, you are becoming more and more relaxed. Nothing will disturb you, nothing will distress you. All concerns are being left behind . . . as you become more and more relaxed . . . relaxed . . . relaxed.

With every breath you take, you are becoming more relaxed . . . and more prepared to be at one with the Great Mystery.

Now feel the blanket moving slowly over your chest, your arms, your back, your stomach, removing all tensions, all stresses. Everywhere the blue blanket touches you, you feel a wonderful relaxing energy moving throughout every cell of your body. Everywhere the blue blanket touches you, you feel relaxed . . . relaxed . . . relaxed.

As the blue blanket moves over your neck, relaxing all the muscles, visualize the blue-colored blanket of the Sky Father transforming itself into a hood that covers your head like a cowl. Feel the energy of the Sky Father and the color of blue permeate your psyche and give you the wisdom to experience spiritual shapeshifting from the Great Mystery. Know that the color of blue will accelerate all your psychic abilities. Now feel the beautiful blue cowl of the Sky Father envelope you completely in its peaceful, loving, relaxing energy.

The Shapeshifting Exercise

As you relax under the blankets of rose-colored well-being, green-colored Mother Earth energy, and blue-colored Sky Father energy, you begin to feel a new, warm, tingling energy moving throughout your entire body. You feel the energy moving through your brain, and you feel your unconscious level of reality becoming activated. You sense the energy moving down your spine, bringing power into your entire being. This is the energy of transformation.

Now you feel the energy of transformation moving to the very center of your being, your most secret innerself. You feel the energy of transformation activating the left side of your brain, your conscious reality.

You feel the energy of transformation as it surges through your body, and you are aware of the warmth that brings strength and power to every cell. You feel yourself becoming warmer as exciting waves of pleasure move throughout your entire being. A heightened state of ecstasy is mounting within you, growing higher and higher.

The energy of transformation is vibrating every cell in your body. You feel new energy, new strength, new power moving through your thighs . . . your chest . . . your loins . . . your feet . . . your hands. You feel the energy rhythmically pulsating deep within your body . . . deep within your spiritual essence. Your head, your mind, your body are all one. You are one with the energy of transformation that allows you to shapeshift into the spiritual essence of the wolf.

The energy of transformation fills your brain with the image of Wolf. The energy floods your inner vision with Wolf, the independent spirit . . . Wolf, the teacher . . . Wolf, the strong and powerful . . . Wolf, the caretaker of the forest . . . Wolf, the loyal, the faithful, the dependable . . . Wolf, the fearless, the magnificent.

Your inner vision has become crystal clear. Your hearing is keener, sharper than it has ever been. Your sense of touch is more sensitive than you knew was possible. Your nostrils are experiencing new aromas, previously far beyond your normal spectrum. Your eyes are perceiving dimensions once impossible to see.

You are hearing sounds that only a great wolf can hear. You are seeing, touching, smelling, feeling sensations that only a great wolf can experience. Enjoy the new muscular sensations. Feel the sleek power of the wolf that you are.

Your wolf body is sinewy and strong. You are a magnificent creature, and you have enormous strength and power. You are an ancient spirit, and you have great wisdom and insight.

Visualize yourself moving effortlessly through the forest. See yourself being joined by other wolves. See a full moon overhead that enhances the silhouettes of others of your kind. Feel a surge of power as you become part of the pack. Feel blood course through your body, your legs, filling you with a pounding need to race wildly through the darkened forest. See yourself running as a wolf in wild abandon. See yourself doing that now!

[Pause here for at least two minutes to allow the spiritual shapeshifter to experience the wild abandon of running with the wolf pack.]

When you have enjoyed all that you desire to experience, you have the ability to return to your normal state, knowing that you may return to this pleasurable state of being whenever you wish by allowing yourself to relax and permitting your psyche to become one with the spiritual essence of the wolf. All you need do to become one with the spirit of the wolf is to take three comfortably deep breaths and say softly, "Mother Earth, Sky Father, Great Mystery, Wolf, Wolf, Wolf." At that time you will feel the strength, the power, and the ancient wisdom surge through your mind, body, and spirit.

[If it is so desired, the spiritual shapeshifter may have more time to enjoy the experience of being one with the wolf essence. After a few more minutes, conclude the exercise with the following words:]

Now you are returning to your present reality as a human being named (fill in your name). At the count of five, you will return feeling better than you have in weeks and weeks. At the count of five, you will return filled with the awareness of your spiritual oneness with Mother Earth, Father Sky, and the Great Mystery. At the count of five, you will return with the strength and ancient wisdom of the wolf, viewing all your fellow creatures with respect. You are now coming awake: One . . . feeling very good in mind and body. Two . . . feeling confident and centered in new awareness. Three . . . feeling very, very good in mind, body, and spirit. Four . . . coming awake filled with new insights and knowledge. Five . . . wide awake and feeling great!

Spunkie

The spunkie is a Scottish goblin that particularly has it in for those travelers who venture out after dark. The spunkie is considered so nasty that tradition has it that he is a direct agent of Satan. It hovers about in the darkness, waiting for a traveler to become lost in the night, perhaps during a rainstorm when visibility is especially bad. The goblin manifests a light that appears to the desperate wayfarer like illumination shining through a window pane, thus signalling shelter and a dry place to spend the inclement evening. But as the traveler approaches the light, it keeps moving just a bit farther away. Since the poor, drenched pilgrim has no choice in the darkness but to keep pursuing the light source, the spunkie keeps moving it just a bit farther on—until the evil goblin has lured the unfortunate traveler over a cliff.

SOURCES:

Spence, Lewis. *An Encyclopedia of Occultism.* New Hyde Park, NY: University Books, 1960.

Stumpf, Peter (1525–1589)

Peter Stumpf—or Peter Stubbe—was born in the town of Bedburg near the city of Cologne about 1525, and according to contemporary biographers of this notorious werewolf, he gave himself up in his youth to the pursuit of magic and **sorcery** and, through necromancy, acquainted himself intimately with many spirits and **demons.** While other magicians made their pacts with Satan in order to acquire great earthly riches, Stumpf was interested only in being able to transform himself into a werewolf in order to work harm on men, women, and children.

After his capture and during his trial, Peter Stumpf told how Satan gave him a hairy girdle or belt, which, whenever he wore it:

> . . . transformed him forthwith into the likeness of a greedy devouring wolf. It was strong and mighty, with great eyes which in the night sparkled like brands of fire. Its body was huge, and the mouth great and wide with most sharp and cruel teeth. No sooner should he put off this girdle, but the mighty paws would again become hands, and presently he would appear in his former shape as if he had never changed.

Until he was revealed as a werewolf, Stumpf had appeared to his fellow townsfolk as quite an ordinary man. Few people suspected that Peter was leading such a ghastly double life. Although never a man believed to be concerned with his eternal salvation, few could guess that within his soul lurked a secret nature "inclined to **blood** and cruelty." Later, it was established that all those individuals who had somehow aroused his anger were stalked and viciously attacked, usually as they traveled beyond the edge of the town. When his victims were discovered, their bodies were so badly mutilated that no one could have imagined that their attack had been accomplished by anything other than a savage beast.

Other than those men who had angered him in some way, Stumpf's favorite victims were women and children. According to the old court records, he would "ravish them in the fields" in human form, then transform himself into a wolf and "cruelly murder them."

To add to his roster of outrageous sins against humanity, Stumpf sexually abused his daughter, who had matured into a beautiful young woman. The horrified judges recorded that "cruelly he committed most wicked incest with her. . . . But such was his inordinate lust and filthy desire toward her that he begat a child by her, daily using her as his concubine." And Stumpf's shocking acts of incest did not end with the abuse of his daughter. "Furthermore, this insatiable and filthy beast, given over to works of evil, with greediness lay even with his own sister. He frequented her company long times according to the wicked dictates of his heart."

Stumpf had other women as well. One woman singled out by the court was suspected to be a beautiful shapeshifting demon, rather than an ordinary human female, for Stumpf's "inordinate lust" could hardly be satisifed with any "natural woman."

Grisly acts of **cannibalism** were added to the many charges against the notorious Werewolf of Bedburg. During one brief time period alone he was accused of having slain 13 young women and devoured large portions of their bodies. In this same time frame, Stumpf killed two pregnant women and "tearing the children out of their wombs in most blood and savage sort, he afterwards ate their hearts, panting and raw, which he accounted dainty morsels greatly agreeing with his appetite."

On one occasion, Stumpf ambushed two men and a woman as they were traveling between towns. The werewolf killed and badly mutilated the men, but no trace of the woman was ever found "for she, whose flesh he esteemed both sweet and dainty in taste, the vile monster had most ravenously devoured."

There seemed no end to Peter Stumpf's outrages against civilized society. Although he had been heard frequently to refer to his firstborn son as his "heart's ease," nonetheless, when he was in the form of a wolf, he killed the youth and "next ate the brains out of the boy's head as a most savory meal to assuage his greedy appetite."

Stumpf was finally captured when a party of men with dogs set out to track down a wolf that had been seen to carrying away a small body tending his family's cattle. As they neared a thicket to which the dogs had led them, the men heard the child crying hysterically. Then, they swore to a man, they

THE LIFE AND DEATH OF PETER STUMP

An eight-panel broadsheet from 1590 showing the execution of werewolf and demonic killer Peter Stumpf.

saw first a wolf appear, and as they watched in astonishment the beast shapeshifted into the form of Peter Stumpf. Since the men recognized the human image before them as a citizen of Bedburg, they at first thought that Satan may have presented them with some kind of an illusion. Cautiously, they followed Stumpf back to his house, then decided to take him to the authorities for questioning.

During the questioning, Stumpf was threatened with the rack, and he startled the authorities by immediately confessing to be a sorcerer, a werewolf, a cannibal, a rapist, and an incestuous adulterer. Stumpf's daughter and his mistress were tried with him as accessories, and all three were condemned to death. As the "principal malefactor," Stumpf was given the severest punishment.

On October 31, 1589, in the town of Bedburg, Stumpf was stretched on the wheel and flesh was torn from his body in 10 places by red hot pincers. His arms and legs were severed with an axe; he was decapitated; and his body was burned. Some time afterward, the city erected a memorial of the Werewolf of Bedburg which consisted of a pole supporting the wheel on which Stumpf was broken, a plaque bearing the image of a wolf, 15 wooden portraits representing the monster's verified victims, and impaled at the very top, the lycan-thrope's head.

SOURCES:

Bores, George. *The Damnable Life and Death of Stubbe Peeter*. London Chapbook of 1590.

Hurwood, Bernardt J. *Vampires, Werewolves, and Ghouls*. New York: Ace Books, 1968.

Masters, R. E. L., and Eduard Lea. *Perverse Crimes in History*. New York: The Julian Press, 1963.

Summers, Montague. *The Werewolf*. New York: E. P. Dutton & Company, 1934.

Succubus

According to certain mystical traditions, the lustful **demons** known as the incubi and the succubi were the children of Father Adam's intercourse with a beautiful fallen angel named **Lilith,** who in the view of certain Jewish mystics, was Adam's wife before the creation of Eve. Succubi appear to men as beautiful, sensual women, tempting and promising.

The heavy cloud of sexual guilt that hung over the Middle Ages undoubtedly spawned a million succubi every night. As might be expected, the Christian hermits and monks in their lonely desert hovels or penitential cells were constantly harassed by sensuous succubi, who sought to tempt them into committing carnal sins.

In the Middle Ages, theologians warned against masturbation on the grounds that waiting demons stood ready to transport the wasted semen for their own nefarious purposes. Nocturnal emissions were interpreted as the work of succubi, who excited sleeping males to the point of ejaculation so they might steal away their spent semen.

SOURCES:

Spence, Lewis. *An Encyclopedia of Occultism*. New Hyde Park, NY: University Books, 1960.

Steiger, Brad. *Demon Lovers: Cases of Possession, Vampires, and Werewolves*. New Brunswick, NJ: Inner Light, 1987.

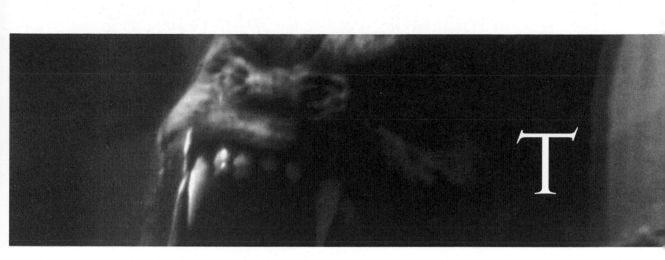

Taigherim

The rites of Taigherim consist of a magical sacrifice of cats that originated in pagan Scotland as a ritual to appease the subterranean gods. Beginning with the Christian era in Scotland, the rite was performed by sorcerers to invoke a special shapeshifting demon which would manifest as a very large black cat. The rites themselves involved the systematic roasting of live black cats on a spit slowly turning over a fire. As each cat was dedicated to the **demons** of darkness, its terrible **howls** of pain were believed to summon a particular monster of demonic power.

After the cruel sacrificial rites had been conducted for many hours, small demons would begin to materialize in the form of black cats and match their cries with the yowls of the unfortunate true cats that were being roasted alive. As the sacrifices continued, celebrated by the screeching of the cat-demons, the sorcerer would at last behold the materialization of a frightful catlike creature of great size, much larger than a black leopard of the jungle. The appearance of the great demon signaled demonic acceptance of the sorcerer's sacrifices, and he was now permitted to make his demands of the huge black cat, whether it be the gift of prophecy, a bag of gold, or the ability to shapeshift into a wolf or black cat.

SOURCES:
Spence, Lewis. *An Encyclopedia of Occultism.* New Hyde Park, NY: University Books, 1960.

Talbot, Lawrence

The annals of werewolfdom and shapeshifters have no Count **Dracula,** a universal figure instantly recognized as the quintessential werewolf as the Count

One of the biker werewolves from the so-bad-it's-almost-good film *Werewolves on Wheels,* which was released in 1971.

is recognized as the ultimate **vampire.** While some devotees of werewolf cinema would vote for Leon, the werewolf portrayed by **Oliver Reed** in *The Curse of the Werewolf* (1961), as the best cinematic enactment of the true lycanthropic legend, the character of Lawrence Talbot created by **Lon Chaney Jr.** in *The Wolf Man* (1941) comes much more rapidly to mind when the conversation turns to werewolves.

Strictly speaking, of course, Talbot is the victim of a werewolf, perpetuating, if not originating, the myth that ordinary people can become werewolves if such a monster bites or scratches them. However, according to ancient traditions, people become werewolves only if they seek to transform themselves into **wolves** through **sorcery** or if they have been cursed to become a wolf through the machinations of an evil sorcerer. Victims of werewolves were mangled into bloody pieces and died from the attack. They did not, as did the victims of vampires, become members of the undead, sustaining their life force by draining the **blood** of subsequent victims. Therefore, contrary to ancient lore, Lawrence Talbot is a victim of a werewolf attack who lived to become himself transformed during periods of the **full moon.**

Clearly, Talbot never takes pleasure in those periods of what could be superhuman lycanthropic empowerment. In each film in which he portrayed Talbot—*The Wolf Man*, *Frankenstein Meets the Wolf Man* (1943), *House of Frankenstein* (1944), *House of Dracula* (1945), and *Abbott and Costello Meet Frankenstein* (1948)—Chaney does an excellent job of convincing the audience that he is a good man who wouldn't bite anyone under normal circumstances and who will do anything to rid himself of the curse of the werewolf. If Talbot had been cursed by an evil practitioner of magic, rather than bitten by a werewolf, he would have been a lycanthrope in the classic tradition. Nit-picking thusly, Leon in *The Curse of the Werewolf* has been made an involuntary werewolf through the circumstances of his birth, and the stages of his development into a raging lycanthrope provide a more complete cinematic fulfillment of the werewolf legend. However, since the true werewolf of tradition actually shapeshifts into a wolf, the lycanthropes of *An American Werewolf in London* (1981), *The Howling* (1981), and *An American Werewolf in Paris* (1997) are even more faithful to the old accounts in appearance, if not in spirit.

Nit-picking aside, the image of Lon Chaney Jr. as the transformed Wolf Man, dressed in dark slacks and shirt, bent over and walking on his tiptoe paws through the mists of Wales, has formed an indelible impression in the psyches of several generations of moviegoers and millions upon millions of horror fans. The sad-eyed, sympathetic Lawrence Talbot, fearful of the full moon and hurting a fellow human, remains the image of the archetypal cinematic werewolf.

Talisman

A talisman is an inanimate object which has come to possess certain supernatural powers which can, in turn, be conferred to the one who wears the object. A talisman is most often a disc of metal or stone engraved with symbols of magical significance and is usually worn on a chain or leather cord that allows it to rest midchest on the magician or supplicant. A talisman is often confused in the general mind with an amulet, which is worn to ward off evil. A talisman's sole purpose is to bring paranormal powers to the wearer. Talismans were often fashioned with lycanthropic designs and wore by those sorcerers who wished to become werewolves.

SOURCES:

Spence, Lewis. *An Encyclopedia of Occultism.* New Hyde Park, NY: University Books, 1960.

Tase

Funerals in Burma (Myanmar) are always loud and noisy with drums, cymbals, shouting, dancing, singing, and banging on pots and pans. Such raucous wakes are for everyone's protection, for it is believed that if the **ghosts** of the recently dead hunger for revenge on their enemies or died with a pique against a member of the family, they can shapeshift into animal forms or hideous monsters. Such vengeful, shapeshifting spirits are known as *tase*, and their living survivors do their best to keep them at bay with loud noises until the soul can find peace and move on to a higher dimension.

SOURCES:

Larousse Dictionary of World Folklore. New York: Larousse, 1995.

Taw

For many years, Harold M. Young, an official of the Burmese government during the period of British control, was stationed among the remote tribes of the Shan of the Lahu. It was among these peoples that Young first heard of—then saw for himself—the strange mountain werewolves that terrorize the Lahu tribe, whose people live in the jungles bordering northern Thailand and Burma (now Myanmar). Manifestations of the supernatural, Young discovered, were daily occurrences among the Lahu. The government official expressed his opinion that the more humanity retreated from nature and hid behind the barrier of civilization, the further we remove ourselves from the basic powers which are the natural heritage of the "uncivilized" human.

Working among the native people, Young had heard about the *taws* for many years. They were always described to him as strange, fearsome creatures with furry hides that at certain times of the month would raid a village and either kill or carry off a victim. He had dismissed all such comments referring to the strange creatures as native superstition, an excuse for carelessness in allowing a wild beast to get past the sentries and into the village. Young was secure in his "educated and civilized" opinion until he was actually confronted by the bloody deeds of a jungle werewolf.

The eerie confrontation occurred in 1960 while he was on a hunting party. His expedition had taken him into Lahu country, high in the mountains that lie to the north of the Burma-Thailand border. The trek had been wearisome, but the thought of some nighttime hunting had adrenalin pumping through his system. As he neared a Lahu village he foresaw no difficulty in obtaining rights for a night shooting; the Lahu and he had always been on friendly terms.

On this night, however, the chief shook his head firmly in denial of his request. He warned Young that the taw were near to the village. It was dangerous to hunt now.

Young was just opening his mouth in protest when a terrible shriek filled the night. His hunter's responses were well conditioned. His hand grasped his pistol firmly as he ran to the thatched hut standing close to the jungle's edge from which the cry had issued. His mind and body alert, he could not help noticing that the chief and other of the men followed him at a distinctly slower pace. He was puzzled by their reluctance to dash after him. He had seen these same men face a snarling tiger without fear—yet now they seemed strangely hesitant about rendering aid. Over and over he heard the whispered word, "taw."

As Young approached the hut, he cautiously slowed his pace. An experienced hunter and adventurer, he could smell danger in the atmosphere of the now ominously silent hut. He tiptoed up to the window and squinted through the aperture.

Later, recalling the incredible experience for writer Ormand McGill, Young said, "There was bright moon that night, and as my eyes became adjusted to the light in the hut, I saw a sight that I shall never forget to my dying day—one that literally lifted the hairs on my head."

Inside the hut was a ghastly creature, chewing slowly on the slashed neck of a dying woman. The hideous beast could only be described as half-human, half-beast. Its body was covered with coarse hair. Its face was grotesque; its eyes small and red. Its mouth showed cruel fangs, dropping **blood** and spittle as it worked deeper into the woman's flesh.

Young had seen enough. His hand automatically brought up the pistol to the window and blasted several slugs at the monster. The beast spun crazily, leaped to its feet with a wild cry, and dashed past the men gathered outside the hut. Within moments it had disappeared into the night.

Young shook his head in confusion. He was an expert marksman, but apparently he had missed the creature at point-blank range, for the thing had vanished into the jungle. Resolved to bring the beast down, he shouted for the men to follow him and they plunged into the darkness after it.

Hours later, their search unsuccessful, they gathered back at the village and huddled around a fire. Talk was scarce; the embers were low. Their nocturnal encounter with the half-human, half-animal being caused more than one tribesman to brood in silence as he awaited the dawn.

With the first light of morning, Young and the Lahu renewed their search. In the clear light, a fresh clue was discovered. Splotches of blood were found leading into a thicket. Young hadn't missed the monster after all. The hunters excitedly followed the trail, which circled the village and re-entered it from the opposite end. Young was baffled. How could the creature have crawled back into the village unnoticed?

The blood trail was traced to a certain hut. With a sudden rush the men tore aside the skin door covering. Inside, lying on a bed, was a dead man. The trail of blood had turned into a stagnant pool that had formed from the blood dripping from a bullet hole in the man's side.

Young could barely speak. This was not the thing that he had seen ripping at the poor woman's throat the night before. This was a man.

The chief leaned forward and spat on the man's face. "Taw!" he uttered with revulsion.

That amazing incident was the only time that Harold Young actually saw the hated and feared taw, but he continued to hear many stories about them during his stay in Burma.

SOURCES:
Dane, Christopher. *The Occult in the Orient.* New York: Popular Library, 1974.

Teenage Werewolves

Early in his career Michael Landon was apologetic about his appearing as a very hairy lycanthrope in *I Was a Teenage Werewolf* (1957). As time moved on and he evolved into one of television's most beloved stars, portraying characters like "Little Joe" in *Bonanza* (1959–1973) , "Charles Ingalls" in *Little House on the Prairie* (1974–1982), and the angel "Jonathan Smith" in *Highway to Heaven* (1984–1989), he developed a more tolerant attitude toward his first starring role in motion pictures. He was, after all, but one of many Hollywood stars, such as Steve McQueen (*The Blob*, 1958), James Arness (*The Thing*, 1951; *Them*, 1954), and Clint Eastwood (*Revenge of the Creature*, 1955) who got their start in horror flicks.

Teenage Werewolf was produced by 29-year-old Herman Cohen, who had studied the results of a marketing survey that indicated that the ages of 70 percent of the moviegoing public lay between 12 and 25. It seemed an inspired bit of moviemaking to apply the classic monster types to new horror films that would feature young people as the creepy creatures. Accomplished character actor Whit Bissell portrayed a psychiatrist who sees in a hostile teenager (Landon) the perfect subject for his experiments in utilizing drugs and hypnosis to blur the line between adolescent and animal. Landon's teenager was neither bitten nor scratched by a lycanthrope, but truly became a werewolf in the classic tradition of being transformed by an evil sorcerer—in this case an unscrupulous psychiatrist.

In his first film appearance, Michael Landon played the lead role in the 1957 film *I Was a Teenage Werewolf*.

The success of *I Was a Teenage Werewolf* encouraged the enterprising Herman Cohen to create *I Was a Teenage Frankenstein* (1957), *Blood of Dracula* (1957), and *How to Make a Monster* (1958). In *Teenage Frankenstein*, Bissell is once again the mad doctor, this time a supposed member of the Frankenstein family tree, who assembles a monster from parts of dead hot-rodders and various other teenage corpses.

Michael J. Fox had already proved his gift for comic timing in the television series *Family Ties* (1982–1989), and the young Canadian actor seemed a natural for big screen success. In 1985, the same year that his engaging role as a teenager in *Back to the Future* boosted him into more stellar roles, the 23-year-old actor played another high school student who inherited lycanthropy from his father (James Hampton) in *Teen Wolf*. Taking a leaf from *The Munsters* (1964–1965), the television series in which a Frankenstein-like monster and his vampiric wife have produced a lycanthropic son and live an ordinary, middle-class life, the bread-winning werewolf (Hampton) in *Teen Wolf* manages a small hardware store and keeps his lycanthropy under calm and assured control.

Teen Wolf is essentially a story of teenage angst in which the horrors of high school and the challenges of gaining peer acceptance are met by Fox with little degree of satisfaction. Then during a basketball game and while under a great deal of stress and frustration, he transforms himself into a werewolf during a pile-up on the court. In conventional horror films, the kids in the gym would have fled in panic at having witnessed such a metamorphosis of basketball player into monster, and the werewolf would charge the crowd and take large, bloody chunks out of those who could not run fast enough to evade his fangs and claws. In *Teen Wolf*, however, the loyal fans on the bleachers quickly recover from their shock at having witnessed one of their school chums change into a very hairy monster in a basketball uniform, and they cheer the wolf's ability to leap high in the air and to sink basket after basket to defeat the school's opponents.

Soon the confused and shy adolescent is a confident werewolf, consistently winning basketball games for the team, walking down high school corridors to the cheers of his fellow students, and high-fiving those who had once ignored him. The film ends with its moral firmly in place as the werewolf learns that the real boy within has many redeeming qualities and that his true friends will love him for who he really is and not because he can transform himself into a werewolf in order to score high points in athletic contests.

While not a hugely successful film and soon overshadowed by Michael J. Fox's star turn in *Back to the Future*, *Teen Wolf* did spawn an animated television series and a big screen sequel, *Teen Wolf Too* (1987), with Jason Bateman as a cousin of the Fox character.

Hollywood's fascination with teenage werewolves continued in 1987 in *Teen Wolf Too,* which starred Jason Bateman (center, dancing) as the young lycanthrope.

The teenage werewolf of the 1990s is the character of Oz (Seth Green) on the popular television series, *Buffy the Vampire Slayer*. Oz, like Michael J. Fox in *Teen Wolf*, is a quiet, unassuming, diminutive high school student until the **full moon** incites his lycanthropic spirit within. However, while Fox's character was a very hairy wolf boy, Oz undergoes the complete metamorphosis into a wolf in the very best of the classic lycanthropic traditions.

Although his powers as a werewolf have come in handy to assist the Slayer (Sarah Michelle Gellar) and her loyal circle of friends, Oz is accustomed to presenting himself to Buffy's Watcher (Anthony Head) to be placed under lock and key until his lycanthropic seizures pass. Oz has a developing relationship with Willow (Alyson Hannigan), an apprentice witch and Buffy's best friend, and a sometimes rivalry with Xander (Nicholas Brendon), who has maintained a lifelong friendship with Willow. An essential part of the charm of *Buffy the Vampire Slayer* is that Buffy, the chosen slayer, Willow the young witch, and Oz the teenage werewolf are also just regular high school students, whose place of learning just happens to be positioned near one of the openings of hell and which attracts a nasty **vampire,** monster, or demon for each new episode.

SOURCES:

Katz, Ephraim. *The Film Encyclopedia.* New York: Perigee, 1979.

Walker, John, ed. *Halliwell's Filmgoer's Companion, 12th Edition.* New York: HarperCollins, 1997.

Thags Yang

The folklore of Tibet includes numerous accounts of malignant, shapeshifting **demons** that lurk near trees, rocks, lakes, and many other places to seize men and animals and suck away their vital breath and life force. One of the most vicious of these entities is the *thags yang,* a demon that can appear as a tiger, a man, or a weretiger. The terrible thags yang follow those travelers who are not sufficiently protected by strong spiritual beliefs and drain their life essence from them. They also lurk near villages, seeking out the weak and the foolish who do not utter their prayers of protection.

SOURCES:

David-Neel, Alexandra. *Magic and Mystery in Tibet.* New York: Dover Publications, 1971.

Theriomorph

A theriomorph is one who has perfected the ability to shift from animal form to human form and back again whenever he or she wishes. A theriomorph who has mastered such physical transformations at will would be a true shapeshifter in the classic sense. Many contemporary students of metaphysics and Native American medicine power term themselves "spiritual theriomorphs," recognizing an inner identification with a particular animal as a guide or mentor, much as traditional **shamans** perceive the transformative powers of their personal animal totem.

Thriller

Michael Jackson's *Thriller* album (1982) produced by CBS Records has sold nearly 40 million copies throughout the world, and the music video of its title song has been hailed as a small masterpiece, complete with Jackson's lycanthropic transformation into a cat-eyed creature and his fabled footwork with a graveyard full of marvelously choreographed dancing corpses. Far from ordinary in any sense of the word, the *Thriller* video is 14 minutes in length and was produced at a reported cost of nearly one million dollars. And yet in spite of all the expense, exhaustive efforts, and excellent production values, the video came close to never being released. Jackson, a devout Jehovah's Witness, became upset when church elders accused him of producing a video that could encourage young people to explore the occult and to fall under the control of demonic entities. Through some persuasive counsel by trusted advisors, Jackson finally agreed to release the video as long as it bore the following disclaimer: "Due to my strong personal convictions, I wish to stress that this film in no way endorses a belief in the occult."

The concept for the video was first born in Michael Jackson's highly creative psyche when he saw and enjoyed *An American Werewolf in London* (1981). He subsequently contacted John Landis, the film's writer/director, and Rick Baker, the makeup/special effects genius, to develop the title song video for his *Thriller* album. After Landis and Baker had participated in a number of conferences with Jackson and were impressed with the extravagance and the scope of the project, they assumed that they were working with a true horror movie buff. Later, they were astonished to learn that certainly was not the case. In fact, Jackson admitted that the only horror films that he had ever seen were *An American Werewolf in London*, *The Hunchback of Notre Dame* (1939), and *The Elephant Man* (1980).

SOURCES:

Skal, David J. *The Monster Show.* New York: W.W. Norton, 1993.

Tiger People

The Khonds are an ancient people who inhabit eastern Bengal and whose traditions include a kind of voluntary shapeshifting that utilizes as its imagery a tiger deity. Some years ago, an Englishman who wished to remain anonymous claimed that he had actually witnessed a Khond transforming himself into a weretiger and swore that his account was true. According to the Englishman, he had spent a good deal of time in India, especially among the Khonds, and had frequently heard stories about the ability of certain individuals to transform themselves into tigers. When he persisted with a number of questions regarding such beliefs, he was informed that there was a place he could go to actually witness such metamorphoses.

Once he had secreted himself at the designated spot in the jungle were such magic was alleged to transpire, he soon began to wonder if he had been played for a fool and was left to spend the night with snakes, wild boars, big cats, scorpions, and a host of other poisonous vermin. But as things turned out, he didn't have long to wait before the would-be tiger man appeared.

The individual was hardly what the Englishman had expected. Not at all fierce in appearance, the man was very young and almost feminine in his mannerisms. Once he reached the edge of the sacred circle, he knelt down and touched the ground three times in succession with his forehead, looking up all the while at a giant kulpa tree opposite him, chanting as he did so in some weird dialect that was unintelligible to the spying Englishman.

Suddenly the jungle seemed to become unnaturally quiet. For some reason he could not understand, the Englishman was filled with a penetrating dread of the unknown. For a moment he wanted to turn and run, but he seemed unable to move. The silence was broken by an eerie half-human, half-animal cry, and there followed the sound of something very large crashing through the jungle.

Whatever the thing truly was, the Englishman saw it manifest before the young supplicant as a vertical column of pure, crimson light about seven feet high. The slim young man knelt before it and scratched a symbol of some kind in the circle and set within it a string of beads. As he began once again to chant, the column of crimson light shot forth a lightning-like bolt of energy to the beads, which instantly began to glow a luminous red. The boy put the beads around his neck, clapped his hands together, and began to chant in a voice that deepened and became more and more animal in tone. There was a shattering roar from the young supplicant's throat and the crimson column of light vanished.

And then the Englishman beheld the young man staring directly at him from the circle, not with the eyes of a human, but with the "yellow, glittering, malevolent eyes of a tiger thirsting for human **blood**."

The Englishman ran for his life toward a tree about 50 yards away. He could hear the tigerman growling behind him. When he reached the tree, the nearest branch was eight feet above him. Resigning himself to his fate, he slumped against the tree trunk as black, gleaming claws came toward him. Then, to his amazement and relief, the tigerman gave a low growl of terror and bounded away in the jungle. Not bothering to speculate why the tigerman had spared him, he ran as quickly as he could back to the village.

The next morning he learned that an entire family had been found in their home, mutilated, torn, and partially eaten. The horrible manner in which they had died indicated that a tiger had attacked them. Significantly, the Englishman learned through village gossip that they had been blood enemies of the young man that he had seen transform himself into a weretiger.

When the Englishman asked a village elder why he thought the weretiger had spared him, the old man asked him for an exact description of where he stood when the man-beast attacked. Listening carefully, the elder explained that he had unknowingly sought refuge at a holy tree that bore an inscription of the name of the god Vishnu's incarnation. Merely touching the tree would

An illustration (c. 1500) showing a German werewolf making off with a small child after killing two other children.

protect anyone from attack by animals. The Englishman concluded his account by stating that he inspected the tree later that day and found upon it an inscription in Sanskrit. He never returned to that village again, but he swore that his witnessing of the weretiger transformation was true.

SOURCES:
Hurwood, Bernardt J. *Vampires, Werewolves, and Ghouls.* New York: Ace Books, 1968

Tigre Capiango

Those individuals in the central provinces of Santa Fe and Cordoba, Argentina, who can change themselves into jaguars through the magical application of great cat skin fragments and incantations, are known as *Tigre Capiango*. In the Quechua region, such jaguar people are known as *Runa Uturunco* and in the Guarani region as *Yaguarete-Aba*. As in the European traditions of lycanthropy, these sorcerers voluntarily seek to accomplish the transformation from human into animal for purposes of individual empowerment.

SOURCES:
Picasso, Fabio. "South American Monsters and Mystery Animals." *Strange,* December 1998.

Tortures of the Inquisition

The common justice of the Inquisition demanded that a witch, a werewolf, or a sorcerer should not be condemned to death unless they convict themselves by their own confession. Therefore, the judges had no choice other than to order the accused tortured so they would confess and thereby permit their execution. In a vicious and most perplexing paradox of justice, the learned tribunals held that even though an accusation by nearly anyone was enough to land witches or werewolves in prison—and if they got as far as prison they were thereby considered guilty—all the testimony counted for naught unless the accused individuals confessed their guilt. No one, under common justice, could be put to death for witchcraft, werewolfism, or **sorcery** on the evidence of another's testimony. What is more, the accused persons must confess without torture.

In order to comply fully with this law, the clever judges turned the accused persons over to eager, black-hooded torturers so that *they* might hack, burn, brand, stretch, starve, and slice away with sadistic fervor until the victims confessed under torture. First, there would probably be the search on the naked body for the "devil's mark," which Satan placed somewhere on all of his children. There would be the insertion of long, sharp pins into the victim's flesh, as the torturers seek for an insensitive spot of flesh that Satan leaves on his chosen ones. Then there is the branding with red-hot irons, the tearing of the nipples with hot pincers. The infamous rack awaits, eager to stretch and snap ribs and dislocate shoulder bones. The alleged children of Satan may have their feet crushed in the iron boot. There may be sulphur in the armpits. Oil may be poured over the head and set aflame. And if the accused are females, there is the bestial lust of the torturers to be sated on their helpless and abused bodies the moment that the priests leave the chamber.

Once a confession had been accomplished under torture, the unfortunate victims were made to stand before the judges (usually standing of one's own volition at this stage was impossible, so the wretches were supported by priests) and confess of their "own free will" *without torture*. There were, then, two confessions—one under the pressure of the rack, the sting of the lash, the bone-crushing embrace of the boot; and the other far away from the torture chamber in the serenity of the courtroom.

Now that the victims of the Inquisition had confessed, they were eligible to be reconciled to the church, absolved of sin, and sent to the stake to be burned. Confessions or not, the accused always found their way to the flaming pyres. The difference in the eyes of the learned men of the tribunals was whether or not the witches, werewolves, and sorcerers went as guilty but penitent or guilty and impenitent.

The Spanish Inquisition seemed to take special delight in the pomp and ceremony of the *auto-de-fe*, during which hundreds, sometimes thousands, of witches, werewolves, and other assorted heretics would be burned at one time. If an auto-de-fe could not be arranged to coincide with some great festival day, it was at least held on a Sunday so that the populace could make plans to attend the burnings. The auto-de-fe began with a procession of the penitent led by Dominican friars. Behind them, bare-footed, stumbling, hollow-eyed with the pain and nightmare of their ordeal, marched the wretched victims of the Inquisition. Those accused of witchcraft were dressed in black, sleeveless robes, and they each carried a wax candle in their hands. The ragged procession of victims was followed by inquisitors on horseback with the inquisitor general on a white horse led by two men with black hats and green hatbands. The penitent were permitted to be strangled before the flames of the stakes were ignited. Those men and women who had somehow resisted the tortures of the holy tribunal were doomed to be burned alive.

Author Kurt Seligmann observes that the persecution of witches and heretics soon became an industry. The efficiency of the church's counterattack against the forces of Satan depended upon judges, jailers, torturers, exorcists, wood-choppers, scribes, and experts on the lore of witchcraft, sorcery, and demonology. With so many people whose livelihood depended upon the Inquisition, it can easily be seen why so few desired an early end to the witchcraft mania. Canon Loos declared that the holy Inquisition had discovered the only true alchemy that really worked, for the inquisitors had found the secret of transmuting human **blood** into gold.

Seligmann comments: "The business became so prosperous that the hangmen's wives arrayed themselves in silk robes, road upon beautifully harnessed horses or in painted carriages. . . . For every witch burned, the hangman received an honorarium. He was not allowed to follow any other profession, therefore he had to make the best of his craft."

It was not long before the torturers had discovered a foolproof method for perpetuating their gory profession. Under torture, nearly any accused witch or heretic could be forced to name a long string of "fellow witches," thereby making one trial give birth to a hundred more.

The Jesuit Friedrich von Spee became an opponent of the witchcraft trials when the wise Duke of Brunswick brought him and a fellow priest into a torture chamber. As the duke and the two priests, who were professed champions of the Inquisition, stood beside a confessed witch who was being tortured further for her increased good soul, the nobleman asked the clergymen if, in their consciences, they could say that the holy tribunals were truly doing God's work. When the Jesuits answered loudly in the affirmative, the duke stepped nearer the poor woman on the rack.

"Woman," he said, momentarily distracting her thoughts from her pain, "look carefully at my two companions here. I suspect them of being witches. Do you recognize them as having cavorted with you to Satan's tune?"

With these words, he indicated to the torturer that the woman should be stretched another notch on their rack. At once she began to scream that the two priests were agents of Satan, that she had seen them copulating with succubi and serpents and had dined with them on a roasted baby at the last Sabbat.

Later, in an anti-Inquisition work, Father Spree declared that he had often thought " . . . that the only reason why we are not all wizards is due to the fact that we have not all been tortured. And there is truth in what an inquisitor dared to boast, that if he could reach the pope, he would make him confess that he was a wizard."

The inquisitors worked terrible vengeance on women, the daughters of Eve, who had caused Adam and thereafter all men to fall from grace. And since it was rumored that female witches gave aid and comfort to Satan by using their very bodies as altars of lust in his pagan rituals, they would use their instruments of torture to disfigure the female form that Satan and his minions found so appealing.

In 1583, Reginald Scot wrote *The Discovery of Witchcraft*, which serves as a kind of answer to Sprenger's and Kramer's *Malleus Maleficarum*. In his opinion, the inquisitors were sexually obsessed madmen, who took delight in inflicting sadistic tortures on their victims. He remonstrated with the holy tribunal for spending too much time examining the naked bodies of young

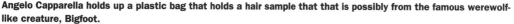

Angelo Capparella holds up a plastic bag that holds a hair sample that that is possibly from the famous werewolf-like creature, Bigfoot.

women for the secret marks of Satan which they insisted might be found on curve or in hollow. When one catalogs the terrible agonies to which the young women were put, Scot argued, who would not confess to anything? And if witches were really as malignant and all-powerful as the inquisitors claimed, why had they not enslaved or exterminated the human race long ago?

Scot's voice was only one of a few sane men who cried desperately in the wilderness of the incredible and disgusting sexual mania that provided the fuel for the witchcraft persecutions. Tragically, the terrible screams and the foul stench of the torture chamber remains all too firmly etched in all too many ways in the collective unconscious of Western civilization.

SOURCES:

Russell, Jeffrey Burton. *Witchcraft in the Middle Ages.* Ithaca, NY: Cornell University Press, 1972.

Seligmann, Kurt. *The History of Magic.* New York: Pantheon Books, 1948.

Trevor-Roper, H. R. *The European Witch-Craze.* New York: Harper & Row, 1967.

Totems

Regardless of our ethnic and cultural origins, almost all of our ancestors employed animal totems, animal spirits, as tools in reaching the supreme being, receiving visions and revelations, and surviving in hostile environments. The spirit helper that will express itself most often in animal form is usually received during the vision quest. **Shamans** advise the supplicants that while on the quest, they are to fast, deny their physical bodies, and pray to the Great Mystery to grant them a spirit helper.

After a few days on the quest, a forest creature may approach the supplicant and offer itself as a guide. Those individuals on the quest are forewarned by the shamans that the temptation to accept the first animal that approaches as one's spirit helper is great. The shamans advise the supplicants that if they are able to endure greater hunger and exposure, the Great Mystery will be certain to send them a more powerful spirit helper, one especially destined for the individual. If one could endure, according to some traditionalists, the true spirit helper would appear as if it were glowing, as though it were composed primarily of light.

In *Warriors of the Rainbow,* William Willoya and Vinson Brown state that the traditional Native Americans used the animal spirit to reach the "source of the world" and to purify the soul. This was not idol worship, they insist, "but something far deeper and more wonderful, the understanding of the Spirit Being that manifests itself in all living things."

Grandmother Twylah, repositor of wisdom of the Seneca wolf clan, commented on the tragedy that the invading European, in the early days of conquest and missionary work, saw the native people interacting with their totem animals and became convinced that the tribespeople worshipped idols and a hierarchy of gods. While the traditionalist does most certainly believe that the Great Mystery manifests itself in a variety of forms, it must be understood that to see the expression of deity in everything is not the same thing as seeing everything as deity.

As Walking Buffalo attempts to explain in *Tatana Mani, Walking Buffalo of the Stonies,* the white missionaries misinterpreted the native people's belief that the Great Spirit existed in all things as the worship of idols. "We saw the Great Spirit's work in everything, and sometimes we approached him through our totem animals."

For those early missionaries who truly listened and paid attention to the words of the shamans, there was never any misconception that the native people were worshipping animals as deities. As early as 1742, missionary David Brainerd states in his *Life and Travels* that the Delaware did not suppose a divine power in animals, but that "some invisible beings communicate to these animals a great power and make these creatures the immediate authors of good to certain persons." And perhaps those early men of the cloth who understood recalled the passage in the Book of Job (12:7–8): "Ask the animals, and they will teach you, or the birds of the air, and they will tell you; or speak to the earth, and it will teach you, or let the fish of the sea inform you."

In his *Man, God, and Magic*, the brilliant ethnologist Ivar Lissner ponders the mystery of why the anonymous Franco-Cantabrian cave artists of over 20,000 years ago painted strange and ghostly two-legged creatures with the heads of animals and birds. Despite what appears to be quite remarkable artistic gifts, our Stone Age ancestors chose not to share a depiction of their own features but confined themselves to portraying entities that were half-human, half-animal. Lissner speculates that perhaps, after all, the ancient artists were portraying themselves, "but in animal guise, ecstatically or shamanistically." Perhaps these shamans of the Stone Age may have believed that "the road to supernatural powers is easier to follow in an animal shape and that spirits can only be reached with an animal's assistance." Perhaps the totem animals are "intermediary beings," stronger than mere mortals and "able to penetrate more deeply into the mysteries of fate, that unfathomable interrelationship between animals, men, and gods."

Beginning perhaps as early as the second century of the Christian era, those European shamans who sought their animal totems were condemned as witches and servants of the devil. By the time of the demon-obsessed Middle Ages, those who expressed confidence in their spirit helpers were actively hunted down and burned at the stake as witches and heretics. Those shamans who lived deep in the forests and explored other dimensions with the assistance of their animal totems were declared enemies of the church, active members of Satan's minions, and put to the torture and the flames. Those herbalists and teachers of the old ways who wore animal skins for clothing and elected to be close to nature and apart from the congestion of growing cities were branded werewolves.

SOURCES:

Lissner, Ivar. Translated by J. Maxwell Brownjohn. *Man, God, and Magic.* New York: G. P. Putnam's Sons, 1961.

Steiger, Brad. *Totems: The Transformative Power of Your Personal Animal Totem.* San Francisco: HarperSanFrancisco, 1997.

Trolls

If you really think that trolls are those cute, redheaded little critters from Denmark with large eyes, turned-up noses, and wide, ear-to-ear smiles, you have a major culture shock in store. Right away you have to start thinking, "The Three Billy Goats Gruff" and the nasty troll under the bridge who wanted to eat them. Once you are visualizing "nasty," then forget about little and cute. In Old Norse, the term "troll" is applied only to hostile giants. By the time of the High Middle Ages, trolls had become a bit smaller and more fiendish, capable of working black magic and **sorcery.** In more contemporary times, the troll is regarded as a denizen of mountain caves, larger than the average human, and exceedingly ugly. Somewhere along the way, the Danes started considering the *huldrefolk*, an elflike or brownie-type being as a kind of troll— and that's where the cute little redheaded creatures originated. Just don't go around the mountainous regions of Scandinavia and shout out any challenges to the trolls. The ugly brute that comes charging out of the cave will bear absolutely no resemblance to that little smiling doll your parents bought for you when you were a kid.

SOURCES:

Simek, Rudolf. Translated by Angela Hall. *Dictionary of Northern Mythology.* Rochester, NY: Boydell & Brewer, 1993.

U

Ukumar

Ukumar is the name the native people of the northwestern area of Argentina given to the half-man, half-beast werebear that is feared for its propensity to kidnap women and children. This "Bigfoot-type" entity has also been seen in the Andean regions of Bolivia and Peru, and it is most often described as a cross between a human and a bear. Claims have been made that such a beast was actually captured near the Tafi Valley in Tucuman. In his *Chronicles of Peru*, Pedro Cieza de Leon stated that a Ukumar had been killed near Charcas, Bolivia, in 1549. Friar Pedro Simon reported the killing of a hairy monster 12 feet tall by soldiers in Venezuela. Recent accounts of the Ukumar in Argentina were reported in 1989.

SOURCES:
Picasso, Fabio. "South American Monsters and Mystery Animals." *Strange,* December 1998.

Underwater Woman

Among the Carib people of Guyana, the great Anaconda, chief of the water spirits, has a number of daughters who can shapeshift into human form to entice unwary fishermen to their death. In some accounts, worthy men have married one of the water chief's daughters and have prospered as a result of their alliance. In most instances, however, the most fortunate of the fishermen who have been seduced by Anaconda's daughters find themselves enslaved— while the unfortunate meet swift and cruel deaths.

In other variations of the tales, the encounter with the underwater woman becomes a ritual of shamanic initiation. The apprentice **shaman** is attracted by the beautiful singing of women rising from the river. As he comes nearer, he is met by Amana, the principal daughter of the water chief. If the young man is deemed worthy of her attention, she takes him with her to spend three days in her underwater kingdom. Here, he learns the special songs and chants which will grant him the power to communicate with spirits. He is also given special tobacco and the magical rattle that he will henceforth use in all shamanic rites.

SOURCES:

Bierhorst, John. *The Mythology of South America.* New York: William Morrow and Company, 1988.

Universal Pictures

For horror movie buffs, Universal Pictures is the magical, monstrous kingdom from which their favorite werewolves, vampires, monsters, mad doctors, and other assorted creepy creatures crawled out of crypts and vaults and into their neighborhood theaters. During the 1930s and 1940s, if it was a spooky movie, it was most likely to have come from Universal. All of the classic horror films— *Dracula* (1931), *Frankenstein* (1931), *The Mummy* (1932), *The Invisible Man* (1933), **The Wolf Man** (1941), and *The Creature from the Black Lagoon* (1954) — were the products of cinematic masters of fantasy at Universal Pictures, who employed such genius directors as James Whale, Roy William Neill, Tod Browning, George Waggoner, and Karl Freund; accomplished screenwriters, such as Curt Siodmak and Willis Cooper; and the master of makeup for nearly three decades, Jack Pierce. The Universal Pictures' Horror Movie Hall of Fame includes such regulars as **Bela Lugosi,** Boris Karloff, **Claude Rains, Lon Chaney Jr.,** Colin Clive, Mae Clarke, Edward van Sloan, John Carradine, Dwight Frye, **Evelyn Ankers,** Patric Knowles, **Maria Ouspenskaya,** Lionel Atwill, Glenn Strange, Richard Carlson, and Richard Denning.

The seed that grew into Universal Pictures was planted by Carl Laemmle in 1909 when he founded his Independent Motion Picture Company of America (IMP). In 1912, Laemmle filmed **Dr. Jekyll and Mr. Hyde,** starring King Baggot and Jane Gail. In that same year, he joined with half a dozen other small independent film companies to form Universal Pictures. In 1915, in order to consolidate their cinematic operations, Universal City was constructed in Los Angeles.

A rather cautious studio, Universal concentrated on low-budget films during the silent era of motion pictures, but the studio also produced some of the greatest hits of Erich von Stroheim, Valentino, and Lon Chaney. With the advent of the talkies, Universal became a significant player in the A-movie arena with the classic film version of Erich Maria Remarque's highly acclaimed novel *All Quiet on the Western Front* (1930), starring Lew Ayres, Louis Wolheim, Slim Summerville, Ben Alexander, and Beryl Mercer.

A scene from the 1970 film *Cry of the Banshee*.

Unfortunately, Universal's skills on the corporate management level did not match their successes at the box office, and they were forced to sell off its theaters during the early years of the Depression. At the same time, however, in the financial chaos of the Depression, Universal began creating its classic horror films, providing escapist fears that allowed the mass audience to forget for a time the unpaid bills and lack of work. The studio also produced a number of successful low-budget comedies with W. C. Fields, and with the Sherlock Holmes mystery series, starring the quintessential Holmes, Basil Rathbone.

By 1936, Laemmle was forced out of the company that he had founded, and the new management achieved sudden success by producing cheerful and positive family fare starring such musical stars as Deanna Durbin. During World War II, the comedy team of Abbott and Costello became the box office champions, and their films, together with the steady issuing of reliable horror movies, combined to produce boom years for the studio.

In 1946, Universal merged with International Pictures and became known as Universal-International, but by the early 1950s, the studio had entered its bleakest period. The audiences were no longer lining up to see Abbott and Costello or the classic movie monsters. In 1952, Decca Records bought the studio and changed its name back to Universal. The Music Corporation of America (MCA) bought Decca in 1959 and began the climb that would once again make Universal a major motion picture and television production company. In addition to having produced a number of megahits such as *Airport* (1970), *The Sting* (1973), *American Graffiti* (1973), *Jaws* (1975), *Field of Dreams* (1989), *E.T., the Extraterrestrial* (1982), *Back to the Future* (1985), and *Jurassic Park* (1993), Universal Studios is also one of Los Angeles' greatest tourist attractions.

SOURCES:

Katz, Ephraim. *The Film Encyclopedia.* New York: Perigee, 1979.

Siegel, Scott, and Barbara Siegel. *The Encyclopedia of Hollywood.* New York: Avon Books, 1990.

Walker, John, ed. *Halliwell's Filmgoer's Companion, 12th Edition.* New York: HarperCollins, 1997.

Uvengwa

Among the native people of West Africa, the *uvengwa* is an entity that inspires great fear. It is believed to be the self-resurrected spirit of an individual who, for some reason, lies restless in his grave. The uvengwa itself is white in color, but it can shapeshift into many forms and seldom appears as it did when human. The most common manifestation of the entity is that of a large, web-footed, white-colored being with one eye in the center of its forehead. It makes no sound, but it wanders the jungles, looking curiously about, as if seeking some as-yet-unknown person or thing.

SOURCES:

Nassau, Rev. Robert Hamill. *Fetichism in West Africa.* New York: Charles Scribners Sons, 1904; Negro Universities Press, 1969.

V

Valhalla

Valhalla (in Old Norse, "hall of the slain") is the name of Odin's stately home in Asgard where the father of the gods gathers the spirits of all the brave warriors who have fallen in battle. Although there are 540 gates to Valhalla, the gate through which the Vikings pass is called *Valgrind*, and it is guarded by a great wolf and watched by an eagle soaring above. Valkyries escort the *einherjar* (slain warriors) through Valgrind and seat them at the great banquet table set before Odin. Once the drinking horns have been filled with mead, the Valkyries serve the heroes meat from a boar, tasty flesh that constantly renews itself. In Valhalla, there will always be plenty of meat, mead, and wine in a feast of celebration that continues unabated. At Odin's side are the great **wolves,** Geri and Freki, eating only from their master's hand and surveying steadily the warrior spirits arrayed before them. During the day, the einherjar fight among themselves, choosing sides, battling fiercely, perfecting their warrior's prowess. At sunset, those who were killed in the intermural battles come alive again, and all return to Odin's banquet hall for more eating and drinking. Valhalla is truly a warrior's dream of a perfect paradise.

SOURCES:

Simek, Rudolf. Translated by Angela Hall. *Dictionary of Northern Mythology.* Rochester, NY: Boydell & Brewer, 1993.

Valkyries

Far from those voluptuous blondes with the jutting breastplates and the enormous wingspan familiar to devotees of Wagner's operas and Scandinavian mythology, the Valkyries originated in ancient days as **demons** who dined on the warriors fallen in battle. In Old Norse, *Valkyrjar* derives from *valr,* which refers to the corpses that remain at the scene of a battle, and *kjosa*, "to choose," thus, "those who chose the slain." The Valkyries were seen haunting the battlefields, their coats of lustrous black feathers rippling in the wind. Because of their black feathers, they were also known as *kraken*, or ravens. Warriors who fell in battle and whose bodies could not be reclaimed by friends or family were known as *hrafengrennir*, "raven feeders."

When the concept of **Valhalla** evolved from a battlefield to a paradise for warriors, the Valkyries became supernatural, super-endowed female warriors who lead the heroes fallen in battle to the reward that the father of the gods had awaiting them in his mansion in Asgard. As the Valkyries shed their demonic taint and became more humanlike, they occasionally assumed the roles of guardian spirits and even became shapeshifters capable of falling in love with humans. The great Danish hero Sigurd was the son of King Ragnar Lodbrok and the Valkyrie Krake, a shapeshifter who could choose to be a beautiful maiden or a raven.

SOURCES:

Davidson, Ellis H. R. *Gods and Myths of the Viking Age.* New York: Barnes & Noble, 1996.

Simek, Rudolf. Translated by Angela Hall. *Dictionary of Northern Mythology.* Rochester, NY: Boydell & Brewer, 1993.

Vampires

On Monday, January 15, 1991, the day following the premiere of the new primetime *Dark Shadows* television series featuring actor Ben Cross as the vampire Barnabas Collins, a bearded man approached a 42-year-old woman in a library parking lot in Missoula, Montana, and demanded money. The woman complied and handed him two dollars. Then the man pulled her hair back, cut her neck with some kind of sharp object, and kissed the open wound. Police detectives launched an intense manhunt for the grisly vampire bandit.

In February 1991, a jury in Australia convicted Annette Hall of stalking and killing Charles Reilly so her vampire lover, Susi Hampton, could drink his **blood.** Hall described in detail how her girlfriend had gone into a "feeding frenzy" after she had stabbed Reilly over a dozen times. Ms. Hampton, a self-confessed vampire who lives on human blood, pleaded guilty and both women were sentenced to life in prison.

For Anne Rice, author of such bestselling novels as *Interview with the Vampire*, the vampire is a "romantic, enthralling" figure. She perceives the vampire's image to be that of a "person who never dies . . . takes a blood sacrifice in order to live, and exerts a charm over people." In the view of Rice and the millions of readers who enjoy her novels, the vampire is a "handsome, alluring, seductive person who captivates us, then drains the life out of us so that

Vampires and werewolves (and often other monsters) frequently go hand-in-hand in Hollywood, as was the case in the wonderfully awful 1965 film *Orgy of the Dead*, which was directed by cult figure Ed Wood Jr.

he or she can live. We long to be one of them, and the idea of being sacrificed to them becomes rather romantic."

The vampire legend, like that of the werewolf, is universal. The villagers of Uganda, Haiti, Indonesia, and the Upper Amazon all have their local variety of nocturnal blood sucker. The Native American tribes, the Arctic Eskimos, and many Arabian tribes know the vampire well and have as many elaborate precautions against the undead as do the inhabitants of Transylvanian villages.

In the eighteenth century, the highly respected French philosopher Jean Jacques Rousseau wrote: "If there ever was in the world a warranted and proven history, it is that of vampires; nothing is lacking, official reports, testimonials of persons of standing, of surgeons, of clergymen, of judges; the judicial evidence is all-embracing."

Theories to explain the universality of the vampire myth are many and varied. All cultures, regardless of how primitive, have come to understand the basic fact that blood is the vital fluid of life. To lose one's vital fluid is to lose one's mortality—the spark of life. Such knowledge would be a powerful stimulant to fear in the primitive mind and the creation of hideous monsters intent on draining one's life essence would not be long in coming.

In appearance, the traditional vampire is a grotesque, demonic presence, perhaps best captured cinematically in *Nosferatu* (1922). A newly rereleased Werner Herzog version of *Nosferatu the Vampyre* (1979), starring Klaus Kinski, was praised by Michael Sauter in the February 5, 1999, issue of *Entertainment Weekly:* "Like Max Schreck's original Nosferatu, Klaus Kinski's Transylvanian count is a far cry from the **Bela Lugosi** model. Sporting sunken eyes, devil ears, and talons, he lurks in Herzog's expressionistic shadows like some oversize vermin."

The classic vampire is also a shapeshifter, able to transform itself not only into the familiar form of the bat, but also into a wolf—and it was able to command the rat, the owl, the moth, the fox. The vampire of tradition is able to see in the dark and travel on moonbeams and mist. At times, the vampire could vanish in a puff of smoke. The hypnotic powers of the vampire are irresistible. And woe to anyone who boldly grabbed hold of the monster, for it has the strength of a dozen men.

After Bram Stoker's novel *Dracula* (1897) became a popular play and a classic motion picture version with Bela Lugosi as Count **Dracula,** the image of the vampire transmuted from hideous demon to a suave, sophisticated, handsome, well-dressed fellow who would fit right in at the very best parties. And his sisters and mistresses of the night are beautiful, sensuous, voluptuous creatures who fill out their evening dresses in the most delightful ways. With few exceptions, contemporary audiences know the vampire only as an attractive and seductive presence, an emissary of the dark side who presents a very compelling case for letting him or her bite your neck so that you may join the ranks of the undead. Of course days at the beach and power breakfasts are now out of the question.

On the other hand, the fact that the modern vampire is virtually undetectable from the rest of us—with the exception of the aversion to sunlight and the hunger for blood—preys upon another basic fear of humankind. The menace of a monster hidden among us can oftentimes be more horrifying than a grotesque, easily identified creature that lurks out there in the darkness. The ever-present thought that your congenial chess partner who always seems to arrive late at the club, or the attractive pale-complexioned man who kept trying to get you to dance with him out on the terrace, or the beautiful lady who will only meet you after dark might be a member of the society of vampires can be a very frightening thought. How can we fight vampires if we can't tell them from our friends?

Well, of course, there's wolfbane, the lotus flower, wild **garlic,** and sacred objects such as the crucifix and holy water. But do they really render a fanged fiend powerless? Maybe it would best to be prepared like Buffy the Vampire Slayer and always carry a couple of wooden stakes in your purse or attache case. A stake in the heart just has to work. Of course that is best applied, according to tradition before and after *Dracula* and Hollywood, when the vampire lies at rest in his coffin during the daylight hours. Or if you're not quite up to the stake in the heart bit, you can destroy his coffin while he's on his nocturnal hunt and let the rays of the early morning sun scorch him to ashes.

Even at the dawn of the scientific age, scholars and members of the clergy were convinced of the vampire's existence. In the eighteenth century, a Benedictine monk, Dom Calmet, turned his attention to the subject of vampires and tried to offer a "scientific" explanation:

> Chemical substances of the soil may conserve corpses indefinitely. By the influence of warmth, the nitre and sulphur in the earth may render liquid coagulated blood. The screams of the vampires [caused no doubt when vigilante vampire hunters went about driving stakes in the chests of suspect corpses] are produced when air passing through their throats is stirred by the pressure which the stake causes in the body. Often people are buried alive, and certain dead, such as the excommunicated, can rise from their tombs; but it is not possible to leave the grave bodily without digging up the soil, and none of the stories about vampires mention that their tombs were disturbed.

When we begin to examine the spark of truth behind the legend of the vampire, we soon discover that the myth disguises a very morbid reality. Today medical science recognizes a vampire psychosis wherein troubled individuals may become convinced that their life depends upon drawing fresh blood from human victims. The persons suffering from such a psychosis may, in extreme cases, actually believe themselves to be dead.

The sexual metaphors to be found in the many cinematic and literary portrayals of the vampire's seductive bite are many and are undeniably a large part of the appeal of the vampire in contemporary popular culture. And while the sexual symbolism may be sensually appealing when a sophisticated Count Dracula or a cultured and stylish Barnabas Collins emerges from the shadows and bites his beautiful victim's bare throat, the bloody accounts of real-life vampires reveal that they seldom act with such dignity and poetry.

A classic case of vampirism was that of Vincent Verzini, who terrorized an Italian village during 1867 to 1871. Verzini's method of attack was to seize a victim by the neck, bite her on the throat, then suck her blood. He murdered two women and victimized many others before he was apprehended.

Although Verzini's examiners found "no evidence of psychosis," there can be little doubt that his vampirism was the expression of deep derangement and sexual perversion. That such was the case is shown lucidly in Verzini's own words:

> I had an unspeakable delight in strangling women, experiencing during the act erections and real sexual pleasure . . . I took great delight in drinking . . . blood . . . It never occurred to me to touch or to look at the [women's] genitals . . . It satisfied me to seize the women by the neck and suck their blood.

John George Haigh was a British vampire who, it is said, acquired a taste for blood when he accidentally tasted his own while sucking a scratch. Intoxicated by the act of drinking blood, he was soon "tapping" the jugular veins of his victims so that he might indulge both his perverse thirst and his fanaticism.

In keeping with the religious bent of his illness, Haigh evolved a ritual. First he would sever the jugular vein of his victim, then he would carefully draw off the blood, a glassful at a time. The actual drinking of the blood was observed with great ceremony. Haigh later became convinced that his faith could only be sustained by the sacrifice of others and by the drinking of their blood.

For nearly a week in February 1960, women in the town of Monteros in Argentina were terrorized by the nocturnal attacks of a vampire. At least 15 women were victimized by the midnight marauder, who crept into bedrooms through windows left open because of a heat wave. Hysterically, the women told police of savage teeth biting deeply into their throats and drawing blood.

When officers managed to track the vampire to his lair, they discovered a young man sleeping in a coffin which he had secreted in a cave on the outskirts of the city. He lay swathed in a black cloak, his eyes closed in deep sleep. On his lips was the dried blood of his most recent victim.

In police custody, the real-life Dracula identified himself as Florenico Fernandez, age 25, a stonemason. He was at a complete loss to present an intelligible explanation for his sadistic attacks.

On October 30, 1981, James P. Riva II, a self-proclaimed vampire, was convicted in Brockton, Massachusetts, of murdering his grandmother by shooting her with gold-tipped bullets, then attempting to drink her blood from the wounds. Riva's mother, Janet Jones of Middlebury, Vermont, testified that her son had believed himself to be a vampire for four years. According to Mrs. Jones, Riva had told her that voices informed him that he was a vampire and insisted that he must drink blood.

Defense psychiatrist Dr. Bruce Harry testified that Riva was insane at the time that he murdered his grandmother. According to the young vampire, the voices had told him that he could not become a good person until he killed someone and drank their blood.

John T. Spinale, defense attorney, explained to the court that Riva felt that he needed human and animal blood in order to survive. Riva truly believed that he was a vampire who must roam the countryside in search of his demonically prescribed "food." According to Spinale, Riva did not eat normal meals. He ate what he could find in the evening, then went in search of animal blood.

Superior Court judge Peter F. Brady sentenced the 24-year-old James Riva II to a mandatory life sentence at Walpole State Prison on the charge of second-degree murder.

On February 12, 1998, a 12-member jury heard graphic testimony from self-professed teenage vampire Rod Ferrell to help them decide whether he should be sentenced to death or jailed for life without parole. The 17-year-old Ferrell, the leader of a coven of vampires, pled guilty to the murders of Richard and Naoma Ruth Wendorf on November 25, 1996. Ferrell said that he had initiated the Wendorf's 15-year-old daughter into the cult with a blood-drinking ritual in a graveyard. Ferrell's mother, Sondra Gibson, was also a member of a vampire cult and had pleaded guilty in 1997 to attempting to seduce a 14-year-old boy as part of a vampire ritual.

The late parapsychologist Stephen Kaplan, director of the Vampire Research Center in Elmhurst, New York, stated c. 1982 that his research indicated that at that time there were at least 21 "real" vampires secretly living in the United States and Canada. Some of these vampires had admitted to Kaplan that, on occasion, they had even murdered humans to obtain blood. He also stated that some of the vampires may truly have been as old as 300 years, but still appeared amazingly youthful, due to the blood they ingested. Or at least the vampires believed that "there are some elements in the human blood that slow down the aging process," enabling them to live far longer than nonblood drinking humans.

At that time, Kaplan's survey found that the vampires were distributed throughout North America, but Massachusetts was in the lead with three self-proclaimed vampires, followed by Arizona, California, and New Jersey, with two each.

Kaplan told of one vampire who worked as a technician in a hospital. He simply took blood from the hospital's reserves whenever he needed it. Although the man was nearly 60, Kaplan said, he passed as a man in his early twenties.

The vampire researcher met a vampire in Arizona who looked like a teenager, but who was actually in his late thirties. He posed as a university student and lured people into the desert to drink their blood.

One attractive blonde vampire appeared to be in her vigorous twenties, but was really in her sixties. She exchanged sexual favors in return for blood from her dates. Kaplan said that he was present on one occasion when such a barter occurred: "I watched her drink blood from a willing victim. I watched her use a scalpel to make several incisions in the body and drink some blood."

Kaplan found that the blood needs of the vampires varied considerably. Some required two pints a week; others, half-gallon. Some vampires admitted that they would sometimes render a victim unconscious to take some blood, but that they always left their unwilling donors alive. Those who confessed to having killed humans for blood insisted that they preyed mostly on hitchhikers, the homeless, and people they assumed to be transients with few family associations.

Although it appeared that the vampires he interviewed were long-lived, Kaplan stated, they were not immortal. They slept in beds, rather than coffins. They possessed no preternatural ability to transform themselves into bats, **wolves,** or other animals. They could function equally well in daylight or in darkness, and they had absolutely no fear of a crucifix.

Kaplan came to believe that true vampirism is a genetic disorder, that people were born into it. "Their mothers and fathers were vampires," he said, "and it appears that their children are always vampires."

SOURCES:

"Gruesome Evidence Heard in Florida 'Vampire' Case." Reuters, February 12, 1998.

Masters, R. E. L., and Eduard Lea. *Perverse Crimes in History.* New York: The Julian Press, 1963.

Melton, J. Gordon. *The Vampire Book: The Encyclopedia of the Undead.* Farmington Hills: Visible Ink Press, 1998.

Steiger, Brad. *Bizarre Crime.* New York: Signet, 1992.

Vanamanushas

In 1965, the Indian village of Talah Malkoti in the district of Chamoli was invaded by the *vanamanushas*, the "wicked wild men" from the hills, strange apelike creatures that have become increasingly bolder over the years. Chamoli, which lies in the lower reaches of the western Himalayan range, is a mountainous region with heavy forests. For generations, for hundreds of years, the villagers have waged a series of skirmishes with the mysterious wild men. Efforts by the authorities to track the creatures down have always proved futile.

The native population of the Chamoli district describe the vanamanushas as very hairy and well-built, with arms so long that they touch their knees when they stand erect. The villagers complain that the creatures raid their crops and haunt the jungles near their communities. Although unable to speak, on occasion the vanamanushas approach the villagers, making gestures indicating that they want food. There have also been many complaints of the monsters carrying off women during their midnight attacks.

SOURCES:

Norman, Eric. *The Abominable Snowmen.* New York: Award Books, 1969.

Vasaria

Vasaria is an imaginary village concocted by **Universal Pictures** for such films as *Frankenstein Meets the Wolf Man* (1943). Although *The Wolf Man* (1941) is set in Wales, the village beyond Talbot castle with its strange mixture of cultures and accents has always seemed like the prototype for Vasaria. One even reads in respectable and otherwise quite accurate books on the history of horror films that *The Wolf Man* takes place in Transylvania. There are abundant reasons for the confusion, and quite likely the real-life horrors of World War II played a large part in Hollywood's desire to create a fantasy world where there were only vampires, werewolves, and monsters to deal with—rather than bombs, concentration camps, and mass slaughter of civilians.

The "Europe" of the horror films of the 1940s takes place in "Vasarian" villages where there is a multiplicity of accents, costumes, architecture, and ethnic types. The houses, market places, and inns make one feel as though the characters are moving through Ireland, Switzerland, Germany, and Transylvania as they walk down the street. Some of the extras wear leiderhosen side by side with others in costumes ranging from medieval to modern, and the natives speak in accents ranging from Hungarian to American. And just when you assess the nationality of a man dressed in what is surely a German police officer's uniform, he speaks in a broad British accent. And that is Vasaria, a strange mysterious village in which Frankenstein's castle with its laboratory-assembled monster can play host to **Dracula** and the Wolf Man.

Volsunga Saga

The *Volsunga Saga* (c. 1300) tells the story of the Norse King Volsung who had 10 sons and one daughter, Signy, who was married to King Siggeir. Siggeir later proved to be a most untrustworthy son-in-law when he murdered Volsung and placed his 10 sons in the stocks. Then to add to the horror, Siggeir allowed his mother, a werewolf, to eat his brothers-in-law. However, Signy, his wife, the daughter of Volsung, was not without magical powers of her own, and she managed to arrive in time to save Sigmund, the tenth son, from being devoured by the voracious she-wolf. Then, sharing her witchcraft with her brother, Signy enables Sigmund to slay the werewolf who has consumed the other nine siblings.

A 1901 illustration by S. H. Vedder showing a werewolf making its way home through the snow.

Later, after Sigmund has gone into hiding to escape the revenge of Siggeir, Signy exchanges physical form with a sorceress and has a son, Sinfiotli, by Sigmund. Sigmund and his son, who are outlaws in the eyes of the populace that remains under Siggeir's influence, assume the wandering life. On one of their journeys, they come upon a hut in the forest where wolf skins hang above two sleeping men. In the Norse tradition, the transformation into werewolf is accomplished by donning the *ulf-har*, literally, "wolf's hair," a belt of wolf's leather, representing the *ulfhamr*, the wolf's skin. Since Sigmund and Sinfiotli had been following the werewolves, they knew that when the men donned the ulfhamr they were werewolves for nine days and men on the tenth.

Sigmund and Sinfiotli put on the wolf skins and found that they were unable to remove them. Since they were now werewolves, they made a solemn pact between them to abide by certain rules when they fought other men: They would speak only in the wolf language which they both understood. While each should be prepared to take on as many as seven men at once, that number should be the limit. If one or the other was ever outnumbered, he must call out for the other's help in wolf-language only.

Later, when Sigmund learns that his son has slain 11 men without howling for his help, he angrily strikes Sinfiotli for breaking the vow and wounds him. Dismayed at what he had done and what they have both become, Sigmund stays with his son until he is healed and until the cycle is fulfilled when they can remove the wolf skins. They agree to lay them aside forever and burn them in the fire.

SOURCES:

Davidson, Ellis H. R. *Gods and Myths of the Viking Age*. New York: Barnes & Noble, 1996.

Simek, Rudolf. Translated by Angela Hall. *Dictionary of Northern Mythology*. Rochester, NY: Boydell & Brewer, 1993.

von Sacher-Masoch, Leopold (1836–1895)

The study of human psychology has defined a *sadist* as one who derives sexual satisfaction from inflicting physical pain and humiliation on others. A *masochist* is one whose sexual satisfaction depends upon receiving pain or humiliation. A *sado-masochist* is a disturbed individual who must receive pain and at the same time inflict physical cruelty on another in order to achieve sexual satisfaction. In all the grisly history of human perversion, inhuman acts of cruelty, and savage werewolf-like attacks on unsuspecting victims, the vast syndrome of unnatural and perverse deeds that were termed sadistic or masochistic were not named after a monstrous emperor, a brutal conqueror, or a sullen and vengeful king, but after two authors, the marquis **Donatien Alphonse Francois de Sade** and the chevalier Leopold von Sacher-Masoch.

Leopold von Sacher-Masoch was born in Galicia, Austria, on January 27, 1836, the son of Johann Nepomuk von Sacher, a police official who had been knighted by Emperor Francis I, and Charlotte von Masoch, daughter of the vice-chancellor of Lemberg University. A scholar who earned doctorates in law and in literature, Leopold studied history at the University of Vienna and, at the age of 20, published monographs on the Flemish uprising against Charles V and the downfall of Hungary and Maria of Austria. At the same time, he continued his father's military tradition; and in 1866, when he was 30, he earned the Austrian medal for valor in the battle of Solferino. Soon after the end of the war, Leopold began writing the novels that would make him famous.

Don Juan von Kolomea (1866) was, for its time, an audacious attack on the institution of monogamous marriage. His best-known work, *Venus in Furs* (1870) portrays a man dominated by his "Venus," a man who receives sexual satisfaction from pain and humiliation. In his childhood, Chevalier von Sacher-Masoch admitted that he had been fascinated by tales that detailed the tortures and sufferings endured by the early Christian martyrs. Since puberty, he had dreamed of being in the control of a cruel woman who would keep him in chains and beat him. His first great love, Franny von Pistor-Bogdanoff, finally grew bored with Leopold's desire to be mistreated and humiliated by her. He would arrange long journeys by rail, paying all the expenses, but acting as her subservient and uniformed footman.

And always Chevalier von Sacher-Masoch dressed his ladies in furs, often having them photographed so adorned and with him lying at their feet, an adoring servant. His first wife, Wanda Rumelin, discovered on their wedding night that she was to wear a fur-lined dressing gown and speak harshly to her husband if she wished to please him. Rumelin grew more perplexed when she was instructed to treat him as her slave, to beat him for any real or imagined shortcomings, and to torture him with jealousy by committing adultery in his presence. For a young woman of petty-bourgeois origins with the equivalent of an elementary school education received in a Roman Catholic convent school, Rumelin was completely confused that she must brazenly achieve complete marital independence and be free to cavort with lovers in full view of her husband's approving eyes.

Later, in her own book, Rumelin told of her husband's favorite game, a variation on "hide and seek" that he insisted upon playing whenever there were a number of ladies present as their houseguests. Leopold would dress all the women in fur coats or wraps and set them to seeking him in his hiding place. He would be easily found, and then the fur-covered ladies were to throw themselves on him as if they were wild beasts, scratching and biting at him.

Leopold von Sacher-Masoch's second wife, Helene Meister, was no young convent-schooled girl who could be intimidated to assume the role of dominatrix to his enactment of the cringing slave. Her stolid common sense appeared to calm him, and he lived the quiet life of a country squire and author until his death on March 5, 1895.

SOURCES:

Eisler, Robert. *Man into Wolf.* London: Spring Books, n.d.

Hunt, Morton M. *The Natural History of Love.* New York: Grove Press, 1959.

Voodoo

Voodoo is a strange and colorful mixture of certain African tribal beliefs and rites with Roman Catholic ritual and practice. The early slaves, who were snatched from their homes and families on Africa's West Coast, brought their gods and religious practices with them. Plantation owners, who purchased the slaves for heavy physical labor, were compelled by order of the lieutenant-general to baptize their slaves in the Roman Catholic religion. The slaves suffered no theological conflict. They received the white man's baptismal water and quickly adapted the hierarchy of saints into their old jungle family of nature gods and goddesses.

The connotations of evil and fear that are generally associated with voodoo has its primary origin in the white plantation owners' constant concern over the threat of slave rebellions. The owners and their overseers were outnumbered at least 16 to one by the black field hands whom they worked unmercifully in the broiling Haitian sun. As the black population increased and the white demand for slave labor remained high, voodoo began to take on an anti-white liturgy. Several messiahs rose up among the slaves, valiant men with vision who were subsequently put to death by the whites in the big houses. In an effort to prevent slave revolts, a number of laws were passed forbidding any plantation owner to allow "night dances" among his field hands.

In 1791, a slave rebellion took place under the leadership of Toussaint L'Ouverture, which was to lead to Haiti's independence from France in 1804. Although the charismatic L'Ouverture died in a Napoleonic prison, his generals had become sufficiently inspired by his courageous example to continue the struggle for freedom until the whip-enforced myth of white supremacy, along with the whites themselves, was banished from the island.

After the Concordat of 1860, when relations were once again established with France, the Roman Catholic priests who came to Haiti found that the vestiges of their religion had been kept alive in voodoo. Although the orthodox clergy fulminated against voodoo from their pulpits, they did not actively campaign against their rival priesthood. After all, the Roman Catholic clergy concluded, the people seemed devout enough. Surely, with the passage of time, voodoo would be forgotten.

Nearly 40 years later, in 1896, an impatient Monseigneur attempted to organize an anti-voodoo league; but it really wasn't until 1940 that the Roman Catholic Church truly launched a rigorous campaign of renunciation directed at the practitioners and adherents of voodoo. Once their crusade that been initiated, the priests went about their methodic attacks with such zeal that the government was forced to intercede and instruct them to temper the fires of their missionary endeavors.

Today, voodoo continues to be tolerated in Haiti. Enterprising members of the priesthood in Haiti, New Orleans, and certain other areas where voodoo is held in high esteem have even taken to staging watered-down rituals for the tourists who want to see some real black magic women and men doing some authentic voodoo dances.

A male practitioner of voodoo is called a *hungan*; his female counterpart, a *mambo*. The "church" where voodoo is practiced is a series of buildings called a *humfo*. The priest and priestess serve a "congregation" called a *hunsi*, and the voodoo clergy cure, divine, and care for them through the good graces of their *loa*, their guiding spirits. It costs a hungan a great deal of money to set up a voodoo practice, but he doesn't have the problem that a conventional doctor sometimes faces in convincing patients delinquent in their bills to pay up. If someone he has cured refuses to pay, his loa will cause a relapse of the malady.

The worship of the supernatural loa is the central purpose of voodoo. They are, in essence, the old gods of Africa, blended with local nature spirits, who occupy a position of power to the fore of God, Christ, the Holy Mother, and the saints. The practitioners and adherents of voodoo adamantly refuse to accept the Church's position that the loa are the "fallen angels," who rebelled against God. The loa do good and guide and protect humankind. Certainly there are **demons,** but a decent hungan or mambo has nothing to do with those entities from the dark side.

The loa communicate to the faithful by incarnating themselves in the bodies of the supplicants during trance, by appearing in their dreams, or when they are dancing in the humfo. During the ritual dancing, each participant eventually undergoes a personality change and adopts a unique trait of his or her particular loa. The adherents of voodoo refer to this phenomenon of the invasion of the body by a supernatural agency as that of the loa mounting their "horses."

There is a great difference, the hungan insists, between **possession** by one of the loa and possession by an evil spirit. An evil spirit would bring chaos to the dancing and perhaps great harm to the one possessed. The traditional dances of voodoo are conducted on a serious plane with rhythm and suppleness, but not with the orgiastic sensuality that one may have observed in certain motion pictures allegedly depicting authentic voodoo rituals.

Twins are believed to be endowed with supernatural powers in voodoo with special access to the loa. It can be very difficult being the parents of twins, for a spanking by a hasty father or mother may result in sudden illness or failing strength that can only be restored by placating the offended spirit that watches over the children. If another child should follow the birth of the twins, this one is regarded as having even greater powers. A child who preceded twins is not looked upon with any deference at all.

Those who serve the loa do not obtain their good will without obliging them with numerous sacrifices and offerings at regular intervals. All voodoo ceremonies must be climaxed with sacrifice to the loa. Chickens are the most common sacrificial victims, although the wealthy may offer a goat or a bull. Participation by all members of the hunsi in the drinking of the sacrificial **blood** is required. On occasion spices are added to the vital fluid, but usually it is drunk "straight." **Zombies,** those blank-eyed, shuffling dread creatures of the undead, well-known elements in tales of jungle voodoo, are the slaves of dark-side sorcerers.

Proving the point that voodoo may be used for good, in 1996, High Priestess Sallie Ann Glassman called upon the gods of voodoo to help rid their New Orleans neighborhood of drug dealers and crime. Sallie Ann and her business partner Shane Norris, both practitioners of voodoo, had enough of the soaring crime rate when they were robbed and attacked. About 100 people gathered outside their store one night and they led a procession to the nearest corner. They set up an altar in the middle of the street using a sewer cap as its base. Against the background of beating drums and flaming torches, Sallie Ann performed a ritual to dispel any evil intent. Then she knelt before the altar and made an offering of rum, cigars, and bullets to Ogoun La Flambeau, the voodoo god of war, fire, and metal.

Within a very short period of time, the voodoo ritual had worked wonders. The crime rate dropped from 70 burglaries per month to about six. Before the ceremony, crack could be bought at seven houses, soon it was down to one. Captain Lonnie Smith of the New Orleans police department, who witnessed the voodoo rite, agreed that something seems to have worked. "And as long as we are getting positive results from [voodoo], I'm all for it."

SOURCES:

Hubbard, S. D., "Crime-Infested Neighborhood Fights Back with Voodoo—& It Works!," *National Enquirer,* 27 February 1996.

Huxley, Francis. *The Invisibles: Voodoo Gods in Haiti.* New York: McGraw-Hill, 1969.

Steiger, Brad. *Monsters Among Us.* New York: Berkley Books, 1989.

Warren, Ed (1926–) and Lorraine (1927–)

North America's best known lay demonologist is Ed Warren of Monroe, Connecticut, who, with his talented clairvoyant wife Lorraine, have been the directors of the New England Society for Psychic Research since 1952. In that time, they have investigated over 4,000 hauntings, as well as cases of real-life werewolves and vampires, such as the astonishing account of the **possession** that transformed **Bill Ramsey** into a real "Werewolf of London." The Warrens were the psychical investigators in the famous Amityville Horror haunting, and their book, *The Haunted*, about a Pennsylvania family under diabolical attack, was made into a television movie by Fox Television in 1991.

Ed says that he grew up in a haunted house from the time he was five until he was 12. His father, a police officer, kept insisting that there was a logical reason for the phenomena, but Ed notes that the elder Warren never quite came up with the logical explanation.

Ed and Lorraine met when they were both 16, and he was an usher at a movie theater in Bridgeport. Ed enlisted in the navy on his seventeenth birthday. Four months later, after his ship sank in the North Atlantic and he was home for a 30-day survivor's leave, Ed and Lorraine were married. After World War II ended, Ed supported his wife and baby girl by selling his paintings to tourists who visited the New England area. Strangely enough, it was through his paintings and sketches that the Warrens began their psychical research. Whenever Ed heard of a haunting, they would travel to the location and he would sketch it. When the home owners saw his painting of their home, they would invite the young couple inside to investigate the ghostly manifestations. Soon Lorraine would be picking up highly accurate clairvisual and clairaudient impressions of the entities.

When the New England Society for Psychic Research was established in 1952, its initial goal was to investigate reports of haunting phenomena. As their reputation grew, Ed and Lorraine would sometimes research an alleged haunted house with as many as four clairvoyants, a number of physical scientists with state-of-the-art equipment, and an ecumenical assortment of clergy. Some critics have called Ed an eccentric because he believes in devils and **demons.** He quickly admits that he has no doubts about the reality of negative entities: "I learned about them as a child, and as a man I have proved beyond a shadow of a doubt that they exist. If you don't want to call them devils and demons, just call them evil, I don't care. Religions are man-made, but spirituality isn't."

The Occult Museum has been a special project of the Warrens for many years. Tours are available by appointment, and serious visitors are allowed to study the vast collection of artifacts, books, pictures, masks, and idols they have collected during the course of their 50-year investigation of the unexplained. Ed does not recommend, however, that anyone touch the objects they have assembled in the museum. "Some are so dangerous that just in touching them you could be very badly affected. They are the opposite of what you would touch in a church were the statues, the crosses, and the holy relics have been blessed. The things in the museum were used in black **witchcraft,** magic, **sorcery,** and curses."

SOURCES:
New England Society for Psychic Research, P.O. Box 278, Farmington, CT 06034.
Warren, Ed and Lorraine, P.O Box 41, Monroe, CT 06468.

The Werewolf of London

The first full-length cinematic treatment of the werewolf legend presented a rather sanitized version of the lycanthrope. *The Werewolf of London* (1935) includes none of the traditional elements of **sorcery, satanism,** sadism, **cannibalism,** or sexual perversion. Although in the folklore of most cultures, the **vampire** and the werewolf play off one another to the point where they often indistinguishable one from the other, *The Werewolf of London* establishes the wolfman in the cinematic mold of the Jekyll/Hyde process of transformation. In the new mythology of the werewolf fashioned by **Universal Pictures,** a person who is bitten or scratched by a werewolf becomes a two-legged man-beast who sprouts thick facial hair, long fangs, and dangerous claws, but retains the basic human shape, complete with clothing. There is no total shapeshifting into a four-legged wolf. This Hollywood formula for the making of a werewolf was applied to **Lon Chaney Jr.** in *The Wolf Man* (1941) and to **Oliver Reed**

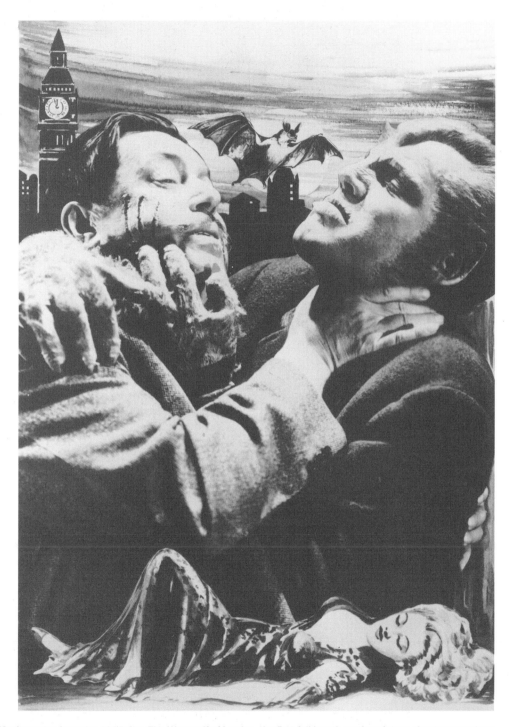

Movie poster from the 1935 film *The Werewolf of London,* the first full-length motion picture about werewolves.

in ***The Curse of the Werewolf*** (1961) and to most cinematic lycanthropes until ***The Howling*** and ***An American Werewolf in London*** in 1981 when astonishing special effects allowed audiences to witness complete transformations of the bitten or scratched victims into demonic wolf creatures.

The Werewolf of London casts the superb character actor Henry Hull as Dr. Wilfred Glendon, an English botanist who has traveled to Tibet in search of the Marifasa lupina, a rare flower that blooms by moonlight only on the Tibetan plateau. While on safari, Glendon manages to find a specimen of the flower, but he is bitten by a strange creature when it rises up to attack him. Ignoring the wound in his triumph of discovery, the botanist returns to his laboratory in London. To his utter despair and confusion, he finds himself changing into a werewolf during the next **full moon.** As if this were not disheartening enough, the scientist knows that he was the man-beast who attacked and killed a woman in the darkened streets of London. A mysterious Asian gentleman named Yogami (Warner Oland) seeks out Dr. Glendon and informs him that he was bitten by a werewolf in Tibet and, since he survived, he is now destined to undergo the transformation to the wolfman each full moon. The only known antidote, Yogami explains, is the moon poppy, the Marifasa lupina.

Although Dr. Glendon tries his best to resist the effects of the curse, he runs amok on the following night and kills again. When it appears that London is under siege by two Jack-the-Ripper-type monsters, Dr. Glendon knows that there must be two werewolves stalking the darkened streets of the city. Yogami admits that he is also a werewolf, and the two man-beasts fight for the possession of the one antidote that can return them to normalcy. The scientist manages to eliminate Yogami, but before he can ingest the flower, his befuddled werewolf mind has him about to tear out the throat of his own beloved wife (Valerie Hobson). The London police arrive with few moments to spare and shoot the Werewolf of London, who, in his dying gasps, reverts to his human form as Dr. Wilfred Glendon.

Henry Hull made his stage debut in 1911 and became a leading man in such silent pictures as *A Square Deal* (1917), *Little Women* (1918), and *The Hoosier Schoolmaster* (1924). His highly successful portrayal of "Magwitch" in the film version of Charles Dickens's *Great Expectations* (1934) no doubt won him the role of Dr. Wilfred Glendon in *The Werewolf of London*. Excellent character actor that he was, the Kentucky-born Hull did not really fit the role of a supercilious English botanist, decked out in cap and tweeds, who suddenly found himself changing into a werewolf. In addition, he had no desire to emulate such horror masters as Boris Karloff or Lon Chaney Sr. and appear on camera in the kind of grotesque monster makeup effects that had made them famous. Neither did he have any wish to submit to long hours in makeup, sitting patiently while Jack Pierce labored to transform him into a lycanthrope.

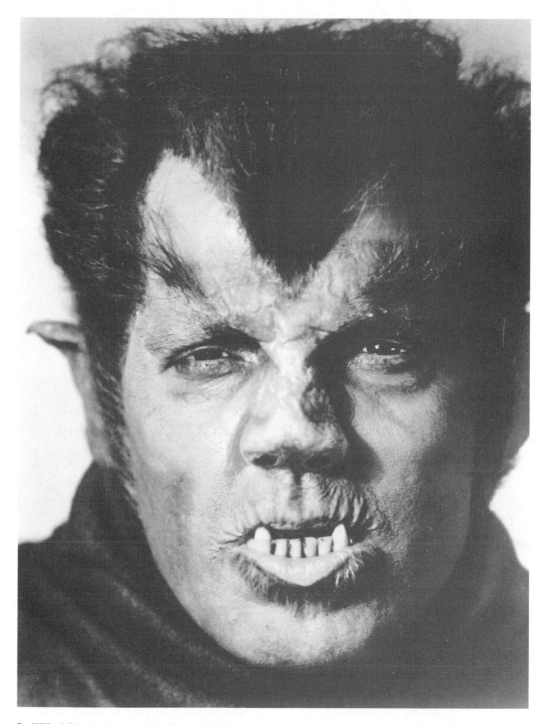

Dr. Wilfred Glendon (portrayed by Henry Hull) transforms into a werewolf in the film, *The Werewolf of London.*

Faced with his star's recalcitrance, Pierce was presented with the challenge of devising a very light werewolf makeup that could be quickly applied to Hull before his scenes as a werewolf stalking the London streets. Unable to create the convincing facial transformation into a man-beast that he would later achieve for Lon Chaney Jr. in *The Wolf Man*, Pierce did the best he could under the circumstances, though some viewers perceived his valiant efforts as having made Hull appear more like a batlike vampire than a werewolf. Henry Hull enjoyed a long career as an actor and went on to appear in such successful films as *The Great Waltz* (1938), *Jesse James* (1939), *High Sierra* (1941), *Lifeboat* (1944), *The Great Gatsby* (1949), and *The Buccaneer* (1958).

Although he was Swedish, actor Warner Oland played the title role of the notorious Fu Manchu in *The Mysterious Dr. Fu Manchu* (1929) and *The Return of Dr. Fu Manchu* (1930). He assumed the persona of the beloved Chinese detective Charlie Chan in *The Black Camel* (1931) and *Charlie Chan Carries On* (1931), and continued playing the wise Asian crimebuster until his death in 1938. By the time he enacted the role of Yogami in *The Werewolf of London*, he had already been typecast as an Asian.

SOURCES:

Clarens, Carlos. *An Illustrated History of the Horror Film.* New York: Capricorn Books, 1968.

Katz, Ephraim. *The Film Encyclopedia.* New York: Perigee, 1979.

The Werewolf of Paris

In 1933, **Guy Endore** published his novel, *The Werewolf of Paris*, based on the life of **Francois Bertrand,** a sergeant in the French army who desecrated a number of graves in Paris before being apprehended in 1840. Although Bertrand was really more ghoul than werewolf, the elements of mutilation worked upon the corpses and his sadistic turn of mind, combined with possible acts of **cannibalism,** move him into the lycanthropic arena. The novel also served as the inspiration for *The Curse of the Werewolf* (1961), starring **Oliver Reed.**

Werewolf Rock

Outside of the village of Eggenstedt, near Sommerschenburg and Schoningen, Germany, stands a large rock that has been called Werewolf Rock for many centuries. According to the legend, a mysterious figure known simply as "the Old Man" would venture out from the Brandsleber Forest and offer to perform tasks for the villagers, such as watching over their flocks of sheep. On one occasion, as he herded sheep for a shepherd named Melle from Neindorf, the Old Man asked for a particular spotted lamb as payment for his work. Melle refused, as he particularly prized that lamb. The Old Man repeated his request many times, and Melle always denied his wishes.

When it was time to shear the flock for the wool, Melle hired the Old Man to help out. Later, when the work was completed, the shepherd found that both the mysterious old fellow and his prized, spotted lamb had disappeared. Many months went by without a trace of either the Old Man or the lamb. Melle concluded the obvious: his hired helper had taken his lamb and eaten it.

One day as he grazed his sheep in the Katten Valley, Melle was surprised by the sudden appearance of the Old Man, who mocked him by sneering that his spotted lamb sent its regards. Enraged, the shepherd raised his crook to give the Old Man a clout, but the strange man from the woods changed his shape into that of a wolf. Melle was frightened, but his dogs came to his rescue and attacked the wolf with fury, causing it to flee.

Melle pursued the wolf until it reached the vicinity of Eggenstedt where the dogs trapped and surrounded it. At that point, the werewolf returned its form to that of the Old Man, who begged to be spared. Melle would not be deceived by such pleas, and he began furiously to beat the man with his crook. An accomplished shapeshifter of the highest prowess, the Old Man assumed the form of a sprouting thorn bush. Knowing now that he was faced with an adversary of great supernatural powers, Melle did no back off, but continued to strike away at the branches of the thorn bush.

The shapeshifter, realizing that a mortal had hardened his heart and was determined to kill him, once again changed its form to that of the Old Man and begged for his life. Melle the shepherd continued to ignore his pleas and kept flailing away with his crook. The shapeshifter changed back into a wolf, planning to run away and escape in its four-legged form, but a fatal blow from Melle suddenly snuffed out its life. The spot where the creature dropped dead will be named Werewolf Rock throughout all time.

SOURCES:

Grimm, Wilhelm, and Jacob. Translated and/or edited by D. L. Ashliman. "Der Werwolfstein." *Deutsche Sagen,* (1816/1818) No. 215.

Werewolf: The Apocalypse

Werewolf: The Apocalypse is a role-playing game from White Wolf Game Studio, the creator of the popular *Vampire: The Masquerade* role-playing game. The premise of the game is actually simple. Each player takes on the persona of a werewolf, or Garou. The Garou have been charged with protecting Gaia, or Mother Earth, from destruction by the evil power of the Wyrm, and they are failing. Despite the best efforts of the Garou, the Apocalypse is coming.

Werewolf: The Apocalypse is set in the World of Darkness, which is a darker, more Gothic version of Earth. Things are much darker on the world inhabited by the Garou—cities are dark foreboding places, and, as the creators say, an edge of *film noire* inhabits everything in the Garou world. The rich are more likely to be corrupt, the poor more numerour and poverty more horrific. It is not a pleasant place to live.

The Garou are divided into three breeds—homids, who were born and raised as humans; lupus, who were born and raised as wolves; and metis, deformed half-breeds who are the product of one Garou mating with another (which is forbidden). All Garou, no matter what breed, live in tribes. There are 13 main tribes, which include:

- Black Furies—these Garou originated in Greece and are almost always female. They defend the rapidly disappearing wilderness in the World of Darkness.

- Bone Gnawers—urban street-dwellers who are the lowest of the 13 tribes. They resemble jackals and are universally hated by other Garou.

- Children of Gaia—a peaceful tribe that seeks to gain and promote harmony with Gaia. If the need arises, however, they will act mercilessly.

- Fianna—Celtic Garou who are known as storytellers and singers. They record and preserve the Garou history and prefer to spend their days drinking and singing.

- Get of Fenris—war-like Garou who live for combat and destruction. Members are fierce warriors who are always first in line to fight evil of the Wyrm.

- Glass Walkers—the only tribe to truly adapt to the vast cities of the World of Darkness. Tribe members work with technology and finance, which causes other tribes to mistrust them.

- Red Talons—this tribe includes only lupus members; tribe members hate all hominids. Members thrive in the wilderness and are the most bestial of the tribes.

- Shadow Lords—powerful, arrogant leaders who seek to take over Garou and human society. They are natural fighters who are highly ambitious, for better or worse.

- Silent Striders—a mysterious travelling tribe that moves from caern to caern (a caern is a type of holy spot in Garou society), Some think they have psychic powers.

- Silver Fangs—members of the Silver Fang tribe are the equivalent of Garou royalty. Noble leaders who are beginning to suffer from a strain of madness.

- Stargazers—mystical martial arts experts who roam the World of Darkness, often protecting others from the powers of the Wyrm.

- Uktena—a remnant of a previously great Garou tribe, the Uktena are extremely cunning and secretive and possess strong magical powers.

- Wendigo—a tribe that has its roots in Native American culture. The Wendigo were nearly wiped out hundreds of years ago, but those that survive are strong in the ways of war and spiritualism.

To play the game, one storyteller is chosen to lead a group of players. The Storyteller creates the story and the physical "world" in which the players will undertake their adventures. Each player then uses books and other guidelines to create a Garou being that is his or her alter ego—players choose a tribe and endow their character with positive and negative attributes that determine how he or she interacts with other players. Games can be played at various level of role-playing reality, from playing the game as a tabletop game with dice, to actually acting facets of the game out.

Werewolves of *Dark Shadows*

Gothic romances, those spooky stories that usually feature a young and attractive female, a creepy mansion, and a mysterious, brooding, handsome master of the manor, were extremely popular in the mid-1960s. I can clearly remember editors advising authors to get aboard the "gothic gravy train" and churn out such tales for the mass market audience, and many male authors of my acquaintance adopted female pseudonyms and got "on board," just as their editors and agents advised. Producer Dan Curtis had his fingers on the pulse of a large portion of the public *zeitgeist* when he decided that the time was right in June 1966 to launch *Dark Shadows*, an afternoon gothic soap opera on the ABC television network. Although supernatural elements were gradually added to the plotlines, ratings were just so-so until he decided to add a **vampire,** Barnabas Collins (Jonathan Frid), in April 1967. With a true monster lurking in the shadows, the series became a major hit that skyrocketed far beyond the expected parameters of an afternoon soaper.

Although to most people the vampire Barnabas Collins is synonymous with *Dark Shadows*, another branch on the Collins family tree bore the fangs, claws, and extreme hirsute countenance of a werewolf. Introduced late in 1968, Quentin Collins, a family member from the 1890s, was afflicted with the curse of the werewolf. Desperate for storylines to keep pace with the demand for five half-hour episodes a week, the scriptwriters had already moved the various characters of the series back and forth in time. Barnabas, who had lived in the 1790s and been revived in 1967, was transported back to 1897 to encounter Quentin. It was not long before Quentin Collins (David Selby) was the second most popular character in the series. His romantic theme music, which issued from an old Edison disk phonograph and to which he softly spoke the lyrics in a dream-sequence with one of his lovers, enraptured so many viewers that 20 recordings of the ballad were made by various artists.

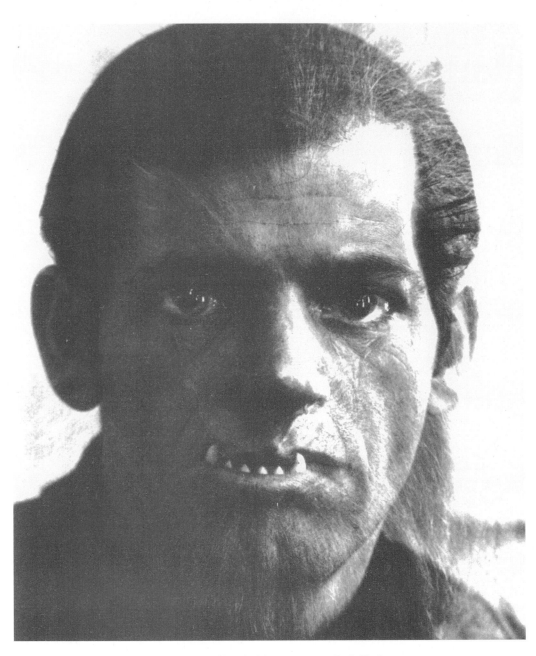

Alex Stevens portrayed a werewolf on the gothic television soap opera *Dark Shadows*.

In 1969, a second, contemporary, werewolf was added to the cast in the person of Christopher Jennings (Don Briscoe), who struggled Talbotlike with the dilemma of lycanthropy. The werewolf lore that figured in the plotlines of

Dark Shadows was drawn essentially from the classic werewolf movies, and the poem uttered by Maliva the gypsy in **The Wolf Man** (1941) was spoken as if it were some kind of biblical malediction:

> Even the man who is pure in heart
> And says his prayers at night,
> May become a wolf when the wolfbane blooms
> And the moon is clear and bright.

One became a werewolf after being bitten or scratched by a lycanthrope; only a silver bullet in the heart could kill such a beast; and after the transformation, the werewolf was still very discernable as a man-beast, who even wore the same suit of clothes without stretching them out of shape. All these truths about werewolves were gleaned from the **Universal Pictures** series of classic horror movies, and were spoken by various characters in the series as though they were dictates from ancient dogma. Christopher Jennings was even presented with the "moon poppy" cure, borrowed from **The Werewolf of London** (1935), the first full-length feature film treatment of lycanthropy.

While Barnabas Collins and an occasional new vampiric character dominated the series until it drew to a close after its 1,245th segment on April 2, 1971, the shadowy Collinswood Estate did experience two werewolves to add to its extraordinary popularity as a supernatural soap opera.

SOURCES:

Melton, Gordon J. *The Vampire Book: The Encyclopedia of the Undead.* Farmington Hills: Visible Ink Press, 1998.

"Werewolves of London"

Singer/songwriter Warren Zevon has developed a loyal following in the world or rock music thanks to his insightful (and often quirky) lyrics and strong musicianship. His songs—such as "Roland the Headless Thompson Gunner" and "Lawyers, Guns, and Money"—are often full or mayhem or violence, but the darkness is almost always offset by a wicked sense of humor. In 1978, Zevon became forever connected to the world of lycanthropy when his song "Werewolves of London" off the *Excitable Boy* album became a surprise radio hit. Full of humorous images ("I saw a werewolf drinking a pina colada at Trader Vic's/And his hair was perfect") and a hard-to-forget piano line, the song remains Zevon's only Top 40 hit.

The fact that the song contained any reference to werewolves was really an accident. While goofing around with a group of fellow musicians one night, Zevon came up with the song almost out of nowhere. As he tells it: "Waddy (guitarist Waddy Wachtel) walked in and said, 'What are you doing?' And I said, 'We're doing the Werewolves of London.' And he said, 'You mean, 'Ah-wooooooo, the Werewolves of London?" And we said, 'Correct.' We didn't see ourselves retiring on the BMI earnings from the song. It's a novelty, but it's not a novelty the way, say, Steve Martin's "King Tut" is."

The song gained further noteriety in 1986 when it was included on the soundtrack of the film *The Color of Money*. The movie, which was a sequel to the classic film *The Hustler*, starred Paul Newman and Tom Cruise. The song was featured in a particularly memorable scene in which Cruise displayed the depths of his talents at the billiards game of 9-ball.

Weyer (Weir), Johann (1515–1588)

All too seldom amidst the screams of pain rising from the torture chambers and the stakes of the Inquisition, a voice of reason would sound—if only fleetingly and in vain. Such a voice of protest against the ghastly machinery of the grand inquisitors was Johann Weyer, a pupil of the famous platonist Cornelius Agrippa of Nettesheim and a medical doctor who had studied in the humanist France of Francois I and practiced in Holland when it was under the enlightened influence of the scholar Erasmus. Agrippa had incurred the wrath of the Inquisition by defying it, shaming its "workers in its slaughter houses" for ignoring the baptism in Christ that would prevent the innocent from suffering from the baseless accusations of heresy. Dr. Weyer admired his teacher's courage and his skepticism.

In 1550, Dr. Weyer was invited to accept the protection of the tolerant Duke of Cleves, Julich-Berg-Marck, William V, and encouraged to write a work critical of the terrible ministrations of the Inquisition. In 1563, at the age of 48, Dr. Weyer published *de Praestigiis Daemonum*, a work that would earn him notoriety throughout Europe and the accusation by famed jurist **Jean Bodin** that the author of such a foul book was a patron of witches and an accomplice of Satan.

While later generations would hail Johann Weyer as the father of modern psychiatry, even the good doctor's friends told him that he must immediately rewrite the book or destroy it before it fell into the hands of the powerful church hierarchy who all championed the Inquisition and the torture and burning of heretics, werewolves, and witches. While there were a few fellow physicians who hailed him as a prophet of enlightenment, the great majority branded him a lunatic. The book was burned by the Lutheran University of Marburg, denounced by the French Calvinists, and placed on the Index by the Roman Catholic governor of the Netherlands, the Duke of Alba, who finally managed to accomplish Dr. Weyer's dismissal from the Court of Cleves.

Lest we paint too fine a picture of Dr. Johann Weyer and portray him as a bold thinker centuries ahead of his time, it must be understood that he by no means denied the reality of witchcraft, werewolves, **demons,** and the vast universe of platonic spirits and entities. In fact, he firmly advocated the existence of the satanic monarchy and its attendant demons; and he, himself, catalogued the evil workings of many of them, declaring that, not counting Satan himself, there were 44,435,556 demons roaming earth, seeking whom they might possess and afflict. Where he displayed his greatest insight was in arguing that the poor wretches who were being dragged to torture chambers by the thousands and burned as witches and werewolves were not true agents of Satan. On the contrary, they had been deceived by the hellish monarch into believing that they had supernatural powers. They were not heretics, they were fools. Their supposed powers were not based on any true knowledge or gifts from Satan. Their magical abilities were merely works of fantasy. They had no ability to fly through the air, to heal, to change their human form into animal shapes. They only imagined such things. Or—and here Dr. Weyer presented great psychological acumen—these so-called witches and werewolves suffered from confused mental states, and they should not be condemned by either civil or ecclesiastical courts, for even a child's or a melancholic's bad and ineffectual wicked intentions are not legally punishable.

SOURCES:

Russell, Jeffrey Burton. *Witchcraft in the Middle Ages.* Ithaca, NY: Cornell University Press, 1972.

Seligmann, Kurt. *The History of Magic.* New York: Pantheon Books, 1948.

Trevor-Roper, H. R. *The European Witch-Craze.* New York: Harper & Row, 1967.

Wild Hunt

Common folk kept themselves well hidden behind closed and locked doors on those dark and stormy nights when Wodan and his **wolves** were abroad on their Wild Hunt. While some anthropologists have suggested that this old folk legend can be explained by assuming that the simple forest people were merely frightened by the noises of a violent storm moving through the trees, **Robert Eisler** scoffs at his colleagues' theories. Men and women who lived in huts in the forest would be quite familiar with the sound of wind and lightning in the trees, he states firmly. In his opinion, the legend began when primitive hunting tribes, armed only with sharpened staves, ran through the forests in lupine packs seeking fresh meat. When they found their prey, whether animal or human, they would kill and dismember their victims as much with their teeth and claws as with their weapons. Other more passive tribes knew that they had better stay hidden in the darkness when the lycanthropic packs were on the hunt.

Centuries later, in complete defiance of the game laws decreed by the lord of the manor, gangs of poachers with their packs of hunting dogs crashed through the night, driving their quarry before them, closing in on it before dawn, then feasting on large sections of their prey in the bloody archetypal way. Once again, the common folk knew enough to stay hidden inside their huts, for they fully realized that the lupine packs of poachers would not hesitate to chase and to kill any humans who happened to get in their way.

Interestingly, the German resistance movement raised against Napoleon I in 1813 was known as the Wild Hunt, in an obvious historical allusion to the legend of Wodan hunting at night with his wolves. The black uniform of the *Schutz-Staffeln*, the dreaded S. S. of **Adolf Hitler**'s troops, with the skull and crossbones on their caps were inspired by the nightly terror visited on the people by the Wild Hunt and by the skeletons of the dead left in Wodan's wake. Hitler gloried in what he delighted in expressing as the brutal, wolflike political measures he would visit upon those who opposed him. His very title, "Fuhrer," denotes the wolf that is the leader of the pack.

SOURCES:

Eisler, Robert. *Man into Wolf.* London: Spring Books, n.d.

Russell, Jeffrey Burton. *Witchcraft in the Middle Ages.* Ithaca, NY: Cornell University Press, 1972.

Wild Women

The *Wilde Frauen* or Wild Women were highly regarded by the rural folk of old Germany. A species of nature spirits that manifested in the form of beautiful women with long, flowing hair, the Wild Women seemed quite benevolent and even somewhat pious of character to those who encountered them. The chief haunt of the lovely nature spirits was said to be on the great moor near Salzberg in an area known as the Wunderberg. It was here that the Wild Women and Dwarfs lived under the earth in magnificent palaces and watched over their treasures of silver and gold. Boys and girls sent out to tend their families' flocks claimed that the Wild Women appeared often and generously gave them sweet tasting breads to eat.

The single flaw in the Wild Women's interaction with humans lay in that unfortunate elfin trait of kidnapping children. In those instances when they made off with small boys and girls, the Wild Women shouted at the parents that the children would be better off with them in their underground kingdom.

SOURCES:

Spence, Lewis. *An Encyclopedia of Occultism.* New Hyde Park, NY: University Books, 1960.

Windigo

Throughout the tribes of the Native American people there are numerous stories of **shamans** with shapeshifting abilities. Generally, the talent of assuming other forms is used for purposes of spiritual enlightenment, healing, gaining insight into tribal problems, and personal awareness. Even when the power to

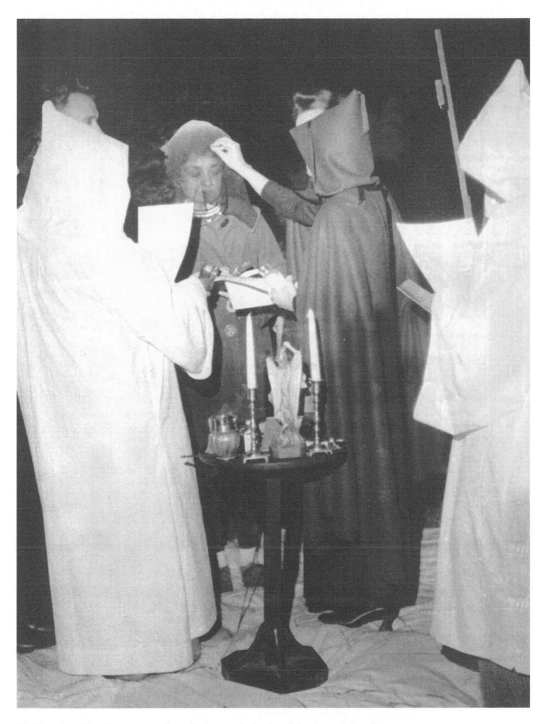

Zia Rose (marking the cross on the veiled woman's forehead) leads a witchcraft ceremony.

transform is used for evil by those sorcerers and witches who have chosen the dark side of medicine, there are few accounts of people being attacked, mutilated, or killed by the shapeshifting. A true savage, cannibalistic, werewolf-like monster is the *windigo*, a creature that hungers for human flesh.

According to Algonquin tradition, the windigo was once a brave warrior, respected by his people. Then, after a fierce battle against tribal enemies, he showed his contempt for the fallen foes by cutting off a piece of flesh and eating it. Unfortunately, the warrior developed a taste for human flesh, and his fellow warriors were horrified when they discovered him several days later roasting another portion of a fallen enemy. Warnings by shamans and chiefs had no effect on the warrior, who ceased hunting game and began to prey upon the people of other tribes for sustenance.

After a time, the Master of Life decreed that if the warrior chose to live like a savage beast, he should appear as a monstrous creature—and the Great Spirit Being transformed him into the windigo. Driven away from the fires of all tribes, the windigo prowls the desolate forests and frozen wastes of northern America, always starving for human flesh.

Among the Chippewa/Ojibway people, the legend of the windigo is used more as a bogeyman to warn children against wandering too far in the forest away from their parents. Some say the story was also used in earlier times as an admonition against the abhorrent practice of eating of human flesh.

SOURCES:
Emerson, Ellen Russell. *Indian Myths*. Minneapolis: Ross & Haines, 1965.

Witchcraft

Witchcraft, as it was defined by the grand inquisitors, is inseparable from werewolves and other shapeshifters. To the church of the Middle Ages, the emissaries of Satan on earth were the witches and heretics who worshipped **Diana,** who sought to transform themselves into **wolves,** cats, and other animal **familiars,** and who practiced **human sacrifice** and **cannibalism.** To the church tribunals, witchcraft, the old religion, was synonymous with **satanism.**

The late witch and authority on the craft, Dame Sybil Leek, once remarked that witchcraft as it is usually portrayed in motion pictures has about as much relation to actual craft practices as Gomer Pyle has to the U.S. Marines. "Mind you, satanism does exist," she added. "But it's not the worship of some medieval devil with horns and cloven feet, but of evil for evil's sake."

If one were to judge the practice of witchcraft according to most television and motion picture depictions, one would believe that witches, the practitioners of the old religion, mock Christ and the Christian Church, desecrate the holy ground of other religions, and seek young virgins to bear the Anti-Christ.

"Nonsense," replied Raymond Buckland, a witch and a former director of the Buckland Museum of Witchcraft and Magick. "What sort of ceremonies do we have? First of all, there is no kissing of goat's buttocks, spitting on crosses, or any of other nonsense associated with witchcraft in the popular mind. Ours is a religion like any other in that we are a group of people meeting together to worship in our particular way. We have prayers and chants; we go through different ceremonies at different times of the year; we do good, so far as we are able, and we abhor and fight evil."

Continuing his remarks concerning a clarification of the true practices of witchcraft, Buckland said:

> We are polytheistic. We believe there are many gods. Perhaps this would not be so difficult for an outsider to understand if he made a comparison with the one Christian god and the large number of Catholic saints. In the same way, we have one principal god and the rest are minor, and, in fact, nameless. Along with our principal god, however, we also have a goddess. Because ours was originally a religion extremely close to nature, we feel there must always be male and female in all things—even in our deities.

In spite of a growing awareness of what witchcraft is really all about and somewhat more accurate portrayals of the old religion on television and in the movies, most witches still practice their faith in secret. As one witch once said to me, "If many of my neighbors knew that I was a witch, the first time they experienced bad luck or their child became ill, they would scream, 'Burn, witch, burn!' They do not know how many times they have actually been helped by a witch."

The thing that seems most to annoy contemporary witches is that the average person retains a conception that witches worship the devil. I have yet to meet a true witch who even believes in Satan, so how did witchcraft come to be portrayed as disciples of the evil adversary of all Christendom?

According to Bill, a young witch who stoutly defends his faith:

> So many paintings and woodcuts from Medieval times picture the Horned God as a devil, so I suppose that modern people are just showing the results of several centuries of brainwashing. Of course there was Pan, the lusty, goat-footed god of the Witches of Thessaly. Some scholars have tried to prove that witchcraft was a Christian fabrication that took form during the Middle Ages. While Satan, enemy of the church, may have been born in Medieval times, these learned scholars are way off base if they believe witchcraft was also fashioned in the Middle Ages. They have forgotten about all the witch cults which were in existence in ancient Greece long before the birth of Jesus. Witchcraft, as we practice it today, is the culmination of the traditions and customs of many centuries.

A descendent of a hereditary witch family that goes back to 1734 stated his conviction that witchcraft, the Faith of the Wise (Wicca, Old English for "wise," gives us "witch"), is concerned only with total truth. In his view, not only is witchcraft one of the oldest of religions, but it is one of the most potent, "bringing as it does, man into contact with gods and man into contact with self." In his view, witchcraft has, in common with all great religions, an "inner experience that is greater than the exterior world, and a discipline that creates from the world an enriched inward vision. Witchcraft can and does embrace the totality of human experience from birth to death, then beyond."

I remember clearly when Gavin and Yvonne Frost of the Church and School of Wicca telephoned to express their excitement and satisfaction over receiving a letter on August 31, 1972, which granted them federal tax exempt status on the basis of witchcraft having qualified as a religion. For centuries witches had been trying to convince the religious and political establishments that their mode of worship really was a true religious experience and should be recognized as such. The Frosts told me that they would charter churches across the United States and that their doors would be open to all who might wish to come, so long as they observed the normal courtesies of reverence and respect:

> A Wiccan church will have to have a coven as a guiding element, and the people who lead the coven will have to be initiated witches. Wicca has no church hierarchy, no king and queen of the witches, no clerical board of supervisors. A coven and its church can go off in its own direction. We believe that as soon as a group has orders coming down from on high, it will die. As long as the coven running the church is composed of initiated witches, they will be on their own.

In October 1998, Phyllis Curott, an Ivy League–educated lawyer who wrote of the inspiration that she had found in witchcraft in her *Book of Shadows*, claimed that Wicca is the fastest growing spiritual practice in the United States, with approximately 400,000 adherents.

Citing the new image of witches as powerful, sexy women in such motion pictures as *Practical Magic* (1998) and the television series *Sabrina, the Teenage Witch* and *Charmed*, entertainment analyst David Davis said: "Suddenly, witches are younger and cuter. . . . Hollywood is good at picking up trends, and horror is big right now. By making the witches cuter and more huggable, they can appeal to a larger audience, including women and younger kids." According to Phyllis Curott, in the 1990s, women are embracing the designation of "witch" as a term of empowerment: "The next wave of feminism . . . is the witch next door."

In spite of such positive responses to witchcraft in the United States, witches still have reason to keep a very low profile in other nations. Regional police chief Exaud Mmari stated in March 1998 that 64 elderly women had been killed in north Central Tanzania on suspicion of practicing witchcraft. In the Northern Province of South Africa, 1,000 cases of "witch purgings" were reported to police and other authorities in 1998. Most victims of the purgings are banished from their homes, which are then set on fire to exorcise **demons** dwelling inside. Many accused witches have been burned alive

A scene from the very disturbing 1922 silent film *Haxan (Witchcraft Through the Ages)* in which a demon leads a Black Mass and commits a ritual murder.

according to ancient beliefs that fire will destroy the soul and thus prevent the witch's spirit from returning to seek revenge. Since the early 1990s, more than 300 South Africans accused of witchcraft have been killed.

In October 1998, it was revealed that masked death squads in eastern Indonesia had slashed to death more than 100 victims who were accused of being black magic sorcerers. The masked executioners conducted the midnight murders over a four-month period, plunging the remote Banyuwangi district in East Java into panic.

SOURCES:

Hainer, Cathy, "The New Face of Witches," *USA Today,* 29 October 1998.

Schuettler, Darren. "Modern S. Africa Battles Deadly Witch Hunts." Reuters/CNN, June 21, 1998.

"64 Suspected Witches Murdered in Tanzania." AFP's People Wire, March 22, 1998.

Steiger, Brad. Personal interviews and correspondence.

Tabloid New Service/Jakarta. "Black Magic Massacre!" October 7, 1998.

Witchie Wolves

David A. Kulczyk provided an account to *Strange* magazine that told of a legend that came to life—to the genuine fear of those who trespassed sacred ground. According to Kulczyk, on the eastern shore of Lake Huron, approximately 34 miles north of Bay City, Michigan, located a few miles from a small town named Omer, is a wilderness area of scrubby pines and swampland known as Omer Plains, the home of the "Witchie Wolves." According to local Chippewa legend, the Witchie Wolves are the invisible guardian spirit dogs that watch over the graves of ancient warriors, attacking any foolhardy enough desecrate the sacred ground.

Kulczyk states that he and friends went twice to Omer Plains, but nobody in his vehicle was brave enough to get out. They could all hear the "hideous, high-pitched laughing bark that came from all directions out of the near total darkness." Visiting Omer Plains became a kind of male teenager rite of passage, Kulczyk said, but few were foolish enough to get out of the their cars. However, he writes:

> Several times a year, a skeptical youth, usually an athlete or an outdoorsman type, would take the dare and get out of the car—only to be violently knocked to the ground by what always seemed to be an invisible wolf or dog, snarling and snapping at the victim's head. Screaming and scrambling back into the car, nobody ever stuck around long enough to see what else would happen. I have seen tough guys cry while telling of their experience. I have heard claims of torn clothes, and I have seen scratches and dents on roofs of cars which the owner, straight-faced and sober, would claim weren't there before the Witchie Wolf attack.

SOURCES:
Kulczyk, David A. "The Witchie Wolves of Omer Plains." *Strange,* spring 1995.

Wolf

Two-time Academy Award–winner Jack Nicholson once cut his acting teeth in such Roger Corman low-budget horror films as *The Terror* (1963) and *The Raven* (1963) playing opposite such legends in the creepy genre as Boris Karloff, Peter Lorre, and Vincent Price, so it was time that he apply his "werewolf smile" and grow some fangs to portray a werewolf in *Wolf* (1994)—especially after he did such a masterful job playing a horny little devil in *The Witches of Eastwick* (1987). Nicholson portrays Will Randall, a rather meek and mild book editor of a New York publishing company, who hits a large animal with his car while driving on a snowy, stormy night. As he gets out of his car to investigate and bends to see to the animal, he discovers that it is a wolf—and he is bitten. Slowly, as the transmutation begins, the Clark Kentish Randall begins to evolve into a lupine superman, for, as he must eventually acknowledge, he was bitten by no ordinary wolf.

Wicca practitioner Yvonne Frost performs a ritual at the School of Wicca.

John Stanley writes, "Amazing, isn't it, when skilled filmmakers can take an old B-movie plot, update it, give it modern sensibilities, and presto—a tired old idea lives again in exciting, new form. This is nothing more than a remake of ***The Wolf Man*** [1941] . . . . "

Well, yes, but as **Lawrence Talbot** began to succumb to the lycanthropic impulses surging through his body, he was never as cool, sassy, and stylish as Nicholson's Will Randall. True, Randall does have his moments of introspective anguish, but he also enjoys his moments of lycanthropic triumph, such as the perverse manner in which he marks his territory in his office. And never did Talbot as the Wolf Man have to go fang to fang in a fight to the death with another werewolf (James Spader) over his lady love (Michelle Pfeiffer).

The touch employed by Mike Nichols, accomplished director of such classics as *Who's Afraid of Virginia Woolf?* (1966), *The Graduate* (1967), and *The Bird Cage* (1996), elevates what could have been another romp down cinematic werewolf lane into a film of high caliber and superb taste. Makeup master Rick Baker, known for films like *Star Wars* (1977), ***An American Werewolf in London*** (1981), and *Harry and the Hendersons* (1987), provides werewolf transformations that fulfill all expectations, and the script by Jim Harrison and Wesley Strick is well done with very effective dialogue that never overindulges in werewolf cliches.

Nicholson's costar Michelle Pfeiffer had portrayed a shapeshifter early in her career when in *Ladyhawke* (1985) she transformed each day into a hawk while her lover (Rutger Hauer) transmutated into a wolf each night, an evil spell keeping them forever apart—until a young squire (Matthew Broderick) helps break the curse. In *The Witches of Eastwick* she fell under a spell once again, this time cast by seductive devil Jack Nicholson. And in *Batman Returns* (1992), her Cat Woman practically stole the film from Batman (Michael Keaton) and the Penguin (Danny DeVito).

SOURCES:

Katz, Ephraim. *The Film Encyclopedia*. New York: Perigee, 1979.

Stanley, John. *Creature Features*. New York: Boulevard, 1997.

Walker, John, ed. *Halliwell's Filmgoer's Companion, 12th Edition*. New York: HarperCollins, 1997.

Wolf Belt

According to the folklore of northern Europe, one of the most common methods by which one transformed himself or herself into a wolf was to put on a wolf belt. The belt was basically a strip of wolf hide with the hairs still attached. Some men put on such a belt simply to become more wolflike, to summon courage and to display savage prowess in battle or to bring about extraordinary strength while performing tasks of heavy labor. Such applica-

Academy Award-winning actor Jack Nicholson put a modern spin on the werewolf legend in the 1994 film *Wolf*.

tions of the wolf belt were acceptable, even common, and were considered charms or **talisman**s. When, however, the wolf belt had received the magical ministrations of a sorcerer, it bequeathed to the wearer the ability to shapeshift into the form of a wolf. The basic motivations for such transformations were to enable the wearers of the belt to go out into the night and attack their enemies or their enemies' livestock.

The Wolf Man

While more contemporary movie audiences have thrilled to the awesome lycanthropic transformations achieved by special effects and makeup geniuses Rick Baker (***An American Werewolf in Londo***n, 1981) and Rob Bottin (***The Howling,*** 1981), the image that still best captures the essence of the werewolf legend for millions of horror fans around the world is that of **Lon Chaney Jr.** loping through the psuedo-Welsh mists in *The Wolf Man* (1941).

Universal Pictures had been considering a film entitled *The Wolf Man* since 1933, though they had no script or any clear concept of what the film would be. The French-born director, Robert Florey, who had come to Hollywood in 1921 and had worked as a scriptwriter on *Frankenstein* (1931), thought the notion of a classic werewolf tale would be an ideal vehicle for Boris Karloff as a follow-up after the Frankenstein Monster and the title role in *The Mummy* (1932). Curt Siodmak, the younger brother of director Robert Siodmak, had left his native Germany and arrived in Hollywood in 1937. Siodmak had written the scripts for *The Invisible Man Returns*, *Black Friday*, and *The Ape*, all released in 1940, so he felt a special challenge in developing the Wolf Man to achieve the status of Hollywood's latest horror icon. It was Siodmak who created the "authentic ancient gypsy malediction" for the character of Maleva to utter:

> Even the man who is pure at heart
> And says his prayers by night
> May become a wolf when the wolfbane blooms
> And the moon is clear and bright.

Although the story was set in Wales, it might as well have taken place in **Vasaria,** the fictitious, multicultural land where a number of the other Universal Pictures monster films would occur.

The plot of the film goes like this: **Lawrence Talbot** (Lon Chaney Jr.) has come home to Wales from the United States where he has received an education, thus accounting for his American accent. Chaney's accent was not the only one out of place for a Welshman, for other alleged lifelong residents of the little Welsh village, such as Warren Williams, Ralph Bellamy, and Fay Helm were also Americans. It didn't matter that Maleva (**Maria Ouspenskaya**), the gypsy fortune teller, spoke with a Russian accent, for, of course, she was a mysterious "foreign" woman. And who would quibble that her son the werewolf (**Bela Lugosi**) spoke what few lines he had with a Hungarian accent?

After Lawrence has installed a large telescope in his father's library, he tests it on the village below and focuses in on an attractive shopkeeper (**Evelyn Ankers**). The young man visits the shop, flirts with Gwen Conliffe, buys his father a gift of a walking stick with a silver wolf's head ornament, and makes a casual date to visit the gypsy camp that evening. As Gwen's friend, Jenny Williams (Fay Helm), is having her fortune read by Bela (Bela Lugosi), the gypsy marks her as the next victim for his lycanthropic bloodlust. Talbot interrupts the attack, but Bela, in the form of a wolf, wounds him, thus infecting him with the curse of the werewolf. When the **full moon** rises, Talbot undergoes a process of transformation that pays tribute to the makeup wizardry of Jack Pierce, setting the standard of such cinematic transmutations for decades to come. Ironically, it is Sir John's silver-headed cane that strikes the

Lon Chaney Jr. terrorizes a helpless woman in a publicity photo from his most famous film, *The Wolf Man*.

fatal blow on the rampaging werewolf that has been stalking the misty Welsh moors, and the Lord of Talbot Castle is shocked to discover, as the transformation reverses from monster to man, that he has killed his own son.

Talbot did not stay dead. Universal resurrected the character in **Frankenstein Meets the Wolf Man** (1943), *House of Frankenstein* (1944), *House of Dracula* (1945), and **Abbott and Costello Meet Frankenstein** (1948), each time with Lon Chaney Jr. portraying the anguished and sympathetic Talbot, seeking somehow to stay the lycanthropic curse and stop killing people.

Evelyn Ankers, the attractive British leading lady who left the Isles for Hollywood, to become the motion picture Scream Queen, appeared in a number of films in the horror genre, including *The Ghost of Frankenstein* (1942), *The Mad Ghoul* (1943), and *The Frozen Ghost* (1945).

Patric Knowles, the handsome British leading man who stole Olivia de Havilland's heart away from Errol Flynn in *The Charge of the Light Brigade* (1936), returned with Chaney/Talbot in *Frankenstein Meets the Wolf Man* as Dr. Mannering, who tries to help his friend break the curse of the werewolf but who becomes distracted while following Dr. Frankenstein's notes to rebuild the monster.

The distinguished actor **Claude Rains** had already appeared in the title role as *The Invisible Man* (1933) and *The Man Who Reclaimed His Head* (1934) among many other films in the mystery or horror genre before playing Sir John Talbot. He received Academy Award nominations for *Casablanca* (1942), *Mr. Skeffington* (1944), and *Notorious* (1946).

The Wolf Man created a number of werewolf traditions for the film that became cinematic werewolf dogma in many horror films to follow:

- People become werewolves after being bitten or scratched by a werewolf.

- Upon the rising of the first full moon after surviving the attack by the werewolf, the victims are themselves transformed into werewolves. Such shall be their fate forever.

- The process of transformation causes fangs and claws to grow, hair to sprout all over the body, and human compassion to be clouded by bloodlust. Werewolves retain an upright, two-legged human body shape and continue to wear the clothing in which they were attired before the transformation began. Shoes are the only items of wearing apparel discarded before the lycanthropes terrorize the moonlit countryside.

- **Wolfsbane** is very effective at keeping a werewolf at bay. **Garlic** is also a pretty good werewolf deterrent, and a **pentagram** might save your life if it is made of silver and displayed prominently where the beast can see it before it tears out your throat. There is a troublesome contradiction here, for a werewolf also sees the sign of the pentagram over its next victim.

- An object made of silver is the only thing that can kill a werewolf. (A silver bullet in heart would be added in *Frankenstein Meets the Wolf Man.*)

With these rules for lycanthropic behavior, manners, and mores firmly established in *The Wolf Man*, Universal rewrote centuries of werewolf lore and legend; and since millions of moviegoers receive their basic instruction in nearly all historical matters from the cinema, such dogma went unchallenged for decades and for dozens of horror movies in which werewolves were central or important characters.

SOURCES:

Skal, David J. *The Monster Show.* New York: W.W. Norton, 1993.

Stanley, John. *Creature Features.* New York: Boulevard, 1997.

Walker, John, ed. *Halliwell's Filmgoer's Companion, 12th Edition.* New York: HarperCollins, 1997.

Wolf, the Grand Teacher

For many traditional people, wolf is the sage, the grand teacher. One of the most popular of all clan and totem animals among Native Americans, the wolf was also the sacred totem of many European clans. **Romulus and Remus,** the legendary twin founders of Rome, were suckled by a she-wolf. Tu Kueh, fabled founder of the Turkish nation, later married the divine she-wolf who suckled and reared him. Siegfried, one of the mightiest of the Teutonic heroes, who conquered dragons, the Queen of the **Valkyries,** and hundreds of warrior opponents, had been nursed by a she-wolf after his mother died in childbirth.

The **shaman** Ghost Wolf says that the old tales give the wolf the credit for teaching humans to live in harmony in "the beginning time." In the *Wolf Lodge Journal*, Ghost Wolf states:

> It was wolf who taught us how to form community upon this earth, for **wolves** have an intuitive knowledge of order . . . and they possess the ability to survive change intact. Wolf medicine is very ancient and born of living experience. Wolf will look deep into your heart and share the greatest of knowledge, but will demand full participation and absolute sincerity. Wolf . . . will rekindle old memories within your soul.

Wolf Moondance, an Osage shaman, reminds us how strong is the parenting instinct in wolves. They are natural mothers and fathers and remain faithful to one another throughout life. Wolf Moondance offers the following advice:

> When you are in need, when you are in danger or feeling separated and abandoned, you can transmit psychic energy and pull to you the energy of the she-wolf. You can allow the feeling of that desire to draw you into the principle of the mother embracing the child.

In his recent book *Evolving Brains*, biologist John Allman of the California Institute of Technology agrees with the ancient legends that portray the wolf as the great teacher of humankind. By forming a partnership with the canines more than 140,000 years ago, early humans became better hunters and gained an advantage that enabled them to outlive the Neanderthals and other hominid species. Primitive *Homo sapiens* likely learned the rules of cooperative living from observing the harmony of a wolf pack.

Grandmother Twylah, a spokesperson for the Wolf Clan of the Seneca, has said that from the wolf the native people learned forethought before decision, the importance of family loyalty and unity, and the knowledge of a great deal of medicine power.

SOURCES:

Steiger, Brad. *Indian Medicine Power.* Atglen, PA: Whitford Press, 1984.

Wolf Wives

Because of the harmony and partnership between early humans and wolves as they hunted and lived together, it became common among many tribes around the world to believe that their ancestors had once been wolves. At first, the old stories said, humans also walked on four legs. Over time they began to develop more humanlike appendages—a toe here, a finger there, smaller ears every now and then. Although there were advantages to being able to stand upright, sitting upright posed the problem of what to do with the tail, so, gradually, it was eliminated—although one could always borrow one from a wolf, coyote, or fox.

Legends grew, and it was supposed that the greatest warriors had either bears or **wolves** for mothers. And fortunate was the man who won the love of a spirit that could appear both as a beautiful woman and a wolf. As a wolf, she could use her sharp sense of smell to lead him to the best game. As a beautiful woman, she would be a marvelous lover and bless him with children that would combine the best of wolf and human traits.

German legends advise that a man throw a piece of iron or steel over a wolf that is suspected of being a werewolf. If his suspicions were correct, the beast will immediately change into its human form. One man suspected that a particular high-born and beautiful woman was able to transform herself into the same wolf that occasionally stole a lamb from his flock. One night as the wolf was about to snatch a meal from his flock of sheep, the shepherd sprang from his hiding place and threw his steel pocketknife over its head. At once the beautiful woman stood there naked before him, and he promised to keep her secret if she would marry him.

Another old folktale tells of the poor farmer who lived with his wife in poverty and bemoaned the fate that had made him a pauper even though he

A woodcut illustration by Henry Anelay from the book *Wagner the WehrWolf (1846–1847).*

worked hard in the fields. At the same time, he counted his beautiful wife his dearest blessing, for she never complained about their crude lifestyle and she somehow always managed to have delicious fresh meat on the table for his dinner.

One day he decided to spy on his good wife in an attempt to learn just where she acquired the choice cuts of meat. He was astonished when his beloved tied a **wolf belt** around her waist as she approached a flock of sheep and transformed herself into a wolf. Stunned beyond speech, the farmer watched as his wolf-wife selected a fine lamb, then fell upon it. At that point, however, a pack of dogs and a shepherd came running at the wolf, intent upon doing it the greatest harm within their power. The farmer called out his wife's name to warn her, and she immediately changed back into her human form, standing naked before her husband, the shepherd, and the growling dogs. The farmer quickly threw his coat over his wife's nakedness and led her away from the confused shepherd and his baying dogs. The farmer won a promise from his wolf-wife never to do such a thing ever again—at least not in the daylight when she could be so easily sighted.

SOURCES:

Emerson, Ellen Russell. *Indian Myths.* Minneapolis: Ross & Haines, 1965.

Spence, Lewis. *An Encyclopedia of Occultism.* New Hyde Park, NY: University Books, 1960.

Wolfsbane

If applied in fatal dosages, wolfsbane would truly repel a werewolf or any other physical being, for it is extremely poisonous. Perennial herbs of the buttercup family (*Ranunculaceae*) are divided into two genera, *Aconitum* and *Eranthis*. The flowering *Aconitum* branch, which includes wolfsbane or monkshood, is the deadly one for it exudes the substance aconite. In Nepal, where the most poisonous variety grows, warriors used the flower to tip their arrows or to turn their enemies' wells into lethal water supplies.

In the skillful, caring hands of an herbalist, however, proper dosages of wolfsbane can be a very effective pain reliever or a tonic. Since so many of the witches of the Middle Ages were accomplished herbalists, it is easy to assume that they knew well how to apply wolfsbane for curative or destructive purposes. While the fabled ointment that could transform the sorcerer into a werewolf is sometimes thought to be wolfsbane, the potion would have to have been mixed with extreme care or certain death would have resulted. It is possible, of course, that the correct proportions could have created an hallucinogenic effect that might have caused the initiate to believe that he had shapeshifted into a wolf.

SOURCES:

Larousse Dictionary of World Folklore. New York: Larousse, 1995.

Wolfstone

According to very old accounts in the Fichtel Mountains of Germany, a shepherd had grown very disgruntled with **wolves** carrying off his sheep. It seems as though, try as he might, he was never able to catch the creatures in the act so that he might kill it. Then, one day, he saw a large wolf creep out of the forest and snatch a lamb from the flock. The shepherd ran after the beast, but the wolf was much too fast, even as it ran with its prey.

The next day the shepherd acquired the services of an expert huntsman to accompany him to the pasture. Although the huntsman was known to be an excellent shot, when the wolf approached to steal another lamb, the bullets he fired seemed to be of no avail.

The next morning the shepherd noticed that an elderly woman long suspected of practicing evil **sorcery** was limping. When he inquired of her injury, she snapped at him angrily that it was none of his business and hurried away. Suspecting that she could have transformed herself into a wolf, the shepherd reported her, and the old woman was interrogated, flogged, and chained securely in a cell. But when the jailers went to look in on her, they discovered to their amazement that she had totally disappeared, leaving the chains behind.

A few days later, the shepherd spotted the same large wolf creeping out of the forest. This time, however, the beast came not for a tender lamb, but to work revenge on the shepherd. The man fought as best he could against the ferocious werewolf, but he would surely have been killed if the huntsman had not happened upon the scene of the deadly struggle. Although his bullet seemed to have little effect on the monster, his silver-bladed knife proved to be the better weapon. The instant that **blood** began to flow from the wolf's side, the creature was transformed into the form of the old woman, writhing and twisting in her death throes.

The two men administered the final fatal blows and buried the werewolf 20 feet beneath the earth. Once this task was completed, they erected a large stone cross, which they called the Wolf Stone on the grave. Although the werewolf was dead and buried beneath the stone cross, local residents claimed that strange phenomena continued to manifest in the area of the monster's grave.

SOURCES:

Sponholz, Hans. Translated by D. L. Ashliman. *Der verwunschene Rehbock: Sagan aus Bayern um Wald, Wild und Jagd.* Oberfränkische Verlagsanstalt und Druckerei, 1981.

Wolves

According to an analysis published in *Defenders*, 8,000 years ago the gray wolf, *Canis lupus*, as many as 20 million strong, roamed much of the northern hemi-

Nona Foch in the 1944 film *Cry of the Werewolf*.

sphere, ranging from the regions we now call southern Mexico, the Arabian peninsula, and the Gangetic Plain of India to arctic Alaska, Canada, Greenland, and Siberia. As has now been established, wolves lived in harmony with the early human hunting societies.

Evolutionary biologist John Allman states in his recent book *Evolving Brains* that it was wolves that helped early humans survive. According to Allman, a California Institute of Technology researcher, early humans became better hunters after they domesticated wolves about 135,000 years ago. The wolf's strength, stamina, and acute hearing and sense of smell helped humans to hunt prey and to overcome predators, especially those beasts that stalked the two-legged species at night. It was the wolf, Allman suggests, that helped *Homo sapiens* outlive the Neanderthals.

When their two-legged partners began to practice agriculture and domesticate livestock, such as cattle, goats, and sheep, the wolves suddenly found themselves transformed from helpers and teachers into ravenous monsters and sinister villains. By the Middle Ages, the wolf had been demonized as an agent of Satan, the vicious monster in folktales, and the werewolf shapeshifter of evil sorcerers. Massive extermination campaigns were begun that reduced wolf populations to mere fractions of their former numbers.

According to *Defenders*, wolves were basically eliminated from western Europe—except in Italy and Spain—by 1950. The last Japanese wolf was shot in 1905.

The world's present population of gray wolves is estimated to be about 200,000 in 57 countries. Of those 57 nations, fewer than half provide the gray wolf with any kind of protection against hunters. And only a mere handful have any kind of nationwide wolf management programs.

The North American continent has the largest number of wolves with approximately 11,000 in the United States and about 60,000 in Canada, the largest number in any single country. The reason why Canada harbors so many wolves is due to the fact that so much of its 3.5 million square miles is so sparsely populated, allowing the wolves to run free to hunt their natural prey.

Since the early 1970s, wolves have been protected under the Endangered Species Act in the lower United States. Unfortunately Alaska and Canada observe no such protective legislation and thousands of wolves are slaughtered annually with few restrictions applied to those who would kill the animals indiscriminately.

As far as wolf populations in other parts of the world, scientists have not documented the sighting of a wild wolf in Mexico since the 1970s, but the Mexican government has pledged to work with the U.S. in reintroducing wolves along the border.

Russia, including Siberia, has around 40,000 wolves spread across 12 time zones and 6.5 million square miles.

The largest western European wolf population is in Spain. Although the 2,000 Spanish wolves have little protection, they are classified as game animals with a legal hunting season and limits are enforced. Such countries as Denmark, Finland, Norway, Sweden, Germany, and France average around 30 wolves each.

Italy protects the 400 to 500 wolves within its borders, and their numbers are increasing.

Latvia has an estimated 900 wolves, but the laws permit about 400 to be killed each year. Poland established a nationwide protection of its wolves in 1998, and because of this legislation, the country probably has a stable population of around 800 wolves.

Portugal has tried to protect its approximate 300 wolves, but illegal hunting continues to decimate their numbers.

In the Middle East, Israel has protected its wolves since 1954 and is building a stable population of around 200.

In Egypt, what few wolves remain exist only on the Sinai Peninsula and are steadily dying out. Iran has a stable population of approximately 1,000 wolves. Jordan's remaining wolves are afforded no protection and are routinely killed by farmers and hunters.

Among the Asian nations, only China and India protect their wolves. India has about 1,300, but the number are declining because of loss of habitat. China's wolf population of around 6,000 appears relatively stable.

Although Mongolia may have as many as 30,000 wolves, the government offers the animals no protection and habitat losses will begin to diminish their numbers.

SOURCES:

Hinrichsen, Don. "Wolves around the World: A DEFENDERS Survey Finds the Top Canine Carnivore Still Holding On in at Least 57 Nations." *Defenders: The Conservation Magazine of Defenders of Wildlife,* fall 1998.

Wraiths

Although in the popular parlance a wraith has become another word for a ghost, it is actually a very special kind of ghostly manifestation. A wraith is a person's spiritual double (the German *doppelganger*) that may appear so lifelike that the witness to the phenomenon mistakes the apparition for the actual person. In folklore, when a wraith of an individual is perceived, it is an omen that the actual person represented by the manifestation has just died or soon will.

Modern parapsychology terms this phenomenon either a "crisis apparition" in which a recognized apparition is seen, heard, or felt when the individual represented by the image is undergoing a crisis, especially death; or a "postmortem apparition" in which a recognized apparition is seen or heard long after the person represented by the image has died.

There are instances when a person very much alive has encountered his *doppelganger*. Perhaps the most famous instance occurred to the great German poet Goethe, who had the astonishing experience of meeting himself as he rode away from visiting Frederika at Strassburg. The phantom wore a pike grey suit with gold lace that Goethe had never before seen. Eight years later, as he was on the same road going to visit Frederika, it suddenly occurred to Goethe that he was presently wearing the same suit that his phantom had been wearing on that earlier occasion.

Dr. Edward Podolsky has recorded the experience of a man from Chicago who returned home after a hard day at the office with a splitting migraine. As he sat down to dinner, he saw, sitting opposite him, an exact replica of himself. The astonishing double repeated every moment he made during the entire course of the meal. Since that time, the man has seen his double on a number of occasions—each time after an attack of migraine.

Samuel V. of Kansas City, Missouri, was startled to see an exact double of himself duplicating his every moment as he went about his gardening chores. The double was visible for about two hours.

Rather unsettling is the case of Mrs. Jeanie P. As she was applying makeup, she saw an exact duplicate of herself also touching *her* features. When she reached out to touch her double, the image also reached out to touch her. Mrs. P. swore that she actually felt her face being touched by her mysterious double.

Dr. Podolsky terms such phenomena "autoscopic hallucinations," and he offers two theories to explain them: The double seen is "the result of some irritating process in the brain," particularly of the parieto-temporal-occipital area [the visual area]; and the double seen is the result of the "projection of memory pictures" that have been stored in the brain. Dr. Podolsky maintains, "When conditions of stress or other unusual psychological situations arise, these memories may be projected outside the body as very real images."

SOURCES:
Podolsky, Dr. Edward. "Have You Seen Your Double?" *Fate,* April 1966.

Y-Pora

According to the legends of the Guaranies Indians of South America, the Y-Pora is a mysterious ghost that haunts the waterways. It can manifest as an amorphous cloud of mist drifting over the waters, but it can also appear as a half-human, half-fish creature.

SOURCES:
Picasso, Fabio. "South American Monsters & Mystery Animals. *Strange,* December 1998.

Yaksha

Among the magical, mythical kingdoms of the world, *Alaka,* hidden away in the Himalayas, is populated by the *yakshas*, nature spirits whose protection may be sought by humans who desire their guardianship for their city or village. Kubera, the chief ruler of the yakshas, sees to it that his followers first fulfill their basic duty of guarding treasures buried within the earth before they hire out to protect human enterprises. The female yakshas appear to human eyes as beautiful women bedecked with lavish and exquisite jewelry. Yakshas are generally considered to be benevolent entities, although it has been noted that offended or discontented female members of their kind may steal a human child and make a meal of it.

SOURCES:
Larousse Dictionary of World Folklore. New York: Larousse, 1995.

Yeren

After more than 200 reports of "wildman" sightings had been filed, an active search for China's *yeren* was begun in 1959. As is typical in such searches for

Bigfoot- and yeti-type creatures, casts of footprints, hair samples, and feces are plentiful, but no one has yet captured a yeren or obtained good photographs of the man-beast. In 1977, 1980, and 1982, expeditions searching for the man-beast set out to track down their quarry in the Shennongjia Forest Park in western Hubei province. In September 1993, a group of Chinese engineers claimed to have seen three yeren walking on trails in the Shennongjia Forest Park.

In October 1994, the Chinese government established the Committee for the Search of Strange and Rare Creatures, including among its members specialists in vertebrate paleontology and palaeanthropology.

A loose consensus among interested members from the Chinese Academy of Sciences maintains that the yeren are some species of unknown primates. The largest cast of an alleged wildman footprint is 16 inches long, encouraging estimates that the yeren itself would stand more than seven feet tall and weigh as much as 660 pounds. The scientific committee has also studied and examined eight hair specimens said to have come from yeren ranging through China and Tibet. The analyses of the hairs, varying in color from the black collected in Yunnan province and the white collected in Tibet to the reddish brown from Hubei, indicate a nonhuman source, but no known animal.

In April 1995, a yeren expedition 30 members strong led by Professor Yuan Zhengxin set out for the Hubei mountains. Although the enthusiastic Professor Zhengxin expressed confidence that the well-equipped group would capture a yeren within three years, by July most of the expedition members had returned to Beijing with little more than some possible hair samples to show for their three-month monster safari.

In January 1999, in spite of an official pronouncement from the Chinese Academy of Sciences that neither the **yeti** nor the yeren exist, anthropologist Zhou Guoxing reminds his colleagues that unidentifiable hair specimens and 16-inch casts of footprints had been found during scientific expeditions to the Shennongjia region. "Even if 95 percent of the reports on the existence of the wild man are not credible," Guoxing says, "it is necessary for scientists to study the remaining 5 percent."

SOURCES:

"China Bans Yeti-Hunting Safaris." Agence France Presse, 14 January, 1999.
"Man-Beast Hunts in the Far East." *Fortean Times,* October–November 1995.

Yeti

For centuries the people of the Himalayas have reported sightings of the *yeti,* a wild, humanlike creature that many researchers believe to be an unidentified species of ape. In 1920, due to a mistranslation of *yeti,* the Tibetan word for the mysterious creature, the term "**Abominable Snowman**" was coined as a general name for such unknown man-beasts around the world.

In August 1981, Soviet mountain climber Igor Tatsl told the *Moscow News Weekly* that he and his fellow climbers had seen a yeti and that they wished to attempt a "friendly, spontaneous contact" with the creature. Tatsl, a factory worker from Kiev, expressed his opinion that it was probably impossible to capture a yeti, but they hoped to make friends with one.

Tatsl went on to state that his team had made a plaster cast of an imprint of the yeti's foot that they had found on a tributary of the Varzog River. This particular river rushes through the Gissar Mountains in the Pamiro-Alai range of Tadzhik in Soviet Central Asia. In 1980, fellow climber Nina Grineva saw a yeti during a night vigil. Several other members of their expedition had also experienced eye-witness sightings.

Tatsl's considered opinion was that the yeti may quite likely be humankind's closest evolutionary relatives. He further believed that their senses were more highly developed than those of our species. "They may sense danger in our intentions," he says. "When they see us carrying cameras, flashes, or other equipment, we never sight them."

In his interview in the weekly news magazine, Tatsl reminds readers that Soviet scientists had sponsored serious efforts to track down the yeti for more than 20 years. Although each Russian province may have its own name for the mysterious giants of the mountain—in Dagestan, *kaptar;* in Azerbaijan, *mesheadam;* in Georgia, *tkys-katsi;* while the Chechens, Ingushes, Kabardins, and Balkars call it the *almasti* —each startled eyewitness seems to be describing the same strange beast.

In January 1999, Feng Zuoguian, a zoologist for the Chinese Academy of Sciences, announced through the state-run *China Daily* newspaper that China was officially proclaiming its firm opposition to any outsiders who attempted to organize safaris to capture the yeti. According to the official proclamation, members of the Chinese scientific community had debated the issue of the yeti's existence in December 1998 and decreed once and for all that the creature does not exist.

SOURCES:
"China Bans Yeti-Hunting Safaris." Agence France Presse, 14 January 1999.
Norman, Eric. *The Abominable Snowmen.* New York: Award Books, 1969.
Steiger, Brad. *Monsters Among Us.* New York: Berkley Books, 1989.

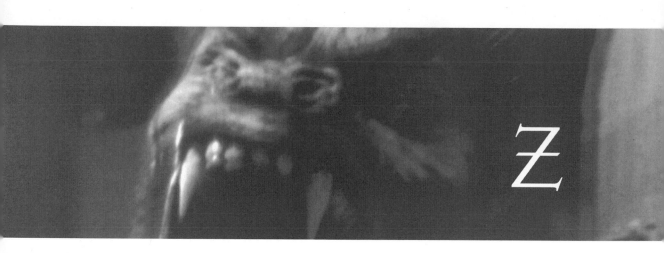

Zana

In 1964, Professor Boris Porshenev excavated the grave of a female "wild woman of the mountains," called an *almasti,* in the Caucasus Mountain region of Russia. According to Porshenev, the bones that he disinterred in the village of Tkhina were those of a female creature and his preliminary investigation of the skeleton determined that its skeletal structure was different from that of a female member of *Homo sapiens*.

Porshenev's discovery brought to mind the claims made c. 1864 by a man named Genaba who said that he returned to Tkhina with a bizarre gift from his friend Prince Achba, an avid sportsman, who had caught a humanlike female being while hunting in the woods. Genaba named the wild woman Zana, and he constructed a special hut for her made out of woven twigs and grasses.

At first he kept her guarded, but eventually Zana grew accustomed to people and was allowed to move about freely in the village. Genaba received Zana's full obedience, and he succeeded to some extent in domesticating her. He tutored her in the crafts of preparing firewood, carrying water, and toting sacks of grain. Zana was of an enormous and powerful build and was capable of tremendous physical labor.

The description of Zana that has come down over oral history appears to tally exactly with the great number of descriptions of the almasti that have been recorded over the past 200 years or more. Her body was covered with thick black hair, and she at first refused to wear clothing of any kind. It was only by exercising the greatest patience that Genaba was able to train Zana to wear a loincloth. However, no amount of patience or attempted schooling could teach Zana to talk. She seemed capable only of mumbling and squealing.

Cleanliness was not a problem with the wild woman. One of her favorite pastimes was her daily bath in the village spring that still bears her name. Winter or summer, Zana could be seen at her daily ritual of washing herself in the icy water.

Zana also enjoyed gathering rocks and attempting to chip them. When the creature had completed her regular duties on Genaba's estate, she would scurry off to her favorite rocks and spend hours arranging them into piles and attempting to chip them in a particular manner that seemed to have some special significance for her.

Elderly residents of the village maintained that while in captivity, Zana gave birth to five children. If true, the implications of Zana's having bred with men of the village are really quite staggering. If the wild woman truly did conceive with human males, then she was not an ape.

Of course the stories of Zana's children may only be legend, added bits of fantasy to make the take of the wild woman even more remarkable as it was told and retold through decades of long, cold Caucasus winters. According to the villagers, four of the children died before their mother, and the fifth answered the shrill call of his mother's people and fled to the mountains.

Zana died in the 1880s and was mourned by the entire village of Tkhina. She had been a gentle creature, amiable in manner and devoted to her master Genaba. Her bones lay forgotten outside the village until the persistent Professor Boris Porshenev unearthed them for examination.

During World War II, Dr. V. S. Karapetyan, a lieutenant-colonel in the medical service of the Soviet army, reported that an infantry battalion near Buinaksk captured a wildman and did not have any idea what to do with him. Dr. Karapetyan was summoned to examine the creature and to give his medical opinion as to whether the soldiers had encountered some strange, wild creature or whether they had apprehended some fantastically disguised secret agent.

When the doctor arrived at the camp, he was informed that the prisoner was kept in a cold shed because he sweated so profusely and seemed to become ill in a warm room. Dr. Karapetyan found the subject in question to appear to be a naked human in form, male, and covered with a shaggy dark brown hair.

According to his report, he said that the man-beast stood erect with his arms hanging, and his height above average. "He stood before me like a giant, his mighty chest thrust forward. His fingers were thick and strong, and exceptionally large. His eyes told me nothing. They were dull and empty—the eyes of an animal. And he seemed to me like some kind of animal and nothing more."

Dr. Karapetyan told the military authorities that their prisoner was no disguised spy, but a "wild man of some kind." The doctor returned to his unit and said that he never again heard anything about the strange prisoner.

SOURCES:

Norman, Eric. *The Abominable Snowmen.* New York: Award Books, 1969.

Zingua

Queen Zingua of Angola, who came to power in 1632, was one of **Donatien Alphonse Francois de Sade**'s favorite historical personages. He most admired her for her ability to extract three pleasures from every man she took as a lover: 1) she witnessed the defeat and death of his opponent in hand-to-hand combat; 2) she commanded his energetic performance on her royal couch; 3) after she had taken her pleasure, she watched him tortured to death.

The African Queen on her bloody throne had everything that a sadist would admire and envy. She had complete control of life and death over her subjects; she could order hideous tortures and executions for the most minor infractions of her decrees; and she was responsible to no other authority than her own. She was completely free to torture and torment, poison and persecute, beat and burn whomever she wished. Although none can dispute Zingua's cruelty and her **cannibalism,** neither can they dispute the fact that she remains as one of the most outstanding monarchs in Africa's history. Some historians have ranked her as an equal to that other famous African Queen, Cleopatra. But movie producers aren't likely to film an epic detailing Zingua's life and loves—not unless it is a horror film.

Tall, darkly beautiful with a regal bearing, she had little difficulty gathering accomplices to help remove her brother the king from power. In an effort to eliminate the male competition in the royal bloodline, the king had previously executed his elder brother and Zingua's son. He should never have underestimated the power of his sister, who had him assassinated in 1632 so that she might ascend to the throne. A devoted respecter of the tradition of ancestor worship, Zingua vetoed the suggestion put forth by one of her advisors that the king's body should be thrown to the jackals. She solemnly announced that she would dry her brother's bones and keep them in a silver box. She and her sorcerers would use them to help guide her important decisions in ruling Angola.

Once a neighboring chieftain, who had little use for a matriarchy, openly accused her of having murdered her brother. Zingua did not bother to deny the charge, but insisted that her brother bore her no ill will. To prove such a claim, she ordered her sorcerers to unpack the oft-consulted bones from the silver box and to arrange them in a magic circle. According to the story, the skull spoke to the chief and his representatives from the neighboring kingdom and told them to continue to trade with the queen. "It is true she murdered me," the skull admitted with a sigh, "but she makes a far better ruler than I ever would have."

Although Zingua's penchant for torturing her lovers to death was well known, it is also a matter of record that she kept a "harem" of men in her royal entourage. She referred to her corral of captive lovers as her "wives," and they were always on call to satisfy her desires. The queen's sexual appetites were matched only by her appetite for human flesh. One court holiday alone required the flesh of 113 children to prepare one of her favorite delicacies.

In keeping with her own view of personal morality, the capricious queen passed a law that commanded all women in her kingdom to be available to any man who might ask, but, at the same time, it was forbidden that any woman should become pregnant outside of wedlock. And Zingua put real teeth into her laws. Her emissaries traveled the entire kingdom and saw to it that every unwed mother was pounded or ground to death in huge mortars. She once told a shocked Portuguese missionary that there were two things in her kingdom which were strictly forbidden: virginity and unwed mothers.

The missionaries were constantly working on Zingua to convert to Christianity, and finally she allowed herself to be baptized. Although the teachings of the gentle Jesus seem far removed from the cruel queen's worship of ancestors and primitive forces, as a matter of political expediency to get the Portuguese off her back, Zingua loudly proclaimed herself a Christian, but continued her worship of idols. It was not until her late seventies that Zingua proclaimed that she had undergone a true conversion. She adopted the Christian name of Dona Ana de Souza, and she scattered all the members of her harem except for one young man whom she married with the church's blessing.

Her subjects had now come full circle under the reign of their ever-zealous Zingua, who so ardently embraced whatever cause she was currently preaching. Whereas it was once punishable by death to remain a virgin in her kingdom, the death penalty was now invoked if a young bride were not a virgin. Whereas human flesh was one the *piece de resistance* of every feast day, anyone who indulged in a little "sweet meat" would have his lips and tongue sliced off.

Dona Ana de Souza, alias Zingua, died at the age of 80 and was borne to her final resting place on a bower of multicolored flowers. Some of those who attended her funeral said that the smooth placidity of the queen's still royal countenance was broken only by a saintly, beatific smile. Others described it as somewhat more mischievous and devilish.

SOURCES:

Masters, R. E. L. and Eduard Lea. *Perverse Crimes in History.* New York: Julian Press, 1963.
Steiger, Brad. *Fatal Females.* Chicago: Merit Books, 1965.

Zombies, like the one shown on the right (from the 1958 film *How to Make a Monster*), have been linked to the werewolf legend.

Zodiac

Every so many years police officers across the nation ask themselves whether or not the mysterious, almost supernatural mass murderer, Zodiac, has returned from whatever nether region he inhabits and come to their city to select new victims. "Zodiac," like "**Jack the Ripper,**" is an appellation that has been given to an unknown werewolf-like sadistic murderer, who, also like the anonymous "Jack," has inspired a good many copycat killers. The original Zodiac terrorized the San Francisco Bay area for more than three years, employing what appeared to be some monstrous murder-by-chance process in the selection of at least 10 victims.

As far as we know, one of Zodiac's first murders occurred on the night of December 20, 1968, when a young teenaged couple from Vallejo, California, were returning home after attending a concert in San Francisco. Bettilou

Jensen, 16, and her companion, Thomas Faraday, 17, parked near a lake reservoir about 11:00 P.M. A half-hour later, their bodies were found by a passing motorist. Faraday had been shot through the head. Jensen, who had apparently attempted to escape, was found about 30 feet from the car. She had been shot five times in the back. There were no clues as to who killed them or what the possible motive might have been.

On the evening of July 4, 1969, a 22-year-old waitress and her boyfriend parked beside the shores of Lake Herman, near Vallejo. Suddenly a fusillade of bullets ripped into the parked car. The young woman was killed instantly. Her date was wounded by four nine-millimeter slugs. After many weeks of critical surgery, he survived.

Shortly after he had attacked the couple on the shore of Lake Herman, Zodiac called the police and taunted them by announcing his deed and telling them where they would find the bodies. Pleased with his bloody work, Zodiac laughed as he explained how he had riddled the couple with nine-millimeter bullets. The murderer had now begun his campaign of terror in full force. Again and again the authorities were to hear his diabolical laughter as the phantom killer telephoned information about his latest grisly slayings. It would not be long before the police realized that they were dealing with a vicious mass murderer with deep roots in the occult.

Taking a leaf from Jack the Ripper's scrapbook of sadism, Zodiac also began to write letters to the city's newspapers. In a letter to the *San Francisco Chronicle*, he cruelly suggested that school children made such nice targets. "I think I will just wipe out a school bus some morning," he wrote. "I'll just shoot out the tires and pick off the kiddies as they come bouncing out."

Officially, the authorities credited five deaths to Zodiac, but then there was his initial letter to a newspaper that stated: "My name is Zodiac! I've killed 10 people. I will kill more!" His "signature" was a cross within a circle, an insignia taken from the Egyptian *Book of the Dead*, where it was used as a symbol of death.

The police could determine no sensible sequence to his actions. Zodiac was completely unpredictable, although the authorities began to suspect that his murders were being scheduled according to some special interpretation that he was giving to the astrological signs. In certain of his letters, Zodiac claimed that he was killing select individuals to serve as his slaves in the afterlife. Some of his correspondence with the authorities also included hieroglyphics from South American Indian cultures and dead civilizations in Asia and Africa. It was quite obvious that Zodiac had an excellent knowledge of mythology and ancient history.

Eventually Zodiac was seen near the scene of one of his terrible crimes, and witnesses were able to provide a partial description. Zodiac is probably a Caucasian male of medium height with red hair. He is huskily built, weighing approximately 200 pounds. At that time, he appeared to be in his mid-thirties, making him in his mid-sixties today. He wore his hair in the crew-cut style popular in the late 1950s, and some witnesses swore that they heard his voice, which they described as slightly high-pitched.

In the opinion of the police psychiatrists, Zodiac stalked his human prey because he enjoyed playing God. He may also have been killing innocent people to avenge a real or imagined rejection by society. In certain of his statements to the media, Zodiac admitted that he suffered recurrent headaches that were nearly unbearable. Perhaps it was such a condition that drove him to a killing frenzy.

The police hoped that they had at last received a break in the case when they were able to link the murderous phantom of the night with the brutal slaying of beautiful, 18-year-old Cheri Jo Bates, a college coed in Riverside, California, that had occurred two years before the reign of terror had begun in San Francisco. After a session of study in the campus library at Riverside College, Bates was abducted from her car (which had been sabotaged so it would not run), savagely beaten, and stabbed. Her mutilated body was found in a ditch.

Shortly after the senseless slaughter of the young coed, a newspaper in Riverside received a typewritten confession of the murder. Pounded out in capital letters, the investigators reviewing the case noticed the similarity of the prose to the style in which Zodiac taunted the police in his epistles to the media. A condensed and edited version of what was probably Zodiac's first public declaration is quoted herewith. Spelling and grammatical errors have been corrected and lurid phrases have been deleted:

> She was young and beautiful, but now she is dead and battered. She is not the first, and she will not be the last.
>
> I lie awake nights, thinking about my next victim. Maybe she will be that beautiful little blonde that babysits near the little store and walks down the dark alley each evening about seven. Or maybe it will be the shapely, blue-eyed brunette that said no when I asked her for a date in high school. But maybe it will not be either one.
>
> Don't make it easy for me. Keep your sisters, daughters, and wives off the streets or alleys or . . . .
>
> [Cheri Jo Bates] went to the slaughter like a lamb. She did not put up a struggle, but I did. First I pulled the middle wire from the distributor [on her car], then I waited for her in the library and followed her out after about two minutes. The battery must have been dead by then. I offered to help. She was then very willing to talk with me. I told her that my car was down the street and that I would give her a lift home.

When we were away from the library, walking, I said that it was about time. She asked me, "About time for what?" I said, "It's about time for you to die." I grabbed her around the neck with my hand over her mouth and my other hand with a small knife at her throat.

I am not sick. I am insane, but that will not stop the game. Beware, I am stalking *your* girls now!

A month after the letter was received by the newspaper, a janitor in the college library discovered what may have been another clue relating to the killing of Cheri Jo Bates. At first the poem appeared to be a meaningless jumble of words that had been scratched into an old desk top by some sophomoric student who valued his artistic expression above vandalism. Later, police investigators thought otherwise. The poem, quite likely scrawled with knife point as he waited for Bates in the library, reads as follows:

Living
Unwilling to Die
cut
Clean.
If red!
blood spurting, dripping, spilling
all over her new dress.
Oh well,
it was red anyway.
Life draining into an uncertain death,
she won't die this time,
someone will find her.
Just wait till
next time.

The poem had been signed with the letters "rh." Investigators wondered if that could be the initials of Zodiac's name or if his preoccupation with the blood of his victims led him to sign "rh" for the "rh factor" in blood. Eerily, the evidence that linked the killing of Cheri Jo Bates with Zodiac meant that the confident, boastful murderer had already eluded police for two years before he began his rampage against the women of San Francisco.

Crafty, cunning, a diabolical genius, Zodiac openly left a number of intriguing clues to his true identity. While admitting his insanity, Zodiac stated that he would continue his "game" of murder as long as possible. To date, 30 years after his trail of terror in San Francisco, no one has deciphered the meaning of the cryptic clues he left behind or captured the monster in his lair.

Could the murderer have decided to halt his crimes of his own accord? That seems unlikely. He enjoyed too much the game of killing, the mystique of being a night-stalking werewolf with occult powers. He may well have decided to move elsewhere, however, and play his murderous game in another city under another persona. Or, possibly, he is serving a prison sentence for some other crime. At any rate, thus far the "Zodiacs" who emerge in various cities from time to time are copycat werewolf killers who attempt to adapt his mystical tools of astrology and the occult to their own sick crimes.

SOURCES:

Lane, Brian. *Forces from Beyond.* New York: Avon Books, 1997.

Steiger, Brad, and Sherry Hansen Steiger. *Demon Deaths.* New York: Berkley Publishing, 1991.

Zombie

The zombie, those dread creatures of the undead who prowl about at night doing the bidding of the dark priests of **voodoo,** are a well-known element of jungle **sorcery** and folklore.

Some impressionable writers and tourists have perpetuated the myth of the zombie after they witnessed an elaborate Haitian funeral. At the conclusion of a series of rituals, the *hungan*, the priest-practitioner of voodoo, waves away spectators and approaches the corpse for the purpose of setting the *loa*, the guardian spirit, free from its former physical servant. The hungan straddles the corpse—and at his sharp command, the cadaver appears to raise its head and shoulders in a convulsive shudder.

Sincere eyewitnesses have testified to seeing a dead body suddenly sit up and release its spirit. Other reports have told of seeing the hungan jerk the body upright with his own hands. Mystical hanky-panky on the priest's part is not intended, according to some authorities on voodoo. The entire ritual is to be regarded as symbolical.

Voodoo lore actually has two types of zombie—the undead and those who died by violence. Haitians are very cautious in their approach to a cemetery, for it is there that one is most likely to encounter the unfortunate **wraiths** who died violently and without adequate time for a proper ritual.

There is a third spirit who may be classified as a zombie—that of a woman who died a virgin. A terrible fate awaits her at the hands of the lustful Baron Samedi, Master of the Netherworld.

For those who embrace the teachings of voodoo, the zombie, the living dead, are to be feared as very real instruments of the hungan who have yielded to the seduction of evil and allowed themselves to be possessed by negative loa and become practitioners of dark side sorcery. It is as terrible a thing to become a zombie as it is to become one of its victims. The dead are meant to rest, not to be forced to prowl around at night as slaves doing the bidding of dark sorcerers.

The ritual that creates a zombie demands that the sorcerer unearths a chosen corpse and wafts under its nose a bottle containing the deceased's soul. Then, as if he were fanning a tiny spark of fire in dry tinder, the sorcerer nurtures the spark of life in the corpse until he has fashioned a zombie.

In Haiti the deceased are often buried face downward by considerate relatives so the corpse cannot hear the summons of the sorcerer. Some even take the precaution of providing their dearly departed with a weapon, such as a machete, with which to ward off the evil hungan.

Haiti is filled with terrible tales of the zombie. One hears eyewitness accounts from those who have discovered friends or relatives, supposedly long-dead, laboring in the fields of some sorcerer. One story that made the rounds a few years back had the zombied corpse of a former government administrator—officially dead for 15 years—toiling for an old hungan in a remote village in the hills.

Upon investigation, many of these zombie often are found to be idiots, imbeciles, or persons suffering from mental problems who only resemble the alleged deceased victim of voodoo. Certain investigators have made a strong case for the fact that it would not be terribly difficult for an unscrupulous hungan to take advantage of someone with mental problems or deficiencies and turn them into virtual zombie.

On the other hand, it may well be that the voodoo priests centuries ago discovered the secret and the utilization of many powerful drugs that could produce a deep state of lethargy in a victim and erode the will to resist. Such application of hypnotic drugs could produce the blank-eyed, shuffling, obedient zombie.

Or even worse, perhaps centuries ago voodoo priests discovered the terrible secret of the reanimation of corpses, thus fulfilling all the awful requirement of the making of a true zombie.

If you should be confronted with what you feel is the genuine article—not a lunatic, not a moron, not a drug-enslaved wretch—be assured that the zombie is generally docile unless you should happen to give it some salt. Even a single grain of salt will penetrate the sorcerer's spell, and the zombie will suddenly realize that it is a corpse without a grave. With this terrifying knowledge erupting in it shriveled brain, it will go berserk in its attempt to return to its burial place. According to voodoo legend, nothing can stop it—surely not you!

SOURCES:

Huxley, Francis. *The Invisibles: Voodoo Gods in Haiti.* New York: McGraw-Hill, 1966.
Steiger, Brad. *Monsters Among Us.* New York: Berkley Books, 1989.

WEREWOLF RESOURCES

The Werewolf Resources gathers together information that is currently available on werewolves in a number of mediums. Included is a guide to sites on the World Wide Web; a list of novels and other works of fiction that feature a werewolf, werewolves, or other shapeshifters as a central part of the plot; a list of nonfiction works about werewolves and other lycanthropes; and a filmography that covers —with descriptions, whenever possible—every werewolf or shapeshifting film of note in the twentieth century.

Web Sites

Crystalinks Shape Shifters
http://www.crystalinks.com/shape_shifters.html

Darke Dreams
http://home.it.net.au/~darke/

Foxy's Alternate Realty
http://www.cymax.com/wolf/index.shtml

GarouMush
http://www.garoumush.org/garoumush/

Halloween Maven
http://www.halloweenmaven.com/werewolves.htm

Halloween on the Web
http://www.halloween.com/witch.html

Hellsgate Werewolves
http://www.hellsgate.com/

Horror Awaits
http://members.aol.com/Horror25/EEindex.html

Lycanthrope
http://www.lycanthrope.org:4242/

Lycanthropes and Furries
http://webhome.idirect.com/~twessner/index.html

The Lycanthropic Book List
http://doncaster.on.ca/%7Evampyre/lists/listb010.html

Monsterland
http://www.monsterland.com/index1.htm

Mysts of Darkness
http://www.vampyra.com/index1.htm

Mythology Web
http://www.mythologyweb.com/

Nightmare Factory
http://www.nightmarefactory.com/vampire.html

Of Weres & Wolves
http://www.best.com/%7Ebrokken/wernwolf.htm

Paraweb Online
http://theparaweb.com/Creatures/
Werewolves/

Real Werewolves
http://members.aol.com/Spidey481/

Shadow Realms
http://shadowrealms.org/

Vampires, Werewolves and other Nasties
http://www.pibburns.com/vampires.htm

Weres and Wolves
http://www.timberwolf.org/wernwolf.htm

The WereWeb
http://www.swampfox.demon.co.uk/
utlah/humour/

Werewolf: The Apocalypse
http://www.ascgames.com/werewolf/

Werewolf Legends from Germany
http://www.pitt.edu/~dash/
werewolf.html

Werewolf Links
http://www.malcop.u-net.com/
werwolf.htm

The Werewolf Page
http://www.rscreations.com/werewolf/
index2.html

Werewolves
http://gwis.circ.gwu.edu/~humsci/wolf.
html

Werewolves and Beyond
http://www.geocities.com/Area51/Cav-
ern/5037/index.html

Werewolves—Lycanthropy
http://www.crystalinks.com/werewolves.
html

Werewolves Myth and Legend
http://w1.303.telia.com/~u30305356/
Werewolves.html

Werewolves on the Web
http://theo6.physik.uni-
siegen.de/bock/wwolves.html

Werewolves in Suburbia
http://www.werewolves.org/

White Wolf
http://www.white-wolf.com/

WolfFang's Night Retreat
http://204.133.195.2/users/wolffang/

Works of Fiction

Adams, Douglas. *The Long Dark Tea-Time of the Soul*. New York: Pocket Books, 1991.

Ahern, Jerry & Sharon Ahern. *Were-wolveSS*. New York: Pinnacle, 1990.

Ahlberg, Allan. *Woof!* New York: Viking, 1986.

Akers, Alan B. *Werewolves of Kregen*. New York: New American Library, 1985.

Aldiss, Brian. *Helliconia Spring*. New York: Berkely, 1984.

———. *Helliconia Winter*. New York: Berkley, 1987.

———. *Helliconia Summer*. New York: Berkley, 1988.

Almquist, Gregg. *Wolf Kill*. New York: Pocket Books, 1985.

Anderson, Poul. *Brain Wave*. New York: Ballantine, 1985.

———. *Operation Chaos*. New York: Baen, 1992.

Anthony, Piers. *Split Infinity*. New York: Ballantine, 1987.

———. *Robot Adept*. New York: Ace Books, 1989.

———. *Unicorn Point*. New York: Ace Books, 1990.

———. *Blue Adept*. New York: Ballantine, 1991.

———. *Juxtaposition*. New York: Ballantine, 1991.

———. *Out of Phaze*. New York: Ace Books, 1994.

———. *Phaze Doubt*. New York: Ace Books, 1994.

Barker, Clive. *Cabal*. New York: Pocket Books, 1989.

Barnes, Steven. *The Kundalini Equation*. New York: Tor, 1986.

Bassingthwaite, Don. *Breathe Deeply*. White Wolf Books, 1995.

Baum, Frank L. *The Lost Princess of Oz*. New York: Ballantine, 1990.

Beagle, Peter S. *The Innkeeper's Song*. New York: New American Library, 1994.

Bell, Clare. *The Jaguar Princess*. New York: Tor, 1994.

Boyd, Donna. *The Passion*. New York: Avon Books, 1998.

Cadnum, Michael. *Saint Peter's Wolf*. New York: Carroll & Graf, 1991.

Caine, Geoffrey. *Wake of the Werewolf*. New York: Diamond, 1991.

Callahan, Jay. *Night of the Wolf*. New York: Leisure Books, 1979.

Case, David. *Wolf Tracks*. New York: Leisure Books, 1984.

Chronister, Alan B. *Cry Wolf*. New York: Zebra Books, 1987.

Collins, Nancy A. *Walking Wolf*. Mark V. Ziesing Books, 1995.

Danvers, Dennis. *Wilderness*. New York: Pocket Star, 1992.

David, Peter. *Howling Mad*. New York: Ace Books, 1989.

Davis, Brett. *Hair of the Dog*. New York: Baen, 1997.

Dawson, Saranne. *Secrets of the Wolf*. New York: Leisure Books, 1998.

———. *Heart of the Wolf*. New York: Leisure Books, 1993.

de Lint, Charles. *Wolf Moon*. New York: Signet, 1988.

Dean, Pamela. *The Dubious Hills*. New York: Tor, 1995.

———. *Tam Lin*. New York: Tor, 1992.

Deitz, Tom. *Stoneskin's Revenge*. New York: Avon, 1991.

DiSilvestro, Roger. *Ursula's Gift*. New York: Donald I. Fine, 1988.

Doyle, Debra and James MacDonald. *Hunter's Moon*. New York: Berkley Books, 1995.

Dreadstone, Carl. *The Werewolf of London*. New York: Berkley Books, 1977.

Endore, Guy. *The Werewolf of Paris*. New York: Citadel, 1992.

Ergas, Elizabeth. *The Shapechanger*. New York: Pinnacle, 1989.

Flanders, Rebecca. *Secret of the Wolf*. Harlequin, 1995.

Forsythe, Richard. *Fangs*. New York: Leisure Books, 1985.

Franklin, Pat. *Embrace of the Wolf*. New York: Diamond, 1993.

George, Stephen R. *Dark Reunion*. New York: Zebra Books, 1990.

Goddin, Jeffrey. *Blood of the Wolf*. New York: Leisure Books, 1987.

Grant, Charles L. *The Dark Cry of the Moon*. New York: Berkley Books, 1987.

———. *Watcher*. New York: Harper Prism Books, 1997.

Green, Sharon. *Hellhound Magic: The Far Side of Forever 2*. New York: DAW Books, 1989.

Greenburg, Martin H., ed. *Werewolves*. New York: DAW Books, 1995.

Hautala, Rick. *Moondeath*. New York: Kensington, 1986.

Hodge, Brian. *Nightlife*. New York: Dell Books, 1991.

Hodgell, P. C. *Dark of the Moon*. New York: Berkley Books, 1987.

Holt, John R. *Wolf Moon*. New York: Bantam Books, 1997.

Housman, Clement *The Werewolf*. Arno Press, 1976.

Huff, Tanya. *Blood Trail*. New York: DAW Books, 1997.

Keesey, Pam ed. *Women Who Run with the Werewolves*. Cleis Press, 1996.

Kelly, Ronald. *Moon of the Werewolf*. New York: Zebra/Kensington, 1991.

King, Stephen. *Cycle of the Werewolf*. New York: New American Library, 1989.

———. *It*. New York: Signet, 1987.

Klause, Annette Curtis. *Blood and Chocolate*. New York: Delacorte Press, 1997.

Koontz, Dean. *Midnight*. New York: Berkley Books, 1995.

Krinard, Susan. *Prince of Wolves*. New York: Bantam Books, 1994.

Krueger, Terry. *Night Cries*. New York: Dell Books, 1985.

LeGuin, Ursula K. *A Wizard of Earthsea*. New York: Bantam Books, 1975.

Lee, Tanith. *Heart-Beast*. London: Headline Books, 1992.

Levy, Edward. *The Beast Within*. New York: Berkley Books, 1981.

Martindale, Chris T. *Where the Chill Waits*. New York: Warner Books, 1991.

Massa, Jack. *Mooncrow*. New York: Berkley Books, 1979.

Masterton, Graham. *Prey*. New York: Mandarin Books, 1992.

McCammon, Robert. *The Wolf's Hour*. New York: Pocket Books, 1989.

Moore, James A. *Hell-Storm*. New York: Harper Prism, 1996.

Murphy, Pat. *Nadya*. New York: Tor Books, 1996.

Murray, Doug. *Call to Battle*. New York: White Wolf Books, 1996.

Norton, Andre. *Fur Magic*. New York: Signet Books, 1988.

Packard, Edward. *Night of the Werewolf*. New York: Bantam Books, 1995.

Pascal, Francine. *Love and Death in London*. New York: Bantam Books, 1994.

———. *Date with a Werewolf*. New York: Bantam Books, 1994.

———. *Beware the Wolfman*. New York: Bantam Books, 1994.

Paxson, Diana L. *The Wolf and the Raven*. New York: Avon Books, 1994.

Peel, John. *Dances with Werewolves*. Archway, 1995.

Philbrick, W.R. *Night Creature*. New York: Scholastic Books, 1996.

———. *Children of the Wolf*. New York: Scholastic Books, 1996.

———. *The Wereing*. New York: Scholastic Books, 1996.

Powers, Tim. *The Anubis Gates*. New York: Ace Books, 1983.

Preiss, Byron, ed. *The Ultimate Werewolf*. New York: Dell Books, 1991.

Pronzini, Bill, ed. *Werewolf*. New York: Harper & Row, 1980.

Ramsay, Jay. *Night of the Claw*. New York: Tor Books, 1996.

Robbins, David. *The Wereling*. New York: Leisure Books, 1983.

———. *The Wrath*. New York: Leisure Books, 1988.

Saberhagen, Fred. *Dancing Bears*. New York: Tor Books, 1996.

Sackett, Jeffrey. *Mark of the Werewolf*. New York: Bantam Books, 1990.

Scotch, Cheri. *The Werewolf's Kiss*. New York: Diamond, 1992.

————. *The Werewolf's Touch*. New York: Diamond, 1993.

————. *The Werewolf's Sin*. New York: Diamond, 1994.

Shinn, Sharon. *The Shape-Changer's Wife*. New York: Ace Books, 1995.

Skipp, John and Craig Spector. *Animals*. New York: Bantam Books, 1993.

Somtow, S.P. *Moon Dance*. New York: Tor Books, 1989.

Stableford, Brian. *The Werewolves of London*. London: Pan Books, 1990.

Strieber, Whitley. *The Wolfen*. New York: Dell Books, 1992.

Tan, Cecelia. *The Beast Within: Erotic Tales of Werewolves*. Circlet Press, 1994.

Tem, Melanie. *Wilding*. New York: Dell Abyss, 1992.

Tessier, Thomas. *The Nightwalker*. New York: Berkley Books, 1989.

Toombs, Jane. *Under the Shadow*. New York: New American Library, 1992.

————. *Gathering Darkness*. New York: New American Library, 1993.

Van Belkom, Edo. *Wyrm Wolf*. New York: Harper Prism, 1995.

van Vogt, A.E. *The Silkie*. New York: Ace Books, 1969.

Vance, Steve. *The Hyde Effect*. New York: Leisure Books, 1986.

————. *Shapes*. New York: Leisure Books, 1991.

Vaughn, Evelyn. *Waiting for the Wolf Moon*. Harlequin, 1993.

Vinge, Joan. *Ladyhawke*. New York: Signet, 1985.

Vinicoff, Eric. *The Weighter*. New York: Baen, 1992.

Von Allman, Stewart. *Conspicuous Consumption*. New York: Harper Prism, 1995.

Weaver, Michael D. *Wolf-Dreams*. New York: Avon Books, 1987.

Weick, Stewart, ed. *When Will You Rage?*. White Wolf Books, 1994.

Weinberg, Robert. *The Devil's Auction*. New York: Leisure Books, 1988.

Whitten, Leslie H. *Moon of the Wolf*. New York: Leisure Books, 1992.

Williamson, Jack. *Darker Than You Think*. New York: Dell Books, 1979.

Wind, D. M. *The Others*. New York: Leisure Books, 1993.

Wolfe, Gene. *Soldier of the Mist*. New York: Tor Books, 1986.

Woods, Jack. *Wolffile*. New York: Pageant Books, 1988.

Yarboro, Chelsea Quinn. *The Godforsaken*. New York: Warner Books, 1989.

————. *Beastnights*. New York: Warner Books, 1989.

Yolen, Jane, ed. *Shape Shifters*. New York: Clarion Seabury, 1978.

———— and Martin H. Greenbburg, eds. *Werewolves*. New York: Harper & Row, 1988.

THE ANIMORPH SERIES

Described as an *X-Files* for kids, *The Animorph* series tells the tales of Jake, Rachel, Cassie, Tobias, and Marco, who can "morph" into any animal they touch, thus enabling them to combat an alien threat to Earth.

Applegate, Katherine A. *The Invasion (No. 1)*. New York: Scholastic Books, 1996.

————. *The Visitor (No. 2)*. New York: Scholastic Books, 1996.

————. *The Encounter (No. 3)*. New York: Scholastic Books, 1996.

————. *The Message (No. 4)*. New York: Scholastic Books, 1996..

———. *The Predator (No. 5)*. New York: Scholastic Books, 1996

———. *The Capture (No. 6)*. New York: Scholastic Books, 1997.

———. *The Stranger (No. 7)*. New York: Scholastic Books, 1997.

———. *The Alien (No. 8)*. New York: Scholastic Books, 1997.

———. *The Secret (No. 9)*. New York: Scholastic Books, 1997.

———. *The Android (No. 10)*. New York: Scholastic Books, 1997.

———. *The Forgotten (No. 11)*. New York: Scholastic Books, 1997.

———. *The Reaction (No. 12)*. New York: Scholastic Books, 1997.

———. *The Change (No. 13)*. New York: Scholastic Books, 1997.

———. *The Unknown (No. 14)*. New York: Scholastic Books, 1998.

———. *The Escape (No. 15)*. New York: Scholastic Books, 1998.

———. *The Warning (No. 16)*. New York: Scholastic Books, 1998.

———. *The Underground (No. 17)*. New York: Scholastic Books, 1998.

———. *The Decision (No. 18)*. New York: Scholastic Books, 1998.

———. *The Departure (No. 19)*. New York: Scholastic Books, 1998.

———. *The Discovery (No. 20)*. New York: Scholastic Books, 1998.

———. *The Threat (No. 21)*. New York: Scholastic Books, 1998.

———. *The Solution (No. 22)*. New York: Scholastic Books, 1998.

———. *The Pretender (No. 23)*. New York: Scholastic Books, 1998.

———. *The Suspicion (No. 24)*. New York: Scholastic Books, 1998.

———. *The Extreme (No. 25)*. New York: Scholastic Books, 1999.

Nonfiction Works

Adams, Douglas. *The Beast Within: A History of the Werewolf*. New York: Avon Books, 1992.

Andrews, Ted. *Spirit Masks and the Art of Shapeshifting*. Life Magic, 1998.

Cohen, Daniel. *Werewolves*. Cobblehill, 1996.

Cooper, Basil. *The Werewolf in Legend, Fact, and Art.* 1977

Douglas, Drake. *Horror!* New York: Collier Books, 1966.

Eisler, Robert. *Man into Wolf*. London: Spring Books, circa 1950.

Gould, Baring. *The Book of the Werewolves*. London, 1865.

Hurwood, Bernardt J. *Vampires, Werewolves, and Ghouls*. New York: Ace Books, 1968.

———. *Terror by Night*. New York: Lancer Books, 1963.

Jamal, Michele. *Deerdancer: The Shapeshifter Archetype in Story & in Trance*. New York: Viking Pen, 1995.

Kriss, Marika. *Werewolves, Shapeshifters & Skinwalkers*. [NEED PUB DETAILS]

Masters, R.E.L. and Eduard Lea. *Perverse Crimes in History*. New York: The Julian Press, 1963.

Noll, Richard (ed.) *Vampires, Werewolves, and Demons: Twentieth Century Reports in the Psychiatric Literature*. 1992.

———. *Bizarre Diseases of the Mind*. New York: Berkley Books, 1990.

Otten, Charlotte F. *A Lycanthropy Reader: Werewolves in Western Culture*. Syracuse: Syracuse University Press, 1986.

Spence, Lewis. *An Encyclopedia of Occultism*. New Hyde Park, NY: University Books, 1960.

Steiger, Brad. *Demon Lovers: Cases of Possession, Vampires, and Werewolves*. New Brunswick, NJ: Inner Light, 1987.

Summers, Montague. *The Werewolf*. London: Kegan Paul, 1933.

Warren, Ed and Lorraine Warren. *Werewolf: A True Story of Demonic Possession*. New York: St. Martin's, 1993.

Werewolf and Shapeshifter Filmography

The werewolf and shapeshifter filmography is a concerted effort to include all commercially released movies that feature a werewolf or a shapeshifter as the central character or a key character integral to the plot. The filmography also includes a wide variety of other were-creatures, including those morphing entities that come from outer space.

Entries are listed alphabetically. Each entry contains the name of the film, a brief description of the plot (when available), and other names by which the film was released. Additional information includes (where known) the date of the original release; whether the film is black and white (**B**) or in color (**C**); the country of origin; the production company [in brackets]; principal cast members and the director. If no country is listed, the film was produced in the United States.

Abbott and Costello Meet Frankenstein

The classic Universal monsters had lain dormant for three years when someone had the inspired idea to team the Big Three of Monsterdom—Frankenstein's Monster, the Wolf Man, and Dracula—with the popular comics Bud Abbott and Lou Costello. When the formula proved successful, it wasn't long before the two comedians had resurrected more monsters than Dr. Frankenstein could ever have imagined, for their meeting of the Big Three produced such sequels as *Abbott and Costello Meet the Invisible Man [1951], . . . Dr. Jekyll and Mr. Hyde [1953], . . . the Mummy [1955]*.

1948 B [Universal] **Cast:** Bud Abbott, Lou Costello, Bela Lugosi, Lon Chaney Jr., Glenn Strange, Lenore Aubert, Jane Randolph. **Director:** Charles T. Barton.

Adventures of a Two-Minute Werewolf

A charming film based on the children's book by Gene De Weese in which a 13-year-old turns into a werewolf.

1985 C [Video] **Director:** Mark Cullingham.

The Alligator People

Even when they have the most noble of intentions, reclusive scientists with experimental serums are to be carefully watched—and probably avoided altogether. In this film, the fine character actor George Mcready is the scientist who believes that his alligator extract will bring renewed strength to accident victims. Tragically, the miracle cure only brings an unwanted transformation to an alligator creature to a newly-wed Richard Crane. Lon Chaney Jr. does not morph into any kind of werebeast, but he plays another kind of sinister, two-legged swamp creature.

1959 C [Cinemascope] **Cast:** George Mcready, Richard Crane, Beverly Garland, Bruce Bennett, Lon Chaney Jr. **Director:** Roy Del Ruth.

An American Werewolf in London

Together with *The Howling*, this highly successful film brought werewolves to contemporary audiences on a scale not achieved since the peak of the Universal monsterfests in the 1940s. No longer were horror movies simply for the buffs or relegated to creature features on latenight television. Mass audiences were lining up to see Rick Baker's extraordinary Academy Award-winning special effects twist and turn and distort that pleasant Dr. Pepper guy, David Naughton, into a savage werewolf. Once again, a light touch to the script helps balance the moments of graphic, numbing horror. Two American students traveling on the cheap across England are attacked by a werewolf, who kills one and mauls the other. The dead Yank continues to visit his live friend and warns him that he will soon become a werewolf—which turns out to be no idle prophecy.

1981 C [Lycanthrope Films] **Cast:** David Naughton, Jenny Agutter,

Griffin Dunne, Brian Glover, John Woodvine. **Director/Writer:** John Landis.

American Werewolf in Paris

Three recent American college graduates are celebrating their self-proclaimed maturity by conducting a "Daredevil Tour of Europe" when one of them(Tom Everett Scott) interferes in a young woman's suicide attempt off the Eiffel Tower. Although she (Julie Delpy) appears to be the Gallic girl of his dreams, he soon learns that she had good reason for attempting to end it all. She is trapped in the living nightmare of lycanthropy and seeking to escape the dark underworld of Paris werewolves.

1997 C [Hollywood Pictures] **Cast:** Tom Everett Scott, Julie Delpy, Vince Vieluf, Phil Buckman, Pierre Cosso. **Director:** Anthony Walker.

The Ape Man

No, we aren't referring to Tarzan. This time it is Bela Lugosi who transforms a man into an ape when he injects the subject with an experimental drug designed to infuse humans with the strength of their simian cousins.

1943 B [Monogram] **Cast:** Bela Lugosi, Wallace Beery, Henry Hall, Louise Currie, Emil Van Horn. **Director:** William Beaudine.

Attack of the Swamp Creatures

They laughed at the mad scientist who believed that he could create a race of superbeings from catfish serum, so he injected himself and changed into an alligatorlike monster. This film is also known as *The Blood Waters of Dr. Z* and *ZAAT*.

1975 C [Thrillervideo] **Cast:** Frank Cromwell. **Director:** Arnold Stevens.

Bad Moon

While on an expedition in Nepal, a scientist (Michael Pare) and his girlfriend are attacked by a werewolf that kills her and bites him. The researcher moves back to the Pacific Northwest to live in isolation with his lycanthropy until his well-intentioned sister (Mariel Hemingway)invites him to stay with her and her son (Mason Gamble) to get over the grief of losing his lover. Things soon begin to go bad, especially when the family dog, a big German Shepherd named Thor, just can't accept the werewolf among them. Interestingly, the novel *Thor* by Wayne Smith on which the film is based tells the story from the dog's viewpoint.

1996 C [Morgan Creek/Badwolf Productions] **Cast:** Michael Pare, Mariel Hemmingway, Mason Gamble. **Director:** Eric Red.

The Bear

A fanciful film with high production values, the story is based on an old Polish folktale of a man who is part bear. The film is sometimes known as *Lokis*.

1970 C Poland Cast: Josef Duriasz, Edmund Fetting. **Director:** Janusz Majewski.

The Beast Must Die

Based on James Blish's novelette, "There Shall Be No Darkness," a millionaire invites a number of people whom he suspects of being a werewolf to his mansion so he can try out his special electronic lycanthrope-detecting devices. This film is also known as *Black Werewolf*.

1973 C [Starmaker] **Cast:** Peter Cushing, Calvin Lockhart, Charles Gray, Anton Diffring. **Director:** Paul Annett.

Beast of the Yellow Night

A man sells his soul to Satan in exchange for the ability to transform himself into various creatures of the night, including a werewolf.

1971 C Philippines [United] **Cast:** John Ashley, Eddie Garcia, Mary Wilcox. **Writer/Director:** Eddie Romero.

The Beast Within

A woman sexually assaulted by an evil spirit gives birth to a son who provides a new fleshly home for the entity. As the boy matures into a teen, he becomes a tool for the demon's terrible deeds. Excellent special effects by Thomas Burton allow the audience to see the shape-shifting transformations the demonic spirit achieves in the teenaged boy's body before his homicidal attacks on the townspeople. Writer Tom Holland adapted the screenplay from a novel by Edward Levy.

1982 C [MGM/USA] Cast: Paul Clemens, Bibi Besch, Don Gordon, R. G. Armstrong, L. Q. Jones. **Director:** Philippe Mora.

Beauty and the Beast (1946)

The classic fairy tale of a man transformed into a werewolf by a curse and redeemed by love was made into a brilliant motion picture by Jean Cocteau. Actor Jean Marais accomplishes a *tour d'force* by appearing as the beast, Belle's arrogant village suitor, and the prince who awaits restoration by the charming Belle.

1946 B France [Embassy] Cast: Jean Marais, Josette Day, Marcel Andre, Mila Parely. **Director:** Jean Cocteau.

Beauty and the Beast (1963)

A modern retelling of the classic fairy tale has a prince afflicted by werewolfism on the nights of the full moon.

1963 C Cast: Eduard Franz, Mark Damon, Joyce Taylor, Michael Pate. **Director:** Edward L. Cahn.

Beauty and the Beast (1976)

George C. Scott assumes a boar's head mask and, together with his wife, Trish Van Devere, fashion a stylish presentation of the classic fairytale for television. Scott was nominated for an Emmy for his interpretation of the Beast.

1976 C Cast: George C. Scott, Trish Van Devere, Virgina McKenna, Bernard Lee, Patricia Quinn. **Director:** Fiedler Cook.

Bela Lugosi Meets a Brooklyn Gorilla

Comedy team Duke Mitchell and Sammy Petrillo (Dean Martin and Jerry Lewis wannabes) manage to get stranded on a jungle island where a mad scientist (Bela Lugosi) just happens to be conducting experiments with a serum that can transform humans into gorillas. This film is also known as *The Boys from Brooklyn.*

1952 B [Jack Broder Productions] Cast: Bela Lugosi, Duke Mitchell, Sammy Petrillo, Muriel Landers. **Director:** William Beaudine.

Blood of Dracula's Castle

The Count and Countess Dracula have relocated to a castle in the Mojave Desert, complete with a basement that their butler keeps well-stocked with fresh victims. A werewolf appears to disturb the vampire's desert paradise.

1969 C [A and E Film Corporation] Cast: Alex D'Arcy, Paula Raymond, John Carradine, Lon Chaney Jr. **Producer/Directors:** Al Adamson, Jean Hewitt

Bloodspell

A teenager confined to a school for disturbed youngsters inherits his father's evil spirit, thus transforming him into a monster with psychokinetic powers.

1988 C [Forum] Cast: Anthony Jenkins, Aaron Teich, Alexandra Kennedy, John Reno. **Director:** Deryn Warren.

Bloodstalkers

Hairy manbeasts that the rural inhabitants call "Bloodstalkers" attack two couples vacationing on their swampy turf in the Florida Everglades. This film is also known as *The Night Daniel Died.*

1976 C [Vidmark] Cast: Jerry Albert, Kenny Miller, Celea-Anne Cole. **Director/Writer:** Robert W. Morgan.

Bloodsuckers from Outer Space

As this film demonstrates, it is not a simple matter to blend comedy and science fiction horror. The invisible alien intelligence has the ability to take over a human body, eject the blood, and reanimate the physical shell to do its bidding, thus totally confusing already befuddled mad scientists and army officers.

1984 C [Lorimar/Warner Bros.] Cast: Pat Paulsen, Laura Elis, Thom Meyers. **Director/Writer:** Glen Coburn.

The Blue Monkey

One might expect such bizarre hazards in outer space, but when a man pricks his thumb on a thorn on good old planet Earth, you just don't expect him to regurgitate a wiggling larva that transforms itself into a bizarre insect. When the thing is inadvertently sprayed with a "lifeforce accelerator," it instantly matures into a full-blown monster. Not surprisingly, this film is also known as *Insect*.

1987 C [RCA/Columbia] **Cast:** Steve Railsback, Gwynyth Walsh, Don Lake, John Vernon, Susan Anspath, Joe Flaherty. **Director:** William Fruet.

Body Snatchers

The third adaptation of science fiction writer Jack Finney's classic paranoid novel of pods from outer space transforming themselves into exact—but emotionless—duplicates of our friends and neighbors. This version chooses a military base as a setting, thus supplanting the previous locales of a small California town and San Francisco.

1993 C [Warner] **Cast:** Gabrielle Anwar, Meg Tilly, Forest Whitaker, R. Lee Emery. **Director:** Abel Ferrara.

Born of Fire

This film presents audiences unfamiliar with certain aspects of Eastern mysticism the opportunity to observe a *djinn* at work as its assumes the shapes of humans, snakes, scorpions, and anything else it wishes.

1984 C India [Vidmark] **Cast:** Peter Firth, Oh-Tee, Suzan Crowley, Rabil Shaban. **Director:** Jamil Dehlavi.

The Borrower

Unfortunately for hapless Earthlings, this insectlike monster borrows human heads to place atop his own stubby neck, thereby also absorbing the unwilling noggin lender's personality and identity in the bloody process. Two cops set out in pursuit of the extraterrestrial shapeshifter, but it is difficult to keep up with a thing that can assume so many identities.

1989 C [Cannon] **Cast:** Rae Dawn Chong, Don Gordon, Neil Glumtoli. **Director:** John McNaughton.

The Boy Who Cried Werewolf

A 12-year-old boy experiences the horror of witnessing an attack by a werewolf on his father. Later, when it is evident that the werewolf virus has infected his dad, no one will believe the boy's warnings.

1973 C [Universal] **Cast:** Kerwin Matthews, Scott Sealy, George Gaynes, Elaine Devry, Robert J. Wilke, Jack Lucas. **Director:** Nathan Juran.

Bride of the Gorilla

Lon Chaney Jr., the quintessential werewolf, gets to watch Raymond Burr undergo a transformation from man to ape. The storyline has the foreman (Burr) of a jungle plantation murdering his boss to get his voluptuous wife (Barbara Payton). A witch slips a potion concocted from the "plant of evil" into the foreman's drink, and he becomes the gorilla man that must be tracked down and killed by the police commissioner (Chaney).

1951 B [Jack Broder Productions] **Cast:** Raymond Burr, Barbara Payton, Lon Chaney Jr., Tom Powers, Woody Strode. **Director-Writer:** Curt Siodmak.

Captive Wild Woman

A mad scientist (John Carradine)turns an orangutan into exotic starlet Acquanetta, who then transforms herself into a woman who goes berserk with unrequited love. Two sequels were cloned from this wereoranguatan, *Jungle Woman* and *Jungle Captive*.

1943 B [Universal] **Cast:** Acquanetta, John Carradine, Evelyn Ankers, Milburn Stone, Lloyd Corrigan. **Director:** Edward Dmytryk.

The Cat Girl

If nothing else, this film is noteworthy for being future Scream Queen Barbara Shelley's first British film. Ms. Shelley inherits a family curse that causes her to crave warm raw flesh and blood, preferably obtained from human victims. The film was also released as *The Cat Woman*.

1957 B British Cast: Barbara Shelley, Kay Callard, Paddy Webster. **Director:** Alfred Shaughnessey.

The Cat People (1942)

Although the transformation of woman into cat is never witnessed by the movie goer, this film has become a classic supernatural thriller. The lovely European bride (Simone Simon) fears that she is transformed into a black panther whenever her sexual desires are aroused. Her patient husband (Kent Smith) and those who may become potential victims are aware only of something sinister moving just out of sight. Excellently wrought cinematography creates an atmosphere of eerie tension throughout the entire film.

1942 B [RKO] **Cast:** Simone Simon, Kent Smith, Tom Conway, Jane Randolph, Jack Holt.
Director: Jacques Tourneur.
Producer: Val Lewton.

Cat People (1982)

While the 1942 classic of the same title was dark, moody, and suggestive, Paul Schrader's take on a brother and sister who morph into savage panthers whenever they make love to their victims is graphic, gory, and direct. While the transformation sequences by special effects master Tom Burman are brief, there is no question that these beings come from an ancient line of shape-shifting entities. As bloody and graphic as the original is subtle and shadowy, the film in nonetheless an effective presentation of ferocious and real Cat People at their most dangerous. The opening sequences with David Bowie handling the theme music sets an eerie, other-worldly tone that is sustained throughout the film.

1982 C [Univesal/MCA] **Cast:** Malcolm McDowall, Nastassia Klinski, John Heard, Annette O'Toole, Ruby Dee, Ed Begley Jr.
Director: Paul Schrader.

The Catman of Paris

A confused and tormented man comes to believe that a series of gruesome murders may have been his own gory handiwork when he undergoes transformation into a werecat creature.

1946 B [Republic] **Cast:** Carl Esmond, Lenore Aubert, Adele Mara, Douglass Dumbrille, Gerald Mohr.
Director: Lesley Selander.

Children of the Full Moon

An anthology film that includes a segment in which a seemingly kindly nanny looks after two werewolf offspring—with the usual dire consequences to strangers who happen upon their mansion in the forest.

1984 C Great Britain [ITC Entertainment] **Cast:** Diana Dors.
Director: Tom Clegg.

Chimera

A four-hour British television presentation edited to two hours for the U.S. market and originally titled *Monkey Boy*, the plot concerns itself with a group of scientists who set out to create a chimera, that is, a creature composed of two distinctly different organisms. Although the classic Greek mythological entity is made up of lion, goat, and serpent, the scientific experimenters in this case decided that man and monkey may be the simplest subjects with which to begin. Some kind of breakthrough is achieved, but all of the doctors end up dead, thus provoking a very careful investigation.

1990 C Great Britain [Prism] **Cast:** Kenneth Cranhaw, Christine Kavanagh, John Lynch. **Director:** Lawrence Gordon Clark.

The Company of Wolves

This film presents its audience with an interesting mixed-bag of allegory and folklore regarding werewolves. Fairy tales are combined with gore as the classic "Little Red Riding Hood" is recast as an encounter with a lycanthrope, as it was no doubt originally intended. There are several werewolf narratives within other werewolf episodes, many with Freudian implications.

1984 C Great Britain [Palace Pictures] **Cast:** Angela Lansbury, Sarah Patterson, David Warner, Graham Crowden, Brian Glover, Micha Bergese. **Director:** Neil Jordan.

The Creature from the Black Lagoon

Gill Man earns his position in the Pantheon of Classic Movie Monsters in this very effective horror film. Scientists Richard Denning and Richard Carlson head an expedition to the remote rivers of South America in search of a missing link between aquatic pre-humans and their land-dwelling cousins. Lovely Julia Adams unwittingly serves as bait to draw Gill Man into the scientists' nets.

1954 B [Universal] **Cast:** Richard Denning, Richard Carlson, Julia Adams, Whit Bissell, Nestor Piava, Antonio Moreno. **Director:** Jack Arnold.

The Creature Walks Among Us

After scientists Rex Reason and Jeff Morrow capture Gill Man, they think it is a good idea to adapt its lungs so it can live full time on land. Bad idea. The Gill Man is not ready to adapt both its lungs and its newfound emotions to deceitful human company.

1956 B [Universal] **Cast:** Rex Reason, Jeff Morrow, Leigh Snowden. **Director:** John Sherwood.

Cry of the Werewolf

Celeste La Tour, Queen of the Trioga gypsies (Nina Foch), has inherited the curse of the werewolf from her mother—and woe be to anyone who discovers her secret.

1944 B [Columbia] **Cast:** Nina Foch, Stephen Crane, Fritz Leiber, Barton McLane. **Director:** Henry Levin.

Cult of the Cobra

American serviceman run a foul of a snake cult in the Far East and incur the wrath of a beautiful woman (Faith Domergue) who can transform herself into a deadly cobra.

1955 B [MCA] **Cast:** Faith Domergue, David Janssen, Marshall Thompson, Richard Long.

Curse of Demon Mountain

This film will take you by surprise. What begins as a rough-riding Western adventure that follows Confederate survivors of the last battle of the Civil War on their quest to find a lost treasure suddenly shifts gears and transforms itself into a genuinely eerie tale of a cache of diamonds watched over by a mysterious demon hawk with astonishing shapeshifting abilities. A well-written script provides plenty of unexpected twists and turns, and a top-notch cast of accomplished actors splendidly portray the horror that strong men must conquer when they discover their brute strength and firepower are useless against a crafty supernatural being. This film is also known as *Shadow of Chikara*, *Wishbone Cutter*, and *Thunder Mountain*.

1977 C [New World/Mintex/High Desert Films] **Cast:** Joe Don Baker, Sondra Locke, Ted Neeley, Slim Pickens. **Director:** Earl E. Smith

Curse of the Queerwolf

After being bitten by a lycanthropic transvestite, a regular straight guy becomes a drag queen, a queerwolf, when the moon is full. Not that there's anything wrong with that.

1988 C [Pirromount] **Cast:** Michael Pulazzolo, Kent Butler, Taylor Whitney. **Director:** Mark Pirro.

Curse of the Swamp Creature

Deep in the Everglades yet another mad scientist is hard at work creating a reptile man.

1966 C [Video Dimensions] **Cast:** Francine York, Bill Thurman, Shirley McLine. **Director:** Larry Buchanan.

The Curse of the Werewolf

A very loose adaptation of Guy Endore's novel, *The Werewolf of Paris*, the film is distinguished by high production values, the directorship of Terence Fisher, and the powerful acting of Oliver Reed as the werewolf. Born on Christmas Eve, the product of a beggar's rape of a mute servant girl, Leon bears such physical signs of the werewolf as a patch of hair on his arm. Although his childhood passes uneventfully after his adoptive father rescues him from shepherds defending their flocks against the lad's inherited werewolf ways, the beast rises within him during a liason with a prostitute. Only the love of the beautiful Cristina can calm Leon's bloodlust, but her father puts him in prison to keep him away from his daughter. Frustration and anger provide the captive werewolf with the strength to escape and meet his destiny.

1961 C Great Britain [Hammer-UI] **Cast:** Oliver Reed, Yvonne Romain, Catherine Feller, Clifford Evans, Anthony Dawson. **Director:** Terence Fisher.

The Daughter of Dr. Jekyll

When a young woman (Gloria Talbott) arrives in England to receive her inheritance from her father's estate, she is informed by a former assistant (Arthur Shields) that her father was the infamous Dr. Jekyll. When a series of mysterious murders occur, she fears that she has inherited her father's deadly schizoid personality. The real murderer, however, is the late doctor's former assistant, who is actually a werewolf.

1957 B [Allied Artists] **Cast:** Gloria Talbott, John Agar, Arthur Shields, John Dierkes. **Director:** Edgar C. Ulmer.

Dead Alive

A bite from a rat monkey of Sumatra transforms a New Zealand zoo visitor into a raging monster monkeywoman.

1992 C New Zealand [Vidmark] **Cast:** Diana Penalver, Liz Moody, Timothy Balme. **Director:** Peter Jackson.

Death Moon

A dream Hawaiian vacation becomes a nightmare for a businessman whose missionary grandfather was cursed by the native inhabitants of the islands. The malediction had to do with lycanthropy, and it doesn't take long for the Mainlander to discover that he has inherited grandpa's curse.

1978 C [VCL made for TV] **Cast:** Robert Foxworth, France Nuyen, Joe Penny, Charles Haid, Barbara Trentham. **Director:** Bruce Kessler.

Dr. Jekyll and Mr. Hyde (1908)

The first of numerous cinematic incarnations of the famous Robert Louis Stevenson tale of the London doctor who experiments with a drug that frees the beast within to emerge and wreak chaos and death was produced in the United States by the Selig film company in 1908. The following year, a Danish production company filmed the classic story of the warring natures within the human psyche.

Dr. Jekyll and Mr. Hyde (1912-1914)

Carl Laemmle filmed the third version of the Stevenson story in 1912. A fourth and fifth cinematic interpretation of the struggle between good and evil as personified in the character of Dr. Jekyll were filmed in the U.S. and in Great Britain in 1913. A sixth version was produced by Starlight in the U.S. in 1914.

Dr. Jekyll and Mr. Hyde (1921)

The famous actor John Barrymore held audiences in thrall as he distorted his handsome features in full view of the camera to create the monstrous "Mr. Hyde." Nita Naldi, one of Rudolph Valentino's favorite leading ladies, was suitably wide-eyed as a threatened damsel in distress. Four other film versions of the classic story were also filmed that year.

1921 B [Paramount Artcraft] **Cast:** John Barrymore, Nita Naldi, Martha Mansfield, Louis Wolheim. **Director:** John S. Robertson.

Dr. Jekyll and Mr. Hyde (1932)

This superb translation of Robert Louis Stevenson's classic story is ranked Number 73 on *Entertainment Weekly's* "Top 100 Science Fiction Movies." Actor Fredric March, one of Hollywood's greatest actors, underwent on-camera transformations aided by special lenses and Wally Westmore's makeup mastery. The film is a highwater mark for horror/science fiction, for March won the Oscar for his portrayal of the scientist with the splintered psyche.

1932 B [MGM] **Cast:** Fredric March, Miriam Hopkins, Rose Hobart, Holmes Herbert, Edward Norton. **Director:** Rouben Mamoulian.

Dr. Jekyll and Mr. Hyde (1941)

Spencer Tracy, another of Hollywood's most accomplished actors, undertook the dual role of scientist and the monster within. The film's production values are high, and the performances are excellently crafted by some of MGM's top stars, but it does not quite measure up to the 1932 version.

1941 B [MGM] **Cast:** Spencer Tracy, Ingrid Bergman, Donald Crisp, Lana Turner, Ian Hunter, C. Aubrey Smith, Sara Allgood. **Director:** Victor Fleming.

Dr. Jekyll and the Wolfman

It was only a matter of time before someone thought of pairing the two legendary figures who most epitomize and symbolize the beast within. The indestructable Count Daninsky has grown tired of the curse that dominates his many resurrections and seeks out the grandson of Dr. Jekyll for help. The film is also known as *Dr. Jekyll and the Werewolf*.

1971 C Spain [Arturo Gonzalez] **Cast:** Paul Naschy, Shirley Corrigan, Jack Taylor. **Director:** Leon Klimovsky.

Dr. Terror's House of Horrors

An anthology of five separate tales of terror. Horror superstar Peter Cushing is a Tarot reader with uncanny powers who predicts how five passengers aboard a train will die. The segment featuring Neil McCallum ends with his being killed by a female werewolf.

1965 C Great Britain [Amicus] **Cast:** Peter Cushing, Neil McCallum, Christopher Lee, Jennifer Jayne. **Director:** Freddie Francis.

The Dolphin

Recent DNA studies indicate that humans have more in common with dolphins than almost any other land mammal, so who is to say that a woman couldn't give birth to a dolphin man? Well, anyway, not this film.

1987 C Portugal [Fox Lorber] **Director/Writer:** Walter Lima Jr.

Dracula Contra Frankenstein

The eternal Count Dracula is brought back to life by Baron Frankenstein, who demands control of legions of vampires to do his bidding. A werewolf and a human consort attempt to establish a balance of beasties, but it takes a band of gypsies to set fire to the Baron's castle and destroy the monsters. This film is also known as *Dracula Against Frankenstein*, *Dracula Prisoner of Frankenstein*, *Dracula vs. Frankenstein*.

1972 C Spain/France [Fenix/Comptoir Francais Du Film] **Cast:** Dennis Price, Howard Vernon, Alberto Dalbes, Brit Nichols, Brandy. **Director:** Jesus Franco.

El Bosque del Lobo

Based on a novel by Carlos Martinez, the plot tells the story of an epileptic peddler who carries off eleven women and brutally rapes them. Local folklore has it that he is a werewolf, and he is eventually snared in a wolf trap. This film is also known as *The Wolf Forest*, *The Wolfman of Galicia*, *The Ancines Woods*.

1968 C Spain [Amboto] **Cast:** Jose Lopez Velaquez, Amparo Soler Leal, Antonio Casas. **Director:** Pedro Olea.

El Castillo de los Monstros

Apparently inspired by those grand Universal gathering of the monster clans, this production tells of the haunted honeymoon of a couple that encounters the Creature of the Black Lagoon, Frankenstein's Monster, the Mummy, and the Wolfman in a mysterious old castle.

1957 B Mexico [Producciones Sotomayor] **Cast:** Antonio Espino, Evangelina Elizondo, German Robles. **Director:** Julian Soler.

El Hombre que Vino de Ummo

This time the mad scientist is an extraterrestrial who comes from the planet Ummo, and his masterplan to conquer Earth involves landing in Transylvania and reviving Dracula, the Frankenstein Monster, a mummy, and the werewolf Count Waldemar Daninsky. But even aliens cannot predict matters of the heart. The scientist's lovely assistant falls in love with the werewolf, who celebrates his good fortune by killing his fellow monsters. This film is also known as *Dracula vs. Frankenstein*, *Assignment Terror*, *The Man Who Came from Ummo*, *Los Monstruos del Terror*.

1969 C Spain/Italy/West Germany [Producciones Jaime Prades/ Eichberg Film/International Jaguar. **Cast:** Michael Rennie, Karen Dor, Craig Hill, Paul Naschy. **Director:** Tulio Demichelli.

El Hombre y el Monstro

Whenever a talented, tormented pianist plays a particular concerto, the notes somehow transform him into a werewolf, whose murderous impulses can only be extinguished by his mother's loving touch.

1958 B Mexico [Diana Films] **Cast:** Enrique Rabal, Abel Salazar, Martha Roth. **Director:** Rafael Baledon.

El Retorno del Hombre Lobo

Once again the werewolf Count Waldemar Daninsky is resurrected from his cold grave. This time three German women have had him disinterred in order to combat one of the world's most evil women, Countess Elisabeth Bathory of Hungary, who was brought back to life when a contemporary disciple of evil poured blood over the corpse's face. The Count manages to send the Countess of Blood back to her niche in Hell, but he, in turn, is repaid by one of the German resurrectionists with a silver dagger in his heart. This film was also released as *The Craving*.

1980 C Spain [Dalmata Films] **Cast:** Paul Naschy, Silvia Aguilar, Azucena Hernandez, Julia Saly, Beatriz Elorietta. **Director:** Jacinto Molina

El Retorno de Walpurgis

Not to quibble with the film's title, but Walpurgis, May Eve, returns every year—and so, it appears, does the werewolf Count Daninsky. In this outing, the Count is freed from his full moon frenzy when he is done in by a dagger made from a silver cross. This film is also known as *Curse of the Devil, The Black Harvest of Countess Dracula, The Return of Walpurgis*.

1973 C Spain [Loyus Films/Producciones Escorpion] **Cast:** Paul Naschy, Faye Falcon, May Oliver. **Director:** Charles Aured.

The Face of the Screaming Werewolf

Lon Chaney Jr. does double monster duty in this film, also known as *The House of Terror*. A mummy (Chaney) who was afflicted with lycanthropy is brought back to life during a thunderstorm and soon resumes his murderous werewolf ways.

1959 B Mexico [Diana Films] **Cast:** Lon Chaney Jr., German Valdes, Yolanda Varela. **Director:** Gilberto Martinez Solares.

The Faculty

This variation on the basic theme of *Invasion of the Body Snatchers* (1956, 1978) was scripted by Kevin Williamson (*Scream*, 1996), who plays on teenaged paranoia by placing alien shapeshifters in the faculty of a high school in a rural Ohio community. Coach Willis (Robert Patrick) is the first to be possessed by the extraterrestrial parasites and the sweet Mrs. Olson (Piper Laurie) and Principal Drake (Bebe Neuwirth) soon fall victim to the otherworldly visitor. Casey Connor (Elijah Wood) is the bright high school loner who has the obligatory role of frightened witness who first detects the sinister transformations and who must attempt to make others believe him. The suspense intensifies when it becomes apparent that the infected faculty members are methodically claiming members of the student body to join their emotionless hive. Connor's only allies are the gorgeous cheerleader for whom he secretly lusts (Jordana Brewster), the smart aleck troublemaker (Josh Hartnett), the science-fiction buff/alienated loner (Clea DuVall), and the newly arrived sweet and naive Southern belle (Laura Harris)—any one of whom may contain the "Queen Bee" of the body snatchers.

1998 C [Buena Vista/Dimension Films] **Cast:** Jordana Brewster, Clea DuVall, Josh Hartnett, Elijah Wood, Salma Hayek, Famke Janssen. **Director:** Robert Rodriguez.

Fallen

Understandably, it takes awhile for detective John Hobbes (Denzel Washington) to comprehend that an executed serial killer (Elias Koteas) made a pact with the demon Azazel before his death and his spirit can now possess and use the body of anyone who is touched by his demonic presence. The demon can hopscotch from one person to another the very instant that any kind of physical contact is made. Of course any modern detective, such as Hobbes's partner (John Goodman), would go bonkers trying to fit such metaphysical belief constructs into routine police work, and Hobbes has more than his share of befuddlement until he meets a theology professor (Embeth Davidtz) who explains the rudiments of demonology and its power in the modern world.

1998 C [Warner Brothers] **Cast:** Denzel Washington, John Goodman, Donald Sutherland, Embeth Davidtz,

James Gandolfini, Elias Koteas. **Director:** Gregory Hoblit.

The Fly (1958)

Horror classic about an earnest scientist seeking the secrets of teleportation who inadvertently ends up with the head of a fly. The final scene of the fly with the tiny human head crying, "Help me!" as the hungry spider closes in on the victim snared in its web remains firmly fixed in the consciousness of millions of horror fans. *The Fly* is ranked Number 26 on *Entertainment Weekly*'s list of "Top 100 Science Fiction Movies." The film produced two sequels *Return of the Fly* and *Curse of the Fly*.

1958 C [Cinemascope] **Cast:** David Hedison, Patricia Owens, Herbert Marshall, Vincent Price. **Director:** Kurt Neumann.

The Fly (1986)

Chris Walas won an Oscar for special effects as he enables Jeff Goldblum to undergo an exceedingly graphic metamorphosis from scientist to giant flyman. This updated version of the 1958 classic provides us with more recognizable scientific theories regarding DNA and gene splicing and lots more identifiable machines in Goldbum's lab, but the scenes depicting the transformation are filled with gore and gross-out sequences far beyond the imaginings of the earlier film.

1986 C [Fox] **Cast:** Jeff Goldblum, Geena Davis, John Getz. **Director:** David Cronenberg.

Frankenstein Meets the Wolf Man

Universal hyped the film as the "Clash of the Century" as the two classic creatures Frankenstein's Monster (Bela Lugosi) and the Wolf Man (Lon Chaney Jr) met to fight to the death, to lie still until they would be resurrected for the next monster movie. Foolhardy graverobbers open Lawrence Talbot's grave during the full moon and revive the Wolf Man, who, in turn, frees the Frankenstein Monster from his resting place. Dr. Mannering (Patric Knowles) finds Dr. Frankenstein's diary and uses the arcane information contained therein to restore both the Monster and the Wolf Man to super strength.

1943 B [Universal] **Cast:** Lon Chaney Jr., Ilona Massey, Maria Ouspenskaya, Patric Knowles, Dwight Frye. **Director:** Roy William Neill.

Full Eclipse

Would you believe a secret group of werewolf vigilantes within the Los Angeles police force taking a gory bite out of crime?

1993 C [HBO] **Cast:** Mario Van Peebles, Patsy Kensit, Jason Beghe, Paula Marshall. **Director:** Anthony Hickox.

Full Moon High

Perhaps inspired by the comedic elements in *The Howling*, this film predates the more popular *Teen Wolf* with Michael J. Fox in its portrayal of a high school football star (a young Adam Arkin, the serious neurosurgeon on the television series *Chicago Hope*) who receives additional power from a source far spookier than steroids. Arkin's real-life father, Alan, one of Hollywood's greatest character actors is also in the cast to see that things run smoothly.

1982 C [Filmways/Larco Productions] **Cast:** Adam Arkin, Alan Arkin, Ed McMahon, Elizabeth Hartman, Roz Kelly. **Director:** Larry Cohen.

Haxan

An early Swedish silent film that explores the dark side of witchcraft. Also known as *Witchcraft Through the Ages*, the film is a mix of medieval book illustrations and vignettes that dramatize the black arts—witches nibbling on corpse fingers, putting frogs and snakes into the stewpot, that sort of thing. Spooky scenes, including director Benjamin Christiansen as a long-fingered Devil, are mixed with comedy in a pseudo-documentary format that often looks and sounds like an instructional film. Despite the inescapably dated quality of the material, it's so unusual that it's recommended, particularly for group viewing by horror fans.

1927 B Sweden. **Cast:** Maren Pedersen, Clara Pontoppidan, Oscar Striboli, Benjamin Christiansen. Tora

Teje, Elith Pio, Karen Winther, Emmy Schonfeld, John Andersen. **Director:** Benjamin Christiansen.

The Hidden

An extraterrestrial shape-shifter enters humans through the mouth and controls their minds in this very effective sci-fi thriller. Joining the police in pursuit of the violent entity is FBI agent Kyle MacLachlan, a man we come to suspect is more than he appears to be.

1987 C [Video/Laser: Media] **Cast:** Kyle MacLachlan, Michael Nouri, Clu Gulager, Claudia Christian. **Director:** Jack Sholder.

Hidden II

In this sequel to the 1987 film, the shape-changing aliens are back on Earth, and another good-guy E.T. appears to aid terrestrial cops to track them down.

1993 C [New Line] **Cast:** Raphael Sbarge, Michael Nouri, Kate Hodge, Jovin Montanaro. **Director/Writer:** Seth Pinsker.

House of Dracula

The last in Universal's series of all-star monster lineups. This film has a sane doctor (Onslow Stevens) who really wishes to cure the monster's of all their bad habits. She is successful with the Wolf Man, and Lawrence Talbot is freed from the curse of the full moon. Dracula proves resistant to the best of intentions, and the monsters once again end up at one another's throats.

1945 B [Universal] **Cast:** Lon Chaney Jr., Onslow Stevens, John Carradine, Glenn Strange, Lionel Atwill, Martha O'Driscoll, Jane Adams. **Director:** Erle C. Kenton.

House of Frankenstein

When the success of *Frankenstein Meets the Wolf Man* indicated that two monsters were even better than one, Universal added Dracula to the mix and created another opportunity to bring back the horror audience's favorite creatures. Although Boris Karloff is on hand, he has the role of the mad scientist while Glenn Strange portrays the Frankenstein monster.

Dracula's cape was an easy fit for John Carradine, who for the first time on screen portrayed the Count with a mustache, as Bram Stoker had written him. And, of course, no one could sprout werewolf hairs the way that Lon Chaney Jr. could.

1944 B [Universal] **Cast:** Boris Karloff, Lon Chaney Jr., John Carradine, J. Carrol Naish, Elena Verdugo, Lionel Atwill, George Zucco. **Director:** Erle C. Kenton.

House of Frankenstein (1997)

A Los Angeles real estate tycoon who moonlights as a vampire joins forces with a werewolf to seek out the Frankenstein Monster in order to complete their unholy trio.

1997 C [NBC TV miniseries] **Cast:** Terri Polo, Greg Wise, Peter Crombe, Adrian Pasdar. **Director:** Peter Werner.

How to Make a Monster

A disgruntled makeup man (Robert Harris) who specializes in horror films uses his cosmetic skills and hypnosis to transform two actors into the Frankenstein monster and the wolfman. Once he has them under his spell, he commands them to murder the studio heads.

1958 B [American-International] **Cast:** Robert Harris, Paul Brinegar, Gary Conway, John Ashley, Gary Clarke. **Director:** Herbert L. Strock.

The Howling

The storyline is straight enough: A Los Angeles news anchor seeking a breakthrough scoop on a psychopathic serial killer finds herself in a coven of werewolves. Although she manages to escape and burn the colony of lycanthropes to the ground, she herself changes into a werewolf during her newscast. The script, however, is loaded with horror-buff in-jokes and it is apparent that very often writers John Sayles and Terence H. Winkless have their tongues firmly in their cheeks. In spite of the light touch, the movie has a number of genuinely chilling moments, and the special effects by Rob Bottin reveal the transformation from human into werewolf so graphically that audiences may begin to feel their own skin crawl and sprout hair.

1981 C [AVCO Embassy/International Film Investors, Wescom] **Cast:** Dee Wallace, Patrick Macnee, Elizabeth Brooks, John Carradine, Slim Pickens, Dennis Dugan, Belinda Balaski. **Director:** Joe Dante.

The Howling II—Your Sister Is a Werewolf

A "sequel" in title only to *The Howling*, the locale in this film shifts from California to Transylvania as a psychic investigator tracks lycanthropic clues until he arrives in the lair of the Queen of the Werewolves.

1985 C [Hemdale] **Cast:** Sybil Danning, Christopher Lee, Annie McEnroe, Reb Brower. **Director:** Philippe Mora.

The Howling III—The Marsupials

It turns out that there is a vicious tribe of werewolf people living somewhere in Australia. What is more, they seem to have adapted some kangaroo characteristics, such as pouches in which to keep their babies. Where is Crocodile Dundee when we need him?

1987 C Australia [Bacannia] **Cast:** William Yang, Barry Otto, Max Fairchild. **Director:** Philipe Mora.

The Howling IV—The Original Nightmare

When his wife continues to suffer frightening dreams of werewolves, her loving husband diagnoses stress and suggests a holiday to the quaint village of Drago. This proves to be an extremely bad choice for rest and relaxation, for everyone in Drago is a werewolf, thereby transforming her nightmares into self-fulfilling prophecies.

1988 C Great Britain [Allied Entertainment] **Cast:** Romy Windsor, Michael T. Weiss, Anthony Hamilton, Susanne Severeid. **Director:** John Hough.

Howling V—The Rebirth

A moldering castle outside of Budapest has been abandoned since the 15th century when all family members committed suicide in an attempt to end their lycanthropic bloodline. Centuries later, it is learned that an infant survived and perpetuated the curse. And now the present embodiment of the werewolf bloodline is murdering guests in secret chambers of the old castle.

1989 C [Allied Vision/Lane Pringle] **Cast:** Phillip Davis, Victoria Catlin, Elizabeth Silverstein, Ben Cole, Stephanie Shockley. **Director:** Neal Sundstrom.

The Howling VI—The Freaks

A vagabond werewolf is captured by the proprietor of Harker's World of Wonders and put on display with the alligator boy and the other misfits of nature. When disgruntled townspeople storm the carnival, the werewolf, who has learned that his kidnapper is a vampire, kills the man and sets himself free.

1991 C Great Britain [Allied Vision/Lane Pringle] **Cast:** Brendan Hughes, Antonio Fargas, Carol Lynley, Michele Matheson. **Director:** Hope Perello.

Howling VII—The New Moon Rising

A hardnosed cop joins a werewolf-hunting priest who is tracking a suspicious Australian wanderer, who seems the likely suspect for a series of lycanthropic murders around Pioneertown in Yucca Valley, California.

1995 C [New Line] **Cast:** Elizabeth She, Clive Hunter, John Remsen, Jacqueline Armitage. **Director/ Writer/ Producer:** Clive Hunter.

I Married a Monster from Outer Space

Another effective story of shape shifters from another planet who arrive on Earth to assume the forms of unsuspecting humans. The film focuses on newlyweds (Gloria Talbott and Tom Tyron) and the confused wife's difficulty adjusting to married life once her husband has been replaced by an emotionless alien masquerader.

1958 B [Paramount] **Cast:** Gloria Talbott, Tom Tyron, Ken Lynch, Valerie Allen. **Director:** Gene Fowler Jr.

I Was a Teenage Werewolf

When a brooding adolescent (Michael Landon) is sent to a psychiatrist (Whit Bissell) for help controlling his psychotic outbursts, the doctor sees an excellent opportunity to experiment with a new serum. Rather than curing the youth, however, the drug regresses him to a primitive stage where he assumes the appearance and mannerisms of a werewolf.

1957 B [American-International] **Cast:** Michael Landon, Whit Bissell, Yvonne Lime, Guy Williams, Robert Griffin. **Director:** Gene Fowler Jr.

Incubus

Based on Ray Russell's novel about the kind of invisible demon that sexually possesses and molests its victims, the film depicts the struggle that contemporary doctors and police officials endure while dealing with an ancient evil.

1982 C Canada [Vestron] **Cast:** John Cassavetes, Helen Hughes, Dirk McClean, Kerrie Keane, John Ireland. **Director:** John Hough.

Invaders from Mars (1953)

This is one of those movies that has built a cult following because it left an indelible mark on the psyches of millions of babyboomers who have never forgotten the movie that first scared the bejabbers out of them. The plot is simple: A young boy (Jimmy Hunt) is awakened one night by the sound of an extraterrestrial craft landing and submerging itself into the sandy hill near his home. No one will believe him, and he comes to realize that nearly everyone in town—including his parents—have been possessed by alien lifeforms—nasty little buggers that cling to the backs of their victims' necks.

1953 B [Cinecolor 3D] **Cast:** Jimmy Hunt, Helena Carter, Arthur Franz, Leif Erickson, Hillary Brooke, Bert Freed. **Director:** William Cameron Menzies.

Invaders from Mars (1986)

A remarkably faithful adaptation of the 1953 cult favorite, director Tobe Hooper updates the classic with dramatic special effects by John Dykstra and Stan Winston that only heighten the impact of the original. One by one, the boy who witnessed the landing of the spacecraft perceives his teachers, townspeople, and parents becoming possessed by the extraterrestrial invaders. A bonus for movie buffs: The scene in which that cold and rigid nurse from *One Flew Over the Cuckoo's Nest*, Louise Fletcher, swallows a live frog in one gulp.

1986 C [Cannon] **Cast:** Karen Black, Hunter Carson, Timothy Bottoms, Laraine Newman, Bud Cort. **Director:** Tobe Hooper.

Invasion of the Bee Girls

A mysterious force transforms women into giant insects that are determined to sting men to death.

1973 C [Embassy] **Cast:** Victoria Vetri, William Smith, Anitra Ford, Rene Bond. **Director:** Denis Sanders.

Invasion of the Body Snatchers (1956)

This is another film that has built a cult following because of the manner in which it pushes certain fear buttons in the psyche: *Could it be possible that the reason those nearest and dearest to me don't seem to be quite themselves is because they have been possessed by some alien intelligence?* Although the "alien intelligence" in this film happens to arrive on Earth in the form of weird, plantlike pods, the frightening possession of unsuspecting humans really epitomizes the basic dread of any shape-shifting entity that can assume any form it wishes at its will. *Entertainment Weekly* ranks this chilling adaptation of Jack Finney's novel Number Eight on its list of the "Top 100 Science Fiction Movies."

1956 B [Allied Artists/Walter Wanger] **Cast:** Kevin McCarthy, Dana Wynter, Larry Gates, King Donovan, Carolyn Jones, Virginia Christine. **Director:** Don Siegel.

Invasion of the Body Snatchers (1978)

Director Philip Kaufman utilizes only the basic theme of the 1956 original and manages to create his own unique vision of extraterrestrial terror in this stylish update of the shapeshifting pods from outer space. This time the setting is San Francisco, rather than a small California town, and the special effects are memorable as one by one the hero's (Donald Sutherland) friends are replaced by pod people who are their exact duplicates.

1978 C [MGM/UA] **Cast:** Donald Sutherland, Brooke Adams, Leonard Nimoy, Veronica Cartwright, Jeff Goldblum. **Director:** Philip Kaufman.

It Came From Outer Space

Although we learn that their intentions are seemingly benevolent, there are chills aplenty as the giant eyeball monsters from outer space—complete with eerie theme music that signals their presence—demonstrate their ability to shape-shift into any form, including the shapes of friends and neighbors.

1953 B [Universal-International 3D] **Cast:** Richard Carlson, Barbara Rush, Charles Drake, Joe Sawyer.

La Bestia y la Espada Magica

The indomitable, lycanthropic Count Waldemar Daninsky manages to time-travel to sixteenth century Japan to seek out wisemen who may derive a cure for his curse. When the Japanese monks admit failure in curing lycanthropy, the Count returns to Europe, goes on a murderous rampage, and is killed by his Japanese lover. This film is also known as *The Beast and the Magic Sword.*

1983 C Spain/Japan [Aconito Films/ Amachi] **Cast:** Paul Naschy, Shigeru Amachi, Beatriz Escudero, Junko Asahina. **Director:** Jacinto Molina.

La Furia del Hombre Lobo

Still trying to shed his werewolf ways, Count Waldemar Daninsky is back again, this time trying to convince a female doctor to help him. As in the other movies in this series featuring Count Daninsky, all principals are killed before the final credits roll.

1971 C Spain [Maxper] **Cast:** Paul Naschy, Perla Cristal, Veronica Lujan. **Director:** Jose Maria Zabalza.

La Loba

Bizarre tale of werewolves in love. A young doctor, who is also a werewolf, meets the daughter of a colleague who also suffers from lycanthropy. The two fall in love, but are undone and die in each other's arms, killed by a specially trained hunting dog and the doctor's assistant. This film is also known as *The She Wolf* and *Los Horrores del Bosque Negro.*

1964 B Mexico [Producciones Sotomayor] **Cast:** Kitty de Hoyos, Joaquin Cordero, Jose Elias Moreno. **Director:** Rafael Baledon.

La Lupa Mannera

Memories provoked by her sexual urgings force a young woman to remember a past life as a werewolf. When she can no longer resist these dark desires, she transforms into a wolf woman in her present life experience. This film is also known as *Daughter of a Werewolf, Legend of the Wolf Woman, Werewolf Woman.*

1976 C Italy [Dialchi Film] **Cast:** Annik Borel, Frederick Stafford, Dagmar Lassander, Howard Ross. **Director:** Rino di Silvestro.

La Maldicion de la Bestia

His werewolf curse seemingly inactive at last, Count Waldemar Daninsky sets out in search of the Yeti in faraway Tibet. As his ill fortune would have it, a bite he receives from an evil sorceress reactivates the werewolf bloodlust within him. Fortunately, before he is able to ravage all of Tibet, a wise monk is able to cure him of his full moon fever. This film is also known as *Night of the Howling Beast* and *The Werewolf and the Yeti.*

1975 C Spain [Profilms] **Cast:** Paul Naschy, Grace Mills, Castillo Escalona, Silvia Solar. **Director:** Miguel Iglesias Bonns.

La Marca del Hombre Lobo

Paul Naschy portrays the Count Waldemar Daninsky in what will become a series of werewolf pictures. In this first outing, he encounters a pair of Hungarian vampires that he knows he is fated to kill. This film was also released as *The Mark of the Wolfman, The Wolfman of Count Dracula, Frankenstein's Bloody Terror.* The last two titles are particularly misleading since neither Dracula nor the Frankenstein monster appear in the film.

1967 C Spain [Maxper] **Cast:** Paul Naschy, Diane Konopka, Julian

Ugarte, Rossana Yanni. **Director:** Enrique L. Equiluz.

La Noche De Walpurgis

When doctors remove the silver bullet from his heart, Count Waldemar Daninsky is once again resurrected. This time before he himself is dispatched he rescues a young woman from becoming the sacrificial offering during the vampire Waldessa's Walpurgis Night ritual. This film is also known as *Shadow of the Werewolf, The Werewolf vs. the Vampire Woman, The Black Harvest of Countess Dracula.*

1970 C Spain/West Germany [Plata Films] **Cast:** Paul Naschy, Paty Shepard, Gaby Fuchs, Barbara Capell. **Director:** Leon Klimovsky.

Las Noches del Hombre Lobo

The werewolf Count Waldemar Daninsky returns, summoned by a mad scientist to destroy his opponents. The Count manages to slay the evil scientist before he himself is killed.

1968 C Spain/France [Kin Films] **Cast:** Paul Naschy, Monique Branvill, Helene Vatelle. **Director:** Rene Govar.

Le Loup Garou

An angry priest curses a murderer, and the power of his words transforms the criminal into a werewolf.

1923 B France **Cast:** Jean Marau, Madeleine Guitty. The film was also known as *The Werewolf.*

Le Loup des Malveneur

Also known as *The Wolf of the Malveneurs*

1943 B France. **Cast:** Maeleine Sologne, Pierre Renoir, Gabrielle Dorziat. **Director:** Guillame Radot.

The Legend of Boggy Creek

An effective docudrama recounting various local accounts of encounters with the fabled manbeast, Bigfoot.

1972 C [Techniscope] **Cast:** Willie E. Smith, John Hixon, John W. Gates, Buddy Crabtree. **Director:** Charles B. Pierce.

Legend of the Werewolf

Similar in theme to *The Curse of the Werewolf* with Oliver Reed, this film stars David Rintoul as a man who was raised by a wolf pack as a child and, as an adult, is afflicted by lycanthropy when the moon is full.

1975 C Great Britain [Tyburn] **Cast:** Peter Cushing, David Rintoul, Lynn Dalby, Ron Moody, Hugh Griffith. **Director:** Freddie Francis.

The Leopard Man

Another intriguing Val Lewton exploration of the eerie and unknown which he based on the Cornell Woolrich novel, *Black Alibi.* As in his classic film, *The Cat People*, things are not quite what they seem in the small New Mexico town where a series of vicious murders appear to be the work of an escaped leopard.

1943 B [Fox] **Cast:** Dennis O'Keefe, Jean Brooks, Margo, James Bell, Margaret Landry. **Director:** Jacques Tourneur.

Lifeforce

Based on Colin Wilson's novel *Space Vampires*, the film effectively shows the power of alien intelligences to steal the lifeforce energy of humans and to assume their physical forms. There are some grim special effects by John Dykstra and John Gant that have corpses coming back to deadly life, then, when denied the lifeforce, crumbling into disgusting messes. The extraterrestrial shapeshifters turn half of London's population into animated zombies— and it appears they might be soul-stealers as well as energy vampires.

1985 C Great Britain [Vestron] **Cast:** Steve Railsback, Peter Firth, Frank Finlay, Mathilda May, Patrick Stewart. **Director:** Tobe Hooper.

Lion Man

The son of a witch, raised by lions, has developed clawlike hands that can rip and rend an enemy to shreds as effectively as any simba in the jungle. Part bizarre swashbuckler and part horror film, the plot allows the Lion Man to take on and slaughter armies of 100 men singlehandedly.

1980 C Greece [Best Film and Video] **Cast:** Steve Arkin, Barbara Lake. **Director:** Natuch Baltan.

Lycanthropus

The director of a women's reform school has a hidden life as a werewolf, and his jealous and protective mistress will murder anyone who guesses his secret. This film is also known as *Werewolf in a Girls' Dormitory, I Married a Werewolf, The Ghoul in a Girls' Dormitory, Monster Among the Girls*.

1962 C Italy-Austria [Royal Films] **Cast:** Barabara Lass, Carl Schell, Curt Lowens, Maurice Marsac, Maureen O'Conner. **Director:** Richard Benson.

Mad at the Moon

A young frontier bride learns the truth of the old adage that one should never marry in haste. The mild-mannered farmer with whom she rushed into marriage for the sake of name and prestige behaves very oddly when the moon is full.

1992 C [Republic] **Cast:** Mary Stuart Masterson, Hart Bochner, Fionnula Flanagan, Stephen Blake. **Director:** Martin Donovan.

The Mad Monster

Mad scientist (George Zucco) introduces wolf blood into a farmer's (Glenn Strange) bloodstream and turns him into a werewolf. Although his experiment had the patriotic motive of creating more powerful soldiers to end the war, the wolf creature runs amok on the townspeople. In some of the later Universal creature features, Strange would substitute for Boris Karloff as the Frankenstein monster.

1942 B [PRC] **Cast:** Anne Nagel, George Zucco, Glenn Strange, Johnny Downs, Mae Busch, Sarah Padden. **Director:** Sam Newfield.

The Maltese Bippy

Spun off their popular *Laugh-In* television series on which they frequently "bet their bippy," comics Rowan and Martin poke fun at old horror movies in this film that depicts Martin as a movie star who seriously believes that he is turning into a werewolf. This film is also known as *The Incredible Werewolf Murders*.

1969 C [MGM] **Cast:** Dick Martin, Dan Rowan, Robert Reed, Julie Newmar. **Director:** Norman Panama.

The Manitou

Few moviegoers will find it easy to free themselves from the image of a 400-year-old Medicine man bursting free from petite Susan Strasberg's back as he is reborn in modern times. In this adaptation of a Graham Masterson novel, Native American shapeshifting legends are effectively presented with great special effects.

1978 C [CBS/Fox] **Cast:** Susan Strasberg, Tony Curtis, Ann Sothern, Stella Stevens, Paul Mantee, Burgess Meredith, Michael Ansara. **Director:** William Girdler.

The Mermaids of Tiburon

A mermaid swims the California-Mexico coast with her pet shark, evading capture and guarding a fortune in pearls.

1962 C [Fright] **Cast:** Diane Webber, Timothy Carey, Gaby Malone. **Director/Writer/Producer:** John Lamb.

Miranda

Among the most popular of benevolent werecreatures is the mermaid. This British comedy updates the classic tale of the mermaid who falls in love with a land lubber and leaves the sea to dwell inland. Adapted from a stage play by Peter Blackmore, the tale spawned a sequel, *Mad About Men*.

1948 B Great Britain [GFD] **Cast:** Glynis Johns, Margaret Rutherford, David Tomlinson, Griffith Jones, Googie Withers. **Director:** Ken Annakin.

Mr. Peabody and the Mermaid

Obviously 1948 was a good year for reeling in attractive mermaids. In this instance, the stuffy Bostonian who finds the mercreature and places her in his bathtub is already married and turns his life into something of a shambles by choosing to bring home his most unusual trophy.

1948 B [Republic] **Cast:** Ann Blyth, William Powell, Fred Clark, Andrea King.

The Mole People

An expedition enters caves in Tibet where they encounter mutant mole people, werecreatures that have been enslaved by the Sumerians, caucasian inhabitants of an ancient lost city.

1956 B [MCA] **Cast:** John Agar, Cynthia Patrick, Hugh Beaumont, Alan Napier. **Director:** Virgil Vogel.

Monster Dog

Rock superstar Alice Cooper plays rock superstar Vince Raven, who returns to his family mansion to make a video for MTV. Raven shouldn't have come home again, for his latent werewolf tendencies emerge in a series of grisly murders.

1984 C [Transworld] **Cast:** Alice Cooper, Victoria Vera. **Director:** Clyde Anderson.

The Monster Squad

Monster-loving kids save the world with techniques learned from watching horror movies when Dracula returns to activate the Mummy, the Frankenstein Monster, the Wolf Man, and the Gill Man—the Big Four of Universal's golden days of Monsterdom.

1987 C [TriStar] **Cast:** Stephen Macht, Duncan Regehr, Tom Noonan, Andrea Gower, Robby Kiger, Brent Chalem, Ryan Lambert, Ashley Bank. **Director:** Fred Dekker.

Mortal Kombat Annihilation

In this motion picture based on the popular video game, the character Nightwolf makes an appearance as the master teacher who inspires the hero Lui Kang to unleash his animal nature and allow this primal energy to make him a fighter powerful enough to defeat the evil Shao Kahn.

1997 C [New Line/Threshold] **Cast:** Robin Shou, Talisa Soto, James Remar, Sandra Hess. **Director:** John R. Leonetti.

The Mummy and the Curse of the Jackals

In an effort to recapture the mystique of Universal's heyday of monsters, this film pits a resurrected mummy against the Jackal man. It seems that monsters just can't get along without fighting or killing each other.

1969 C [Academy] **Cast:** Anthony Eisley, Marita Pons, Maurine Dawson, Robert Allen Browne. **Director:** Oliver Drake.

The Mutations

Donald Pleasence, who created so many memorable roles in the horror genre, plays a mad biologist who decides the solution to the world's woes is to crossbreed humans and plants, thereby creating some ghastly mutations and flesh-eating plants.

1974 C Great Britain Cast: Donald Pleasence, Michael Dunn, Tom Baker, Jill Haworth, Julie Ege, Brad Harris. **Director:** Jack Cardiff.

My Mom's a Werewolf

Someone's mother has to be a werewolf, what with all the teenaged werewolves rampaging through the theaters. In this far-out comedy, a sexually frustrated single mom changes into a werewolf when she meets a handsome pet shop owner.

1988 C [Image] **Cast:** Susan Blakely, John Saxon, Ruth Buzzi, John Schuck, Marilyn McCoo. **Director:** Michael Fischa.

Night of the Bloody Apes

Contrary to its title, there is only one ape in this film—or ape man, to be correct. A desperate scientist transfers the heart of a gorilla into his dying son. The operation appears to be successful, but then the young man turns into an ape createure who rampages through the streets of Mexico.

1971 C Mexico [MPI] **Cast:** Armand Silvestres, Norma Lazareno, Jose Elias Moreno. **Writer/Director:** Rene Cardona, Rene Cardona Jr.

O Homen Lobo

When this Brazilian father sent his son to boarding school, he did not expect him to contract the werewolf virus and to commit murders that somehow made him the suspect. What could a father do other than to kill his errant heir to clear his own good name?

1971 C Brazil [Pinheiro Filmes] **Cast:** Raffaele Rossi, Claudia Cerine, Lino Braga, Juliana Pitelli. **Director:** Raffaele Rossi.

Okami no Monsho

The literal English title of this Japanese werewolf film is *Coat of Arms of the Wolf*. The motion picture is also known as *Horror of the Wolf, Mark of the Wolf*.

1973 C Japan

Project Metalbeast

In 1974, Operation Lycanthropus obtains blood from a werewolf in Hungary with the intention of using it to create a serum that will transform ordinary men into supersoldiers. Forward 20 years later and a werewolf equipped with experimental metallic flesh becomes a rampaging superbeast.

1995 C [Blue Ridge Entertainment/ Prism] **Cast:** Barry Bostwick, Kim Delaney, John Marzilli, Musetta Vander, Dean Scofield. **Director:** Alessandro de Gaetano.

RatBoy

It is unlikely that half-human, half-rat creatures will ever attain the cinematic popularity of wolf men and women and other shapeshifting beings, but this film presents an interesting contemporary fairy tale of a journalist who finds a ratboy living in a garbage dump and seeks to exploit him.

1986 C [Malpaso] **Cast:** Sondra Locke, Robert Townsend, Larry Hankin, Christopher Hewett. **Director:** Sondra Locke.

The Rats Are Coming! The Werewolves Are Here!

A family of werewolves encounters people-eating rats. This film is also known as *Curse of the Full Moon*.

1972 C [Mishkin] **Cast:** Hope Stansbury, Jacqueline Skarvellis, Berwick

Kaler, Noel Collins. **Director/ Writer/ Producer/Photographer:** Andy Milligan.

Return from the Past

An attempt to fashion an anthology from five stories about vampires, werewolves, zombis, and other assorted monsters, this film is also known as *Dr. Terror's Gallery of Horrors, Alien Massacre, The Blood Suckers, The Witch's Clock*.

1967 B Cast: John Carradine, Lon Chaney Jr., Rochelle Hudson. **Director:** David L. Hewitt.

The Return of the Vampire

Bela Lugosi plays Armand Tesla, a vampire who preys upon London with his faithful werewolf (Matt Willis) at his side, until he is killed with the traditional stake through the heart by a professor wise in the ways of vampire hunting. Years later, during the London Blitz of World War II, a bomb unearths the vampire's grave, dislodges the stake, and frees him to seek revenge on the professor's associate (Frieda Inescort) and her daughter (Nina Foch).

1944 B [Columbia] **Cast:** Bela Lugosi, Frieda Inescort, Matt Willis, Nina Foch, Roland Varno, Miles Mander. **Director:** Lew Landers.

Revenge of the Creature

Gill Man is captured in his primordial Black Lagoon and transported to a sea world park in Florida. It wouldn't be a horror movie if the big guy was contented to remain in his new pond. Soon he is carrying the heroine off to the Everglades. Clint Eastwood made his film debut as one of the lab technicians.

1955 B [Universal] **Cast:** John Agar, John Bromfield, Lori Nelson, Nestor Pavia. **Director:** Jack Arnold.

Santo y Blue Demon contra Dracula y el Hombre Lobo

Santo and his buddy the Blue Demon save the world from the terrors of Dracula and the Wolf Man.

1971 C Mexico [Cinematografica] **Cast:** Alejandro Cruz, Santo, Aldo Monti. **Director:** Miguel Delgado.

Scream of the Werewolf

At the same time that a writer is being stalked by a werewolf, the manbeast is also being tracked by a big game hunter who wants a one-of-a-kind trophy for the wall of his den before hanging up his guns.

1974 C [Made for TV movie available on video] **Cast:** Peter Graves, Don McGowan, Clint Walker, Philip Carey. **Director/Producer:** Dan Curtis.

Seedpeople

Centuries ago a meteor crashed to the earth and spread its deadly spores over a peaceful valley. When a man returns to his home town after several years away, he discovers that something deadly has taken its toll on his old friends and neighbors—they now sprout fangs and drip slime from their gaping mouths.

1992 C [Paramount] **Cast:** Andrea Roth, Sam Hennings, Bernard Kates, Dane Witherspoon, Holly Fields. **Director:** Peter Manoogian.

Serpent Warriors

This movie is worth watching just to see sexy songstress Eartha Kitt transform into a snake goddess who is determined to use her serpent warriors to drive construction workers away from a site sacred to her tribe.

1986 C Cast: Eartha Kitt, Clint Walker, Anne Lockhart, Chris Mitchum. **Director:** Niels Rasmussen.

Shadowzone

During a series of scientific experiments in deep sleep states conducted in an underground laboratory in Nevada, the subconscious mind of one of the volunteers opens a doorway to another dimension and permits a shapeshifting monster to step through and proceed to stalk all victims in sight.

1989 C [Paramount] **Cast:** Maureen Flaherty, David Beecroft, Louise Fletcher, James Hong, Shawn Weatherby, Miguel Nunez. **Director/Writer:** J.S. Cardone.

The She Wolf of London

Cruel mind games by the true murderer preying on Hyde Park attempt to convince the attractive young member of the Allenby family (June Lockhart) that she has fallen victim to the ancestral curse of becoming a werewolf. While there are no wolves in this motion picture, it would not be too many more years before Ms. Lockhart was overseeing Lassie, the most incredibly gifted canine on television.

1946 B [Universal] **Cast:** June Lockhart, Don Porter, Sara Haden. **Director:** Jean Yarbrough.

Silver Bullet

Based on Stephen King's novelette *Cycle of the Werewolf*, Corey Haim portrays a paraplegic boy who becomes convinced that a real werewolf is responsible for the gory murders that have been taking place in their small North Carolina town. Only his sister believes him when he describes how he damaged the werewolf's eye during a near-fatal encounter. They eventually track down a likely suspect for the lycanthropic slayings, then hope their befuddled uncle (Gary Busey) can protect them with a silver bullet.

1985 C [Paramount] **Cast:** Corey Haim, Gary Busey, Everett McGill, Terry O'Quinn. **Director:** Daniel Attias.

Sleepwalkers

In this original screenplay by Stephen King, two shapeshifting monsters, who may or may not be mother and son, seek to live among human society undetected. When her "son" falls in love with a mortal, "Mom" begins to run amok. For no readily apparent reason, the two monsters have a morbid fear of cats, and it is a massive gathering of felines that manages to put the two creatures away.

1991 C [RCA/Columbia] **Cast:** Brian Krause, Alice Krige, Madchen Amick, Ron Perlman—and a number of in-joke cameos by the likes of Clive Barker, Joe Dante, John Landis, and Stephen King.

The Snake Woman

In the 1890s, a British herpetologist injects his mentally ill wife with snake poison in his belief that such treatment will heal her psyche. When the couple's child is born, they discover that their daughter has many reptilian characteristics. Since she matures into an attractive young woman, her altered genes are masked—until it is too late for her victims.

1960 C Great Britain [Cinemacabre] **Cast:** Susan Travers, John McCarthy, Geoffrey Denton, Else Wagstan. **Director:** Sidney J. Furie.

Snowbeast

Snowbound skiers find refuge only in the lodge as a Bigfootlike creature begins turning the ski runs bloody.

1977 C [TV movie; Worldvision] **Cast:** Bo Svenson, Syliva Sidney, Clint Walker, Yvette Mimieux, Robert Logan.

Something Is Out There

A Xenomorph, an extraterrestrial shapeshifter, has escaped from an alien prison ship and come to Earth to rip folks apart with extreme prejudice. An attractive alien humanoid is in pursuit, and soon she and a police detective are on its trail. Rick Baker designed the Xenomorph, and John Dykstra created the outer space effects.

1988 C [A four-hour TV miniseries intended to be the pilot for a series] **Cast:** Maryam D'Abo, Kim Delaney, Joe Cortese, Robert Webber, George Dzundza. **Director:** Richard Colla.

Splash

In interviews about the time of this movie's release, Daryl Hannah stated how, as a child swimming in the family pool, she always envisioned herself as a mermaid. Her childhood fantasies certainly enriched her performace as a mermaid who rescues a human from drowning when he is just a boy, then falls in love with him when he becomes an adult. This Disney comedy presents a charming updating of the classic tale of folklore in which a creature of the sea leaves its natural environment to embrace land and a landlocked lover.

1984 C [Touchstone] **Cast:** Daryl Hannah, Tom Hanks, John Candy, Eugene Levy, Richard Shull, Dody Goodman. **Director:** Ron Howard.

Splash, Too

Amy Yasbeck is a worthy successor to don Daryl Hannah's mermaid tail, but the storyline is disappointly weak compared to the original. There seems lost opportunities in the story of a yuppie and his mermaid mate settling into life in Manhatten, and there little comedic response to a nasty scientist who mistreats dolphins.

1988 C [Disney TV movie] **Cast:** Amy Yasbeck, Todd Waring, Donovan Scott, Rita Taggert, Dody Goodman. **Director:** Greg Antonacci.

Sssssss

A herpetologist slowly turns a young man into a king cobra—with dire consequences. The premise may sound hokey, but a good cast emphasizing their acting skills above the limited special effects, provide some genuinely effective and eerie moments.

1973 C [Fox] **Cast:** Strother Martin, Dirk Benedict, Jack Ging, Heather Menzies, Richard B. Shull. **Director:** Bernard L. Kowalski.

Starman

Excellent special effects by Rick Baker, Stan Winston, and Dick Smith show us how a crash-landed extraterrestrial is able to translate the DNA from a lock of hair into the elements of total transformation into the image of an earthwoman's deceased husband. An effective and emotional outer-space love story superbly enacted by Jeff Bridges as the Starman with powers of resurrection and by Karen Allen as the widow who comes to care for the entity who has usurped her husband's lifeform. *Starman* was ranked Number 76 on *Entertainment Weekly's* "Top 100 Science Fiction Movies."

1984 C [RCA/Columbia] **Cast:** Jeff Bridges, Karen Allen, Charles Martin Smith, Richard Jaeckel. **Director:** John Carpenter.

Teen Wolf

Bringing the same energy and high-voltage charm to this film that he delivered in *Back to the Future* (released the same year), Michael J. Fox tries his best to make as much as possible of a shaky plot that has a high school student dealing with the old family curse of changing into a werewolf during moments of stress.

> **1985 C** [Atlantic] **Cast:** Michael J. Fox, James Hampton, Scott Paulin, Susan Ursitti. **Director:** Rod Daniel.

Teen Wolf Too

There is no Michael J. Fox in this sequel, but another television teen star, Jason Bateman, assumes the role of a kid with werewolf genes running in the family. Puzzled that he is accepted into college on a boxing scholarship, the Teen Wolf soon learns that the university hopes that he has the same werewolf powers as his cousin, the famous Teen Wolf.

> **1987 C** [Atlantic] **Cast:** Jason Bateman, Kim Darby, John Astin, Paul Sand. **Director:** Christopher Leitch.

Terminator 2: Judgment Day

This popular action film, featuring Arnold "I'll be back" Schwarzenegger as the indestructible cyborg—this time on the side of good—introduces a villain who is composed of liquid metal capable of assuming any form, thus becoming a deadly shapeshifting antagonist. The computerized technology utilized in this film allows the audience to view the startling details of each and every metamorphosis that T-1000 (Robert Patrick) chooses to assume. Director James Cameron utilized an earlier version of the fluid morphing technique in *The Abyss*, but after *Terminator 2* and the fine-tuning of the process by Stan Winston and Dennis Muren, the transformation sequences for werewolves, shape shifters, and other monsters have reached a level of sophistication far beyond the previous special effects and makeup tricks.

> **1991 C** [Video/Laser] **Cast:** Arnold Schwarzenegger, Robert Patrick, Linda Hamilton, Edward Furlong, Joe Morton, S. Epatha Merkerson, Castulo Guerra.

Terror House

The terror in this film is psychological rather than transformational, but James Mason gives an excellent performance as a man who believes that he becomes a compulsive murderer under the light of the full moon. Eerily set on the Yorkshire moors and punctuated with dark and stormy nights, the tale, based on a novel by Alan Kennington, places a lovely young schoolteacher (Joyce Howard) and her companion in a mansion with a sinister hermit who may be a frenzied killer. This film is also known as *The Night Has Eyes*.

> **1942 B Great Britain Cast:** James Mason, Joyce Howard, Mary Clare, Wilfrid Lawson, Tucker McGuire. **Director:** Leslie Arliss.

The Thing

While the 1951 version arrived in theaters during the early days of the flying saucer scare and has become a classic chiller, John Carpenter's interpretation is much closer to the original concept of writer John W. Campbell's novella, *Who Goes There?* on which both movies were based. Carpenter stresses the ability of the exterrestrial invader to shapeshift into any lifeform, including the scientists' sled dogs and the scientists themselves, to defeat the members of an isolated Antarctic research station. Rob Bottin's special effects intensify some startling scenes. This movie was ranked Number 30 on *Entertainment Weekly's* "100 Best Science Fiction Films."

> **1982 C** [MCA] **Cast:** Kurt Russell, Wilford Brimley, Richard Masur, Richard Dysart. **Director:** John Carpenter.

Track of the Moon Beast

The legend of the Lizard God is invoked during an asteroid shower over New Mexico. When a fragment of the asteroid strikes a man and lodges in his brain, he is transformed into a reptilian lizard man.

> **1976 C** [Prism] **Cast:** ChaseCordell, Donna Leigh Drake. **Director:** Dick Ashe.

The Undying Monster

Based on a novel by Jessie Douglas Kerruish, the film focuses on the Hammond family of Cornwall and their centuries' old lycanthropic curse. Also titled *The Hammond Mystery*.

> **1942 B** [Fox] **Cast:** James Ellison, Heather Angel, John Howard. **Director:** John Brahm.

The Werewolf (1913)

No known copy exists. Drawing upon Navajo legends of witchcraft and human-to-animal transformations, the film portrays a witch who turns her daughter into a werewolf so that she might attack the invading white settlers. An actual wolf was utilitized in the transformation scenes.

1913 B Canada [Bison Films]

The Werewolf (1932)

Adapted from the novel *Der Schwarze Mann* by Alfred Machard, this is the first motion picture of the sound era to deal with the werewolf theme.

1932 B German Cast: Magda Sonja, Vladimir Sokolov. **Director:** Friedrich Feher.

The Werewolf (1956)

Scientists hope to cure a man's radiation poisoning by injecting him with an experimental serum. Unfortunately, the cure doesn't take and the man (Steven Ritch) is changed into a deadly, rampaging werewolf.

1956 B [Columbia] **Cast:** Steven Ritch, Don Megowan, Joyce Holden. **Director:** Fred F. Sears.

Werewolf (1987)

This made-for television movie was the pilot for a proposed series. With overtones of *The Howling* and *An American Werewolf in London,* together with the excellent Rob Bottin-Rick Baker effects, the story depicts a graduate student who becomes a werewolf after being bitten by a lycanthrope. In spite of some truly grotesque werewolf makeup applied to television regular Chuck Connors, the numbers for *Werewolf* weren't deemed high enough to gamble on a series.

1987 C [Fox TV] **Cast:** John York, Lance LeGault, Chuck Connors, Raphael Sbarge, Michelle Johnson. **Director:** David Hemmings.

The Werewolf of London

While in Tibet in search of a rare flower, a botanist (Henry Hull) is attacked by a werewolf (Warner Oland). When he returns to London, the scientist is himself transformed into a werewolf during the next full moon. In addition to dealing with such an unwelcome metamorphosis, the botanist must also confront the werewolf, who travels to London from the faraway land to challenge him for the possession of the Tibetan flower, the only known cure for lycanthropy. The botanist manages to kill the werewolf, but he is, in turn, shot by the London police.

1935 B [Universal] **Cast:** Henry Hull, Warner Oland, Valerie Hobson, Spring Byington. **Director:** Stuart Walker. **Werewolf makeup:** Jack Pierce. Available on video from MCA.

The Werewolf of Washington

Versatile actor Dean Stockwell plays a presidential aide who is bitten by a werewolf while on assignment in Hungary. When he returns to Washington, he begins prowling Capitol Hill for likely victims.

1973 C [Millco] **Cast:** Dean Stockwell, Jane House, Michael Dunn, Biff McGuire, Clifton James. **Director/ Writer/Editor:** Milton Moses Ginsberg.

The Werewolf of Woodstock

Woodstock '69 wasn't just a time when flower children and music stars gathered to celebrate the Age of Aquarius. Lurking in the woods near the event is a hippie-hating farmer who has been turned into a werewolf by a stray bolt of lightning.

1975 C [ABC movie made for TV] **Cast:** Meredith MacRae, Michael Parks, Tige Andrews. **Director:** John Mofitt.

Werewolves on Wheels

The motorcycle gang, Devil's Advocates, are plenty tough dudes and biker chicks, tearing up the countryside, intimidating the local residents, and hosting raucous orgies whenever their hormones so move them. When they try to rough up some monks, however, they pick on the wrong crowd. One of their motorcycle mamas (D.J. Anderson) is transformed into a werewolf who kills the gang members one by one.

1971 C [Southstreet Productions] **Cast:** Steven Oliver, D.J. Anderson, Billy Gray, Barry McQuire. **Director:** Michel Levesque.

Wilderness

When her lover will not accept her claims that she is a werewolf, a tormented young woman relocates to an isolated part of Scotland and there achieves a complete transformation into a wolf.

1997 C **Great Britain** [Made for TV] **Cast:** Johanna Benyon, Mark Caven. **Director:** Ben Bolt.

Wolf

A movie reviewer once commented on Jack Nicholson's "werewolf smile," and he certainly gets to use it to good advantage in this excellent updating of the classic wolfman legend. Rick Baker's makeup and special effects accentuate the internal anguish (a'la Lawrence Talbot) that Nicholson's character undergoes as his transformation from man to wolf becomes undeniable. Supported by an excellent cast and top-grade production values, Nicholson makes the ancient legends of werewolves as contemporary as the Internet.

1994 C [Columbia] **Cast:** Jack Nicholson, Michelle Pfieffer, James Spader, Kate Nelligan,Christopher Plummer, Richard Jenkins. **Director:** Mike Nichols.

Wolf Blood

After receiving a transfusion of wolf's blood, a man becomes a werewolf.

1925 B [Lee-Bradford] **Cast:** George Chesebro, Marguerite Clayton, Ray Hanford. **Director:** George Chesebro.

The Wolf Man (1941)

The classic motion picture that established Hollywood werewolf lore and featured Jack Pierce's time-lapse transformation of man into werewolf. While visiting a gypsy camp with an attractive shopkeeper (Evelyn Ankers) from the village, Lawrence Talbot (Lon Chaney Jr.) is attacked by a werewolf (Bela Lugosi). Although Talbot is a virtuous man, the aged gypsy fortuneteller (Maria Ouspenskaya) warns him that a good heart is no defense against the curse of a werewolf's bite. When the full moon occurs, Talbot undergoes the terrible metamorphosis of man into beast. After a few nights of terrorizing the countryside, the senior Talbot (Claude Rains) kills the werewolf with his silver wolf's head cane and is astonished to discover that he has slain his own son.

1941 B [Universal] **Cast:** Lon Chaney Jr., Evelyn Ankers, Ralph Bellamy, Maria Ouspenskaya, Bela Lugosi. **Director/Producer:** George Waggoner. Available on video from MCA.

The Wolfman (1915)

1915 B [Reliance-Mutual]

Wolfman—A Lycanthrope (1979)

In turn-of-the-century Georgia, a man inherits his father's curse as well as the family estate. It's not long before the full moon has him transformed into a full-fledged werewolf.

1979 C [Thom EMI] **Cast:** Earl Owensby, Kristina Reynolds, Maggie Lauterer. **Director:** Worth Keeler.

Wolfman—A Cinematic Scrapbook (1991)

Selected film clips from the cinematic careers of such professional werewolves as Lon Chaney Jr., Oliver Reed, John Carradine, Bela Lugosi, and others.

1991 C/B [Rhino Home Video]

Wolfen

Very loosely based on Whitley Streiber's novel, the film reveals an ancient species of wolves that are possessed of superintelligence and who regard humans as careless interlopers on Earth. All this gets somewhat jumbled in the movie, however, and we are left with a thriller about a police detective investigating a series of murders that are attributed to a mysterious pack of wolves running wild in the Bronx. Somehow the super species of wolves gets blended together with the plight of Native Americans who also had their territory usurped by newcomers to the scene.

1981 C [Orion] **Cast:** Albert Finney, Diane Verona, Gregory Hines, Edward James Olmos, Tom Noonan. **Director:** Michael Wadleigh.

This filmography was created with the help of the sources below:

Clarens, Carlos. *An Illustrated History of the Horror Film*. New York: Capricorn Books, 1968.

Douglas, Drake. *Horror!* New York: Collier Books, 1969.

Halliwell, Leslie. *Halliwell's Film Guide, Sixth Edition*. New York: Charles Scribner's Sons, 1987.

Hardy, Phil. *The Encyclopedia of Horror Movies*. New York: Harper & Row, 1986.

Maltin, Leonard. *Leonard Maltin's 1999 Movie and Video Guide*. New York: Signet, 1998.

Stanley, John. *Creature Features: The Science Fiction, Fantasy, and Horror Movie Guide*. New York: Boulevard, 1997.

VideoHound's Golden Movie Retriever. Farmington Hills, MI: Visible Ink Press, 1999.

VideoHound's Horror Show. Farmington Hills, MI: Visible Ink Press, 1998.

PHOTO AND ILLUSTRATION CREDITS

Photos and illustrations used in The Werewolf Book were reprinted
with permission from the following sources:

AP/Wide World Photos: 5, 37, 73, 179, 227, 256, 285

David del Valle Archive: 3, 9, 11, 16, 21, 25, 27, 31, 35, 42, 50, 51, 55, 59, 64, 67, 79, 81, 84, 90, 92, 97, 100, 102, 106, 111, 113, 118, 129, 134, 139, 143, 145, 151, 159, 163, 171, 174, 181, 192, 197, 203, 207, 216, 231, 241, 244, 246, 249, 253, 270, 275, 277, 291, 295, 311, 313, 318, 327, 331, 333, 340, 353

The Kobol Collection: 54

Mary Evans Picture Library: 41, 46, 75, 120, 125, 166, 177, 186, 237, 267, 281, 302, 337

Brad Steiger: 199, 219, 323, 329

PHOTOS USED IN THE COLOR INSERT

David del Valle Archive: Jack Nicholson (both photos); Phil Buckman; John Malkovich; Jannie Fauerscuou; Jens Okking; Chuck Connors (both photos); Alex Stevens; *Curse of the Cat People; The Catman of Paris; I Was A Teenage Werewolf, The Wolf Man; The Boy Who Cried Werewolf; Wolfman; The Monster Squad; Fright Night II* (all three photos); Mark Dacascos; Mary Nash

The Kobol Collection: David Naughton (both photos); Albert Finney; Jeff Bridges and Karen Allen; Sandra Locke and Robert Townsend; Susan Strasberg; Michael J. Fox; Nastassia Kinski; Kurt Russell; Megan Follows, Gary Busey, Corey Haim; David Thewlis; Amanda Donohoe; Dirk Benedict; *The Howling*